The Generation of 1914

Robert Wohl

HARVARD UNIVERSITY PRESS
Cambridge, Massachusetts
1979

Library of Congress Cataloging in Publication Data

Wohl, Robert.
    The generation of 1914.

    Includes bibliographical references and index.
    1. Europe—Intellectual life—20th century.
2. Youth—Europe—History. 3. Conflict of
generations. 4. European War, 1914-1918—Influence
and results. 5. Youth in literature. I. Title.
CB203.W63   909.82′1   78-21124
ISBN 0-674-34465-0

For Birgitta,
who lived it

Acknowledgments

TO acknowledge individually all those people who helped me in this project and to indicate with any fairness how they shaped the book would be to tell the story of my life during the last ten years. Despite the evident temptations of such an enterprise, it is better left to another time. There are some cases, however, where my debt is so great that not to acknowledge it would both deprive me of a pleasure and rob the reader of a clue that might facilitate his understanding of the book. At a very early point, Eugene Anderson planted in my mind the idea that the book should not take the form of a series of parallel biographies. Whenever tempted by this way of structuring my materials, I remembered his advice. Eugen Weber watched the book develop, read it in its various drafts, and knew when to be encouraging and when to tell me in straight language that I was straying from the right path. The style, form, and content of the manuscript have all benefited from his freely and promptly given suggestions; and if he likes the book, I shall be pleased. The late Jean Touchard and René Remond of the Ecole des Sciences Politiques in Paris spent a rainy afternoon orienting me in the French materials. They directed my attention to "le phenomène Montherlant"; the reader will see that I profited from their suggestion. Gunnar Myrdal arranged an important interview and shared with me his own thoughts on the generation problem. We disagreed; but the areas of disagreement later turned out to be important in shaping my approach. Sir Oswald and Lady Diana Mosley talked with me at length on several occasions and furnished me with letters of introduction that were invaluable in following the traces left by Drieu la Rochelle. Lucienne Didier described the Drieu la Rochelle whom she had known and made it possible for me to meet two of his closest friends, Jean Bernier and Gaston Bergery. Later Bertrand de Jouvenel, Alfred Fabre-Luce, and Philippe Barrès took the time to evoke for me the

France in which Drieu grew up and lived. Leo Valiani, Piero Melograni, and Renzo de Felice gave me important leads regarding the Italian materials. Giuseppe Prezzolini renounced the pleasures of an Easter Sunday afternoon in Lugano to answer my questions about the period of *La Voce*. Consuelo and Juan Gil arranged interviews in Spain; Soledad Ortega gave me access to vital correspondence from the Ortega archives and comfortable circumstances in which to peruse it; Julián Marías, Luis Aranguren, and Pedro Laín Entralgo offered invaluable suggestions with regard to the interpretation of the intellectual world in which Ortega moved. I thank them all for their patience and their hospitality.

My research assistants, Kathy Flanagan-Hoffman and Barry Silver, traced down the most inaccessible materials and often provided me with rich insights bearing on their interpretation. Hayden White read the manuscript at a critical juncture and brought home to me that I was writing intellectual history at a time when I still thought of myself as working on the refinement of a sociological model. Under his influence, I became increasingly aware of the structural continuities in generational literature. Lauro Martines saw something in the first version of the manuscript that I had missed entirely: namely, that I was engaged in demystifying a cluster of ideas and images that were gathered together under the label of the "generation of 1914." He urged me to ask why these myths had been created, who their inventors were, and what the relationship was between these myths and the politics of the time. The final version of the manuscript was written with his questions constantly in mind. Victor Wolfenstein showed an uncanny ability to enter into my work and to discuss it with me when discussion was needed. Many of my ideas came in response to his questions or objections. Annie Kriegel was, as usual, a splendid host and an inexhaustible mine of research leads and ideas in Paris. And were it not for the generous assistance of James L. Mairs, Riccardo Scrivano, José Alfonso Sánchez, Wolfgang Beck, Wilhelm Heinz, Pietro Omodeo, Paola Monti, Yves Gérard, and Sir Geoffrey Keynes, my photographic documentation of the generation of 1914 would be less complete than it is.

I have benefited inordinately from the criticism of friends and acquaintances who took time to read the whole or parts of a long manuscript. J. G. Bell, Elisabeth Sifton, and Donald Lamm read an earlier version of *The Generation of 1914* and made helpful suggestions for its revision. Ted Bogacz was kind enough to read the English chapter and to share with me his immense knowledge of the English war poets and the circumstances within which their poetry was written. Vittoria Omodeo provided me with a photograph of her father and a most useful line-by-line commentary on the pages I devote to his book on the life of the Italian combatants during the Great War. Peter Goldman gave the manuscript the kind of searching critique that only a friend dare give and caused me to rethink the way in which I formulated my conclusions. Camille Smith of Harvard University Press labored at the ungrateful task of preparing the manuscript for publication. Though not readily encapsulated in a sentence, her contribution was enormous. As for my editor, Aida Di Pace Donald, my debt to her is even greater than she knows. She trod the narrow path between encouragement and criticism with sure-footed grace. All authors should be as fortunate in finding the right editor as I was. Finally, I wish to thank my wife, Birgitta, who never ceased to believe in the book and whose faith in its validity and importance kept it alive under the most adverse of circumstances. Her desire to read the finished manuscript seems, in retrospect, the only thing that brought this potentially eternal project to an end.

Contents

Illustrations

Rupert Brooke's grave on the island of Skyros
Love and Death by G. F. Watts
We Are Making a New World by Paul Nash
Siegfried Sassoon in the early 1920s
Wilfred Owen with fellow officers in 1916
Erich Maria Remarque in the early 1930s
Henry Williamson at a meeting of the British Union of Fascists in the late 1930s
Vera Brittain at a meeting of the P.E.N. Club in the 1930s
T. E. Lawrence with his brothers when Lawrence was an undergraduate at Oxford
Sir Oswald Mosley addressing a meeting of the British Union of Fascists in the late 1930s

Following page 152
Miguel de Unamuno in 1917
Ramiro de Maetzu in the 1920s
Pío Baroja about 1900
Azorín about 1920
Ortega reading the news of the outbreak of war in August 1914
Ortega in 1925
Ortega after his speech calling for the "rectification" of the Republic in December 1931

Following page 192
Giovanni Papini
Giuseppe Prezzolini
The first number of the Florentine journal *Leonardo*
Benito Mussolini leading the march on Rome in October 1922
The union of older and younger generations in the Fascist militia
Adolfo Omodeo during the Great War
Antonio Gramsci shortly before his arrest in 1926
The first page of Gramsci's *Prison Notebooks*

Daring as never before, wastage as never before.
Young blood and high blood,
fair cheeks, and fine bodies;

fortitude as never before

frankness as never before,
disillusions as never told in the old days
hysterias, trench confessions,
laughter out of dead bellies.

There died a myriad,
And of the best, among them,
For an old bitch gone in the teeth,
For a botched civilization . . .

   Ezra Pound, 1920

In Search of the Lost Generation

. . . Think now
History has many cunning passages,
   contrived corridors
And issues, deceives with whispering
   ambitions,
Guides us by vanities.
   T. S. Eliot, 1922

GENERATION OF 1914—close your eyes and a host of images leaps to mind: of students packing off to war with flowers in their rifles and patriotic songs on their lips, too young, too innocent to suspect what bloody rites of passage awaited them; of trenchfighters whose twisted smiles and evasive glances revealed their close companionship with death; of pleasure-seekers in the 1920s, cigarettes hanging from the corner of their mouths, defiance and despair showing in the directness of their stares and the set of their faces; of Communists, heads bobbing in a sea of masses, prisoners of the movement they claimed to guide; of Fascists, tight-lipped, stiff-postured, without pity for others or themselves; of pacifists campaigning belligerently against war; of veterans unable to forget the grandeur of the trenches; of wasted women who had become widows before becoming wives; of a generation missing, sacrificed, decimated, destroyed "for an old bitch gone in the teeth, for a botched civilization." [1]

These images have a privileged place in our conception of the early twentieth century. They color our memories and creep into the best of our books. They are the prisms through which we view the years between the two world wars. Films, novels, poems, autobiographies, songs, remembrances have pressed these images indelibly into the deepest layers of our minds. Who can forget Remarque's young soldiers lamenting that, live or die, their world was lost forever; Hemingway's Jake Barnes drowning with alcohol the memory of the man he once had been and would never be again; or Robert Graves saying goodbye to all that and abandoning a declining England for the pagan pleasures of Majorca?

Yet despite the spell these images exercise over us, despite the hold with which they grip our imaginations, despite the depths of consciousness in which they dwell, their status is uncertain. They hover strangely, like the shades of dead soldiers, in a no-man's-land between literature and legend. Some are mutually contradictory. Others clash with what historians know. All suffer from the general confusion as to what a generation is. Asked what the phrase "generation of 1914" meant, pressed for a definition, how many of us could compress our images into a coherent picture that would have anything to do with history as it is now being written? How many of us could pass from the names of writers, vague notions about fate, remembered generalizations about casualty lists (very long) and the impact of the war (very great) to a satisfactory interpretation of the period in which these men lived and the role they played in it? For that matter, how many of us could even identify with any degree of certainty the so-called "men of 1914"? Indeed, one would be tempted to argue that if the war generation is "lost," it is lost because it has no history; lost because its history is overlaid with myth.[2]

My purpose in writing this book was to rescue the generation of 1914 from the shadowland of myth and to restore it to the realm of history. Such a venture seemed well worth undertaking. A history of the generation of 1914 might illuminate in unsuspected ways the origins of the Great War and its impact on those who fought it. It held the promise of helping us to understand such critical developments as the spread of pessimism and despair, the waning of liberal and humanitarian values, the rise of the Communist and Fascist movements, and the sudden eruption of violence in Europe's most progressive countries during the years between 1914 and 1945. One might even hope that such a history would yield a new perspective on the period as a whole—or at the least, a finer sense for its conflicts and concerns.

Yet how was such a history to be written? Who were its protagonists to be? A study of generational theories persuaded me that no available model of generation was flexible enough to encompass the baffling variety of ways in which the term "generation of 1914" and its synonyms had been used in the discourse of early twentieth-century Europe. Theorists had naturally tried to be consistent; but the most striking thing about the generation of 1914 seemed to be the indeterminacy of the social group to which the phrase referred. For some time I searched for a solution that would do justice to the complexity of the facts. The one I chose was to abandon theoretical and lexicographical consistency as standards and to try to find out what people living in early twentieth-century Europe had meant by the "generation of 1914." After all, the generation of 1914 was an idea. Why not approach it as such and attempt to determine how and in what contexts people used it, to what individuals or groups it referred, what shifts if any occurred in its usage, why (and which) people found it indispensable, and what interests—hence what politics—lay behind it.[3]

This strategy appeared all the more appropriate when I realized that the most important generational theories were themselves products of the period between 1910 and 1933. It was fair to assume that they had been influenced, if not inspired, by the example of the generation of 1914. It seemed equally likely that they bore within them some element of distortion, if only deriving from the circumstances in which they had been formulated. These distortions could be exposed and the insights that the theories contained about the generation of 1914 could be rescued by testing theory against social reality whenever possible. Where the theories deviated from historical fact, as I suspected they would, I would seek the reasons for this divergence. These factors of distortion would be bound to cast some light on the history of the generation of 1914—or so I supposed.

The kind of study I envisaged could not be confined to a single European country, because the idea of the generation of 1914 came to imply a unity of experience, feeling, and fate that transcended national borders; because different national experiences brought out different aspects of the generational phenomenon; and because generational theory had been formulated in a number of countries and from a variety of national perspectives. On the other hand, and for some of the same reasons, the story of the generation of 1914 had to be told from a national point of view. Otherwise, the peculiarities of national experience would be buried beneath a false universalism. I resolved therefore to generalize about the generation of 1914 as a whole only after building up a series of national foundations for these generalizations. Hence the book is European in scope and comparative in method, though national in structure. Throughout I have tried to remember with Ortega that the secret to the study of European history is *"Eadem sed aliter:* the same things, but in another way."[4]

My source material consists of what contemporaries thought and said about the generation of 1914. But thought has been defined as broadly as possible. I have subjected to scrutiny novels, poems, memoirs, autobiographies, philosophical essays, sociological treatises, university lectures, private letters, personal notebooks, newspaper articles, political speeches, conversations when recorded—indeed, anything that might throw some light on the generational phenomenon. When possible I have interviewed the people who figure in the book—or talked to friends who were close to them during the period under study. I discovered that different nationalities had a tendency to express themselves in different forms. Thus the Germans were more likely to produce full-fledged social theories dealing with the generation problem, whereas the English wrote poetry, novels, memoirs, and letters commenting on their generation's fate. The French were given to generational portraits organized around groups of writers; the Italians excelled in essays analyzing the politics of the generation of 1914. In Spain Ortega presented his most important generational theories in public discourses and university lectures designed to be heard rather than read. The chapters reflect these differences. But the focus nonetheless remains the same. In each case I am looking for the effort of consciousness to come to grips with and to understand a social phenomenon that was one of the most prominent characteristics of the age.

The argument of the book therefore proceeds nationally, topically, and to some extent chronologically. France comes first because the generation of 1914 made a spectacular and much commented upon debut in France during the years just before the outbreak of the Great War; because the first important statement of twentieth-century generational theory by François Mentré was a direct response to this event; and because later generational theorists attempted to take into account what had happened in France. Germany follows because the next great burst of generational theorizing occurred there in fundamentally changed conditions during the decade and a half after the war. The focus then shifts to England where I seek to reconstruct the history, and account for the longevity, of the legend of the "lost generation." The setting of the next chapter is Spain, and the theme is José Ortega y Gasset's series of attempts to formulate a comprehensive generational theory within the framework of his philosophy of human existence and against the background of national and then general European political and cultural crisis. Turning then to Italy, I describe the situation within which Antonio Gramsci reached his important insights into the generational phenomenon and I seek to show how they can be used to provide a necessary corrective to Ortega's approach to the problem. A final chapter brings together the various strands of the argument, enlarges the context of the discussion to Europe as a whole, and presents my own reflections on the generation of 1914.

M Y aim throughout has been to probe behind poetic and political imagery and the propositions of social theory in order to discover the life experience that inspired their authors to produce them. This gives the book an aspect of collective biography. But I have in no way sought to represent in all its social variety the age-group of Europeans born in the late nineteenth century. I tell the story of the generation of 1914 in terms of the individuals who identified themselves or were identified by others as belonging to it and in some way exemplifying it. For reasons that will become evident, these people tended to be males from the middle layers of society whose main activity was writing. Much of the book deals with their intuitions, feelings, and ideas. It is a study of mentalities, both individual and collective, and of the efforts made by some to use these mentalities as the basis for a reorganization of national life. I should like it to stand or fall on its ability to illuminate the politics of early twentieth-century European intellectuals. Some of the people I discuss are currently much admired; others are currently much disliked. I should therefore make explicit my view that the book has neither heroes nor villains. Only by acknowledging the extent of our alienation from the past can we hope to repossess it. The key to understanding the generation of 1914 is to recognize that their world was very different from ours. That shrewd explorer of early modern sensibility Lucien Febvre once remarked that the historian is not he who knows, but he who seeks. This book is about such a search, a quest for the realities behind the myths of the lost generation.[5]

CHAPTER ONE

France:
The Young Men of Today

We are a sacrificed generation.
  Henri Massis, 1914

H ISTORICAL generations are not born; they are made. They are a device
   by which people conceptualize society and seek to transform it. But what
people? In early twentieth-century Europe generationalists* were almost always
literary intellectuals living in large cities. They were members of a small elite
who were keenly aware of their uniqueness and proud of their intellectual superiority. What concerned these writers or would-be writers was the decline of
culture and the waning of vital energies; what drove them together was the
desire to create new values and to replace those that were fading; what incited
them to action was the conviction that they represented the future in the
present; what dismayed them was their problematic relationship to the masses
they would have liked to lead. Whether they called themselves Expressionists,
Futurists, or Fabians, they felt above all like "young men of today."[1]

  It is in these groupings of intellectuals that we shall find the first traces of the
"generation of 1914," and nowhere more clearly than in France, where a flurry
of inquiries into the "miracle" of the new youth appeared in the years just
before the outbreak of the Great War. Books were written; articles appeared in
the influential reviews; newspaper surveys of opinion were compiled, then released with great éclat. Of these newspaper surveys or *enquêtes*, the one that
generated the most discussion, indeed the one that can be said to have
launched the new French generation on its course and to have given it its attributes and profile, was that conducted in 1912 for the Parisian daily *L'Opinion*
and published the following year under the title *Les Jeunes Gens d'aujourd'hui*
[The Young People of Today].

  The classical pseudonym under which *The Young People of Today* was

---

* I shall use the term "generationalist" to designate someone who is inclined to the use of the
generational concept and "generationalism" to designate the phenomenon of generational thinking.

published—Agathon, Socrates's disciple, "good, brave in war"—concealed the identity of two young French intellectuals, Henri Massis (1886) and Alfred de Tarde (1880).* De Tarde was the son of the well-known sociologist Gabriel Tarde, who held the chair of modern philosophy at the Collège de France until his death in 1904. Tarde had been a pioneer in the development of social psychology and was remembered chiefly for his concern about the breakdown of the French family and his refutation of Emile Durkheim's notion of collective mentalities, an idea closely related to the generational concept. Massis was younger than de Tarde, more precocious, and destined to have a longer and more brilliant career. To place him properly in the topography of French intellectual life before 1914, one might say that he was neither an original thinker like Henri Bergson, nor a poet like Paul Claudel, nor a political journalist like Charles Maurras—all writers whom he admired—but an aspiring man of letters who throbbed with the ill-concealed ambition of becoming a leader of youth and a spiritual guide. Once a worshipper at the altar of Anatole France, the reigning literary deity at the century's turn, Massis had transferred his allegiance to Maurice Barrès, whose integral but republican nationalism had provided the inspiration for a small book in which Massis had confessed his intellectual debt and that of "the best among us" to the "prince of youth" and self-proclaimed "professor of energy." [2]

In 1912 Massis and de Tarde were fresh from a brilliantly successful campaign against the professors of the "new Sorbonne," whom they accused of "germanizing" French culture and of replacing classical learning with Teutonic sociology and meaningless erudition. At issue in this campaign against the giants of the French academic world—among them, the historians Charles Seignobos, Alphonse Aulard, and Ernest Lavisse, the literary critics Gustave Lanson and Ferdinand Brunot, and the sociologist Emile Durkheim, all founding fathers in their disciplines, all men whose works we still read and respect today—had been the ideology of the Third Republic and the objectives of its educational establishment. Agathon accused these professors of having failed to fulfill their mission as educators and shapers of the nation's youth. They had not provided their students with ideals or with faith in their country's future; nor had they taught them to appreciate their cultural heritage, which required, in Massis and de Tarde's view, a mastery of Greek and Latin and a knowledge of the French classics. Instead, in their zeal to create a democratic and cosmopolitan elite, they had turned their students into notetakers, bibliographers, and intellectual technicians. They had sullied the nation's cultural heroes by means of the techniques of literary criticism instead of teaching their students to honor them. Massis and de Tarde had been particularly incensed by the professor of literature who had run into his class on Pascal proclaiming gleefully that "this time we have him dead to rights." By the end of 1911 the

_____
* Dates in parentheses following names designate year of birth.

Parisian intellectual community had taken sides, with the majority of the Academy and the Institute supporting Agathon and the Left rallying to the cause of the Sorbonne. The debate had even been carried to the floor of the Senate, where one incensed legislator had insinuated that Agathon's campaign was nothing less than a blow against "that religion of which Reason is the goddess and Renan the prophet." [3]

The inquiry into the opinions and life-styles of "the young people of today" followed logically from the first campaign. The Sorbonne professors had failed, according to Massis and de Tarde, because they were unable or unwilling to administer to the spiritual needs of the twenty-year-olds who were flocking to their classrooms in search of a faith and emerging full of bitterness at the superficiality of modern learning. As one of them put it in a letter to Agathon, "At the age when one is anxious for notions that have some application to life, at a time when we looked to our teachers for the prestige of a spiritual authority asking them to help us find ourselves, what did we discover? An empty science that failed to take into account the needs of the intelligence, a pedantic materialism, a skeptical mode of inquiry that degrades and diminishes. Everything in their teaching forced us to serve as inert slaves or to exasperate ourselves in rebellion." [4]

Massis was impressed by the novel features of these young men; the difference between them and their supposed teachers and guides was not one of degree or of age, but of kind. They seemed to possess a physiognomy of their own and to be moving in a common direction. What was taking place, he concluded, was nothing less than a "transformation of character," a mutation of species. For a time Massis played with the idea of writing a novel that would exemplify their spiritual itinerary and end with a "song of confidence" in action and their destiny. But the nature of his talent, more polemical than imaginative, and the desire to reach a larger public encouraged him to frame his portrait in the form of a newspaper enquête. The campaign against the Sorbonne had been a great success. Enquêtes were all the rage. Why not revive Agathon and present the public with a composite image of the generation of 1912 that would have the prestige and the added impact of a documented, hence scientific, survey? Massis approached de Tarde; talked to him about some of his friends who, in Massis's view, incarnated the new mentality; and showed him some articles from reviews that younger men were launching. Together they agreed to conduct a survey of Parisian students between the ages of eighteen and twenty-five at the elite preparatory schools and the university faculties, as well as the Grandes Ecoles, in order to determine to what extent their impressions could be generalized. [5]

From the beginning this second collaboration between the two men was difficult. Just past thirty, de Tarde approached Massis's young men with curiosity, with sympathy, but also with skepticism. For him, secular, solidly republican, and a believer in the methods of social science, they were subjects to be studied whose statements had to be carefully controlled. He suspected, rightly, that his young collaborator was writing his autobiography in the form of an enquête. In short, he had to be convinced, and the evidence was not always forthcoming. Massis, scarcely twenty-five, identified with the new youth; was himself going through a spiritual crisis that would lead to his conversion to Catholicism; had grave doubts about the Republic; and was more concerned that the portrait they were drawing should be sharply etched than that it should be rigorously or scientifically accurate. After all, he was no aspiring social psychologist; his ambitions did not lie in the University; this was no state doctorate. Barrès, not Durkheim or the elder Tarde, was his model. He wanted to shape opinion, not to measure it, and de Tarde's detachment annoyed him. The wonder is that the partnership did not collapse, as they put Massis's general impressions to the test of facts, soliciting letters, collecting the testimony of teachers, and cornering spokesmen of "representative" groups to whom they read excerpts from the works of Anatole France, Renan, and Barrès, with the purpose of recording their reactions. That the collaboration did hold, despite numerous disagreements, was because Massis and de Tarde were united by a common aspiration—to see France revive, to see it regain its former grandeur—and also because the great majority of facts that they collected seemed to confirm the initial thesis that something had changed, that the new youth were indeed different.[6]

No question: French youth were different, if only because more of them were now going to universities.[7] But the overwhelming impression Agathon's enquête gave was of a group of young men (for that was what Massis and de Tarde meant by "jeunes gens") who spoke out with a single voice and possessed a single set of values. Massis and de Tarde began their book by contrasting the young men of today with the generation of 1885. The generation of 1885, they said, had been pessimistic, self-doubting, morally flabby, overly intellectual and introspective, relativistic, incapable of energetic action, lacking faith, obsessed with decadence, and ready to accept the defeat and eclipse of their country. All these traits converged in a debilitating dilettantism. "Dilettantism," wrote Agathon, "is the unconcentrated being in whom the bundle of energy relaxes; it is the inability to choose, or to put it better, it is the lack of love." The young man of 1912, on the other hand, had "exiled self-doubt" and was a sportsman. Airplanes, automobiles, and football attracted him more than books. He was a patriot in the sense that he was prepared and even eager to give up his life, if that sacrifice would lead to the revival of his country and the throwing off of the unbearable German yoke. He was tired of relativism, hankered after absolutes, and inclined toward Catholicism because it offered him the faith and discipline he craved as well as a basis for coherent action. He cared little for ideology and was pragmatic when it came to politics. He read less than his elders; traveled more; was chaster in his morals; married younger; was quicker to accept financial and familial responsibilities; and was more likely to have children. He tended to be hostile to the Republic in its present form, in great part because he was disgusted with the morals of its leading representatives. If he was not a follower of the Action Française, it was because he was skeptical of institutional reform and considered monarchism, the doctrine of the Action Française, "an intellectual chimera" out of keeping with his sense of political realities. Among French intellectuals the men he admired and recognized as his guides were Charles Maurras, Henri Bergson, Charles Péguy, and Georges Sorel. Above all, he was an organizer and a man of action who lived according to an inner, self-imposed code, while he waited for a chance to submit his country to a new political discipline. "In all matters, it is his distinguishing characteristic to create order and hierarchy, just as his elders created disorder and ruins."[8]

The novelist and deputy Maurice Barrès was the pivotal figure in Agathon's analysis. Barrès (1863) was a member of the generation of 1885, which Agathon termed "the sacrificed generation." While young, Barrès had drunk deeply and self-consciously the dregs of relativism bequeathed to his generation by their teachers Ernest Renan (1823) and Hippolyte Taine (1828). He had known the excitement and the desperation of a life in which there was no transcendence, no absolute, nothing to cling on to but the mechanical agitation of the sensibility and the cult of the existential self in its multiple, successive, and contradictory incarnations. The creed of the young Barrès had been "to feel the most while analyzing the most"—to sweep up experience so that it could be processed by intelligence. His individualism and his separation from all communities—from what he called "the Barbarians"—had been total and irrevocable. But Barrès had escaped from nihilism and reconstituted the unity of his self. He had overcome his sense of decadence and gotten a firm grasp on life. And this itinerary from dreams to reality, so elegantly and ironically described in his novels and essays, was what made his life exemplary for the young men who came after him. For Barrès had made his way through an exhausting self-analysis to a rediscovery of the collectivity, an affirmation of the nation as the ultimate reality that men may know, and a commitment to tradition that expressed itself in a reverence for the land and the dead of former generations, especially for the land and the dead of Lorraine. These values—or better, the acceptance of this determinism, the determinism of France, the determinism of having been born in Lorraine—had given Barrès a zest for action and had freed him from the heavy chains of ideas and opinions, always less real in his mind than feelings and emotions. Thus the lesson of Barrès's career, as read by Agathon, was the need for choice and commitment as an antidote to dilettantism.

All this sounds literary, and in one essential respect it was: Massis was using the generational idea as a sledgehammer with which to dismantle the reputations of his predecessors and to get his literary career underway. We have here, then, what appears to be an example of the eternal battle of literary generations, the changing of the literary guard. What was the "generation of 1885," except a handful of writers, loosely grouped and vaguely defined, with whose values Massis disagreed? This was so. But it is also true that Massis would not have drawn the contrast between the generation of 1885 and the young men of 1912 as sharply as he did and proclaimed so confidently the coming of a new generation if he had not experienced directly and witnessed in his closest friends the changes and the crises he was describing. Agathon's enquête may have been a literary act, but it corresponded to a reality in Henri Massis's life: his salvation from the spiritual quagmire of fin-de-siècle French intellectualism.

While still a student at the Sorbonne, Massis had begun to frequent Anatole France, whose kind and playful skepticism both excited and confused him. At twenty he emerged from the relationship, according to his own account, "with his mind distraught, his heart beating fast, and his hands empty." It was about this time, in 1905, that he approached Barrès and showed him his first literary effort, a modest essay in criticism entitled *Comment Zola composait ses romans* [How Zola Composed his Novels]. The master, then at the height of his fame, was encouraging and arranged for Massis's second work, a caricature based on his philosophy teacher Alain, to be published. In 1907 Barrès introduced Massis to his nephew Charles Demange, an elegant young man with ambitions in literature and politics and the means to pursue them. Massis was immediately taken by the brilliance of Demange's mind, the range of his culture, and the refinement of his manners. Demange vibrated with sensibility, lived exclusively according to the passions of the spirit, and was determined to avoid any reality that might demean him. For Massis it was friendship at first sight, and Demange seems to have reciprocated his feelings. Two years later Demange put a bullet through his brain in a provincial hotel. Why? Both his literary and political careers seemed assured; he had money, manners, charm, wit, the connections required for success—everything, except the will to live. The ostensible reason for the act was a disappointment in love. Barrès and Massis, however, saw Demange's suicide differently. They blamed it on his nihilism and his overcultivation of the ego. Demange, they believed, was an example of dilettantism carried to the point of sickness; he was the bundle of energies gone slack; he was force and talent with no goal, no organizing principle; he was the early Barrès, without the salvation of the roots Barrès had found in France and Lorraine. There was no doubt in Massis's mind: Demange had died of oversensibility and an overly rich diet of ideas. "He was too much in a hurry to live; and this fever in him had something frightening about it. He had excellent nerves, but he abused them." In short, this splendid young man, full of force and potential brilliance, had been a victim of the "cult of the self." He had analyzed and felt too much instead of living.[9]

Whereas Demange provided a negative example for Massis and verified his worst fears concerning the evil influence of relativist ideas, Ernest Psichari

(1883) stood for the positive model of action, asceticism, discipline, and renunciation that Agathon contrasted with the best among the men of 1885. Massis met Psichari in 1906. He was immediately enchanted by the childlike candor of his eyes, the vitality of his physical presence, and the simple, unpretentious kindness of his manners. "He opened himself to you completely on the first meeting." In other words, Psichari was the opposite of Charles Demange. He was a man of action and not a man of words. He lacked *façons*—those complicated and deceptive manners that the fin-de-siècle mentality cherished and that we find so alien today. But Psichari had not always been so sure of himself; nor had he always presented such a picture of overflowing spiritual and physical health.[10]

Like Demange, Psichari was born into the inner circles of the French literary elite. His father Jean Psichari was a well-known poet and professor of Greek philology at the Ecole Pratique des Hautes Etudes. His mother Noèmi was the daughter of Ernest Renan, author of the heretical *Vie de Jésus* and living incarnation of republican intelligence. The mere mention of Renan's name in fin-de-siècle France suggested the academic establishment, religious skepticism, and a mocking epicurean relativism that took pleasure in the contradictions of human thought and conduct and that despaired of establishing any absolute truths, whether religious or simply moral. "We live," Renan had written in 1876, "on the shadow of a shadow. On what will one live after us?"

It was in this world, surrounded by intellectual and political personalities of the first rank, that Psichari grew up and formed his first impressions of culture and politics. Then, even more than now, sons and grandsons of famous men were cut out from the common herd and given educations where they were likely to fall in with young men like themselves. While in *lycée* Psichari met and became fast friends with Jacques Maritain, the grandson of Jules Favre, another eminent figure of the Third Republic. With Maritain, one year his elder, he shared the passions of their progressivist, republican, and highly intellectual milieu around the turn of the century. He was a fervent supporter of Dreyfus; he met and admired Jaurès at his family's table; he leaned toward a broadly construed humanitarian socialism of the Jauresian type; and he spent his Sundays in good progressivist fashion teaching in the Popular Universities to raise the cultural level of the masses so that they too could one day move on the intellectual heights inhabited by the Psicharis.[11]

Progressivist opinions, however, did not save Psichari from the spiritual crisis that afflicted so many young intellectuals of his time. Like Demange, he lived like a dandy and labored over sentences that oozed with tenderness, weakness, irony, and passion; and also like Demange, he contemplated self-destruction. In 1903 he tried to end his life when Maritain's sister, whom he loved with all the desperation of his twenty years, married another man. Foiled in his suicide attempt, Psichari abandoned his home, went out into the streets of Paris, and tried to dull his sorrow with the pains of hunger and the aches of physical labor. For a time at least, he knew the misery of a penniless vagabond with no reason for living other than a vague literary ambition and a desire to commit his life to some worthy cause. A dandy cohabiting with a populist; a man of action with no ideal toward which to bend his will.

Ten years earlier Psichari might have become an anarchist or a Socialist; coming along as he did in 1905, he took another course, though one that given the conditions of his upbringing was no less radical. Determined to escape from the disorder of his life, he joined the army. The cure was so effective that after a year of service he reenlisted and transferred to the colonial artillery, a strange and even shocking choice for the son and grandson of university professors whose antimilitarism was well known. In 1906, after having earned the rank of sergeant major, Psichari made his first trip to Africa, where he spent eighteen months surveying unexplored regions of the Congo that were claimed by France. The experience was overwhelming, exhilarating, life-transforming. Psichari had fled the lies and ugliness, the skepticism and irony, the large stomachs and vain speeches of Paris. He had wanted at all cost to escape from a world of capitulation and heavy good sense. In Africa he found natives, unhampered by the burden of civilization, who reminded him of what Europeans must have been like before "the vices of decadence" had weakened their resolve and robbed them of their force. Africa was a great adventure, a great voyage, an education in primeval and uncomplicated emotion. Colonial service there, he wrote, "makes us better; it exalts us, raises us above ourselves, in a tension of the soul where dream and action interpenetrate and become one." In Africa Psichari came to know and venerate the "knights of death," those soldiers and travelers who had of their own free will given up the comforts and safety of their native land in exchange for the risk of dying an obscure death among strange and uncomprehending peoples. Contact with such men gave Psichari the feeling that he had penetrated to "the very source of life," for "such passing figures suffice to fix in a noble and heroic beauty the most fluid of universes." When he returned to Paris he was able to proclaim that he had "conquered a belief" and hoisted his dream "above all doubt and relativities."[12]

In 1909 Psichari, now a second lieutenant, went out to Africa a second time, with Mauritania as his destination. His three-year sojourn in the desert brought him into contact with muslims and inspired him to meditate on the relationship between authority and religion. He became convinced that there was a necessary connection between the army and the church. A soldier, like a priest, was a man of fidelity. One could not accept the authority of the army without at the same time accepting all authority, both human and divine. Surrender to one absolute led inevitably to surrender to the other. What could be more beautiful, what could bring man closer to the infinite, Psichari mused, than a battle mixed with prayers? Observing the peoples of Islam at first hand, the young officer began to reflect on the relationship between civilizations and the religious traditions that underlay them. He came to view Catholicism as a religion of sacrifice that valued the martyr and the crusader above the mystic or the sage. He believed that through contact with the Moors he had rediscovered his own country, a France of purity and faith that lay hidden beneath the other France of lies and laziness "that he had cursed at the very moment he had left it, perhaps forever." [13]

Yet Psichari, unlike his friend Maritain, was slow to receive the grace to believe. He hungered after faith long before he achieved it. Thus he adopted the peculiar stance of a Catholic who did not believe in the church's essential dogmas. "I am, if I can say this absurd thing, a Catholic without faith," he wrote Maritain from Africa in June 1912. Such a paradox had to lead in one direction or the other: toward either spiritual surrender or the recognition of his inability to believe. For Psichari, who suffered actively from the lack of a faith, the outcome was clear. In 1913, shortly after his return to France from Mauritania, he converted and received communion under the guidance of Maritain and his wife Raïssa. The grandson of Ernest Renan, symbol of modern skepticism, had returned to the most ancient of French communities: the army and the church. [14]

Massis's admiration for Psichari rose in direct proportion to the plunge in morale and self-confidence he felt after Demange's death. Here was a young man who had freed himself from the confusion of ideas and won himself a faith. Moreover, Massis soon discovered that Psichari was not alone. While home on leave his friend introduced him to Maritain (1882) and to Charles Péguy (1873), editor of the *Cahiers de la Quinzaine* and implacable critic of republican culture. Maritain, already making a reputation for himself as a Thomist scholar and an opponent of Bergson, awed Massis by his calm spirituality and his mastery of philosophical thought. In Maritain Massis discovered a Catholic convert who could meet and vanquish the scholars of the Sorbonne on their own intellectual grounds, someone who knew the sources not just as well but better than they did. Like Psichari, Maritain leaned toward royalism and had been influenced by the writings of Charles Maurras, whom he considered France's outstanding political thinker. Péguy, well past thirty but full of robust energy and capable of igniting the enthusiasm of younger men, had abandoned the socialism of his youth for tradition and was rallying a nucleus of Parisian intellectuals around his program of patriotism and Catholic faith without Catholic dogma. His journal was more than a review; it was a gathering point for all those gadflies like himself who were dissatisfied with the way France was and wanted her to be different.

It was also about this time that Massis met Henri Franck, Bergson's nephew. To Massis, Franck (1889) represented the realism and antibookishness of the younger generation. Though acclaimed for his scholarly successes and his poetic gifts, Franck feared that his mind had been deformed by too much culture. He longed to get into contact with "reality," which he identified, somewhat surprisingly, with the life of army camps. In letters to his friends he proclaimed the end of "the reign of theories" and confessed his eagerness to begin his military service. "During an entire year, to run, to walk, to carry burdens, and *to laugh with simple folk*, oh! what a good experience and how healthy it will be!"

Unfortunately, Franck's delicate constitution made it impossible for him to put this "theory" into practice. He died of tuberculosis in 1912, soon after completing his studies at the Ecole Normale Supérieure. Before disappearing from the scene, though, he played an important role in Massis's life and left his imprint on *The Young Men of Today*. A fervent patriot who believed that the future of liberty in the world would be decided on France's eastern frontier, Franck accepted the necessity of war with Germany. "And the sooner the better. With the handsome aloof English and the splendid Italians, we'll get the better of these gross Barbarians, and if not we might as well be dead." Franck also encouraged Massis to think in terms of generations; indeed, Franck's greatest talent seems to have been for bringing together young men of similar leanings and revealing them to themselves. "In his liquid and deep glance, sheltered by long eyelashes, we found brought back to life the reflection of our own faces: we were all illuminated by it." Through this impresario of elective affinities Massis came to know Jacques Rivière (1885), aspiring literary critic and future coeditor of the *Nouvelle Revue Française*. After 1918 Massis and Rivière would become archenemies; but in 1912 they shared a passion for Barrès, a past of neurasthenic dandyism, a newly gained respect for the nation, the army, and the church, and a belief that the younger generation had shaken off the torpor of fin-de-siècle pessimism. "We are men," Rivière would write in 1913, "for whom the novelty of living has been reawakened." [15]

Massis, Psichari, Maritain, Franck, and Rivière had all known the crisis of fin-de-siècle amoralism. All had peered into the Barresian abyss. All had been touched by the epidemic of despair that had led Charles Demange to put a bullet through his brain. All were simultaneously attracted to and frightened by the intense life in which one surrendered the stability of the self to the dispersion of experience and the contradictions of passion and feeling. Barrès's novel, *Sous l'oeil des Barbares* [Under the Eye of the Barbarians], Rivière warned his friend Alain-Fournier in 1905, was not just literature to be criticized like any other book. It was the novel of his inner life; and he had lived personally the struggle for selfhood and authenticity that Barrès had transformed into fiction. [16]

Massis, as we have seen, felt the same way. Yet the emphasis in *The Young People of Today* was on the transcendence of the fin-de-siècle mentality. What distinguished the new generation "from even the best among their elders," said Massis and de Tarde, was that they were beginning where Barrès had left off. What Barrès and his disciples had striven for, questioned, and finally accepted, they took for granted and felt no need to discuss. They possessed Barrès's values without having had to endure the agony that Barrès had suffered in achieving them. They had been born into the world knowing the value of tradition and the vanity of ideas without action. Their patriotic faith was calm; their Catholic religion, deeply felt and uncomplicated; their morals, austere and puritanical; their politics, realistic and antiideological. "These traits emerged from all our accumulated observations as the superimposed portraits of the same family form a collective face: they compose the resemblance of the new generation." Later Massis would add that above all it was "realism" that had characterized the young men of 1912, a state of "spiritual health" that contrasted sharply with "the pessimism, the lacking energy, the moral disarray of their elders." "The rugged will to make France live had acted on the elite of youth like a powerful reminder to return to reality. In the space of a few seasons, youth had proceeded to examine their conscience and to revise privately all their values . . . A clear view of patriotic necessities had secretly prepared them to accept a whole series of parallel truths in the moral, intellectual, literary, and political domains . . . This is what we had wanted to show in order to increase their contagious virtue."[17]

Between 1912 and 1914 dozens of articles were devoted to Agathon's enquête. The subject became unavoidable and spilled over into every important Parisian newspaper and review, where men whose opinions carried weight debated the newness of French youth. "What must one see in Paris these days?" a French journalist was asked in London. "Their young men," he responded frivolously, but not without good reason. Novelists felt compelled to work the theme into their plots and to arrange for a fateful encounter of the old and new generations. In the final installment of his novel-sequence *Jean-Christophe*, written in 1911–1912, Romain Rolland (1866) introduced a representative of the younger generation, born in 1893, whom he described as "full of joie de vivre, superficial, enemy of all spoilsports, passionately in love with pleasure and violent games, easily duped by the rhetoric of his time, inclined by the vigor of his muscles and the laziness of his mind to the brutal doctrines of the Action Française, nationalist, royalist, and imperialist." Rolland contrasted these attitudes and qualities to the romantic idealism, aestheticism, political radicalism, cosmopolitan humanitarianism, and free spirit of Jean-Christophe, who viewed with alarm this rising generation that was more desirous of acting than of understanding and hungrier for possession than for truth. Looking at his work from the vantage point of 1912, Rolland concluded that in telling the story of Jean-Christophe he had written "the tragedy of a generation that is about to disappear." Roger Martin du Gard (1881) also made much of the young men of today in *Jean Barois*, the novel he published in 1913. His Dreyfusard hero undertakes an enquête into the attitudes of the "new youth," only to be told curtly by two young students from the Ecole Normale Supérieure that his generation consists of "dreamers, incapable of willing or acting," whose anarchistic values must now be superseded. Annoyed and discouraged, unwilling to acknowledge that his lifelong struggle for reason and social justice has been futile, Barois consoles himself with the thought that the new generation represents a brief swing of the pendulum, an ebbing of the wave of progress, and that the movement toward a better, freer, juster life will resume again. "A moment to wait: the sea rises nonetheless!" [18]

Although many French intellectuals were offended by the description of the "generation of 1885" and though others deplored the antiintellectualism, the careerism, the pragmatism, the athleticism, and the militarism of the young men of 1912, few disagreed with the general outlines of Agathon's portrait. Small wonder that Massis considered this enquête his greatest literary and moral success and came back to it in work after work of memoirs. The great men of French letters had acknowledged him as a spokesman for the younger generation. After some initial hesitation, Barrès (1863) agreed that the young men of 1912 seemed to have left behind the destructive and negative tendencies that had haunted his own generation. They had surmounted nihilism as a healthy body overcomes a debilitating disease. "The new generation now ascending," he confided to his journal, "announces itself as one of the best that our country has known. Long live French youth!" Bergson (1859) conceded, when queried, that the new youth were truly a "miracle" and added, from the point of view of a specialist in matters of mind and spirit, that what had occurred was nothing less than a mutation in temperament, one of the rarest and most mysterious of events. Paul Bourget (1852), an early opponent of the relativism and nihilism presumed by Agathon to be typical of the generation of 1885, rejoiced that "new generations" had emerged for whom "the sky is once more populated with stars," generations "that reattach themselves resolutely to the philosophical and religious tradition of the old France." Emile Faguet (1847), dean of French enquêteurs, the literary Gallup of his time, grudgingly acknowledged the reality of the phenomenon, while adding, in ill-concealed annoyance, that Agathon had distorted and underestimated the achievement of his elders and overconcentrated on literary youth. "The young men Agathon knows are pure, full of elevated feelings, ardent, courageous, in love with life and confident, devoted to the *patrie*; and all that has to delight us and render less melancholy our approaching departure from the scene. But, by Jove, they aren't modest!" [19]

One of the central themes of Agathon's enquête was the acceptance of the necessity of war with Germany and the prestige of arms among elitist youth. War, Massis and de Tarde had claimed, was no longer anticipated with fear or bitterness; it was now longed for with "secret hope." They quoted in support of this conclusion a statement by a student of rhetoric who wrote, with clear evidence of his course of study, that it was "in the life of camps and under fire that we shall experience the supreme expansion of the French force that lies within us." [20] Many students may have felt this way. Yet the first effect of the war when it arrived in August 1914 was not to increase French power but to threaten the French nation with humiliating defeat and to decimate the ranks of French manhood. Losses were especially high among men of Massis's circle. Charles Péguy fell in the first few weeks of the fighting with a bullet through the head. Psichari died on August 21, shot in the temple as he retreated down an open road after a futile attempt to stop the German advance with the artillery under his command. Alain-Fournier, Rivière's young novelist friend, was reported missing in action on September 22. Rivière himself was taken prisoner and interned in a German camp for the remainder of the war. A shiver of terror ran through the civilian population, as the list of casualties mounted and the government was hurriedly transferred to Bordeaux in the midst of a panic-ridden night. But the French army held at the battle of the Marne, Britain rushed troops to the Belgian frontier, the front was stabilized, and what had begun as a breathtaking war of movement settled into a depressing and seemingly endless war of entrenchment.

We remember the mobilization of armies in August 1914; we forget the mobilization of minds. The one was no less devastating to European civilization than the other. Everywhere in Europe intellectuals militarized themselves, shed their civilian values as volunteers shed their civilian clothes, donned the arms of cultural combat, and set to work to justify their country's action. The idea of generation was one of many peacetime concepts adapted for military use. Massis, who though called up had not seen action, was quick to establish a connection between his young men of 1912 and the army that had saved the country from German domination. "There are few generations," he wrote on a September Sunday in 1914, "that have begun their lives with such a feeling of renunciation and of humility; and that is precisely the meaning of these words that one of our men uttered one day: 'We are a sacrificed generation.'" It would be a mistake, Massis continued, to discern in this remark the least regret or undertone of self-pity. To say that the men of 1912 were a sacrificed generation meant that from the beginning they had gladly accepted a sacrifice to which they were predestined: They had employed their intelligence and their will to prepare themselves for an event of which they would be an instrument, and which would result in the revival of their country. Massis read these lines to a young writer friend, soon to fall in combat, whose only reaction (as recorded by Massis) was to say with a trembling voice, "We shall live our entire lives with what we have done during this war."[21]

The idea was credited, the image was consecrated, and thousands of pages were dedicated to the young men of 1914 whose readiness to die and surprising success in withstanding, if not defeating, the German hordes gained them the temporary status of mythological heroes. Barrès himself devoted his entire literary effort during the war years to this work of consecration; he became the chronicler and poet of the men of 1914. But in the midst of this general acceptance of the idea of a sacrificed generation, a subtle change took place; or better, an ambiguity crept in, unnoticed, which would confuse the issue of the war generation from 1914 on. Massis and de Tarde had studied a small minor-

ity. Their enquête was addressed to young men in the Parisian elite schools
who had been born between 1887 and 1894, men who were still in school or
had recently graduated. The portrait they produced therefore described at the
most a few thousand privileged youths in a country of forty million. But the
French army that manned the trenches consisted of a mass born between 1870
and 1900, not to mention older men who had finagled their way into the service. What this mass shared was an experience, a fate, an adventure, a
trauma—not a youth, a set of ideals, or a common age group of fathers, guides,
and teachers against whom they were reacting. To be sure, they learned to live
together, suffer together, drink together, complain together, even die together;
but only their uniforms and the amalgam of mud and fear that veiled their
faces gave them the semblance of a common physiognomy, and, if they returned, their pattern of action would vary, depending on their politics, their provenance, and their social status. No matter. The identification would be made:
After 1914 French intellectuals, following Massis's lead, would use the term
"generation of 1914" inconsistently to refer both to small groups of writers
united by common age and sensibility and to the mass who had fought in the
war.

Thus out of the ideological campaigns of the prewar decade and the mobilization of French society to stop the Germans at the Marne was born the image
of a sacrificed generation, an army of different ages, classes, and opinions—
young and middle-aged, bourgeois and peasant, urban and rural, royalist and
anarchist—that became identified with an age group, an experience, and a state
of mind. Few, perhaps not even Massis himself, had occasion to remember
that the term "sacrificed generation" had first been used by Agathon to charac-
terize the men of 1885.

M ORE than two decades passed before Massis got around to subjecting his
portrait of the young man of today to a critique, and even then he
approached the task in the spirit of a painter retouching here and there a flawed
but essentially master work that was destined to live in the memory of men. [22]
In the meantime, however, the French generational writings of the first two decades of the twentieth century had inspired an inquiry of a different sort that
sought to give some intellectual respectability and theoretical rigor to the generational idea. In 1920 François Mentré (1877) published a lengthy volume entitled *Les Générations sociales* [Social Generations], which bore a dedication
"to the new youth." Mentré's book had been conceived before 1914 and (as the
dedication suggests) was deeply influenced by the movement of cultural revival
that had produced Agathon's enquête. But writing after the war, Mentré also
felt compelled to make some effort to take into account the new idea of generation as a mass of men of widely differing ages and backgrounds bound together
by a common experience and striving together toward a common end. The

result, as Mentré himself acknowledged, was run through with unresolved contradictions and cluttered with untied ends. [23]

A sociologist in the tradition of Alfred Espinas and Emile Durkheim, Mentré came to the generation problem as someone seeking to comprehend the mechanism of intellectual innovation and social change. Though trained as a philosopher and out of sympathy with the efforts of the scholars of the "new Sorbonne" to reduce knowledge to the history of knowledge, Mentré was nonetheless impressed by the fact that the generational idea had haunted the nineteenth-century imagination. He therefore began his book with a survey of "prescientific" generational theories. After discussing briefly the pages that Plato, Auguste Comte, John Stuart Mill, Antoine Cournot, and Durkheim had devoted to the subject, he gave extended treatment to the more elaborate constructions of the Frenchman Justin Dromel, the Italian Giuseppe Ferrari, and the Austrian Ottokar Lorenz, figures who were as obscure to Mentré's readers as they are to us today. Both Dromel and Ferrari had attempted to account for the sequence of revolutions in nineteenth-century France by means of the generational idea. Political change ensued, they argued, when one generation displaced another. This happened very fifteen years according to Dromel; every thirty years according to his Italian contemporary. Yet both agreed that political attitudes were determined by the structure of human life, and both believed that generations possessed a unity of thought and action. Lorenz approached the problem from a different perspective. A genealogist and statistician, he thought that it was possible to calculate the average difference in age between fathers and sons and thus to establish scientifically the existence of generations and, beyond this, the operation of long-term cycles in history. While critical of all these theories, Mentré salvaged from them the idea that the generational concept might be used to explain the mechanism of progress. Did progress not result from the continuous renewal of populations and the passing of "the torch of truth, beauty, and justice" from one generation to the next? If this could be demonstrated scientifically, then progress would cease to be an abstraction and an article of belief and would become instead a social fact. Mentré set out to test this promising hypothesis. [24]

Mentré began by distinguishing carefully between familial and social generations and between coevality and simple contemporaneity. Social generations, he pointed out, cannot be identified with the succession of fathers, sons, and grandsons in the family because new familial generations are being born every day. The movement of population is continuous and uninterrupted. Nor should social generations be defined in terms of all people coexisting in society at any given time, as the lexicographer Emile Littré had done in his authoritative dictionary. Indeed, the whole point about social generations and the reason for the utility of the concept was that contemporaries could be broken up into different age-groups. The division of society into age-groups occurred because the mass of active and productive adults changed totally and regularly every thirty years. With this change in personnel came a change in sensibility. Inspired by Taine and the historian Fustel de Coulange, Mentré insisted that history should study the development of human sentiments and beliefs. Thus he rejected the idea that social generations were determined by the course of political development, the breakthroughs of science, the innovations of technology, the insights of philosophy, or the history of educational systems. A social generation was the product of a spiritual transformation, "a quiet labor of minds that gives birth to a new ideal of human activity." This spiritual transformation took place regularly within the minds and hearts of adolescents and young men. Intellectual life developed through the principle of opposition; and this opposition derived ultimately from the struggle between fathers and their sons. Obeying the obscure yet inexorable law that sets children against their parents, the members of the younger generation revolted against the teaching of their elders and forged out of their experience a new system of values, a new hierarchy of ends, and a new gallery of models. Generation thus could be defined only "in terms of beliefs and desires, in psychological and moral terms." A social generation was not a means of dividing time, but a "spiritual unity." It was "a new way of feeling and understanding life," "an original spiritual milieu," "a collective state of mind incarnated in a human group that lasts a certain period of time." [25]

Like the nineteenth-century generational theorists on whom he based his work and from whom he derived many of his ideas, Mentré assumed that generations had a regular rhythm, and reasoning from what he took to be a man's period of effective social action, he concluded that they lasted about thirty years. He considered briefly, only to dismiss, a suggestion by Durkheim that the concentration of population in large cities would increase conflict between young people and their elders by weakening tradition, and thus speed up the process of generational formation. "There are never more than three male generations in a century; but nowadays they appear to be fragmented into two, three, or four segments, because young people are so anxious to get themselves talked about and encroach easily upon the rights of their elders!" Hence, the apparent acceleration in the coming and going of generations was nothing but an illusion; by arranging human life in such a way that male social and biological "fecundity" coincided, nature had ensured that generations would appear every thirty years. [26]

Yet persuaded as he was that the structure of life determined that social generations would be of relatively equal length, Mentré stressed that the process of generational formation should not be thought of as a steady, regular, unending flow. In the emergence of social generations, some years were more noteworthy than others. Creativity came in spurts; the graph of generational development consisted of mountain peaks, valleys, and slopes. Each social generation had its guides, heroes, and prophets, whose dates of birth tended to cluster around certain decisive years. Other years were "sacrificed" and "sterile" in the eyes of

men living at the time; they gave birth to the deviates, the precursors of generations to come and the stragglers from preceding generations. Discontinuity in
generational matters was the rule; continuity was always the exception. And the
struggle of one generation with another was more violent and thus more evident at some times than at others.[27]

Mentré was struck by the way great men banded together and were related to
another by common styles and themes. Indeed, in his view a school of thought
was a social generation. But great men corresponded to a social need and existed only through and by means of their collaborators and admirers. "Great
works," insisted Mentré, "are accomplished by groups of contemporaries."
Focusing as he did on revolutions of sensibility, the generational historian had
no choice but to be an elitist. He must acknowledge that from the point of view
of the historical generation, many lives simply did not count: one had to know
how to resign oneself to obscurity when one was a mere member of the mass.
"The majority of men," Mentré commented sadly, "play nonspeaking roles in
the great human choir and provide the backdrop for the great dress ball of history."[28]

Mentré believed that every period had a dominant generation that reflected
for a time the beliefs and desires of the entire nation. This generation, he suggested, was like an army that gathered in its ranks all those individuals capable
of bearing arms. It had its generals and its privates, its officers and its noncoms,
its bearded veterans and its new recruits, with the entire intervening gamut of
age groups. "It is a profound mass from which emerge certain heads, and
which confounds in a common fate a multitude of male existences that are not
rigorously contemporary but that obey a single impulse and are animated by
the same ambitions and the same hopes."[29]

Each century contained three such dominant generations. What method
should the historian employ in trying to find them and delimit them? With
what tools should he be equipped? Here Mentré had no hesitation. Given the
elementary state of historical linguistics, literature offered the most comprehensive vantage point from which to study the transformations of sensibility. Not
that literature *determined* social evolution; but it translated and reflected more
accurately than any other form of activity or "series" all aspects of collective
life. It was "the faithful mirror of spiritual changes as well as of the profound
and mysterious tendencies of peoples." Every book was "a fragment of collective psychology and the indication of a generalized mentality; it had been successful because it responded to an expectation." Literature—and the intellectual series in general—were like families; they developed through the law of
opposition. They were subject to the laws of genealogy. And thus the turnover
of generations became especially clear when viewed through the literature of a
period.[30]

Born in 1877 and brought up in the cult of social facts, Mentré was enough
of a positivist to be embarrassed by the scientific shortcomings of the genera-

tional idea. He acknowledged, for example, that it was impossible to determine with absolute precision the duration of a social generation. He also conceded that it was difficult to draw hard and fast chronological boundaries between one generation and another. The perception and description of the generational sequence, he granted, was another sticky problem that was likely to give rise to error and disputation. Yet despite these theoretical stumbling blocks, Mentré was convinced of the utility of the generational idea, for it corresponded to common sense and was a reality for every individual. "When a man refers to his generation, he uses an expression that is perfectly clear, although it is not chronological. He designates by it those who are more or less the same age as he is, his fellow students and his friends, those who were growing up at the same time he was and who shared with him spheres of activity and influence. All the men of a generation are bound together by the community of their point of departure, of their beliefs, and of their desires."[31]

Besides, argued Mentré, shifting to another line of defense, the generational idea was no more imprecise than many of the historian's other methods. The better one got to know the data the more one's doubts about its utility began to disappear. Properly conceived, the notion of generation could be an extremely precious "working hypothesis," an auxiliary, and (in Mentré's view) by no means the least important, principle of historical explanation. With this *fil conducteur* to guide him through the chaos of facts, the historian could understand more completely the activity of a great man, the influence of his work, the curve of his reputation, or even the history of an entire series like the history of science or the history of philosophy, "provided that one had at one's disposal documents that were sufficiently plentiful and detailed."[32]

M ENTRÉ'S book did not receive a favorable reception. When presented as a thesis for the state doctorate at the Sorbonne, it received rough treatment at the hands of Charles Seignobos, the reigning expert on questions of historical method. The upshot was that Mentré's work failed to reach or influence the historians toward whom it was primarily directed. Nor was it much appreciated by those nonacademic but highly influential intellectuals who dictated Parisian literary taste and possessed the power to launch a reputation. Reviewing *Social Generations* for the *Nouvelle Revue Française*, Albert Thibaudet praised Mentré's probity, prudence, and intelligence, then went on to say that Mentré's treatise was nothing but a preface to the book that would one day be written by somebody who was willing to approach *ce beau problème* from a Bergsonian point of view and to conceive of generations as expressions of *élan vital*. For the most part, Mentré's book was simply ignored. This was understandable. Because *Social Generations* did little to clarify the phenomenon of generationalism, as it was presenting itself to French intellectuals during the first three decades of the twentieth century. Instead, it reflected and elevated to the status of scientific hypotheses assumptions that were current among literary intellectuals like Massis and de Tarde.[33]

The most evident problem was that Mentré's theory failed to fit the facts that it had been devised to explain. Anyone trying to understand the sequence of generations in postwar France with the aid of Mentré's book would have been dismayed and confused. We can see why if we take a quick glance at some of the generational writings that appeared in France during the decade of the twenties. Massis, remember, had identified his generation first as those born around 1890, then later as all those who fought in the war. This corresponded more or less to Mentré's calculation that a new generation had appeared between 1910 and 1914. The war had not been over long, however, before it became clear that the combatants could not be treated as a single generational bloc and that the generation of 1910—if it existed—was already being overtaken by its successors. Within the ranks of the French intellectuals who had fought in and survived the war, two age-groups stood out, rendering ambiguous if not downright meaningless the idea of a single "war generation."[34]

The first of these groups consisted of writers like Massis who had been established or on their way to being established when the war broke out. Now they had passed thirty and were no longer young men, particularly not now, after the war, when to be truly young meant to have been too young to fight in the war. In August 1914 they had responded to the call of patriotism and adventure. Many of them had died. But those who had come back bore proudly on their civilian suits the decorations they had won in the field. They were no longer comers or on the ascendancy: They were survivors, and they had arrived. Most of them had been at Verdun in 1916. They knew that war was hell, but they considered *this* war just, because they believed that it had been necessary to remove once and for all the intolerable German menace that had weighed on them during their youth. While in the war they had grumbled like everyone else about the food and the leadership and agreed that it was difficult to tell which was lousier. But damn it, they had won! Now they had come home to claim their "booty" and to live *la belle vie*, and soon they began to complain that their women and their jobs had been taken by draft dodgers of their own age or by unprincipled adolescents who had been too young to fight but not too young to take advantage of their absence. "Hats off before the dead," was a slogan often heard during the twenties. Rhetoric aside, it meant quite simply to give the survivors the places and the power they had earned by their efforts during the war. This first "war generation" found its most eloquent spokesmen in Henri Barbusse (1873), Georges Duhamel (1884), Jules Romain (1885), Roland Dorgelès (1886), and Maurice Genevoix (1890); but no one ever caught the mentality of these survivors better or expressed their sense of grievance more poignantly than André Lamandé (1886) in his best-selling

novel *Les Lions en croix* [Lions on the Cross], which described them melo-
dramatically as victims of routine and oblivion, "poor men with lion's marrow,
nailed on the triple cross of indifference, scorn, and forgetfulness."[35]

The second "war generation" was made up of young intellectuals, mostly
born in the 1890s, who had gone directly from school examinations (which
some of them had failed) to the front and who had come back full of bitterness,
irony, and nostalgia for the transient life of camps and trenches. They saw the
war not as a sacrifice for which they had prepared but as a thunderbolt that had
struck them down or an earthquake that had swept the ground from underneath
them as they ventured out into adult life. They grieved over their lost youth,
complained about the mediocrity of civilian life, and had no places to reclaim,
for they had not yet started careers when the war broke out. Many of them had
not known the élan of August 1914; they had gotten to the front after the battle
of Verdun, when red pantaloons had been replaced by horizon blue, patriotic
slogans were something to be smiled or spat at, offensives were to be feared,
and the only value, other than gallows humor, was comradeship in a slaughter-
house where all expected to die, if not today then tomorrow. They remembered
the war with the same ambivalent affection with which a man recalls his first
mistress, unable to separate the pain they had suffered from the afterglow of
youthful excitement whose warmth they still sometimes felt. They hated their
leaders with a vengeance that often sounded revolutionary even when it was
only bitter; they separated the world into combatants and noncombatants rather
than into nations; they dreamed of turning on the fat civilians who had profited
from their blood; and they believed in nothing but themselves, their comrades
(now mostly dead), and the vague, indefinable insights the war had brought
them. They had lost their faith in words, art, and order, and they were constantly threatening to burn all the bridges, to destroy culture, and to blow society sky high. Nihilism, not patriotism, was the attitude they adopted most naturally. Respect for their elders was not their strength. Once home, one of the
first things these young soldier-intellectuals did was to put Anatole France and
Maurice Barrès on trial for "crimes against culture," by which they meant
crimes against youth. André Breton (1896), Louis Aragon (1897), and Philippe
Soupault (1898) belonged to this group; Dadaism and early Surrealism expressed certain facets of its mentality.[36]

A connoisseur of generational differences, Massis was quick to note the
change in sensibility. It was not long after the war ended, he wrote, before we
noticed the coming of a new generation only a few years younger than ourselves for whom our history was a closed book. "It was as if the victory had
never happened. In the universal negation of all the values that had inspired us
when we fought, before the spectacle of a world that sought the nothingness of
sleep, we quickly came to wonder if our comrades had not died in vain and if
we ourselves did not belong to another world, a world that would always
remain inside of us." By 1935 Massis had concluded that his genera-

tion—whose center he now pushed back from 1910 to 1905—was a generation of "conservers." They had attempted to revise and preserve certain values—country, religion, discipline—from whose constraints the next generation, a generation of negators, had sought to escape.[37]

Massis later wrote that it was on meeting the young war hero Henry de Montherlant, his junior by only ten years, that he first became aware that "I was already a man of another era, of another age." And during the early twenties it was above all Montherlant (1896) who came to represent this younger war generation to the book- and journal-reading public. People who know Montherlant's work, especially his novels and plays, may find it hard to understand how the author of *Les Jeunes Filles* and *Port-Royal* could ever have been considered typical of any social group, least of all his generation. Among the great French writers of the twentieth century, Montherlant was the outsider par excellence. His whole life seems to have been lived against the current. Of noble birth and Catholic upbringing in a middle-class and secular republic, Montherlant resolved at an early age "to dedicate himself entirely to the interests of his mind and soul." The Roman sage and the Catholic saint who set themselves aside from the hurly-burly of their times and devoted themselves to the pursuit of their own perfection were—and remained—his models.[38]

Yet circumstances intervened to identify Montherlant with the war and the generation of younger men who fought in it. An unsuccessful and unenthusiastic student of law, Montherlant was just eighteen when the war arrived. Prevented from enlisting by his mother, who was ill and on the verge of dying, he spent the first year of the war rounding out his knowledge of the classics and pursuing his literary fantasies in the austere reading room of the Bibliothèque Nationale. When his mother died in August 1915, he immediately applied for the army, only to be turned down because of a weak heart. Not until September of the following year did he manage to get passed for service, and even then only the intervention of his grandmother succeeded in getting him assigned to an infantry regiment at the front. By this point the terrible losses at Verdun had called into question the sanity, not to mention the humanity, of the leaders on both sides responsible for the slaughter. The world seemed absurd; death a quasi-certainty; the official reasons being given for the war a ruse designed to conceal something deeper and more fundamental. It would have been hard to regard service in this inferno as anything more than an inescapable and desperate duty, and Montherlant's background had not encouraged the development of patriotic sentiments. Raised in a family so reactionary that they regarded the defeats of the French army in August 1914 as divine punishment for the sins of the Republic, Montherlant went to war without illusions or patriotic faith to sustain him. For him the war was a fate he had freely chosen, a furnace he entered with the intention of forging the outlines of his character and purifying the materials of his soul. Wounded gravely in 1918 and cited for gallantry in action, he lived for two years side-by-side with death. This experience was the catalyst that gave shape to his emerging sensibility. Like many survivors, he apparently came to believe that he had a responsibility to bear witness for the dead and to keep alive their memory. After he was demobilized in 1919, his grandmother secured employment for him as secretary to a commission formed for the purpose of erecting an ossuary as a monument to the dead of Fort Douaumont, scene of some of the fiercest fighting at Verdun. It was from this position and in the guise of an official representative of the French dead that Montherlant published his first books and essays.[39]

It is clear why Massis felt uncomfortable and hopelessly old-fashioned in the company of Montherlant. A realist whose passion for authenticity led him to the brink of nihilism, the younger man lacked completely the happy optimism, the tranquil faith, and the sense of social responsibility that had given rise to the spirit of sacrifice among Massis and his friends. A Montherlant hero risked his life for his country without believing in the justice of its cause. He served, knowing his service would be useless, because he enjoyed the sensation of being free to dispose of his life as he liked. He revered Catholicism, while going out of his way to indicate that he did not believe in God. And he was a dedicated sensualist driven by a "desire without remedy," to whose satisfaction he was nonetheless ready to devote long periods of his life. There was nothing in nature—no matter how violent or cruel—that Montherlant could not affirm. An intrepid toreador, an athlete, and a soldier with scars to document his courage, he possessed an unshakable sense of superiority over other men. Nor did he bother to conceal his scorn for those who had not known and enjoyed physical combat. He was a pessimist whose skepticism spared no value and who delighted in the inconsistencies and contradictions of life, especially his own. Above all, he was an exile in the world of peace, for whom the war had been not a step in the revival of his country but a deeper, truer, more intense way of life for which he would always long. Montherlant had "loved life at the front, the bath in the elemental, the annihilation of the intelligence and the heart." He believed that there would always be wars because there would always be twenty-year-old boys who would start them "by dint of love." Massis's young men had gone off to war with their knapsacks full of values and hopes; when he came home, Montherlant's knapsack was empty, and he made no attempt to conceal that when he traveled, he traveled light. The challenge for Montherlant's heroes was to live life grandly and fully—just as if they believed that their service would be useful. "The knight of nothingness," he called himself in one of his most famous essays—a younger, harsher brother to Psichari's "knights of death."[40]

Montherlant had reservations about the concept of a war generation and warned against the term's abuse. Not so Pierre Drieu la Rochelle, his elder by three years and like him one of the great French literary discoveries of the immediate postwar years. Drieu (1893) returned home from the war determined

Maurice Barrès in the 1890s.

The day on which we discovered Barrès, we discovered ourselves as well.
  Henri Massis, 1909

Henri Massis.

A clever, penetrating, but weak person who would like to impose on others the tutors he himself needs.
    Jacques Rivière describing Henri Massis, 1924

Top: Jacques Rivière about 1920; Ernest Psichari about 1912. Bottom: Alain-Fournier about 1910; portrait of Henri Franck in 1905 by Jacques Briss.

We are men for whom the novelty of living has reawakened.
  Jacques Rivière, 1913

Henry de Montherlant in the 1920s.

To search for a solution, knowing that the problem is insoluble; to serve, while smiling at what one serves; to subject oneself to an iron discipline, without end and without profit; to write, in the profound conviction that one's work has no importance; to know, to understand, and to tolerate, while constantly bearing in mind the painful uselessness of being right . . .

Henry de Montherlant, 1929

Pierre Drieu la Rochelle in the 1930s.

We have been, and above all, after the war is over, we shall be . . . what you dreamt of being.

 Pierre Drieu la Rochelle to André Suarez, 1917

Top: Marcel Arland in 1929. Bottom: Jean Luchaire on the bench of the accused in 1946; Jean Prévost about 1930.

Growing up in a lost Europe of blood and hate, amidst demented or terrified men, what direction, what support could our youth find?
    Marcel Arland, 1926

to bear witness for his friends, "for the young men, for those who fought, for those who died. We haven't said our last word. More than one people will perish before we do."[41] A student at the posh Ecole des Sciences Politiques in 1912, Drieu may have been among those queried by Massis and de Tarde. If he was, his answer should have given them cause to make some substantial modifications in their portrait of the young man of the moment. Far from possessing a calm patriotic faith, Drieu lacked confidence in his fellow Frenchmen, suffered from the weakness and diplomatic humiliations of his country, and dreamed of emigrating to America or Australia where he could lead the life of an adventurer and share the fate of the Nordic peoples who dominated the world. He had, it is true, wanted desperately to be an athlete, for team sports evoked thoughts of England, ruddy-faced schoolboys, and military power. Yet the effort to discipline his muscles and learn rugby had failed and left him persuaded of his irredeemable decadence. He remained a man of dreams who was more at home in the café or the drawing room (and later in the boudoir) than on the playing field. When the war came, he was by his own account "a sniffling bourgeois, afraid and pessimistic." A young intellectual closer to the bookish and self-destructive Barrès of the 1880s than to the dynamic life-affirming sportsmen described by Agathon.[42]

The war represented a moment of fulfillment. It had come as a "marvelous surprise" and had temporarily reversed Drieu's feeling of failure and decline. In August 1914 Drieu was under arms and suffering at the thought of three years of tedious military service. He could not really believe that the statesmen of Europe would allow war to happen. "I had placed a bet on it and promised to buy my friends three bottles of champagne if the regiment so much as left its barracks." Then came the great experience beside which all others would always pale. At Charleroi in August 1914 Drieu participated in a bayonet charge and discovered within himself unsuspected reserves of courage. Nailed to the ground in a plain littered with dead bodies, he found himself rising and rushing forward, leading the attack. Inside himself he felt a sudden spurt of life, a shower of ecstasy that revealed to him the person he had sought throughout his adolescence but never found. "Who was it who suddenly emerged? A leader. Not only a man, a leader. Not only a man who knows how to surrender himself, but a man who knows how to take." Henceforth Drieu would always believe in the unity of life and death. He had discovered in that moment of ecstasy that life was a "single stream." He could not ask to live life fully without at the same time accepting the idea of his own annihilation.[43]

Drieu enjoyed the war and the medals he won for fighting in it. He had never been so free before, and he savored the comradeship of soldiers—especially those of his own class who were determined to amuse themselves before they died. But even the war turned out to be an ambiguous experience. For in discovering courage Drieu also discovered fear and the awful inhumanity of war as it was being waged on the Western Front. At Verdun in 1916 a massive shell blast caused him to wet his trousers and tore from him a cry of terror that he would never forget—"that cry of my intelligence in the midst of the bestial silence of soldiers."[44]

Drieu forged his war experiences into a slim volume of poems entitled *Interrogation*, which he published in a limited edition in 1917. Inspired by the odes of Paul Claudel and Futurist in tone and language, Drieu's poems celebrated the virtues of war without concealing its horrors. War, Drieu rhapsodized, had completed the restoration of the body that sport had begun. It had reconciled dream and action. It had brought the bourgeoisie into contact with the common people. And most important of all, it had made possible the return to a tragic vision of life. Do not ask us to regret or to deny this war, Drieu warned. "If you venerate Love, do not insult War." The poems made no display of phony patriotism or of stoic endurance. Drieu confessed that on "that day at Verdun I was the one who cried no to pain." But since Charleroi life for Drieu had become inextricably connected with death, renewal with destruction. "Everything that is new is good, beyond the new there is no health. Humanity can endure only by renewing itself constantly, by killing with years its old age." Perhaps the most striking feature of *Interrogation* was Drieu's claim to speak for all young soldiers of his age group and class—for those he was later to call those adventurers who played out their great game beneath the heavens in a rain of steel. The young men who had fought this war, Drieu wrote, had been transformed by the experience. They bore within themselves a revelation and a revolution. It was time for them "to emit their cry," and it was the turn of the "old men" to hold their tongues. Those at home should beware of the returning warriors. "For these men, in this hour, are suffering from the war because of their strength. Tomorrow they will come back. Only they will leave there, in that country where others haven't been, their fear and the despair that possessed them because they, the strongest, were condemned to pain and suffering. Having rid themselves of their burden, they will be proud of themselves and they will be ferocious. When peace comes the uneasy times will not be over."[45]

Not long after the armistic, however, Drieu began to suffer new doubts about himself and his generation. Like other young returning veterans, he felt that the combatants had "capitulated" and allowed themselves to be absorbed into the miserable banality of everyday existence in peacetime France. Drieu's short stories and novels of the 1920s chronicled savagely and masochistically the aimlessness of young warriors, like himself, who had been "clapped between the hands of the war" and who had come home to find that in their absence life had somehow gone off its track. These men, Drieu lamented, were "poor children, fascinated and lost." They were unable to escape from the memory of the war, and they wondered if they would ever escape from its "mystical dream." Taken unawares by the armistice, they were forced to improvise the peace in the same way that their elders had improvised the war. But the task of reconstruction was beyond them: They had no real education and no sound values. Thus they embarked upon a period of debauch. They spent their time in salons, restaurants, bars, and opium dens. They experimented with pederasty and slept with one another's women out of boredom and in obedience to the law of novelty. They conceived no children, and in their sterility they bled France of the men needed to defend its frontiers and to restore its greatness. Their life was filled with frantic activity, but the reality behind their movement was "depressing immobility, idle contemplation, and sterile expectation." They traveled, but their bags were empty. They were everywhere, but they were nowhere. They remained "outside of everything." They were crushed beneath the new freedom that had suddenly been forced upon them. And the soundest of them fled "stifling in the silence of the woods his lamentation against the unknown, a complex of desires, inevitabilities, and miseries that is striking down the men and women around him."[46]

Yet as quick as spokesmen for the young war generation, like Montherlant and Drieu, were to indict their comrades for capitulation and to describe in painful and self-lacerating detail their failure in civilian life, they could not believe that it was in vain that the combatants had "received the highest exaltation that there is." They waited for the moment when their generation would rise again and take its rightful place. In the meantime, they suffered from the mediocrity of everyday life that fell on their "warm enthusiasm" like a "perfidious, little grey rain." It had taken no more to master them and quench their ardor, they complained, than the signing of the peace and the return of the "bad doctors" who governed France. "But what a sudden desire sometimes comes over us to unbend, to strike the air with our now impotent fists, to spit in disgust. And before the clouds that pass in the sky, what nostalgia rises in our troubled hearts. A strange malaise that numbs us, an unexpressed desire to embrace the unknown, to flee toward faraway lands, to punish our poor bodies for their quiet somnolence by exposing them as in the past to the rigors of the simple elements." No matter what these men were now, their spokesmen claimed, they could not and would not forget the men they once had been. Meanwhile, unyielding writers like Montherlant and Drieu la Rochelle kept alive the memory of their greatness and created lasting literature out of their nostalgia, their anger, and their style of life.[47]

D URING the twenties this generation of young warriors was much discussed. Numerous accounts of the war experience were published. And small groups of men labored, without much success, to turn the veterans' movements into a base for renovating and transforming republican institutions. The veterans, said Marcel Bucard (1895), "intend to play in the peace the role they played yesterday in the war: the first!"[48]

But the thirty-year-olds of 1925—the Montherlants, the Drieus, the Bretons—came close to being shouldered aside and eclipsed by a group of even younger men, who also identified themselves in terms of the war. This generation consisted of young writers, all born around 1900, who had just missed serving in the war. They had accepted the idea of their own death and were surprised and disoriented when the war ended, peace descended, the expected apocalypse failed to materialize, and they suddenly found themselves with lives to lead and careers to make in a world filled with shattered illusions. Few French literary age-groups have analyzed themselves so relentlessly or with such persistent fascination as these talented and tortured young men. The autobiographical essay was de rigueur, and the earlier one wrote it the more likely one was to succeed. Many young writers evidently felt that they had nothing to recount except their own experiences and their search for a stable self. Yet what is noteworthy from the point of view of our theme is their tendency toward *collective* self-analysis. Even when narrating personal and highly individual experiences, the writers of this age-group slipped easily and without embarrassment from the isolation of the first person singular to the community of the generational *we*. Their premise, made explicit by the young Catholic philosopher Henri Daniel-Rops (1901), was that through the play of some obscure awareness men gathered, confronted their fate, and committed themselves on the road of life in groups. "There is no such thing as a loner: Those who appear to be alone are, in reality, the precursors of a slower legion. And human history seems to advance by leaps."[49]

These postwar emulators of Massis differed over what characteristics distinguished their generation. Marcel Arland (1899), a member of the editorial staff of the *Nouvelle Revue Française* and an up-and-coming literary critic, spoke of a new *mal du siècle*. His autobiographical sketch, *La Route obscure* [*The Dark Road*], described the spiritual torment of a young man so lost and uncertain of his own identity that he not only was unhappy; he lacked a desire for happiness. "I've sought desperately a goal to seek, I've waited for something to wait for, I've desired something to desire," he lamented. Arland doubted that the most representative members of his generation would ever overcome their crisis. The circumstances in which they had grown up had compelled them to destroy and to break with the past; the circumstances of the postwar years had made it impossible for them to seize on any values in which they could believe. And yet they wanted desperately to live and to experience life fully. Their negativism and their fierce desire to live, Arland feared, were likely to lead them into desperate adventures and make them prey to dogmatisms of all kinds. Daniel-Rops agreed with Arland that what distinguished the postwar generation was their unrest and anxiety. But he stressed the intense, almost desperate nature of their spiritual quest. The young men of today, Daniel-Rops said, were Hamlets. You could single them out from their elders by their hesitation to act, their insatiable curiosity about themselves, their taste for the absolute, and their religious impulse, which might lead to either a sentimental commitment to an established religion (as in the case of Daniel-Rops himself) or an attraction to some kind of religious surrogate like Communism. Jean Luchaire (1901), a political journalist, came to an almost diametrically opposed conclusion. For him the younger generation was above all realistic. The war had been a "school of facts," and the disillusions of the postwar years had purged the younger generation of its adolescent romantic sentimentalism. If today's young men hesitated to commit themselves, it was because they rejected ideologies, social myths, and mystiques in general. But they would act if they could be effective. André Malraux (1901) doubted that the efficacy of their actions would be determining for those youths who had discovered life in the aftermath of the war. They would act to defend themselves against their own spiritual vacuum and their fear of death. "To what fate then is destined this violent youth, so marvelously armed against itself and delivered from the vulgar vanity of calling grandeur what is actually disdain for a life to which it does not know how to attach itself?"[50]

What all self-analysts of the postwar generation could agree on was the uniqueness of their experience, their skepticism about prewar values, their openness to new departures, and their alienation from returning veterans. The uniqueness of their experience, they held, derived from the fact that they had grown up without the discipline of fathers and teachers. While still adolescents they had had thrust upon them the responsibilities of maturity and the temptations of a wartime society in which money was readily available and women longed for the society of men. Their skepticism about conventions and ideologies and their determination to look the world unflinchingly in the eye no matter what the consequences for themselves or others, they said, were the product of a disillusionment that had begun when they first saw through the lies of patriotic propaganda and that had been capped by the failure of the Allies to make the peace and by the equally shattering failure of revolutionaries to renovate society. Their ambivalence toward returning veterans, they explained, was also the result of disenchantment. Brought up during the war to admire the men in horizon blue and to worship them as heroes, they found those who returned to be immature, insufficiently serious, and hopelessly old-fashioned in their values. Moreover, they were shocked—or claimed to be—by the veterans' frivolity and lack of discipline; put off by their apparent preoccupation with death; disappointed by their powerlessness to effect wide-ranging changes in society; and bored by their obsession with the war. They were ready to concede that these men had lived a great adventure; they were even willing to admit that they might have some grim wisdom to impart. But as time went by, they began to doubt whether these scarred and battered warriors, so obviously fatigued by their efforts and more inclined to linger over memories than to project new ideas, were cut out to lead them in the combats that lay ahead. Commenting on the declaration of a group of veterans that "younger men expect from us the signal indicating a direction," Daniel-Rops asked whether this were true and answered without hesitation: "For them, not for us." There was, he said, an abyss between the two age-groups that the most sincere affection could not overcome. And significantly, when referring to the "war generation," Daniel-Rops and his coevals almost always added the plural *s* and spoke of "war generations," as if to remind the combatants that they too had been formed by the war. [51]

During the late twenties and early thirties the conflict between returning veterans and their younger brothers was a popular literary theme. The veterans, men of responsibility and principle, were contrasted to their precocious juniors, who trampled over other people's lives and were sowers of disorder. [52] Why had postwar youth been moved by such a nihilistic and aimless spirit of revolt? Jean Prévost (1901) and André Chamson (1900) sought to answer this question in generational memoirs published at the end of the twenties. Prévost's study, *Dix-Huitième Année* [When I Was Eighteen], singled out the impact of war hysteria as the cause of his revolt. They taught us, Prévost said, that only one thing was respectable: to fight. We accepted the fact that we were inferior to the combatants and that we would spend the rest of our lives admiring them. We despised civilians and had no respect for old men, teachers, women, or ourselves because none of these groups enjoyed the prestige that came from being at the front. We could see no reason to respect authority because only the combatants deserved to be respected, and the myth of the combatant fabricated by the propagandists of the rear (like Barrès) did not include the virtue of obedience. We learned to admire the airmen on leave who insulted the police and drove their cars on the sidewalk to amuse themselves. We grew up without public spirit because we were used to waiting passively for news of our salvation from the front, where our destiny was being decided. When the war ended, we assumed that everything would change. We would be happy; we would become a serious people like the Americans; we were going to be generous; the *poilus* would come back, and they would cure us of our laziness and serve as our example. Instead, Prévost said, his generation had discovered that nothing was going to change. And when the government reneged on its promises, youth remembered and vowed to take their revenge. "That is why we revolted then or since, without any other program than that of insults for those who lied to us, without any other demand than a justice we did not deserve." Theirs was "the revolt of children, the revolt of witnesses." Witnesses, that is, of broken promises and shattered dreams. [53]

Prévost chose as his theme "the cult of courage detoured by peace into a revolutionary élan." He implied that his experience had been representative of his generation as a whole. André Chamson tried to be more specific. He set out to explain the fate of a part of his generation, those young intellectuals (like Prévost and himself) who had been attracted to left-wing ideas during "the revolution of 1919." Chamson ascribed his own drift toward radicalism to the break in the continuity of generations that had resulted from the war. He and his coevals, he pointed out, had grown up without the guidance of older brothers. There had been no one to discipline the disorderly inclinations of their twentieth year. If these inclinations were rebellious and destructive, it was because he and others like him had internalized the world of war in a way the combatants themselves had not. The combatants at least had carried within them images of a peaceful prewar world to oppose to the images of death that surrounded them; Chamson and his generation, by contrast, had possessed no experience and no solid values with which to defend themselves against the infection of war. Young intellectuals like himself, Chamson suggested, had tended to experience the war as an apocalypse and the end of a civilization. They wanted a purification of the world, a rebirth; they welcomed the coming of an era of austerity and heroism during which the comforts of the old world would be renounced and life would temporarily be impoverished. The strikes and labor unrest of 1919 and the radicalization of the French Socialist party had seemed to correspond to their hope. They joined the Socialist movement and became Marxists. But then they woke up to see that nothing in the world had changed, despite the appearance of revolutionary action. The same men, the same institutions, the same structures prevailed. Yet in the process, youth itself had changed. They had been delivered from the specter of death and the vision of an apocalypse. They had learned to appreciate traditional values, and they had become attached to life in its most unchanging forms. The crisis of adolescence, Chamson concluded, can call into question an entire civilization. In liberating themselves from the myth of revolution, Chamson claimed, he and others like him had also freed themselves from the myth of youth itself. They had finally become adults and were no longer haunted by the images of death that had clouded their adolescence.[54]

André Chamson was more honest than most generationalists of the twenties in admitting that his goal was to describe the experience of only a part of his generation; yet even that part reacted in diverse ways to the events of 1919–1920. Whereas the failure of the Socialist revolution inspired Chamson to liberate himself from the cult of youth and to return to the enduring values of the land, it led his coeval Jean Luchaire (1901) to cultivate the myth of apocalyptic change and to exploit for his own political advantage the hostility felt by young men toward their elders. The son and grandson of university professors, Luchaire had spent the war in Florence where his father was director of the Institute of International Intellectual Cooperation, an organization that fostered cultural and political contacts between France and Italy. An extraordinarily precocious youth whose ruling passion from his earliest years was for politics, he astonished his father by his single-mindedness and his ability to persuade others to underwrite and finance his undertakings. The lack of an assured income and the possession of a facile pen turned him toward journalism, a natural course for a young man who wanted to make his way in politics. His first articles were published before the war. During the conflict he organized the Latin League of Youth to support the French cause in Italy and to encour-

age Italians to fight on the side of their "Latin sister." Disillusioned by the outcome of the war, he returned to France in 1919 and married. Children followed in rapid succession. To support them and to further his political
ambitions, Luchaire worked for numerous Parisian newspapers, among them
Le Matin, Le Petit Parisien, L'Europe Nouvelle, L'Homme Libre, and *La
Volonté.* He came to know the people who dispensed government funds to the
press and was rumored to have excellent relations with the foreign minister,
Briand, whose enthusiasm for the League of Nations he shared.[55]

In 1927 Luchaire launched a new review entitled *Notre Temps: La Revue des
nouvelles générations.* Briand was widely believed to have subsidized it with
government funds, because of Luchaire's strong support for Briand's policy of
Franco-German rapprochement. Among its editors and contributors were Guy
Crouzet, Daniel-Rops, and Bertrand de Jouvenel. *Notre Temps* called for a
bloc of all those belonging to "the younger generations" and aimed at the capture and transformation of the Radical party. By the new generations were
meant those whose mentality had been formed during or immediately after the
war. Luchaire began from the assumption that an uncrossable abyss separated
"those who have lived *before,* impregnated by a past heavy with traditions and
diverse mysticisms, and those who, coming *afterward,* cannot permit themselves to be guided by the intellectual values, ideals, and politics accepted
before the World War." The new generations, claimed Luchaire, were relativistic, associationist, technocratic, nonconformist, and aware that their mission was to prepare a new world that was in the process of being born. The central theme of *Notre Temps* was the necessity for the younger generations to
preserve themselves from compromising and divisive alliances with their elders.
The members of the younger generations must know how to wait. In the meantime, they should not fall into the trap of viewing political life in terms of a
conflict between capitalism and social democracy. Luchaire insisted that the
struggle between the conservative André Tardieu and the old-fashioned, left-
leaning Radical Edouard Daladier, both survivors of the war, was not *their*
struggle.[56]

Indeed, the survivors of the war were treated with especial roughness by
Notre Temps. "We could believe in 1919 that the veterans would regenerate
the world," Crouzet wrote in 1930; "we were ready to take them as leaders and
as guides: in 1930 it is too late. We can no longer have any other attitude than
the one perfectly defined by [the German author] Ernst Glaeser: the war is our
parents. Without denying the cruel cost of their experience, we are going ahead
on our own." Another young man of the "new generation" quoted by Crouzet
in *Notre Temps* was even harsher. "We may have every defect, but we will
never have on our shoulders the terrible responsibility of those who abandoned
the peace after having won the war." The journalist Pierre Dominique replied,
and a polemic ensued concerning the validity of the generational concept. In
an interesting reversal of position, Dominique, who had been one of the prom-

inent generationalists of the twenties, denied that generations existed; whereas *Notre Temps* insisted that the generational idea was the fundamental concept of history and essential for understanding the present balance of political forces in France. "We believe in the generation of 1930," Guy Crouzet retorted; and Luchaire added that the real struggle in France was between the *jeunes équipes* (young elites) and the forty-to-sixty-year-olds, who had been shaped before the war began. Crouzet conceded to Dominique that no movement was "purely" generational. But movements did exist that "in their totality" were expressions of "tendencies" within a generation, tendencies that might be more or less shared by individuals belonging to other generations. It was a question not of drawing strict chronological limits beyond which their generational alliance could not extend, said Crouzet, but rather of insisting that the men most likely to belong to the jeunes équipes were those who had matured after 1918.[57]

Things worked out badly for Luchaire and his generational alliance. Already in May 1930 Luchaire had registered sadly the death of "young Radicalism." The jeunes équipes, he said, had let themselves be taken in by Daladier and had then committed the doubly serious error of confusing their evolutionary program with the doctrines of Socialism. There remained young Radicals, Luchaire predicted, who had not given in to Socialism and around whom the "young realists" of France would gather once they had entered the political struggle.[58]

This prediction takes on an eerie quality in view of Luchaire's own political evolution. Up to 1934 he had been known as an internationalist, a pacifist, and a determined antifascist. In that fateful year he, like many others, began to shift in his political orientation. Observers suspected him of taking drugs and keeping expensive mistresses. Despite the burden of his four children, he was rumored to have a double and even a triple ménage. In 1935 *Notre Temps* floundered when its subsidies were cut off by the new premier, Doumergue. Through the German youth leader Otto Abetz, who had married Luchaire's secretary and become a close personal friend, Luchaire repaired his fortunes. His belief in Franco-German cooperation slipped toward sympathy for the Nazis. After the defeat in 1940 he was given a high office in the Vichy government and managed the French press in the northern zone. He used his pen promiscuously to serve the German cause; later he was accused of having collaborated with the gestapo in the hunting down of resisters. He found little sympathy among his countrymen after the liberation and was condemned and executed in 1946. Thus ended the most consistent and ambitious proponent of a generational politics in interwar France.

G ENERATIONS in postwar France, then, did not behave as Mentré said they had in the past or as he predicted they would in the future. Instead of a large generational army moving slowly across a landscape of thirty years, we find three shorter generations—more like guerrilla bands—with a dubious and yet-to-be-established relationship to a larger mass. Observe the evidence. First come the men of the prewar revival, heralded by Agathon and represented by Massis and Psichari; then the column of young warriors in 1920–1925, with Montherlant and Drieu la Rochelle bearing their standard; then, fast on their heels, the paladins of anxiety in 1927–1930 like Jean Luchaire, Marcel Arland, and Henri Daniel-Rops, who insist that they and they alone speak for youth and the younger generation. The difference among these generations is the difference in their relationship to the war. The first generation grew up under its menace and prepared to fight it; the second was caught up by it like a leaf in a hurricane and had no choice but to yield to it and to derive what lessons it could from the experience; the third missed serving in it but was marked forever by its passions and the disillusionment and disorder that followed in its wake.

The pattern, then, is jagged and irregular. We have three generations that appear and noisily proclaim their programs in a period of exactly fifteen years. Three generations that identify their fate with the First World War. Three generations that are so tightly packed together that they could easily be present in the progeny of a single family. Three generations, finally, that can no more be fitted into Mentré's theory than the feet of Cinderella's ugly stepsisters could be squeezed into Cinderella's glass slipper. Unless, that is, we assume that these three generations were all waves of a single war generation. But how then can we account for the fact that they felt themselves to be so different? Perhaps Durkheim was right in his suggestion that the interval between generations was shortening because of factors at work in the structure of modern society? Or perhaps Mentré was wrong in his conception of a generation? Let us investigate more closely this second possibility.

Mentré defined a generation as an attitude toward life, a nuance of sensibility, and a collective state of mind. This last idea, reminiscent of Durkheim's concept of collective representations, was suggestive and full of promise.[59] But Mentré rendered it unusable and undermined its credibility by going on to argue that every generation expressed itself in an ideal, a movement, and a school of thought. He further hurt his case by adding that three such schools or movements occurred in every century. His assertions implied that a generation was bound together by a unity of doctrine. It is difficult to understand how a man of Mentré's intelligence and commitment to empirical observation could have advanced a hypothesis that clashed so evidently and so hopelessly with the facts. Both before and after 1914 French youth were divided when it came to the espousal of ideals and doctrines and membership in movements.

Henri Massis himself is an excellent example of the diversity and divisiveness of French cultural and political life. A man who dreamed of rallying his generation around a common program, he soon fell out with all the friends who had provided models for the generation of 1912. Henri Franck disapproved of the attack on the professors of the Sorbonne and even went so far as to draft a reply to Agathon's accusations. Psichari deplored the antiintellectualism of *The Young People of Today* and prayed God to preserve French youth from the pragmatism and "intense life" that Agathon's young men appeared to covet. As for Rivière, unlike Psichari and Massis, who sought the reassurance of a faith, he remained true to the early Barrès, who had prized sincerity and psychological experimentation with the self above fixity of character or the acceptance of determinisms like nation and race. In 1924 Rivière felt compelled to denounce Massis publicly as "an intellectual gendarme," incapable of growing up and unwilling to let others do so. Even Jacques Maritain, the inspiration for Massis's belief in a Catholic revival, broke with Massis during the twenties when the Action Française was condemned by the Vatican. By 1930 Massis felt abandoned and alone. In 1912 he had been representative—but only of a sector of his generation, a sector of bourgeois and conservative youth that was losing faith in the Republic and moving in the direction of the Action Française.[60]

Mentré's mistake was in trying to locate the unity of a generation in a doctrine or a movement. Massis and de Tarde came closer to the mark when they wrote in the preface to *The Young People of Today* that a generation "supposes a community of traits, a bond, a secret entente, a whole within which each individual moves in solidarity with the other's effort." Hence a common physiognomy, the awareness of a common bond, and a common pattern of action.[61] This approach has the merit of shifting the discussion from the realm of ideas to that of feelings and similarities in modes of action. Even so, Massis and de Tarde, like Mentré, came at the problem from the wrong end of the causal chain. What created the "secret entente" among Agathon's young men was not a doctrine or idea but their position in society and their placement in the flow of history. All products of an elitist educational system, all "heirs" to French culture, accumulated property, and positions of leadership in society, they shared what Barrès called "prejudices, a vocabulary, and objects of disdain."[62] They had read the same books, been trained by the same teachers, developed the same ambitions and expectations, and worried over the same problem of French decline. What distinguished them from their elders and created a further bond between them was their feeling that they were to be the beneficiaries—or perhaps the victims—of rapid and irrevocable change. This feeling of change and of their mission to oversee it was inspired, on the one hand, by the introduction of team sports and the invention of new means of transportation like the automobile and the airplane; and on the other, by the widespread awareness that war with Germany was an imminent possibility and that if it came they would have to fight it. These two factors—the breakthrough in technology and styles of life and the expectation of an epoch-making conflict—gave the young men of 1912 the assurance that their world would be different from the one that had preceded it. The experience of the war confirmed that expectation. The world in which they lived their adult lives would be faster and more dangerous than the one in which they had grown up.[63]

Still, the problem with Mentré's theory goes even deeper. A social scientist in his training and aspirations, Mentré was so busy trying to formulate a theory of generations that he devoted little attention to the conditions under which generations had come into existence during his own lifetime. Neglecting (or perhaps not seeing) the evidence before his eyes, he reached the unshakable conclusion that, regardless of appearances, generations emerged automatically every thirty years or so, because thirty years was the normal length of a man's active social life. To ignore the factor of consciousness and to go in search of underlying social laws may have been considered good scientific method when Mentré was trained at the "new Sorbonne." But it was bad history, and thus, inevitably, it produced bad sociology. Mentré's determination to treat generations as an eternal and unchanging characteristic of human society at all times and in all places prevented him from perceiving first, that generation was a means of conceptualizing society and one's place in it; second, that this way of thinking about society was becoming more widespread because of contemporary developments, of which the war was a spectacular example; and third, that the generational idea was being used to mobilize people for cultural and political purposes. In short, Mentré took for social reality what was an attempt to shape, mold, and reorganize social reality. As a practicing generationalist, Massis knew better. He later acknowledged that he and de Tarde had sought in *The Young People of Today* to give French youth "an image of itself in which it would discern more clearly its reasons for action, for committing itself, for living with a sense of power and pride." Their essential aim "was to assemble these forces, to achieve a union, to arouse a spirit of affirmation, of creation, of reconstruction, from which a new France would emerge." Agathon's enquête, then, had been an act of cultural politics, not an effort at objective reportage, and Massis had been aware of this at the time.[64]

Mentré assumed that a generation arose and took shape in opposition to its predecessor. The primary social law, he wrote sadly, was that of oblivion. Sons turned their backs on their fathers. Rejection was the price the members of society paid for progress. This hypothesis sounds reasonable, and immersed in Freudianism as we are, we find it easy, perhaps too easy, to accept. In some circumstances, it undoubtedly describes reality. Yet it would be seriously misleading to interpret the generational writings of Massis and his successors as a rejection of the past. On the contrary, what stands out in these generational manifestos is the continuity of form and content that links them all together and makes them sound like variations on a single theme. When Massis and de Tarde set out to describe the mentality of the younger generation, they had before them a ready-made model. Balzac, de Musset, and Saint-Beuve had all dabbled in generational portraiture. Later, in the mid-1880s, Paul Bourget had made a succès de scandale and clinched his literary reputation with a devastating collective analysis of the generation of 1850. In 1911 Victor Giraud had sought to do the same for Bourget's generation in a widely acclaimed work entitled *Les Maîtres de l'heure* [The Masters of the Hour].[65]

But the most important generationalist in late nineteenth-century France, and the one who had the greatest influence on Massis and his successors, was Barrès. In the 1880s Barrès had consciously struck out to reach a generational clientele and to build a following among elitist youth. His most famous novel, *Les Deracinés* [The Uprooted], published in 1897, had taken the form of a generational portrait. Intuiting and brilliantly exploiting the ambiguities inherent in the pronoun *we*, he had denounced the generation of his elders, spoken to and for youth, stated as an indisputable law that no one could really be understood by the previous generation, and depicted his generation as sacrificed, sterile, and lost, adding that it had a special and unique mission to fulfill. He had also rediscovered the importance of the nation, come to a new appreciation of the role of faith and traditional hierarchies, and denounced the materialistic and corrupt mores of the parliamentary Republic.[66]

These two sets of themes are not coincidentally related. The generational idea feeds on a sense of discontinuity and disconnection from the past. People who suffer from this loss and feel that they must somehow rectify it have two alternatives: They can hurry forward to a new world or seek to return to the old one. In either case, the young men of today—that is, the young generation —are lost by definition. Their mission can only be to prepare the way and to build for their successors. Hence the spokesmen for the present generation, once they begin to think of themselves as belonging to a generation, will represent themselves and their coevals as unique, lost, sacrificed, and charged by history with a special task.[67]

These categories of uniqueness, loss, sacrifice, and mission were all present in Agathon's enquête and, to a greater or lesser extent, in the generational writings that followed it. Indeed, it would be no exaggeration to say that by 1912, when Massis and de Tarde conducted their inquiry, generational portraiture and polemic had reached the status of a literary genre; and that, like all literary genres, the generational manifesto had its rules, its structure, and its themes. One of its rules was the assumption, seldom made explicit because it was taken so for granted, that generations could be reduced to the handful of writers who exemplified them. Mentré, as we have seen, agreed that the outlook of generations was reflected most faithfully in the works of literary intellectuals. Massis and de Tarde also started with this strange assumption. It was true, they said in the preface to their book, that an inquiry addressed to the youth of the workshops, the suburbs, and the fields might have yielded a different image than the one they presented in *The Young People of Today*. "But the numerical majority, as it turns out, has only secondary significance, a significance that can even be deceiving, for it is when a doctrine has gained the crowd that it has begun to die in the eyes of philosophy; its present triumph assures us that it will not dominate the future." If one wanted to understand the future, one turned not to the masses but to the "innovating elite, leaven in the amorphous mass. It is the beliefs of intellectuals that in the long run orient the civic spirit and through it politics, mores, and the arts." Massis and de Tarde quoted with approval Emile Faguet's conclusion, based on his own contemporary enquête, that the rest of the young French bourgeoisie lagged behind "philosophical and literary youth." The implication was that these other bourgeois elements might one day catch up. The remaining social categories who made up the "amorphous mass" would presumably remain permanently outside history.[68]

It would be hard to find a more straightforward statement of literary imperialism. The fact was that in 1912 "philosophical and literary" French youth were especially and dangerously divorced from the social realities of their own country. The most sensitive among them confessed that they suffered from a seemingly unbridgeable chasm between dreams and possibilities for action. Only outside France, and preferably in the colonies, could a young bourgeois intellectual like Psichari discover "reality." Yet what is significant about *The Young People of Today* and what sets it off from earlier generational portraits like those of Bourget and Giraud is that Massis and de Tarde shifted the focus of their investigation from writers to youth. They sensed that youth had become an autonomous and perhaps decisive factor in national life. Elitist as they were, they sought to influence and direct sectors of the population that went far beyond the few thousand "princes of youth" to whom Barrès had addressed himself in 1888. Perhaps they intuited that youth was a social category that was increasing in number and gaining in power and prestige.[69]

The war, with its collective trials and burdens, had the effect of intensifying this tendency toward broadening the concept of generation, which Massis and de Tarde had helped to initiate. In the emergency of 1914, Massis went so far as to extend the concept of the younger generation to the army as a whole, and soon afterward Mentré borrowed the analogy, if only to emphasize the difference between a generation's field commanders and the great mass of simple soldiers who, regretfully, did not count in the production of ideals. Veterans' movements sought to politicize and mobilize this generational mass once the war was over; and journals like Jean Luchaire's *Notre Temps* and Bertrand de Jouvenel's *La Lutte des Jeunes* tried, unsuccessfully, to reach and influence large sectors of youth. Even so, most generational writings in France during the interwar period remained firmly anchored within the tradition of Bourget, Barrès, and Giraud. A generation, Marcel Arland wrote in 1923, could be reduced to the four or five writers who represented it. The idea seemed so natural that few members of the literary establishment thought to object. This explains why most French analyses of the generational phenomenon since Mentré's book have been devoted exclusively to explaining shifts in literary sensibility and styles.

French historians and sociologists remained wary of the concept, precisely because it had been appropriated by the elitist literary culture whose categories they were trying to escape.[70]

By the third decade of the twentieth century, therefore, generational writing in France had achieved the status of a genre, one in which the thematic continuities were often more impressive than the descriptive novelties. The emphasis on the discontinuity of generational experience was, ironically, one of the elements of continuity in the manipulation of the genre. Perhaps Ernest Hemingway, who lived in Paris during the 1920s, had some inkling of this when he insisted testily in his memoir *A Moveable Feast* that, Gertrude Stein to the contrary, "all generations were lost by something and always had been and always would be."[71] He might have added that all generations are sacrificed by someone and charged by history or fate with a special mission. But a genre does not arise, and certainly it does not gain favor with the public, unless it fills some need. What need or needs did generational portraiture and polemic fill in early twentieth-century Europe? The answer is many.

CHAPTER TWO

Germany: The Mission of the Young Generation

Renewal will come through youth or it will not come at all!
   Jonas Lesser, 1932

THE problem of the generation of 1914 is so inextricably connected with the problem of youth that to discuss one means inevitably to discuss the other. This is especially true in the case of Germany. Like "generation," "youth" is an ambiguous word. Throughout the nineteenth century it was used in Germany primarily to designate a stage in an individual's life history. This stage of life was invested by German intellectuals with a range of meanings and a wealth of emotional resonance not to be found in other European countries. Youth suggested poetry, purity, friendship, creativity, Sturm und Drang, the blue flower of endless seeking, the striving for final ends, the search for the whole rather than the part, and early, hence unblemished, death. Even such a relatively restrained and scientifically minded scholar as the educational philosopher Eduard Spranger (1882) fell into lyricism and nostalgia when he described the psychology of youth, finding its defining characteristics in spirituality (*Geistigkeit*), life-drive (*Lebensdrang*), eroticism (*Erotik*), longing (*Sehnsucht*), and an "unrelieved bondage of loneliness" (*unendlich verschlossenen Einsamkeit*).[1]

Spranger's book was published in 1925. Long before that date, however, *Jugend* (youth) had come to have another meaning. It referred not only to a stage of life but to a group or class of individuals who were united by a common age and a common set of attitudes. In other words, "youth" had become a synonym for "generation." The structure of the German language facilitated this transition. *Jugend* could be combined with *Generation* and *Gemeinschaft* (community) to form the compounds *Jugendgeneration* and *Jugendgemeinschaft*, and these linguistic inventions, which would have made no sense in French or English, were used more or less interchangeably with a series of related expressions like *die junge Generation* (the young generation), *die neue Generation* (the new generation), *die kommende Generation*, *die heranwachsende Generation* (the generation now growing up), and *ein neues Geschlecht* (a new race or breed of humanity) to suggest the presence of a mass of young people who represented not merely an age-group but a new and radically different category of human beings.[2]

This innovation in linguistic usage was linked to the appearance of the Youth Movement, which grew during the two decades before 1913 to a loosely organized federation of 25,000 members. Originally founded for the purpose of getting middle-class youth out of large cities into the countryside where they could commune with nature, the Youth Movement soon outgrew the limits and functions of an association of recreation clubs and eventually came to play an ideological and even a political role in pre-1914 German life. Its leaders proclaimed the right of youth to their own realm, their own teachers, their own organizational form, their own dress, their own music, their own mores, and their own values. Theoretically, of course, "the realm of youth" was a neutral concept that merely expressed the desire of young people to enjoy their youthful years untroubled by adult concerns, and perhaps that was the way most members of the *Wandervogel* understood the term in the years before 1914.* But the minority who dominated the movement and gave it its tone made it clear that their aim was to provide an alternative to the values of adult Germany. The summons to the October 1913 meeting of the movement on the Meissner Mountain near Kassel stated provocatively that German youth no longer intended to remain "a dependency of the older generation, excluded from public life and relegated to a passive role." "It seeks, independently of the commandments of convention, to give shape and form to its own life. It strives after a style of life, corresponding to its youth, which however also will make it possible to take itself and its activity seriously and to integrate itself as a special factor in the general work of culture."[3]

It was but one short step from declarations like these to the convictions that youth was superior to age, that old meant evil, and that it was the duty of the young to struggle against and supplant their elders. If this step was taken so readily by some of the movement's leaders—and, to be sure, it was not taken by all—it was because they had responded to and absorbed the critique of Wilhelmine culture and society carried out by mavericks of the older generation during the last decade of the nineteenth century. Far from creating a new, distinctive culture, as some of its enthusiasts claimed it had or would, the Youth Movement became a haven for the amalgam of confused and irrational ideas known in German as *Lebensphilosophie*, in which the ultimate value was vitality and the ultimate standard "the needs of life." Finding the world "cold,"

---

* *Wandervogel* (*Wandervögel* in the plural) was the name of one of the earliest and most important of the youth groups, but it was generally used to describe the movement as a whole, and I shall follow this pattern of usage throughout this chapter.

"static," "desolate," and "deprived of soul," the leaders of the Youth Movement turned to philosophers of cultural renewal. One of the central tenets of this movement of thought, of which Nietzsche was the best known but by no means the most representative exponent, was the need for a rejuvenation of European and particularly German life. Julius Langbehn, author of the phenomenally successful book *Rembrandt als Erzieher* [Rembrandt as Educator], published in 1890, issued repeated incantations to German youth to rise against their fathers and to renew German culture. "Right," he said, "is on their side." Arthur Moeller van den Bruck, another prophet of national revival, also insisted during the 1890s that the nation "needed a change of blood, an insurrection of the sons against the fathers, a substitution of the old by the young." Even Max Weber, who is generally regarded as the representative of the scientific and enlightened impulse in German life, demanded rejuvenation—in his case, through imperial expansion. "We will not succeed in banning the curse under which we stand—that of being the aftermath of a politically great epoch—unless we are able to be something else: precursors of a greater." These beguiling calls to renew German life by infusing it with the virtues of youth found their echo in the summons to the meeting on the Meissner Mountain, wherein it was bluntly stated that the ambition of the Youth Movement was to rejuvenate Germany by introducing into its spiritual life youth's enthusiasm for the highest human tasks and youth's unbroken belief in noble existence. To eliminate the possibility of any misunderstanding of the attitude of youth toward the achievements of the adult world of imperial Germany, the authors of the summons added that there was nothing the German people more urgently needed than "spiritual rejuvenation."[4]

The theme of generational conflict was also common in the literature of the period. Frank Wedekind and Heinrich Mann made their literary reputations in the 1890s by protesting against the oppression of the young by the old, particularly within the school system; and during the years directly preceding the war the Expressionists carried this campaign to the point of portraying, with evident delight, the murder of fathers by their sons. The progress of mankind "upward" toward "highest energy" and "highest freedom," cried the Expressionist playwright Walter Hasenclever in 1914, led through the war of sons against their fathers. The violence of generational rhetoric rose steadily between 1910 and the late 1920s. Arnolt Bronnen's play *Die Geburt der Jugend* [The Birth of the Youth], the sequel to *Vatermord* [Patricide], portrayed roving bands of boys and girls on horseback who galloped over the aged, trampled them to dust, and shouted that they themselves were God. It would be a mistake to write off these expressions of youthful rebellion as meaningless phrasemongering or to identify them solely as angry and irresponsibly formulated demands for the reform of an authoritarian family and school system. Roy Pascal has pointed out that what is distinctive about German literature after 1880 is not the prominence of the theme of youth and its problems, which had been common since the days of Sturm und Drang, but the way that literary works "broaden out, sometimes clumsily, into an attack on the older generation in general, on the ethics of social success and conformity, on conventional sexual ethics particularly; that is, the son-father conflict assumes importance in relation to much bigger and more general issues, so that as a result it acquires the status of a symbol rather than remaining a socio-psychological fact." [5]

By 1914, then, youth had become a symbol. But a symbol of what? We can get an answer to this question if we look at the evolution of Franz Pfemfert, the editor and publisher of the influential Expressionist weekly *Die Aktion*. Pfemfert (1879) began his career as a left-wing critic of German society and politics. He deplored the backwardness of German culture, the cowardice of the German bourgeoisie, the reformism of German Social Democracy, the heavy-handed and dangerous militarism of German foreign policy, the authoritarianism of German schools, the lack of political consciousness among German university students, the dishonesty of the German press—in fact anything and everything that crossed the horizon of his searching gaze during the years before the war. He wanted to shake the Germans out of their "sleeping sickness" and to "revolutionize minds." In late 1912 he discovered youth. He now began to portray official Germany as a "lost generation" that "groped in vain after salvation and self-preservation." Pfemfert warned his readers not to expect anything from the political parties. German Socialists, he noted bitterly, were as reactionary as the bourgeoisie. He laid his hopes for the future in youth—a revolutionary, internationally minded youth dedicated to the values of Spirit. This new youth would not be long in coming, he predicted confidently in December 1912. While waiting, Pfemfert did what he could to speed the new youth's advent. Increasingly, *Die Aktion* began to print articles on the conflict of generations, on the schools, on relations between the sexes, on the family, and on psychoanalysis, which was seen as a weapon for use by children against their domineering parents. Pfemfert publicized and may have given financial backing to a monthly journal for high school students, *Der Anfang* [The Beginning], which called for a new *Kulturkampf*, "the Kulturkampf of youth."* When the Wandervögel held their meeting on the Meissner Mountain in 1913, Pfemfert's enthusiasm was unbounded. It was, he said, the struggle of German youth for freedom from the "crimes of a sinking world." Youth was right to avoid party entanglements on both the right and the left. "Be neither 'radical' in the sense of day-to-day politics nor 'nationalist.' Be young! Struggle for the right to be young against a narrow-minded and ossified world!" To be young in Pfemfert's vocabulary clearly meant to have abandoned the values of "the thoughtless generation" that was ruling Germany. Youth—and with it the generational idea—had been assigned a political value and

---

* *Der Anfang*, May 1913. The Kulturkampf had been a movement of persecution directed by Bismarck against German Catholics.

had begun to serve as a symbol for the renewal of society and culture as a whole.[6]

It is tempting to interpret the Youth Movement and Expressionism as cultural projections of the hostility that young men customarily feel for their parents. In 1913 Pfemfert ran an article by Gerhard Kornfeld (1888), who argued that the conflict of generations was "the cruelest and most fateful" of wars. Apparently unaware of the teachings of psychoanalysis, Kornfeld explained generational conflict by "the grotesque demand of the parent generation for love, gratitude, and piety from their offspring." "The mass of men," he remarked unhappily, "still do not understand how to be and to remain young." Beneath Kornfeld's angry rhetoric there no doubt lies a truth derived from personal experience. The Central European family was a mirror image of the Central European state: stern, authoritarian, oppressive, demanding discipline and obedience, and quick to suppress spontaneity. Ernst Fischer, the Austrian Communist, remembered threatening his father, an army officer, with a revolver at the age of fifteen. Max Weber's revolt against his father, and the anguish it caused him, are well known. It is easy to understand why both the Youth Movement and Expressionism aimed primarily at autonomy, just as it comes as no surprise that Central European society provided the conditions necessary for the discovery and formulation of the theory of the Oedipus complex. Oppressive patriarchal rule was a fact of Central European life.[7]

The aggressive feelings so many young middle-class Germans directed against their fathers and their teachers stemmed above all, however, not from some deep, unconscious, primeval urge toward patricide but from their highly conscious dissatisfaction with the social order in which they found themselves condemned to live. The Reich created by Bismarck in 1871 had turned out to be a disturbingly shaky structure. Well supplied with military and industrial muscle, it throbbed with internal tensions and bubbled with potential social conflict—like a giant afflicted by chronic indigestion. The cult of patriotism, the pursuit of prosperity, and the pretense of grandeur could not conceal the social fragmentation and the political discord that lay beneath the surface of the empire. To contemporary observers it appeared that literature and the arts were dominated by second-raters who paled by comparison with the creative geniuses who had abounded in the miniature states of disunited Germany. Everyone paid lip service to the cult of national unity, but no one could be sure how deeply rooted the feeling of community was among the diverse and quickly growing population. It was understandably weak among the 2.2 million Poles, the 80,000 Danes, the 60,000 Lithuanians, and the 1.5 million inhabitants of Alsace-Lorraine who had been included, willing or not, within the new nation-state. It was not much stronger among the Catholic masses of the south and the workers, who felt themselves excluded from the national community by the unrepresentative political system and by Bismarck's repressive social and religious policies.[8]

Even more troubling was industrialization, with its unsettling effects. In thirty years Germany had become the strongest industrial power in Europe. In itself that was good. It meant that Germany could afford a modern navy; that it could play a premier role in world politics; and that it could claim a share of the imperial profits so long and so unfairly monopolized by England and France. But how could one think about this power without remembering the terrible bargain that Faust had struck with Mephistopheles? The rub was that Germany had been able to become strong only by ceasing to be Germany—or so it seemed to people who associated Germany with medieval towns, with obedient peasants and artisans, and with the first movement of Beethoven's Sixth Symphony. For such people industrialization was a double-edged sword whose blade had started to cut their way. Industrialization, they now realized, drove people from peaceful hamlets into large impersonal cities and increased the number of workers, hence of potential Social Democrats. It gave free rein to the financial operations of rootless and unscrupulous speculators. And it exposed everyone to the threat of economic crises that might sweep from under them the bases of their material and psychological well-being. Where would it all end, and could the German spirit survive the rising tide of materialism, modernity, and cosmopolitanism?

Young people from the middle layers of society were especially sensitive to these issues; they suffered from these anxieties and worried over the future of the nation. The great appeal of the Youth Movement was that it gave them the opportunity to flee from the unpleasant realities and insoluble dilemmas of Wilhelmine Germany into a knightly and rural world of youth where they could dream, untroubled, of cultural renewal. As they hiked through the unspoiled countryside, danced around flaring bonfires, sang folk songs, strummed their guitars, and declaimed Nietzsche's *Zarathustra* and Stefan George's poetry, they could forget the asphalt and the grey working masses of the cities and contratulate themselves on having achieved a true national community or *Volksgemeinschaft* within their marching groups. They believed that they had escaped from the lies and hypocrisy of the adult world, and they fancied that they were laying the foundation for a new and better Germany. Ethical purity and spiritual growth were their objectives, and to the extent that they walled themselves off from the adult world they achieved them. Small wonder, therefore, that they listened with approval to men outside the movement, like the educational reformer Gustav Wyneken and the publisher Eugen Diederichs, who told them that they represented a "new generation" and that they bore within them a revolution of the body against the exaggerated rationalism and the smug self-satisfaction of a soulless epoch. It was easier before than after 1914 to believe that spirit could overcome matter and that inner purity could eliminate social discord and division.[9]

YOUTH, then, had been identified by many, both young and old, as the agent of cultural renewal in Wilhelmine Germany. Yet given the social and political conditions of the period, this idea appeared little more than wishful thinking, a fantasy of young people unable to come to terms with their time. In 1913 there seemed little reason to believe that German life was going to undergo any major change, and even less reason to believe that if a change did occur, middle-class youth would be its beneficiaries. Official Germany held all the levers of political and economic power, while its most serious challenger was working-class Germany, represented by the Social Democratic party with its massive organization. The inner renewal that middle-class Germany had chosen in preference to practical party politics seemed to preclude success. The war provided a solution to this dilemma. By undermining official Germany and discrediting its leaders and institutions, it made possible and even inevitable sweeping structural change. Official Germany crumbled like an ill-constructed building in the earthquake of the war. The collapse of political and social structures opened an opportunity for middle-class youth to seize the leadership of the nation. Yet the price that had to be paid for this opportunity was awesome, for middle-class youth had to fight the war that official Germany had unleashed upon the European continent. Those who came back were bound to be different from those who went.

The first effect of the war was to shore up the wobbly structure of the Reich and to give Germans the intoxicating illusion that the social rifts of the past had disappeared. No social group gave itself more unreservedly to the war effort than middle-class youth. Recruiting officers were mobbed by student volunteers. Nor did any social group show greater readiness to die in the service of the German state. In October 1914 a force of volunteers, composed largely of students and former members of the Youth Movement, stormed a fortified position in Flanders and suffered staggering losses. The "heroes of Langemarck," as they were christened, were said to have gone to their deaths fearlessly and with patriotic songs resounding from their lips. They soon became symbols of a generation of youth who combined gaiety with sobriety and disapproval of society as it then existed with an unqualified, almost lighthearted willingness to lay down their lives for the redemption of their fellow Germans. "What happened there in Flanders," Rudolf Binding later wrote with understandable exaggeration, "was unparalleled in world history." And indeed the casualties suffered by members of the Youth Movement were appalling. Only one-third of the 15,000 Wandervögel who went to war returned alive.[10]

We can gain some idea of why and in what frame of mind these young men went to war from Walter Flex's best-selling memoir about his friend Ernst Wurche, *Der Wanderer zwischen beiden Welten* [The Wanderer between Two Worlds]. The son of a hyperpatriotic secondary school teacher, Flex (1887) resolved as early as 1905 that he would write tragedies about the sacrifice of the individual for the good of the state. The life of the individual, the young Flex thought, took on meaning only when it served as a wheel "in the machinery of the whole." Between 1910 and 1914 Flex was employed as a tutor by the Bismarck family. In his free time he pursued his literary career, although without much success. Like many young men of his age, Flex deplored the lack of devotion to the national interest in the parties of both the Right and the Left. "I see only the two great economic interests, agriculture and industry, which fight each other in the name of conservatism and liberalism and exploit the idealism of the masses with patriotic or democratic phrases." The dangerous growth of the Social Democratic electorate convinced Flex that universal suffrage in Germany would be an absurdity, and perhaps an irreparable mistake. Only a national crisis, caused by an external threat or foreign aggression, could save a people like the Germans who suffered from an excess of cosmopolitanism and a lack of national feeling. "We need a tough, hardhearted national idealism that is prepared for every sacrifice. Traditionally only the enemy has brought the Germans that!" When Germany went to war two and a half years later, then, Flex was quick to interpret the occasion as an opportunity to escape from the morass of party politics and to revive the sense of national purpose. Spared from compulsory military service because of a chronically inflamed tendon in his right arm, he volunteered in August 1914 during the outburst of general enthusiasm and was passed for active service. Standards must not have been very high. While he was in university, Flex's right arm had been too weak to hold a dueling saber. Now it would have to bear a rifle and provide the driving force for a shovel and a pick.[11]

Flex spent the next six months in trenches near Verdun dodging shells, building fortifications, and performing the physically demanding duties of a simple soldier. It was probably the first time this prophet of community had ever found himself face to face and shoulder to shoulder with members of the real *Volk*. He met Ernst Wurche in the spring of 1915 when they were chosen along with other student volunteers to attend an officer training course in Posen. As they marched up the incline that took them away from the front lines, Flex was struck by the unusual bearing of the young man who walked at his side and who was soon to become his friend. "As the slim, beautiful man in the worn-out grey coat climbed the mountain like a pilgrim, his light grey eyes bright and full of longing for clearly defined goals, he was like Zarathustra, who comes from the heights, or Goethe's wanderer." Later the two young lieutenants served together on the Eastern Front, where in August 1915 Wurche was killed while reconnoitering an enemy position. Grief-stricken by Wurche's death and persuaded that he represented the prototype of the future leader who would save Germany from the lies of the parties and the selfishness of the economic interests, Flex decided to erect a literary monument to his memory, so that he would live on in the consciousness of the nation. At first he thought in terms of a collection of letters from Wurche to his parents with commentary by himself; but his publisher convinced him to issue separately his own highly idealized evocation of what his friend had been like. The result, a slender volume published in 1917, went through thirty-nine editions and sold 250,000 copies in less than two years.[12]

Before the war Wurche had been a Wandervogel. His devotion to the movement was so strong that he sent part of his lieutenant's salary to his group so that they could continue their excursions, and he followed the Wandervogel journal even while at the front. Though not himself a member of the Youth Movement, Flex believed that the Wandervogel experience had played an important part in shaping Wurche's extraordinary character. To Flex, Wurche was a living example of the Wandervogel motto: "Remain pure and become mature" (*rein bleiben und reif werden*). This was the spirit, he thought, that the "coming Germany" needed. Readers who approach Flex's book today may find Wurche less mature than confused. A student of theology who carried into battle Nietzsche's *Zarathustra*, Goethe's poetry, and the New Testament, Wurche combined a penchant for broad philosophical generalizations about the ways of God with the good-natured gaiety of a fraternity boy and the blood-thirsty longing for combat of a samurai. Wurche's greatest ambition was to participate in the storming of an enemy position. Whether he survived the attack was of secondary importance to him. This attitude, Flex claimed, was the source of his ascendancy over his fellow officers and men. He appeared indifferent to danger and unafraid of death. According to Flex, Wurche's composure under fire derived from his conviction that the war was a moral test in which both peoples and individuals had a rare chance to prove themselves and to transcend their weaknesses. Viewed from this perspective, service in the war was a rare privilege, for it brought the participant closer to God and his mysteries than ordinary men could ever hope to come. "We ask nothing more from life than that it reveal itself to us; no human being is entitled to demand more. Life has given us more than it has given the others; let us then wait peacefully by to see whether it will not also demand more of us!" Besides, death could not be denied, for it was through death that life was eternally rejuvenated. "For men of great sensitivity," Wurche told Flex, "death is the greatest experience."[13]

Wurche was no ordinary patriot. He disliked the way the war was being represented by the German government and press. Instead of engaging in banalities about the selfless and superhuman heroism of Germany's soldiers, he preferred to speak of their devotion to duty, their obedience to their officers, and their loyalty to the national cause. Wurche was even willing to envisage the possibility that Germany would perish in its struggle, for all things created by God, including nations, were transitory. What mattered was spiritual growth. Flex felt similarly. Indifferent to nationalist goals and uninterested in the expansion of German territory, he believed that the war offered an opportunity for individuals to contribute to the improvement of their country through the demonstration of their *moral* superiority over the enemy. The egoism of the *I* must be sacrificed to the higher cause of the *Thou*. Like Wurche, Flex thought that this demonstration could be made as well in defeat as in victory. To judge from the collection of letters published by Philipp Witkop in 1928, attitudes like these were widespread among German student volunteers during the first two years of war. They were willing to sacrifice their lives because they believed that through fighting, killing, and dying they were contributing to the moral elevation of their country and the progress of humanity. As one young volunteer put it, "we fight for our *Volk* and spill our blood and hope that the survivors are worthy of our sacrifice. For me it is the struggle for an idea, the fata morgana of a pure, true, noble Germany, free from wickedness and deceit. And even if we go down to defeat with this hope in our hearts, it is probably better than to have been victorious and to see that it was only an outer victory without improving men within." [14]

Such interpretations of the war bore little relationship to the motivations of the leaders who had plunged Germany into the conflict or to the annexationist aims for which they were fighting. Nor was it realistic to suppose that the strain of war would elevate the character of the people who had to bear it. Indeed, it would have been wiser to expect the contrary. Consequently, the moral attitude with which many German middle-class volunteers went to war contained within it the potential for enormous disillusionment. Confronted with the reality of war, expended like matériel, reduced to the life of a troglodyte, surrounded by images of ugliness, cut off from the world of civilians, deprived of victory, the volunteer could easily turn against the forces that brutalized him and condemned him to what he increasingly suspected was a meaningless sacrifice. Grown accustomed to the use of violence in the name of an ideal, he might conclude that his anger and his bullets should be directed against those responsible for his suffering.

Attitudes like these spread in the German army in late 1916 and early 1917 in the aftermath of the unsuccessful attacks on Verdun and the tremendous blow absorbed by the Germans on the Somme in the summer and fall of 1916. They can be found in Fritz von Unruh's Expressionist novel *Opfergang* [Way of Sacrifice], which was written in 1916 during the battle of Verdun at the request of the German General Staff, but then suppressed because of its revolutionary overtones. [15]

The son of a Prussian general whose knightly ancestors could be traced back to the age of Charlemagne, Unruh (1885) went to cadet school with the Crown Prince Oscar and served as a page at the Kaiser's court. Brought up to respect and cherish his father's military values, he discovered while in cadet school that his true vocation was for poetry and the drama. In the conditions of Wilhelmine Germany, the careers of a writer and an officer were not easily combined. Officers were not expected to expose their military honor to the hazards of the stage and the shifting taste of the vulgar public. When his father died in 1912, Unruh took sick leave from the army and devoted himself to writing. Though his pre-1914 plays indicated a longing for combat and romanticized death in the service of a patriotic ideal, they also suggested that he saw in war a chance for the transformation of the individual and for escape from an oppressive situation of boredom and stultification all too easily identifiable with the Germany of the Reich. His state of mind appears to have been close to that of his Expressionist coeval Georg Heym (1887), who confided to his diary in 1911, "I suffocate in the superficial enthusiasm of this banal age. For I need tremendous emotions to be happy." [16]

The war supplied Unruh with the emotions and the excitement that he sought. It also brought about his inner transformation and provided him with a cause for which he would henceforth fight with unremitting commitment. Against his mother's protests, he volunteered in August 1914 and saw action with the German cavalry during the first months of the war. While on a reconnaissance ride in Belgium he was shot off his horse, robbed of his uniform and belongings, and left to die. Many years later he described the experience. "I first came to in the light of dawn. And when I looked around, I discovered that I had been lying on the dead body of a French chasseur . . . Suddenly I was seized in the throat by something like anguish, like the grasp of death . . . In this moment the sun broke through the ocean of fog . . . I extended my arms to meet it. And in this godly moment I suddenly realized with clearsightedness . . . that the age-old, so-called 'cowardice' in war . . . was the beginning of a new zest for life. And that the age-old, so-called 'courage' to die in war was in reality only cowardice." By October 1914 Unruh had decided that the artist could not be a soldier, that it was evil to take life, and that the real war was not between the French and the Germans but between the soldiers of all nations and the rulers who had sent them to murder and be killed. It was with these impassioned convictions that he undertook to evoke the battle for Verdun. [17]

Way of Sacrifice bears many resemblances to *The Wanderer between the Two Worlds*. It has the same emphasis on the idealism of the German soldier; the same affirmation of the creative function of death and of the existence of a "holy communion" of the fallen; the same indifference to annexationist war aims; and the same insistence on the moral value of the war. What distinguished Unruh's novel from Flex's work and what caused it to be suppressed was its suggestion that the front soldiers were the bearers of a revelation that might revolutionize civilian life. "What if we brought the light of this hour home with us, where only lamps burn in houses," a platoon leader proposes to his captain. The captain is skeptical and replies, "They will show us the door and diminish everything by a thousand means, until the illumination of this ghastly gully fades away in weariness and disgust." But the platoon leader Clemens is not dissuaded:

Where are those who built barriers among us? I don't see them! Death holds them far from us. Those who lay in chains behind go here free and drunk with prophetic vision among their brothers. Those who sat on thrones behind sit now at telephones, pale and shaking, and wait upon us. We are the decisive factor. Ours is the initiative! No one will ever again take our heart captive! In us lives youth! Behind us lie the old men! I see the flame of our purification rise high above all everyday things, and no common fingers will ever touch it! [18]

However mannered the style, the message was clear. *Way of Sacrifice* suggested that the youth, idealism, and common suffering of the men of the front might combine to form a spiritual purgative that would transform German life back home. Striving to make sense of the slaughter at Verdun, Unruh had intuitively fused the prewar ideas of generationalism, youth ideology, and cultural renewal that were present in the Youth Movement and Expressionism with the notions of the front experience and the brotherhood of soldiers. The distinction between the morally pure and the corrupt, so central in the ideology of the Youth Movement and in Flex's portrait of Wurche, was now translated by Unruh into a rift between the world of the front and the world of the rear. Unruh located the agents of cultural renewal in the survivors of trench warfare. Consigned by fate and cold-hearted rulers to a life of mass destruction and bound forever in a holy communion with their dead comrades, the men of the front would one day return to bring the light of their revelation to the moral darkness of civilian Germany, whose population had not been able to live up to the virtues of their fighting forces. "Do you believe that the youth up there die in vain?" the platoon leader Clemens asks his captain in *Way of Sacrifice*.

That their bright spirit bleeds to gain new lands? Can you not perceive that we struggle in holy community? To make a true fraternity of the spirit, of a people? What do we care about fortresses or lands? And if the world has grown rotten, poisoned, so that corruption eats at the soul, then let it be burned! I want to be the first to throw fire into this nest of consumption! Body, become once more the temple of soul! Were Verdun that promise, then henceforth let every inch of it be covered with weapons! Away with deference and respect! For I foresee the coming of a mighty generation [*Geschlecht*] of men! Today every man feels as I do. It is still silent; but one day the dams will no longer hold! Laugh if you want, the day of judgment is drawing near. Ah, you peoples of the earth, unless we are fighting for the light of your spirit—then all this powder has been shot off in vain! . . . Woe to him who bars our way! [19]

The idea of the front generation and its liberating mission could theoretically have strengthened the socialist Left. Perhaps it did so temporarily between 1917 and 1920. Unruh himself moved toward the Left and became an active supporter of the Weimar Republic. His plays *Das Geschlecht* [The Progeny] and *Platz* [Plaza] expressed continued hopes for a new beginning and a radical transformation of German life. Ernst Toller (1893) also translated the desire for spiritual renewal into powerful Expressionist dramas in the immediate postwar years, as did Walter Gropius (1883) into stunning architecture. The early Communist party was able to channel some of these feelings into a revolt directed against the conservatism of the Socialist leadership; indeed, the German Communist party, like other Western Communist parties, was to a great extent a creation of men who had fought in the war or whose political convictions had been shaped by it.[20]

But despite its apparent left-wing implications, the idea of the front generation was never effectively exploited by the left-wing parties. Instead, it became an important ideological and organizational weapon in the arsenal of the German radical Right. This was because of the implicit tension between the idea of a generational alliance based on common experience and the idea, essential to the Left, of a class alliance based on economic interest; because of the congruence between the nationalist tradition and the myth of a people's front arising from the ashes of the war; and above all, because the men most drawn toward the myth of the young generation and its mission by their background and experience were also those who were most hostile to a revolution carried out under the auspices of the Left.

When the war ended in November 1918 there existed thousands of junior officers who had been promoted on a provisional basis to fill gaps created by losses in the regular officer corps. Most of these young men came from the middle and lower-middle classes. Deeply marked by their war experiences and hostile toward the civilian population, by whom they felt betrayed and abandoned, they returned to find their homeland in the throes of revolution and social upheaval. Confused, embittered, angry, hungry, and with no hope of pursuing military careers because of the limitations placed on the German army by the Treaty of Versailles, these men soon found opportunities to use the destructive skills they had learned at the front. It was they who provided the leadership for the Freikorps groups that were organized in 1919–1920 at the request of the Weimar government to check the revolution and establish order at home. Later they fought against the Poles on the eastern frontier, participated in assassination attempts against Republican officials, and led the resistance movement against the French when French troops occupied the Rhineland in 1923. Some, like Ernst Röhm, joined Hitler's National Socialist party and became active in the Nazi squads. Others, like Franz Seldte and Arthur Mahraun, formed veterans' organizations and *Kampfbünde* or combat leagues dedicated to keeping alive the mystique of the front. Most of these men looked on with sympathy when Hitler tried to overthrow the Republic in the Beer Hall Putsch of 1923. Their common program, insofar as they shared one, was to destroy the Republic, to reestablish the authority of the state, to denounce the Treaty of Versailles, and to eliminate those responsible for fomenting social conflict and undermining the unity of the Volk. Their organizing myth was the creative and renovating force of the front experience. Having learned in the trenches "what fate is, and what man is, and what life is like, and how short the span from life to death is," they believed that they, and only they, were capable of overcoming the antagonisms within the nation and giving to a seemingly absurd time its true meaning. Seldte, the leader of the Stahlhelm, a league of front soldiers, stated their immediate objective with not untypical directness. "We must fight to get the men into power who will depend on us front soldiers for support—men who will call upon us to smash once and for all these damned revolutionary rats and choke them by sticking their heads into their own shit."[21]

Their herald and the person who preeminently incarnated their values was Ernst Jünger, a soldier of extraordinary valor and a writer of equally rare imagination, who forged his war experiences and the ideas of German Neoromanticism into a highly personal and widely influential synthesis during the years immediately following the war. Jünger (1895) grew up near Hanover amidst medieval buildings, memories of Hanseatic grandeur, and ample bourgeois comfort supplied by his father, a successful chemist and businessman who owned pharmacies and speculated in fertilizers. From earliest youth Jünger was a dreamer who believed that life was an adventure and that what most people called reality was a screen that had to be penetrated if one was to unravel the riddles of existence. An avid reader of *Don Quijote, Robinson Crusoe,* and the *Arabian Nights,* Jünger felt "homeless" and stifled in the narrow and finely ordered world of his parents and his class. The ramblings of the Wandervögel offered him a chance to escape from family, school, and city. But organized excursions soon lost their appeal for this independent and headstrong boy. Attracted toward the life of a vagabond, he resolved to leave Europe and to seek adventure in the tropics. The deepest, darkest, most disease-ridden territories of Africa became the focus of his dreams and the object of his longing, because only these unexplored corners of the world held out the chance to escape from the constraints of civilized society and to lead a virile, heroic, and autonomous existence. At seventeen, armed with a guidebook to Africa, a map of the city of Trier, a pipe like Sherlock Holmes's, and a pistol, he ran off to Verdun to join the Foreign Legion. His father intervened and arranged, with the help of the German Foreign Office, for his wayward son to be returned to Hanover; but Africa remained "the promise of happiness" that echoed like a far-off ringing tone "in the sleepy rest of the old city," and Jünger was determined to make his way there as soon as he passed his secondary school exams and received his degree.[22]

Jünger was to discover time and again that life does not allow itself to be planned or plotted. He found the "hot, bold movement" and the "great, lonely adventure" he sought, all right, but not in Africa—instead, on the fields of Flanders and northeastern France. Like Flex, Jünger would always remember August 1914 as a holy moment. The thick walls of the bourgeois world that he felt pressing in upon him suddenly collapsed, the quotidian gave way to the extraordinary, and an entire people surrendered itself to the beckoning fantasy of knightly combat in the service of a great ideal. "Who experienced those days," he later wrote wistfully, ". . . possesses an idea of what life means." The day after the mobilization was announced, he volunteered for service and was accepted in the prestigious 73rd Fusilier regiment of Hanover. After a brief period of training, and provided with a hastily bestowed secondary diploma, he left for the front on December 27, 1914, in a rain of roses and "divine tears" that intoxicated him like wine and shook him to the depths of his being. His mind was filled with images of romantic landscapes, colorful uniforms, unfurled banners glittering in early morning sunlight, neighing horses, trumpets sounding the attack, and flowers stained with the blood of dying heroes. No death, he thought, could be lovelier than this one; the important thing was not to have to stay at home, to be with the others as they marched off to live their dream of power and glory. He was nineteen years old. The national interests and diplomatic entanglements that had brought about the war meant nothing to him.[23]

During the next three and a half years Jünger participated in some of the fiercest fighting on the Western Front, first as a simple soldier, then as an ensign and squad leader, later as a lieutenant and company commander. He was on the Somme in July 1916 when the British delivered what they hoped would be a knockout blow against the outmanned and outgunned German forces; he led storm troop assaults at Cambrai and Passchendaele in 1917 to win back ground lost to the British after their initial breakthroughs; he was in the first wave of attackers in the great German offensive of March 1918; and he served in the front lines during the retreat of July–August 1918, when the German troops lost all hope of victory and isolated units dug in to check the swelling wave of Allied might. There was nothing pretty or romantic about Jünger's war. He saw men blown to bits beside him. He watched as old French and Belgian towns, much like his own, were reduced to rubble. He learned to discern through the night the sweet stench of decaying corpses. He was pursued by the images of men he had killed. He felt his sensibility harden and his memory of fallen comrades fade. He knew that his troops often killed their prisoners and plundered the still-warm bodies of their own dead. He was wounded fourteen times, at least once by one of his own men. He bore twenty scars on his body and untold scars on his mind as souvenirs of his service at the front. Yet at no time, up to the final, exhausting days, did Jünger lose his enthusiasm for the war. Even in the elite regiment to which he belonged he distinguished himself by his indifference to danger and his zest for trench fighting. He was one of fourteen infantry lieutenants during the First World War to receive Pour le mérite, Germany's highest military decoration for heroism. When the war ended he was in Hanover recovering from his latest wounds and making plans to return to the front.

It may seem strange that a lover of fantasy and freedom like Jünger could find fulfillment in the German imperial army of the First World War. How could an individualist who had fled custom and complacency and questioned hierarchy and dicipline when they presented themselves in the form of the father and the schoolmaster resign himself happily to the factory-like slaughter of the Western Front? The paradox is a real one, and Jünger's published war diaries contain ample evidence that he was aware of the contradiction between his anarchistic temperament and the situation in which he found himself.[24] But the force of the contradiction—and hence its importance for understanding Jünger's later attitude—dwindles when viewed in the context of his war experiences, as he reconstructed them in his most famous book, *In Stahlgewittern* [The Storm of Steel]. What had attracted Jünger in Africa was danger, death, and male vitality unrestrained by the codes of European civilization. On the battlefields of the Western Front he lived in close proximity to all three. A student of extreme situations who believed like Ernst Wurche that death was the greatest of all adventures, Jünger felt the need to see men die and if possible to die or nearly die himself. The war afforded him the rare opportunity to live daily on the border between life and death and, on one occasion at least, to have the feeling that he had crossed it, if only for a fleeting instant. Thus the insatiable curiosity of the adventurer overcame the horror of the civilized man and subdued the disgust of the aesthete.

Besides, as a company commander and stormtroop leader, Jünger succeeded in escaping to a considerable degree from the constraints of discipline. His willingness to die earned for him a margin of freedom. As the war progressed and the morale of his troops declined, Jünger distinguished increasingly between those who suffered the war and those who mastered it by the sheer force of their courage. Though not lacking in compassion for the ordinary soldier, *The Storm of Steel* is a celebration of those "princes of the trenches, with their hard set faces, brave to madness, tough and agile to leap forward or back, with keen bloodthirsty nerves, whom no despatch ever mentions." The occasional experience of raiding or storming enemy trenches when "the overpowering desire to kill winged my feet" and "rage squeezed bitter tears from my eyes," and the knowledge that his courage had triumphed over the fear of pain and death allowed Jünger to salvage from the general bankruptcy of ideals his own fantasy of quixotic heroism and to view himself, once the war was ended, as "a freebooter, a wandering knight, who has broken many a lance and whose illusions melted away in sarcastic laughter."[25]

Jünger's extraordinary war record won him the privilege, seldom granted to nonprofessional officers, of staying in the reconstituted and greatly shrunken German army. For five years he availed himself of this option, thus avoiding the chaotic and semioutlaw existence that many of his friends and contemporaries lived after the war. But the bloodthirsty young knight who had loved trench warfare and the sensations it produced was not cut out to be a professional military man. Soldiering in peacetime was both time consuming and boring. There was no adventure in defending law and order against inept civilian putschists or in writing infantry manuals, the two tasks to which he was assigned. At the same time, Jünger discovered that he was gifted as a writer. *The Storm of Steel* was a popular success that continued to sell well throughout the twenties. Besides, leaving aside the lack of enthusiasm Jünger felt for the Republican government he served, his primary concerns during these first postwar years appear to have been to complete his education and to pursue certain cultural interests for which the army left little time. Thus in 1923 he left the Reichswehr and enrolled in the University of Leipzig to study zoology with Hans Driesch. In 1925 he married, broke off his studies without taking a degree, and became a full-time writer, living on his pension as a knight of the order of Pour le mérite and the income from his books and articles. [26]

Only then did Jünger enter politics. In search of a base from which to operate, and persuaded by others that his pen could make a difference, he agreed to contribute regularly to a special supplement of the Stahlhelm's newspaper aimed at young, radical war veterans. During the next four years he produced dozens of essays. By 1929 he had established himself as the leading living spokesman of the front generation. Much of his literary success during this period depended on this identification. Jünger was persuaded that his experience was typical of his generation, that it was a variation on the theme of the time or at most a "special species" that differed in no essential way from "the family of species" to which it belonged. But in the conditions of Weimar Germany, where veterans were divided between the Right and the Left, Jünger's attitude toward his own work contained a serious equivocation. He claimed to speak for a generation of men for whom war was "the father of all things"; but his persistent and confusing use of the egalitarian *we* hid his authoritarian belief that he was able to read the secret riddles of the time and that he had earned the right, precisely because he was not typical, to dictate to others their course of action. His attitude toward the public paralleled exactly his attitude toward the troops under his command during the battles of 1918—one of irritation and patronizing superiority. And just as his coolness under fire and his military prowess had won the admiration of his men and fellow officers, now the firmness of his convictions and the dispassionate and chilling style in which he expressed them captured a public that was looking for an intellectual commander to lead it against the fortifications of the Republic. [27]

Jünger's essays of the twenties expounded on the lessons of the war. They showed what could be made of the ideas of Flex, Wurche, and Unruh once they were stripped of any pretence of religious sanction or civilized morality. Man, Jünger wrote in *Der Krieg als inneres Erlebnis* [War as Inner Experience], was "the most dangerous, the most bloodthirsty, and the most goal-conscious being" that strode the earth. The human race was like a primeval forest from whose dark and misty depths emerged the cry of victims ripped out of their nests by creeping, crawling beasts of prey. To live meant to kill. There was no distinction between men, animals, and inanimate nature. Man would never overcome war, because it was greater than he was; and woe to him if he tried to escape from its grasp, for it was in war that men fulfilled themselves most completely. What, Jünger asked, was holier than a fighting man? What human encounter was more powerful, what exchange more intense, than the meeting of two peoples on the field of battle? War was a "great school," and life expressed itself more deeply and more comprehensively in the actions of a soldier than in the pages of the most learned book. Indeed, one of Jünger's central themes was that the war did not represent a retrogression or a barbarous interlude in Western history, as many pacifists seemed to think; it was not a cause of man's unhappiness, but an expression of his eternally unchanging nature and at the same time a revelation of the face of things to come. War was a creative force. It made men and their times what they were. The creation of new values could not take place without death and sacrifice; continued progress required victims. Western civilization had been threatened by complacency and comfort. The intellect had been overrefined. "Then that secret pendulum that is present in all living things, that incomprehensible principle of reason that is operative in the world, swung to the other side and sought through the power of the fist and through the igniting of a monstrous explosion to create in the rigidified masonry [of the bourgeois world] a breach that would lead to new ways. And a generation, a wave in the sea, called it absurd and without meaning, because they were destroyed in the collapse." [28]

For all his idealization of the trench fighter and his insistence that morale and fighting spirit were more important than numbers or equipment, Jünger recognized that masses and matériel had won the war. The German soldier had been defeated because the largest battalions and the greatest factories had been on the side of the Allies. Yet Jünger believed, like Flex and Wurche, that for those who took the long view the outcome of the war mattered little. On the contrary, the lessons the war had to teach could be learned even better in defeat than in victory. For in the depths of his despair the German soldier had made a precious discovery: He had come to know and worship the nation. He had come to realize that the *I* was nothing and that the *we* to which he belonged was everything. He had liberated himself from the old liberal values and had come to long after a new, tragic form of life. The "new man" would never again be satisfied with the values of the nineteenth century. He fulfilled himself in war and knew that "the dynamic of the cosmos exists in tension, battle, and unrest." Territories and war aims were mere symbols necessary to get men to die. War was an eternal rite in which young celebrants strove after moral perfection. In the performance of this rite, death was unimportant. Those who died left the imperfect Germany of appearances and took their place in the profound reality of "eternal Germany" where they contributed to "the sources of our feelings, acts, and thoughts." Every generation drew upon its predecessor. Nothing was lost. The generations of men were like a coral reef in which no layer could exist without the innumerable already decomposed layers from which it derived its substance. "Man," Jünger affirmed, "is the bearer, the constantly changing vessel, which contains everything that has been done, thought, and felt before him." [29]

This, said Jünger, was the most profound lesson of the war. No one had died in vain. The English, French, and Germans had all been working toward a common goal: a new mode of life. It was true, Jünger confessed, that only a minority of soldiers had understood this lesson; but what mattered was the elite and not the mass. The Zeitgeist was always shaped by the select few who knew how to respond to the demands of their time. The elite of this time, Jünger said, were indisputably the soldiers of the trenches—not the common soldiers who had merely endured the war, but the storm troopers or freebooters who had fought for the love of fighting. These "jugglers of death," these "masters of explosive and flame," these "magnificent beasts of prey" represented a new race. They were the most combative men the world could bear, and they had achieved the highest synthesis ever known of the body, intelligence, will, and sensuality. Now they were dispersed throughout the parties, the veterans' associations, and the combat leagues (*Kampfbünde*). Jünger called on them to unite, to yield to fate, and to turn their efforts to the destruction of the Weimar Republic, so that the new order, which had originated in "elements of earth and fire," could come into being. [30]

M ANY veterans agreed. Jünger's sentiments, or variations on them, were voiced in meetings of ex-servicemen all over Germany. By 1929, however, it was clear that the elite of the returning veterans had failed to live up to the mission that Jünger and others had assigned to them. The two most influential veterans' leagues, the Stahlhelm and the Jungdeutsche Order, had become enmeshed in party politics and shown themselves incapable either of overthrowing the system or of successfully adapting to it. The two parties in which veterans played a leading role, the Nazis on the extreme Right and the Communists on the extreme Left, had waned in influence and lost a great part of their following since their efforts to seize power in the confusion of 1923. With the onset of stabilization and relative prosperity in 1924, people had less occasion to think about the war. When they thought about the men who had survived it, they were more likely to see them with the harsh gaze of Erich Maria Remarque than through the magic lantern of Ernst Jünger. That is, to most people, and especially to those too young to have fought in the war, the veteran was not so much a tragic hero as a malcontent, an enemy of law and order, a tattered figure of violence who could not forget how to hate, a poor student and lazy apprentice who drifted aimlessly from one occupation to another and whiled away his time in bars and cabarets.

No question: The fight had gone out of many of these fighters. Jünger himself abandoned politics in disgust when the veterans' front he called for failed to materialize. "The time of great human and manly dreams had passed. The self-seekers triumphed. Corruption. Misery." For those who could not forget the war, all that remained was "impotence, despair, indifference, and schnapps."

Most frontfighters, of course, had simply melted quietly into civilian life, and many who shared Jünger's convictions wondered where "this mighty war generation, these people of the great battles, these men of the mighty war effort" were hiding themselves and why they did not emerge from their silence and begin to dominate Germany with the same mastery they had shown in standing up to the ordeal of the war.[31]

At the same time, the politically inclined intellectuals who followed with eager eyes the fever chart of Weimar's fortunes interrogated themselves about the attitudes and direction of youth. For by the late twenties it was certain that young people would play an important and perhaps a decisive role in German politics. It was widely recognized that the Republic's greatest failure had been its inability to mobilize the enthusiasm and loyalty of youth. The elections of September 14, 1930, would show that they were being drawn toward the extremist parties. The very word *Jugend* had taken on powerful and irrational overtones. "Youth," sighed one writer of the period. "What heart does not beat joyfully faster when people begin to speak about it!" And by youth he meant not the stage of life to which Eduard Spranger had devoted his famous book, but the great masses of young people who were streaming into leagues and organizations of various kinds. Some of the enemies of Weimar who had earlier placed their hope in veterans now turned their attention to the combat *Bünde*, which had mobilized between 50,000 and 100,000 members and which one Youth Movement publication defined simply as "fate and grace."[32]

The Bünde even had their echo in scholarly circles. In 1927 Eduard Wechssler, professor of French literature at Berlin, proposed redefining generations as youth communities (*Jugendgemeinschaften*). The history of the world, he suggested, could best be understood as an "unceasing change-filled procession of ever new youth movements." On its own ground and in its own terms, Wechssler warned, youth was always right against age, because God was on the side of the *Jugendgeist*, which he defined as "God and Demon, Savior and Destroyer." Wechssler himself counted on intellectual youth, "the simple, noble fool" of Wagner's *Parsifal*, to save Germany from the corrupting influence of Negroes, Bolsheviks, and American technology.[33]

The cult of youth in Weimar had reached such proportions by the mid-twenties that Spranger felt compelled to point out that the Youth Movement had produced no culture worthy of consideration and that young people were unreliable allies in politics because their vision was total rather than concerned with limited objectives and because they resisted organization. But after observing that every generation carried within it a mysterious new "spirituality," he conceded that the militants of the original pre-1914 Youth Movement had been "the secret conspirators of a better world" and suggested that present-day Weimar youth were the bearers of an ideal, nourished by "deep, unconscious life sources," that might transform Germany and save her from materialism and the reign of masses and machines. Yet how could one define youth's new

attitude toward life; and what was youth's relationship to the generation who
had fought in the war?[34]

These questions took on new urgency after 1929, when stabilization gave
way to depression, the Weimar coalition collapsed beneath the pressure of economic decisions that drove unbreachable rifts between the governing parties,
and opportunities arose for an extremist and revolutionary politics. For it was
clear to many observers at the time, just as it is clear to us today, that any truly
new politics would have to command the allegiance of youth and to draw on
the talents and energies of the generation then nearing forty—namely, those
who had served in the war. Hence the spate of articles and books devoted to the
war generation, its failure, and its relations with its elders and its juniors that
appeared in Germany between the outbreak of the Great Depression and the
coming to power of the Nazis, an intellectual reflection of the excitement
generated by the new political circumstances.

The center of this polemic, the driving force from which its participants
derived many of their ideas and much of their inspiration, was the *Tat* circle, a
group of young right-wing intellectuals who wrote for Eugen Diederich's popular monthly *Die Tat* and who fancied themselves the brain trust of the coming
German revolution. The debate extended, however, to other young intellectuals of the radical Right, who were convinced that "the way to the future" led
through a synthesis of Right and Left in a true national socialism, which they
were not ready to identify with Hitler and his party. These young intellectuals
had no political following, no votes, no organization. What they did have was
unbounded ambition, facile pens, and a vision. This vision was grounded in
their hostility to parliamentary democracy and industrial capitalism, their longing for a strong authoritarian state and "folk community," and their conviction
that the "young generation" held the key to the German and European future.
Some of them hoped to build a new political movement between the parties of
the Left and the Right using as an organizational base the veterans' leagues and
the youth Bünde. All of them disliked parties of the traditional type based on
"interests" and favored "organic" forms of political organization, in which
leaders were not elected directly by the mass but emerged spontaneously and
naturally from the body of their immediate followers. Some of these young intellectuals were up-to-date on the latest writings devoted to the generation
problem. They had read Wechssler, Spranger, Mannheim, and Ortega and
were eager to apply their ideas to an analysis of the German political situation.[35]

The discussion was opened and its tone was set by an article entitled "The
Second Wave" that Hans Zehrer, the newly appointed editor of *Die Tat*, published in November 1929. A veteran and former Freikorps volunteer and puts-
chist, Zehrer (1899) was a young man in a hurry who made up in self-confidence and a knack for catchy phrases what he lacked in sound ideas. His
November article, much commented upon at the time, was an attempt to iden-

tify and at the same time to rally the forces of the "young generation," which in his view had its nucleus in young war veterans like himself, who had yet to commit themselves politically. The war generation, Zehrer suggested, should be thought of in terms of assault waves. The first wave had run itself out. It had made the mistake of not entering into its time and of not paying sufficient attention to material and practical details; it had been unable to liberate itself from the memory of the war; and it had taken for granted that recalling the justice of its claims and the authenticity of its experience would be enough to rally the support of the nation at large. As a consequence, it had failed to revolutionize politics, and many of its members had taken refuge in an aesthetic Bohemia. Now this first wave was too played out to rely "on the strength of its arm or the battleworthiness of its staff." It had been defeated. Yet all was not lost, for the second wave of the front generation, the phalanx of those who had taken up occupations, mastered practical methods, and remained silent, was now advancing. These men combined the deep insight of the front generation with a knowledge of how things worked; they, and only they, were in a position to revolutionize Germany. From them would come books not on the front experience as such—Zehrer was obviously thinking of Jünger among others—but on the relevance of that experience to the problems of technology and everyday life. "Germany," concluded Zehrer, "will be rebuilt by these men of the front, or it will not be rebuilt at all."[36]

Eager to pursue this theme and aware that he had touched on an issue of considerable public interest, Zehrer followed his November article on the second wave with another in April 1930 provocatively entitled "The Class of 1902 Disowned." Beginning with a further development of the critique of his own generation that he had initiated in his earlier article, Zehrer shifted sights and ended with a slashing attack on the class of 1902—men born in 1902—and its successors. We took for granted, wrote Zehrer, that we would fight together with our younger brothers against the older generation. Yet we forgot in our impatience for the assault that the battle *for* the young is as important as the battle *against* the old; and although we saw clearly what we wanted to demolish, we had no clear ideas about what we wanted to put in its place. For eleven years we have been sounding the attack without a well-defined objective, and youth has not responded. Though Zehrer was at pains to chide the front generation for its lack of program, his real target was postwar youth itself. The class of 1902, he noted unhappily, has not followed in our footsteps. While we have remained young, they have aged beyond their years. We fought for a new vision of society; they were merely fighting the eternal battle of the generations for privilege and position. They pretended to speak our language; yet when the chance was offered, they capitulated and settled comfortably into the positions that the men of the front had angrily thrust aside. Now, concluded Zehrer, we must face up to a sad but true fact: We are fighting on two fronts. The class of 1902 is more like our fathers than like us. It has inherited everything that we left behind in the war: "the panache, the security, the big words, the care-lessness of judgment, the lightning-fast operation of the brain, the matter-of-factness, and the clownish behavior." The youth of today are not men of the future, but "the errand boys of a dying age."[37]

Zehrer's notion of a second wave or resurgence of the war generation was further and more subtly developed by Edgar Jung, a veteran of the war and the Freikorps movement and the author of the influential book *Die Herrschaft der Minderwertigen* [The Domination of the Inferior], widely known as the "bible of young conservatism." Zehrer had never bothered to define what he meant by the front generation; nor was he much more precise about the boundaries of the postwar generation, which he situated "between us and our sons." Yet it was clear that when Zehrer said "front generation," he was not referring to all the men who had fought in the German army. Jung (1894) attacked this problem of chronological limits in an article published in May 1930, which he entitled dramatically, "The Tragedy of the War Generation." The German participants in the World War, Jung maintained, could by and large be divided into two groups: those who were mature men in 1914 and who experienced the war as an interruption of their peacetime activities; and those born between 1885 and 1900, for whom the war was an introduction to life and adventure. This second group had rediscovered heroism, come into contact with the primitive, and realized that life demands sacrifice—in other words, this second group had had the authentic war experience. Moreover—and this was an essen-tial element in Jung's argument—the younger German front fighters did not merely represent another generation: they were, he said echoing Jünger, a levy of "new men," whose revelation on the battlefields happened to coincide with the collapse of the bourgeois order and the birth pangs of a new era.

Where, though, was this war generation now, and why had it failed to carry out its mission as the midwife of the new order? Jung denied that the war gen-eration had been unable to adjust to civilian life. Rather, he argued, it was the bourgeoisie who had been unable to adjust to the war generation. The middle class disliked the front fighters' idealism because it constituted a threat to a so-ciety based on commercial values. If the front generation had finally turned against the Republic, it was because the Republic had let *them* down and failed to live up to *their* standards. Like Zehrer, Jung viewed the postwar decade as a period of weeding out within the war generation itself. Some veterans had ad-justed. Others had become disillusioned. The "best," however, had steeled themselves. They were still looking for the political form that corresponded to their vision. Their tragedy was that they had not yet carried out their task; the new order had yet to be created. Indeed, they might never see the order they had been called upon to prepare; they might remain until their deaths "wan-derers between two worlds." That, too, was tragic; but had they not learned during the war to lay down their lives for the sake of victories they would never see? "We must wander through gloom so that our children and our grandchildren will be ensured a bright and untroubled existence. We must become a sacrificed generation, not just as we once were in the hot years of the war, but also in the icy cold of a postwar world without gods . . . The war generation died before its time; now it must go on living so that someday in the future it may rise again."[38]

Meanwhile, Zehrer's article in *Die Tat* disowning the younger generation had provoked a reply by a young man named Uttmann von Elterlein, who identified himself with the class of 1902. Elterlein took issue with Zehrer's attempt to relate attitudes to generations. The real distinction, he argued, was not between the war generation and the postwar generation, but between men of the nineteenth and twentieth centuries. Men of the nineteenth century thought in terms of "graspable significance"; those of the twentieth thought rather in terms of "inner value." Zehrer's mistake, according to Elterlein, was to think that the lines between these two camps could be drawn on the basis of age alone. At the moment, disorder prevailed in the sequence of generations. It was difficult to know to what generation any given individual belonged. In general, though, men born before 1880 stood outside the twentieth century's zone of influence. Even among those born during the following decade the new attitude was the exception rather than the rule. The front generation consisted of those born between 1890 and 1900; their tragedy was that they had a foot in each century. Then came the class of 1902, a transitional generation, followed in turn by those born after 1910, whom Elterlein perceived to be "essentially different from us." Even to use the word "generation," Elterlein warned, could thus be confusing; for when one said generation, one really meant the relationship of the twentieth to the nineteenth century, "the relationship of materialism to spirituality, of rationalism to idealism. Thus one doesn't really mean generation at all."[39]

Elterlein's argument was not nearly so clear as I have made it; still, through the foggy mists of his language Elterlein seemed to be saying that men like Zehrer and Jung were using the word generation to get at something that could not really be tied down to age or experience. Hans Hartmann's pamphlet *Die junge Generation in Europa* [The Young Generation in Europe], published the same year, showed that the point was well taken—that indeed the term generation was being invested with meanings that went beyond the limits of age. For Hartmann, an admirer of the Nazis, generations were defined not by their birth dates but by their "rhythm of blood in thought," which in turn arose out of a tension between their subjective "enrootedness" (*Verwurzelung*) and their objective task. The young generation in Europe, which Hartmann wasted no time in delimiting chronologically, was, in his view, European and national, conservative and radical, oriented toward the community rather than toward the individual, and anxious to bring thought into harmony with action. This young generation could be found everywhere in Europe—and indeed the main virtue of Hartmann's pamphlet was to show how extensive the organization of youth had become in Europe—but its vanguard was in Germany. Hartmann wrote mainly about Europeans under thirty, hence born after 1900. Still, the implication of his pamphlet was that youth was more a function of enthusiasm, dynamism, and attitude than of age or even of experience. By 1933, when a second edition of the work appeared, he did not hesitate to affirm that the Nazis (by that time mostly led by men nearing or over forty) represented the very essence of youth. [40]

Frank Matzke, another self-proclaimed representative and interpreter of youth, agreed with Hartmann that age alone did not suffice to define a new generation. Each generation, Matzke submitted in his book *Jugend bekennt: so sind wir!* [Youth Revealed: This Is the Way We Are], contained an underlying form, just as the pyramids were more than blocks of stone. This form was not to be discovered among peasants whose life remained unchanging with the passage of time, or in the masses where modishness and superficiality prevailed. Moreover, it was not even to be found within all intellectuals of a given age-group, because some were stragglers from the previous generation and still others were forerunners of the revolution to come. Nor did any individual incarnate the new form in all its purity. The generational form was a type or *Urbild* that could be described but never defined; it had to be experienced and lived directly. Drawing on his own feelings and experiences and choosing examples from a random sample of writers, painters, and architects whom he admired, Matzke unhesitatingly discovered the new generational form in *Sachlichkeit*, a name given to an artistic movement then in vogue. The Expressionists, the immediate predecessors of the new generation, had, according to Matzke, overpowered *things* with *feelings*. The new generation made a sharp distinction between the two. They were practical, down-to-earth, reserved, distant, and skeptical. They loved what was appropriate to the achievement of an end and hated anything that was superfluous or overblown. They no longer believed in gods or world views and had ceased to worry about essences. In general, they subordinated thinking and theory to experience and blood, and they were not inclined to overrate the value of books and culture. Like pre-1914 youth, they longed after community; but unlike their predecessors, they were not willing to pay the price of subordination to organizations for the attainment of this end. [41]

Characteristically, Matzke's book was lacking in Sachlichkeit as well as common sense. In comparison, the pamphlet Ernst Wilhelm Eschmann wrote for *Die Tat*'s subscribers, *Wo steht die junge Generation?* [Where Does the Young Generation Stand?], was a model of social analysis and without question *Die Tat*'s most thoughtful and intellectually respectable contribution to the debate. Eschmann (1904) was a student of the sociologist Alfred Weber at Heidelberg and displayed familiarity with the ideas of Karl Mannheim, who had been on the faculty at Heidelberg before moving on to a chair at Frankfurt. This background undoubtedly accounts for the refreshing originality and sophistication of Eschmann's analysis. Instead of approaching the problem of the younger generation through the manifestos of its self-proclaimed representatives, Eschmann side-stepped the issue of what the younger generation claimed to be and posed a question about the functioning of the social system as a whole. Why was it, he asked, that the transition between the generations was so much rougher and conflict-ridden in Germany than in England? This comparative and more concrete approach allowed Eschmann to make a distinction that had eluded earlier contributors to the debate. The tension between age-groups that was widespread in Germany, he pointed out, did not necessarily mean that a new generation had arisen. A new generation meant a new beginning, an upheaval in ways of thought and feeling, a destruction of the existing system, and a bringing to the surface of a preexisting but hitherto hidden reality. The appearance of such a new generation was a "gift of history" that welded a people together and set them in motion. Before such a renewal could occur, two preconditions had to be present in a nation's youth: a common direction or tendency and a common experience. A common experience alone did not suffice to produce important political changes. It might leave traces in literature, art, and religion, but it need have no lasting historical effects on the life of a people. In contrast to the majority of commentators on this theme, Eschmann concluded that in Germany, at least up to 1930, there had been no common experience, although he did detect a common tendency. Now, in 1931 in the wake of the Great Depression, he saw signs that a common experience was crystallizing, but on the details of this experience he remained characteristically vague.[42]

Much more worthy of attention than Eschmann's conclusion, which contained that element of speculation and wishful thinking common in almost all generational literature, were some of the observations he made in reaching it. To begin with, he was quick to note that the "younger generation," so much referred to in the press, in political speeches, and in literature, was a simple legend. The substance of this "generation" was a narrow circle of middle-class youth, whose advance in economic and political life had been blocked for various reasons. Any generalization about the younger generation, Eschmann warned, would have to take into account the young Nazis and Communists and the great mass of unorganized youth. Eschmann also had some blunt words on the cult of youth. In Germany, he wrote, there was a lot of talk about youth and its irreplaceable value. "The ideal of 'youth' is becoming a magic formula without which no movement dares to show itself before the public." In reality, Eschmann argued, the rhetoric of youth was a weapon used by the older generation to bar youth from its rightful share in the determination of national policy and the enjoyment of material goods. In comparison to other European countries—Russia and Italy, for example—Germany was still ruled by old men. It was the fact of gerontocracy combined with the myth of youth as a value in itself (*Jugend als Eigenwert*) that made the relations between the generations tense and antagonistic.[43]

The worst victims of the youth cult, Eschmann said, were the front generation, whom he defined as those born between 1892 and 1897. The men born
in these years had been aged prematurely by the war; at the same time in many
respects they were younger—the implication was that they were more immature—than their juniors. Far from acknowledging the younger veterans as potential leaders of a revolution based on a coalition of youth, Eschmann specifically excluded them from membership in the "young generation" and
described them as suspended tragically between the upper and lower age-groups
of the German people. No coalition of war veterans, such as the one that
Zehrer and Jung had called for, existed; nor did Eschmann think one was likely
to arise. Indeed, the period since the war had shown that it was impossible to
create a new state and a new mentality based on the war experience, precisely
because this experience did not have universal validity and was not binding for
the younger age-groups. The front generation deserved their rightful place in
national life, but they must seek it in an alliance with their juniors—an alliance in which Eschmann clearly did not think they were destined to play the
leading role.

Whereas Eschmann's pamphlet rejected Zehrer's claims for the destiny of
the front generation and proclaimed postwar youth's ambitions, E. Günther
Gründel's long and fascinating book *Die Sendung der jungen Generation* [The
Mission of the Young Generation], published the year before Hitler came to
power, attempted to reconcile the differences of these two groups in one of
those solutions of "the higher third" so dear to German intellectuals. The result
was brilliant and at the same time slightly mad—a powerful demonstration of
how longing had come to dominate the sense for political realities of many of
these ideologues of a generational revolution.

Influenced primarily by Wechssler, Gründel submitted that generations were
"waves of humanity," consisting of men born within a band of more or less
thirty years, "in which the cultural-historical action of peoples manifests itself."
These "creative unities" bore the stamp of certain particularly important historical moments or events. The young generation in Germany today, Gründel
claimed, was made up of those born roughly between 1890 and 1920. To be
properly understood, this mass of youth had to be further divided into three
subgenerations: the young front generation (born between 1890 and 1900); the
war youth generation (born between 1900 and 1910); and the postwar generation (born after 1910). Each of these subgenerations had its distinctive experience and characteristics. The first generation, of which the militants of the pre-
1914 Youth Movement had been the vanguard, had inaugurated the struggle
against the chauvinism, matertialism, and class consciousness of the older generation and then had been decimated by the war. The war youth generation
had been subjected to the collectivist spirit of the first phase of the war, the
hunger, distress, and disillusionment of 1917–1918, and the inflation and economic collapse of the early twenties. The postwar generation had grown up in a

relatively untroubled world of booming technology, camaraderie, and sport during the late 1920s; but then the Great Depression had come, and they too had known dismay, doubt, and deprivation. For all their differences, however, the three subgenerations were bound together by their relationship to the war and by their central place in the unfolding of the bourgeois crisis; each in its own way had been given a glimpse into the postbourgeois world; and now instead of bickering with one another and flinging accusations, all three age-groups should work together and join forces against the old.[44]

Gründel agreed with Eschmann that Jünger's generation had been mistaken in assuming that they were destined to lead the coming revolution. Though excellent critics of bourgeois society, the young front fighters were too diminished in their numbers, too single-minded in their preoccupation with death and destruction, too aristocratic in their concept of society, too rigid in their thinking, and ultimately too bound to the nineteenth century to lead the kind of complex and many-sided revolution that history, according to Gründel, had in mind. It was the war youth generation (to which Gründel, born in 1903, belonged) that was best suited for this task.

Gründel's reasons for reaching this conclusion reveal the penetration of psychoanalytic ideas into the discussion of the generation question in Germany. To begin with, Gründel pointed out, the war youth were more numerous than their predecessors and their successors and thus possessed greater reserves of leadership material and vitality.[45] But even more important was the series of experiences that the war youth had undergone. Drawing from the work of Spranger and Carl Jung, Gründel maintained that youthful experiences were more important than those undergone later in life. Nothing experienced in youth was lost. Somewhere in the depths of the soul it remained and led a latent existence, like "tensely strung harpstrings" that could vibrate at any moment in response to other sounds. Gründel was impressed by Carl Jung's assertion that traumatic experiences could either strengthen people or lame them. It was a fact enshrined in all the great folk myths, he recalled, that heroes were men of noble birth whose hard and trying youth had steeled them for their later exploits. The negative type, the man crushed by his experience, appeared first and seemed to dominate, at least in the mass. It was only later, after a certain incubation period, that the stronger type emerged; and it stood to reason that if an entire age-group of young men had come through a hard experience together, the result would be a Jugendgemeinschaft that, bound together by a collective, conscious, and at the same time unified will, could achieve extraordinary deeds.[46]

Gründel took issue with the view, shared by Eschmann and Matzke, that the main characteristic of the young generation was its Sachlichkeit or matter-of-factness. Surveying the cultural attitudes of the late twenties and early thirties, he thought it likely that youth would throw over materialism and nihilism in favor of a new idealism that might contain irrational elements of faith and belief. The young men of 1932, he found, were marked above all by their outer coolness and inner passion; by their matter-of-factness in material things and their heightened feeling when it came to things of the soul. They were collectivists—though by the collectivity they meant something different from the "colorless mass"—and they longed for a community that would be heroic, aristocratic, and personal.[47]

It was essential to Gründel's argument, indeed it was his central theme, that the style of the young generation represented what Spranger had called a "culture-renewing moment" and not just an "age-group movement."[48] Every generation, Gründel wrote, lived in two dimensions. There were short-term generational styles, destined to disappear without leaving a mark on history, and there were styles characteristic of entire epochs. Occasionally, in times of crisis, a new generational style could dominate an entire century. Gründel was convinced that the young generation in Germany stood at such an epochal turning point. The world of the bourgeoisie with its faith in freedom of thought and the domination of matter by reason had been dealt a mortal blow by the war and the depression. The old generation and its values were bankrupt. The day of liberal capitalism and the reign of the trader were over. Now people realized that what the bourgeois revolution had won in breadth and power it had lost in depth and spirit. The new faith would be harmonious wholeness and the organic integration of man. The clearest sign of the bourgeois collapse was to be found in economic life, where people now demanded a planned economy that would serve human needs.

Gründel's vision of the future was dazzlingly precise. As he looked through the "creative fog" of the present, with the aid of Moeller van den Bruck and Edgar Jung, he glimpsed the outlines of a new era, comparable in novelty and significance only to the Renaissance. The center of the new Western revolution lay in Germany, just as the centers of the earlier one had lain in Spain, England, and France. The historical mission of the German revolution was to achieve European unity, for only the Germans possessed the necessary objectivity (Sachlichkeit) for the task. Germany was the conscience of Europe and at the same time its most oppressed nation. France was finished as a great power. Thus the precondition for the creation of Europe was the destruction of the Treaty of Versailles, which Gründel thought might occur without war. First, however, Germany must rebuild itself. The setting up of the Weimar Republic, to be sure, had been a false start. Weimar represented the domination of plutocrats, the rule of the incompetent, and the politics of narrow class interests. German youth wanted a "noble, practical socialism," not to be confused of course with the socialism of a party or a single class. The way of the German revolution unquestionably led through a dictatorship. The authority principle must be reestablished before Germany could get back on her feet. German youth had been the first to understand that democracy must be complemented by the aristocratic principle. This "supplementation" of democracy would take place through education and breeding. The Reich would undertake to form its leadership eugenically and would develop all types necessary for life in a modern society. "Biological man," Gründel pointed out, "is the indispensable raw material, which is shaped and formed by spirit in cultures, states, and nations . . . The conscious cultivation of this raw material has become in the twentieth century an urgent human duty." The resulting society would be divided into three classes: a layer of leaders, distinguished by great intellect and character, who would be recruited from all sectors of the population; a parsimonious, economically qualified middle class, as numerous as possible, that would include skilled workers who were to be paid "as well as possible"; and finally, "an economically thriving, numerically broad peasantry, sound in soul," that would serve as a guarantee for the nourishment of the people and a continuing well of bodily and intellectually healthy population renewal.[49]

Yet what did all this mean in practical terms; and why, if the old was moribund, had the members of the young generation failed to unite and destroy the Weimar Republic? First of all, Gründel thought, echoing Eschmann, because of the confusion of the postwar years and the skill with which the old elite had used diversionary tactics (the cult of youth, the lure of economic reconstruction, the myth of the Republic) to drive a wedge between the front youth and the war youth, thus neutralizing the younger forces and hiding the reality of gerontocracy. Now it appeared that youth had seen through the ruse. The elections of September 1930 had shown that young people were beginning to move toward the extremes and especially toward National Socialism. Gründel saw this movement of youth toward political radicalism as an inevitable and necessary stage in the German revolution, because the great problems of the moment, in the final analysis, would all have to be resolved politically. He was persuaded, however, that neither the Communist nor the National Socialist parties held the key to the German future. Communism had preserved the spirit of nineteenth-century capitalism in its obsession with material progress and represented the revolt of the masses against excellence and personality. Its victory would result in a reverse selection of talent and the destruction of the peasantry. National Socialism was based on an erroneous racial theory and took as its model a soldier-warrior type that was not suited to the modern world. If National Socialism triumphed, Germany would experience a cultural regression and would be governed by terror, which was alien to the German spirit.[50]

Nor did Gründel believe that the veterans' leagues, such as the Stahlhelm and the Jungdeutsche Order, were fated to oversee the German transformation. They lacked a sense for "the whole" and had not yet chosen between the bourgeoisie and revolution. The time for the German revolution, he concluded with calm assurance, was not yet ripe and would not be until the fifth decade of the century. No leader yet possessed the formula that the times demanded. Youth must rely on itself and not abandon itself to false prophets (like Hitler), who embodied the style of today. In the meantime, while waiting for the bourgeois world to collapse, the young generation's task was to prepare, to learn how to master money and technology, to practice true socialism in its daily life, and to train itself to follow, so that one day, having found its Führer, it might lead. The best format for this activity, Gründel thought, was still the Bünde. Unlike the parties, the Bünde stood for ideals rather than for interests, and to this extent they foreshadowed the style of tomorrow, when classes would give way to an elitist Gemeinschaft.

It all sounded so reasonable, so clever, so clear. Alas, within two years of Gründel's shimmering forecast of the future, Hitler had installed himself securely in power, Edgar Jung had been murdered by the Nazis, Hans Zehrer had been forced to withdraw from political journalism, and the veterans' leagues and youth Bünde had been "coordinated" and integrated within National Socialist organizations with which they had little in common. It became part of the mythology of the regime that the Nazi leadership represented the essence of youth. Talk about the conflict of generations no longer had meaning when society was being restructured according to the leadership principle. Indeed, while taking care to project an image of youthful energy, Hitler assured the older generation that under a National Socialist regime young people would be taught to venerate their parents, tradition, and above all the army. Hence, it was the Nazis, rather than the Weimar political establishment, who utilized the cult of youth to neutralize the challenge of the younger generation. Under Hitler youth consciousness became false consciousness. Young people were subordinated to the needs of the regime and lost all claim to autonomy, not to mention the right to dwell in a world of youthful values.[51]

Evidently, Gründel had omitted some essential factor from his analysis: the possibility that once allowed to grasp the levers of state power, the Nazis would not permit themselves to be displaced. The key to the German future lay not in the Bünde but in those unorganized masses of young people whose political importance Eschmann was alone to appreciate among writers of the neoconservative camp. These masses responded to the Nazi message. They wanted jobs, security, and protection from their enemies, whether real or imagined. Above all, they wanted a leader; and Hitler had a diabolical knack for telling them what they wanted to hear. The prophets of a generational politics had no answer to Hitler. They could not outbid him in his appeal to the masses; nor were they willing to resist him. To Gründel as to Edgar Jung, the Nazis appeared the lesser of evils. As a popular movement and an electoral organization engaged in party politics, they were distasteful; but they were preferable to all other existing political solutions. For all their shortcomings, the National Socialists were the mass movement to which the neoconservatives felt closest. Besides, as men who specialized in the anticipation of the future, they *knew* that the Nazis' tenure in power would be nothing more than a prelude to the emergence of a truly new nobility that would find its leaders in the youth of the Bunde. Have illusions ever proved more costly?[52]

Top: Youth Movement group around 1900. Bottom: Youth Movement group on a hiking expedition in 1909.

[*The members of the Youth Movement sought*] *independently from the sluggish habits of the old and from the commandments of hateful convention to give shape and form to their life.*

Summons to the meeting on the Meissner Mountain, 1913

Youth Movement group singing in their "nest" in 1911.

[The members of the Youth Movement strove] after a style of life, corresponding to the nature of youth, which would at the same time make it possible for them to take themselves and their activities seriously and to integrate themselves as a special factor into the general work of cultural creation.

Summons to the meeting on the Meissner Mountain, 1913

Top: Walter Flex during the Great War. Bottom: Ernst Wurche at the front in 1915.

For men of great sensitivity, death is the greatest experience.
    Ernst Wurche to Walter Flex, 1915

Top: Fritz von Unruh in 1920. Bottom: Ernst Jünger during the Great War.

What if we brought the light of this hour home with us, where only lamps burn in houses?

Fritz von Unruh, 1916

German veterans marching in 1930.

We are—that we feel every day with firmer certainty—a new generation, a race that has been hardened and inwardly transformed by all the darting flames and sledgehammer blows of the greatest war in history.

Ernst Jünger, 1930

Karl Mannheim.

Why precisely is it that in most recent times people have become conscious of generational unity?
    Karl Mannheim, 1928

THE writings just considered formed only a small part of the huge body of publications on the generation question that appeared in Germany during the decade before Hitler came to power. The generational method was put to work to illuminate everything from contemporary social conflicts to the history of classical antiquity.[53] Compared to the French generational writings discussed in chapter one, three features of the German literature stand out: a tendency to view youth as a social category and a historical agent in its own right; an awareness that age-groups do not necessarily blossom into "generations," and a concern for the conditions under which a generational change produces a revolution in national life. Whereas Mentré saw generational change as regular and dependent on the length of human life, the Germans emphasized the role of events and experience, particularly youthful experience. For Mentré literature was the most faithful mirror of generational sensibility; for the German writers of the twenties politics was the theater of generational action. For Mentré the agent of generational change was a school of thought; for the Germans it was a youth movement. These differences are differences between France and Germany—and to some extent, differences between 1914 and 1930. What Mentré had taken for granted—the regular turnover of generations and the eternal conflict of fathers and sons—had become uncertain in Germany because of the failure of the war generation to carry out its revolution. Generations, the Germans realized, were a "gift of history." Their formation needed to be explained.

In a country where sociology had arisen to describe contemporary reality, it was inevitable that this situation and these debates would leave their mark on social theory. They did, in Karl Mannheim's now classic essay on the problem of social generations, which he published in two installments in 1928–1929. A former student of Georg Lukács and Heinrich Rickert, the Hungarian-born Mannheim (1893) was an academic sociologist whose primary interest lay in the development of thought. His earliest essays dealt with the classification of world views and theories of knowledge, but he was soon led to grapple with "the monstrous tension" between historicity and timelessness and above all with the relationships among changing cultural styles, political traditions, and social groups. Mannheim was drawn to the generation problem because of a series of scholarly works, which appeared in Germany during the second decade of the twenties, purporting to discover in generations the explanation of the Zeitgeist or the source of cultural styles. Mannheim was highly ambivalent about these efforts, as he was about much in the German cultural tradition. On the one hand, he applauded the attempt to broaden the concept of thinking to include irrational elements, and he considered German thought deeper and more all-encompassing than French and English empiricism. On the other hand, he was concerned about the penetration of neoromantic and irrational ideas into the discussion of a question that should be explored empirically on the mediating level of society, where hypotheses could be subjected to the test of facts. Mannheim himself favored the dialectical method when studying the development of cultural and social thought. At the same time, he was clearly eager to show what a scientific sociology could do when presented with a seemingly insoluble problem. He brought to the task an original mind and a rigorous method of sociological and cultural analysis.[54]

Mannheim began, as was his habit, with a brief but incisive discussion of earlier writings on the topic. These, he said, could be divided into two traditions: the positivist approach and the romantic-historical school. The positivist tradition reached back to David Hume and Auguste Comte through Justin Dromel and Giuseppe Ferrari and had its latest incarnation in Mentré. All these thinkers operated with the insight that the biological nature of man—the relatively fixed length of any single human life, the continuous flow of births, the process of aging—must in some way determine the process of social and cultural change. Their common goal was to discover a general law or historical rhythm based on the vital statistics of life and death. Their problem was to fix quantitatively the length of a generation and to find the point from which one should begin to count in order to establish the sequence of generations. The positivist school had its center in France, and its thinkers were inspired by the unilinear idea of progress. They conceived of time in quantitative terms and saw the secret of history in chronological tables. For this tradition, generations did not interrupt the onward flow of history; they assured its continuity and articulated the movement of society. The generational concept thus became both an explanation and a proof of progress. The romantic-historical approach, on the other hand, originated in Germany and was penetrated by a conservative bias. Its proponents sought a weapon for use against the idea of progress, and they had found it, among other places, in the concept of generations, which (in their interpretation) contained a new and radically different view of time as inner, lived, and hence quantitatively immeasurable experience. For Wilhelm Dilthey, according to Mannheim, contemporaneity was not a chronological fact but an identity of influences, an inner time that could be seized not through numbers but only through the insight of a historically oriented mind.[55]

For Mannheim, the worst offender in this second tradition was not Dilthey, whom he admired, but Wilhelm Pinder, whose attempt to apply the concept of generation to art history was fresh in Mannheim's mind. Pinder (1878), a highly respected professor at the University of Berlin, was fascinated by what he called the "noncontemporaneity of contemporaries." One man's inner time, he noted, was not necessarily identical with another's, even though they lived at the same time. The Zeitgeist was really a polyphony of voices from different generations; it was like the sound achieved by the vocally contrasting members of a trio, with the difference that each singer had earlier sung his predecessor's part and that the harmony achieved was only apparent or superficial. Time was not a point along a horizontal line, but an axis that extended up and down through different age-groups. Generations, Pinder argued, should be thought of in terms of an entelechy, or unfolding process, with its own unity, inner aim, and law of development. The various arts, languages, races, and styles constituted such entelechies. There was also an entelechy for Europe and one for individuals. Entelechies were biologically determined by secret laws that lay buried deep in nature. With respect to generational entelechies, this meant that everything a generation would be or could be had already been decided when its members were born. The historical process was the product of the interplay between chronological entelechies and constant factors, like cultural areas, nations, family, individuality, and types. Applied to art history, this led to the conclusion that art historical phenomena were determined. Events were not reversible. The new cultural history would have to go to the school of biology; spirit was the faithful servant of nature. The ability to explain something was less important than the ability to perceive it.[56]

Mannheim was impressed by Pinder's insight into the noncontemporaneity of contemporaries and by the notion of entelechies, which he identified as an adaptation and extension of Alois Riegl's idea of *Kunstwollen* or "art motifs." These ideas, he said, were valuable and even brilliant. What annoyed him was Pinder's suggestion that the inner laws of these entelechies were generated by some secret natural process and were more important than the things that happened in society. There might well be mysteries in history; there might even be a historical rhythm, and one day we might know it. But the danger of theories like Pinder's, Mannheim felt, was that they distracted researchers from the study of the nonoccult and hence more comprehensible phenomena in society that could be analyzed and understood. Would it not be more profitable, he asked, to inquire whether conflicts, influences, and relationships created "social entelechies"?

Mannheim's criticism of Pinder broadened into an attack on the methods of the romantic school in German intellectual life. This intellectual current, he complained, concealed the fact that there was a layer of socially formed forces between the natural and cultural spheres. The romantics either explained everything in terms of sheer spirit or deduced everything from biological categories, like life, race, generation, and "secret natural processes." Generation, Mannheim hastened to add, was not a useless concept; on the contrary, for those who wished to understand the development of social and intellectual movements, it was an indispensable tool. But in its present form the concept of generation was ill conceived and unscientifically formulated. What was needed, Mannheim concluded, was a new statement of the generation problem that would bring together what was best and most valid in the French and German traditions, discard what was ill founded, and synthesize the findings of the separate branches of scholarship. Sociology was the intellectual discipline best suited to undertake this task, and Mannheim conceived of his essay as a first step in this direction.[57]

The sociologist, said Mannheim, must begin by asking what binds the members of a generation together. If he did this, he would notice that, with a few exceptions like the German Youth Movement, generation was not the kind of social bond that gave rise to a concrete group. A generation was not a community—that is, a group whose unity depended upon the physical proximity of its members. Nor was it a social formation organized for a specific purpose. It was neither a Gemeinschaft like the family nor a Gesellschaft like a political party. What kind of a social formation, then, was a generation? Somewhat surprisingly, Mannheim came to the conclusion that a generation was like a class; it was an objective fact, a *location* in society that did not depend upon the consciousness of its members. This location was based on a biological rhythm in human existence—ultimately on the factors of life and death, a limited span of life, and aging. These biological factors, however, did not explain the social and historical phenomenon of generation; they merely made the generational bond possible. It was in missing this distinction, said Mannheim, that the positivists had gone wrong. Any attempt to deduce attitudes from biological data was bound to lead to confusion and error.

In order to explain the sociological implications of a common generational location, Mannheim imagined a society in which death did not exist and a single generation lived on eternally. This enabled him to plunge to the center of the generation question, avoiding the pseudoissues that had plagued so many of his predecessors. The first feature Mannheim identified in his imagined society was a tendency toward single-mindedness, for without a mechanism of birth there would be no reinvigorating influx of cultural innovators. Indeed, he noted, the most radical changes in perspective had their roots in the biological factors of life and death. It was the "fresh approach" of the oncoming generation—the contact of newcomers with the accumulated cultural heritage—that compensated for the inelasticity of the human mind. Death, moreover, was just as important to the renovation of society as the birth of new minds. Lacking the outflow of dying members, Mannheim's eternal society would have to devise some means of forgetting what it had once learned. Too much experience would be an obstacle to innovation. To be old, Mannheim said, meant above all to live in a specific, self-achieved, predetermining experiential system or network (*Erfahrungszusammenhang*) through which every new experience could be filtered and within which every new experience could be assigned its place. The turnover of generations wiped the slate clean and made it possible for new men to learn from new experiences.

An eternally living generation, Mannheim continued, would also lack the primary characteristic that gives human life its dialectical rhythm: the polarity of experiences arising out of the fact that all men participate in a limited segment of the historical process. The human mind was structured in such a way that some experiences had more force than others. The first experiences, especially those of childhood and adolescence, had a tendency to crystallize into a conception of life. Later experiences were not simply added to this primary layer; they stood in a dialectical relationship to it, either confirming or negating this first conscious world view. The rebel was just as much a prisoner of his first experiences as the conformist; for both oriented themselves, either negatively or positively, in terms of their earliest and least self-conscious visions of the world. The stratification of the mind, argued Mannheim, explained why culture so seldom displayed a linear development. The enemy of the older generation—the pole around which they had organized their program and the foil against which they had formulated their ideas—no longer existed for the younger generation, who were already fighting different foes. Living eternally, all the men of Mannheim's utopian society would have similarly stratified minds; thus their culture would develop relatively linearly rather than through conflicts and returns to past forms.

This identity of mind stratification would eliminate two of the most important aspects of society: the transmission of culture from one generation to the next and the process of interaction and interlearning between generations. Mannheim's utopian society would have no need for cultural transmission. Men would possess their culture consciously. Yet in human beings the deepest layer of consciousness, what later seems most natural, is often inherited from the past and absorbed from the surrounding milieu unconsciously. Taught knowledge is already problematic knowledge. Following Spranger, Mannheim asserted that it was at about age seventeen that men began to pass from a world of unconscious cultural influences to a conscious spiritual life in which they developed original intellectual solutions to the problems posed by experience. Continuing the analysis, he pointed out that such a utopian society not only would lack the security of deep, unquestioned mental moorings; it would also miss the spur of interaction between the generations. Contrary to what most generational theorists had believed, Mannheim insisted that generations, at least in present-day society, were not self-contained units turning over every thirty years. In ordinary times, younger generations must adjust to the way of their elders; in times of rapid change, elders were more open to the wisdom of youth. If there were no generations, there would be no way for new knowledge—that is, the knowledge that comes from fresh experience—to be transmitted and to be assimilated by older age-groups; and at the same time, if it were not for the existence of intermediary generations, cultural transmission could never be accomplished without conflict. A society with generations, then, was not a series of idea-tight compartments (as Pinder had suggested) but an ever moving, mutually influencing flow.[58]

This analysis, though somewhat ponderous and frustratingly abstract, put Mannheim in a position to answer two of the questions at the center of the generation problem: who belonged to a generation and how long generations lasted. In answering the first question Mannheim introduced a narrowing series of distinctions between potential generational locations (*Generationslagerung*), actual generational complexes (*Generationszusammenhang*), and generational units (*Generationseinheit*). If generations were defined in terms of social location, he pointed out, then it was absurd to ask whether the youth of Germany and China belonged to the same generation, for the two groups could not experience the same events and did not have similarly stratified minds. But even a common location did not in itself suffice to create a generational bond. A generation as an actuality—a Generationszusammenhang—arose only when similarly located individuals shared a common destiny and participated actively and passively in the social and intellectual movements that were shaping and transforming the historical situation. Hence peasant and urban youth living in the same period, though similarly located in the historical process, could not be said to belong to the same generational complex because young peasants were not affected by the events that moved the youth of the towns.[59]

What about similarly located individuals who belonged to different ideological camps, like the conservatives and liberals in Europe during the early nineteenth century—could they be said to belong to the same generation? To answer this question, Mannheim introduced the idea of the "generation unit." The generation unit was a widely shared pattern of response to a specific historical situation rather than a concrete group. What gave the concrete group its importance and its binding force on other members of the generation was that it formulated principles that expressed the fresh approach to experience and the mind stratification of the generation as a whole. Thus the Christlich-deutsche Tischgesellschaft, an association of students formed in the early nineteenth century, had developed ideas that later became dominant in German conservatism, a generation unit rather than a group. Mannheim insisted that these generation units should not be confined to any single group. What typified them was precisely that they were collective, that they incorporated certain basic principles or tendencies (*Grundintentionen*), and that they were not dependent on physical contact. One could think like a conservative without ever coming into contact with the members of a conservative group; indeed, one could think like a conservative without being aware that any such thing as conservatism existed.[60]

Having disposed of the problem of how far the generational bond extended and whom it affected, Mannheim turned to the vexing question of how long generations lasted. Theoretically, he admitted, there were as many generational locations as there were birthdates. Not every generational location, though, created new collective impulses and gave rise to generation units. Whether age-groups realized the potential inherent in their location depended on the rate of social change. When social change was rapid, the gradual adaptation of human attitudes and values was no longer possible, and new patterns of experience consolidated, forming a new generational style or a new generational entelechy. If the tempo of social change became too quick, new patterns of experience and feeling might pile up too rapidly, and budding entelechies might be destroyed before they could create distinct styles of life. In such cases, the members of these generations, frustrated in the development of their own entelechies, would attach themselves to an earlier generation that had already achieved a satisfactory form or to a younger generation that seemed capable of achieving a newer life-ideal. Here crucial group experiences could act as "crystallizing agents." Again, Mannheim introduced a distinction between generations that realized themselves intuitively and those that were conscious of their own generational uniqueness. The German Youth Movement and the Burschenschaften in the first half of the nineteenth century were examples of this second, self-conscious type of generational formation.[61]

From all this it was clear, Mannheim concluded, that biological factors need not determine the rhythm of cultural or social change. The chain of births went smoothly and continuously on; the tempo of cultural and social development was erratic. This was where most generational theories had gone wrong.[62] They had jumbled up biological and social factors, failed to distinguish between generational location, generation as actuality, and generation units, and ended up a sociology of chronological tables. Whether new generations appeared every year, every thirty years, every hundred years, or whether they appeared rhythmically at all, depended entirely on the social and cultural process. Mannheim again emphasized the need to study the unfolding of natural factors against the background of history and society. It was true, for example, that men of equal age were drawn together by a natural affinity, but this natural affinity in itself would never produce a social generation. Only history, the unfolding of man's collective fate in a specific social context, could bring these biological tendencies to fruition.

In the final section of his essay, Mannheim sought to clarify the relationship between generations and historical epochs. On the issue of the Zeitgeist and the factors that produced it, he disagreed with both Pinder and Wilhelm Petersen, a professor of German literature at the University of Berlin, who had used the generational concept to define the essence of romanticism in 1926. The Zeitgeist, said Mannheim, could not be reduced to a generational style or principle, as Petersen had sought to reduce it; nor did it disappear in the harmony or cacophony of different generational entelechies coexisting at a given time, as Pinder had claimed. The Zeitgeist arose from the tension of different currents or tendencies, anchored in social classes, which expressed themselves most clearly in political ideologies. There existed a polarity of traditions rather than a succession of types. Generational entelechies, Mannheim thought, developed within these long-term tendencies or streams of thought. The normal, socially anchored individual was shaped not by the Zeitgeist, which was indefinable in itself, but by the ideological traditions in his surroundings. Historians of literature like Petersen had missed this point, according to Mannheim, because they studied "free-swinging" intellectuals, who tended to be relatively free of social moorings. Other social groups did not shift so rapidly in their sensibility and structures of thought. From this Mannheim concluded that generational changes and new generational entelechies could be studied meaningfully only insofar as they expressed themselves within existing intellectual and political currents. [63]

M ANNHEIM intended his essay as an exercise in formal sociology. Hence he made no attempt to apply his categories to the analysis of a given society, although he mentioned that he thought they would be useful for understanding the development of contemporary Europe. In this last supposition, Mannheim was undoubtedly correct, for in comparison to existing generational theories his approach represented a considerable step forward, at least from the point of view of an empirically oriented social science.

For example, by introducing the concept of mind stratification and by setting forth the conditions under which age-group locations gave rise to a distinctive generational mentality, Mannheim accounted, as Mentré had not, for the rapid piling up of generations during the relatively brief period between 1912 and 1927. By violently interrupting the flow of national life, the war created age-group rifts between those who had been too old to fight in it, those who had borne its brunt in the trenches, those who had been too young to be called up but old enough to respond consciously to events, and those whose independent and conscious spiritual life had begun after the war had faded into a historical memory. Each of these age-groups had its mind stratified in a different way, and to observers at the time each seemed to have different characteristics. Mannheim's distinction between generation as location and generation as actuality helped further to illuminate the relationship between the masses and the intellectual and political elites who sought to lead them. The more collective the nature of historical events, the greater the number of people they would affect, hence the larger the potential size of the actual generation. A gale of social change that swept over all sectors of the population, the war had been such a collective event and had therefore, according to Mannheim's theory, created the possibility of a truly mass generation in which elites and subordinate classes would feel bound together by a common experience. Finally, Mannheim's theory explained why the returning veterans—identified by many as the "war generation"—had failed to revolutionize German life, as Jünger and others had predicted that they would. Generations, Mannheim said, expressed themselves through existing political and cultural traditions. The war generation had been divided among many such currents, but above all between those who sought a reactionary solution and those who sought a socialist solution to Germany's problems. Hitler's coming to power and the creation of the Third Reich signified not the victory of the war generation, as the Nazis claimed, but the victory of one part of the war generation over its opponents and the imposition of one interpretation of the war generation's experience on the population as a whole.

One contemporary problem Mannheim did pose, but evidently decided not to pursue, was the question of why people had suddenly become so conscious of the generational bond.[64] This is a large issue and one I shall confront in the conclusion after gathering and analyzing empirical evidence from a greater variety of national contexts. It is a question, I should say now, that has no single answer. But if we narrow the question, rephrase it slightly, and ask why people—and what kind of people—were drawn toward generational politics in the Weimar Republic, then Mannheim's essay provides an important clue.

The most distinctive feature of Mannheim's analysis was his comparison of the idea of generation to the concept of class. Influenced by Georg Lukács, he grasped that, like a class, a generation was a social-historical location that had to be understood in terms of the relationship between social fact and the consciousness of social fact. Just as not all class locations led automatically to a unity of class action and attitude, so not all age-groups would necessarily realize the potential implicit in their situation. Mannheim saw too that generational formation depended on history in the same way that the consciousness of class was sharpened or dulled by historical events; and he perceived that generational locations contained positive tendencies of thought and feeling, as well as negative limitations of action, that were capable of uniting men and women who did not necessarily know each other or ever come into contact. Impressed with the power of the analogy, he even went so far as to argue that, like class ideologies, generational tendencies might appeal to those outside the situation—that is, to older or younger people. Indeed, the core of a generational attitude might be shaped by isolated precursors, just as the men who created socialism, an ideology of working-class liberation, stemmed in great majority from the bourgeoisie. But just as the real locus of class ideology remained the class even when the ideology was created by deserters from other classes, so the real seat of the new generational impulse remained the generational situation, even if members of other age-groups participated in its articulation.[65]

The analogy is enlightening. So enlightening, in fact, that one is inspired to push it further—until one comes up against the differences that set the generational idea off from that of class. The generational approach implies that the historical experiences that bind the members of an age-group together are more important than any social differences that might divide them. The real conflict in society, the generational approach suggests, is not between classes, but between youth and age. Moreover, classes have interests dictated by material realities; generations, by contrast, have values generated by the capacity of the human mind for new departures. In the language of the German intellectual tradition, interests derive from nature; values derive from spirit or Geist. The trouble is that age groups are always divided in their values, just as they are always divided in their social interests. This makes it necessary for generationalists to distinguish between those who possess the "new" generational values and those who do not. Such distinctions appear in all generational writings, but they are particularly prominent in the writings of the German intellectuals discussed in this chapter. Ernst Jünger identified the "new men" as the storm troopers of the Western Front and dismissed the rest of his age-group, including those who had fought in the war, as hopelessly attached to the values of the nineteenth century.[66] Hans Zehrer distinguished the first wave of the front generation, which had either adjusted to bourgeois society or retreated into Bohemia, from a second wave (to which he belonged), which had preserved its enthusiasm and its convictions intact. Edgar Jung singled out veterans who had become disillusioned from those who had been steeled by adversity and were now ready to accept their tragic fate. Frank Matzke classified as authentic members of the new generation only those people who incarnated the kind of cultural outlook he happened to like. And Gründel, who was more aware than most other German writers on generation of the hazards of this kind of generalization, based his entire book on a distinction between those who react positively to early experiences and rise above them, incorporating them into a new world view, and those who are crushed by the force of cataclysmic events. Only Eschmann tried to take into account the unorganized masses who were not covered by these facile generalizations; and he concluded that no younger generation yet existed, although he thought that the depression might create one if it gave German youth a truly common experience and not one as selective and unique as that undergone by young soldiers at the front.

This, comparison of generations to classes helps to explain the function and appeal of the generational concept in Weimar Germany—and in postwar France and other European countries as well. The generational mode of interpreting and organizing social reality was not merely like that of class; it was an alternative to it. It was part of a larger cluster of ideas that members of the middle classes were using to break the iron grip of class interests, and it provided an ideological weapon with special appeal for intellectuals, who were resisting the onslaught of a mass, materialistic society in which they feared that heroic and aristocratic values would be lost, culture would be replaced by technology, and the sense of community would be destroyed. Hence the generational idea appealed to academics like Wechssler, Pinder, and Petersen, who longed after the "whole"; to former officers like Jünger, who missed the adventure, community, and natural hierarchy of the wartime army; to university students and members of the youth leagues, who felt that what divided them from their coevals was less important than what united them; and to "free-swinging" intellectuals, like the men of *Die Tat*, who were seeking a third way between the traditional conservatives of the Right and the radicals of the Left. Cut off from the working class by their elitism and antimaterialism, and hostile to the conservative interests because of their belief that the war had opened up a new era of history in which traditional ideologies would disappear, intellectuals like Jünger, Zehrer, and Gründel were forced to look about for masses who might provide the troops for *their* revolution. They thought that they perceived these masses in the veterans' leagues and in the uncommitted youth who had grouped themselves into Bünde. It was this coalition, glimpsed dimly through "creative fog," to which they were referring when they spoke about the mission of the "young generation."

Viewed retrospectively, these hopes seem more like daydreams and self-indulgent fantasies than like politics. The locus of power in the Weimar Republic remained in the parties, the large economic interests, and the churches. When veterans and students were mobilized politically, it was not by the men of *Die Tat* but by Hitler's smoothly functioning propaganda machine. What can we conclude, then, but that the politics of generation was a politics of illusion? True enough, but wishful thinking, combined with an unrelenting hate for the Republic, was precisely one of the characteristics of political thinking—and especially the political thinking of intellectuals—during the last years of the Weimar Republic. Anything and everything seemed possible; and a chance to shape the future justified every risk. Generational fantasies alone were not sufficient to overthrow the system; they could and did, however, help to prevent the system from mobilizing the support of young people against its enemies. On the level of political fantasy and rhetoric, then, the idea of the young generation and its mission played a modest but by no means insignificant role in the downfall of the Republic.

It is curious that Mannheim never made the connection between the popularity of generational thinking in the Weimar Republic and the transformations that were taking place in society and politics, for he himself had cleared the way for such an insight when he pointed out that key words like "freedom" and "revolution" change their meanings and functions over time and become connected with other ideas, with which they have no logical or necessary relationship. Mannheim's failure to treat "generation" as such a word and subject it to historical analysis appears all the more surprising when one discovers that the topic to which he turned after the generation problem was that of intellectual competition. For the generational idea owed much of its popularity in Germany and elsewhere during this period to its potential as an intellectually respectable competitor of class. It was the favored collectivism of young intellectuals who had lost faith in traditional solutions and who sought to preserve what was best in the past by a flight into the future—a counterutopia that corresponds very closely to the definition of ideology that Mannheim gave in 1929, namely a type of orientation that transcends reality but fails to break the bonds of the existing social order. Or to put the matter differently, the revolution of the younger generation was the utopia of men who were uninspired by the idea of social equality or material plenty and who feared that they would lose their identity and privileges in a society of masses. It was an alternative vision of the future that was never put into effect.[67]

The explanation of Mannheim's failure to make these connections between his own conceptual categories and the problem that engaged his interest at the end of the 1920's may lie in his ambivalence about the German academic tradition and the values that underlay it. Too much of an outsider not to see the ideological coloring of the mainstream of German thinking, he was yet too deeply influenced by its categories of thought and too impressed by its achievements to free himself completely from its grasp. He criticized the concept of generation and insisted that generations must be studied within political traditions and against the background of social class; yet at the same time he conceded that generational entelechies and the Zeitgeist did exist, and he dreamed of the transcendence of political opposites in a higher synthesis by the intellectuals of his generation.[68] Mannheim devised many of the distinctions necessary to transform the concept of generation into a serviceable intellectual tool; but ultimately he remained a prisoner of the idea of the young generation and its mission. After all, born in 1893, he too was a member of the generation of 1914.

CHAPTER THREE

England:
Lost Legions of Youth

The unreturning army
  that was youth;
The legions who have
  suffered and are dust . . .
  Siegfried Sassoon, 1918

THERE is a legend about the history of twentieth-century England. Like all legends, it exists in many variants and was the product of many minds. Though it is nowhere written down in its entirety, fragments of it are to be found in many books and it lives on in the national memory and the oral tradition. It goes something like this.

Once upon a time, before the Great War, there lived a generation of young men of unusual abilities. Strong, brave, and beautiful, they combined great athletic prowess with deep classical learning. Poets at heart, they loved the things of the mind for their own sake and were scornfully detached from the common struggle. Although stemming from all parts of England, they were to be found above all at Oxford and Cambridge, and in the case of the younger men, at the better public schools. When the war broke out, they volunteered for service in the fighting forces and did whatever they could to hasten their training and secure their transfer to the field of battle. Their main fear was that the war would end before they arrived at the front. Brought up to revere England and to do their duty, they embraced their country's cause and accepted lightheartedly the likelihood of early death. Most of them were killed on the battlefields of Gallipoli, Ypres, Loos, the Somme, Passchendaele, and Cambrai. Those who were not killed were mutilated in mind and body. They limped home in 1919 to find that their sacrifice had been in vain. The hard-faced, hard-hearted old men had come back and seized the levers of power. Youth had been defeated by age. Civilization had been dealt a fatal blow. Few in number, tired and shell-shocked, disillusioned by what they found at home, they sat by helplessly during the interwar years and watched the old politicians flounder in incompetence and squander their victory. The peace was lost; English hegemony in the world was lost; the empire was lost; even traditional

English values were lost, as the English submitted to the tyranny of foreign models. Eventually a second war came to seal the disaster of the first, and England slipped pusillanimously into the category of second-rate powers. All might have been different if only the splendid young men of 1914 had not given up their lives on the fields of Flanders and the beaches of Gallipoli. [1]

This myth had its origins in a disillusioning experience shared by many Englishmen of the privileged classes. One man who contributed to it, indeed who in some respects can be said to have launched it, and whose posthumous reputation has subsequently suffered from it, was the poet Rupert Brooke (1887). Brooke's credentials as a prospective English hero in a highly class-conscious and literary age were impeccable. His father was a housemaster at Rugby, where Brooke did his secondary studies; his uncle was dean at Kings College, Cambridge, where the most brilliant Edwardian intellectuals gathered to sharpen their wits and refine their sensibilities in cloistered conversation, an elite within an elite. Brooke's childhood friends were Geoffrey Keynes, James Strachey, and Virginia Stephen (later Woolf); thus he had access at a young age to the group that would later form in Bloomsbury. His family was not rich, but enough money was set aside for him (£150 a year) to spare him the distraction of work. He also possessed surpassing beauty and a clever way with words that convinced him and his literary-minded mother that he was a poet *en germe*. His earliest enthusiasms were for the English Decadent poets of the 1890s: Wilde, Swinburne, and Dowson. Later, with the aid of an older and more authentically decadent friend, he discovered and devoured Baudelaire and the French Symbolists. In some ways, Brooke never outgrew his early passion for fading flowers and delicate and dying poets, though he later struggled manfully to write modern verse. Some critics thought he succeeded too well; they complained, when his first volume of poems was published in 1911, that Brooke was taking the beauty out of poetry by evoking the grosser aspects of day-to-day life. [2]

Brooke went up to Kings College, Cambridge, in 1906. There he came into contact with a group of talented and articulate young people, most of them born as he was during the second half of the 1880s into the educated professional middle class. These privileged young intellectuals were rebelling, with the understatement and good manners typical of the English ruling classes, against the nineteenth century and Victorianism. They got their ethics from G. E. Moore, their politics from the Webbs, their attitude toward relations between the sexes from Ibsen and George Bernard Shaw, their vision of the future from H. G. Wells, and their ideas of what art and literature should be from Roger Fry and E. M. Forster. They wanted to be modern. To be modern, they thought, meant to be socialist, feminist, indifferent if not hostile to religion, irreverent about conventions and traditions, and in favor of natural as opposed to formal manners. It meant to prefer the country to the city and the company of simple people to society; to live chastely while unmarried, but to talk freely and even obsessively about sex; and not necessarily to rise when a lady entered the room. It required being candid even at the risk of seeming rude. Brooke dutifully made himself into a modern young man, turning his back self-consciously upon the aestheticism of his youth and devoting himself (when he was not engaged in theatrical productions or the writing of sonnets) to the reform of society and the triumph of the Fabian brand of socialism, which he studied during summer vacations under the tutelage of the Webbs. His slogan during this period might well have been "new worlds for old," the title of a book by H. G. Wells published in 1908, which he hastened to read and recommended to his friends.[3]

We think of Brooke primarily as a poet; but his friends thought he might become a leader who would leave his mark on public life. As Virginia Woolf, who knew him well during this period, later commented, "He was the type of English young manhood at its healthiest and most vigorous . . . You might judge him extreme, and from the pinnacle of superior age assure him that the return to Nature was as sophisticated as any other pose, but you could not doubt that, whatever he might do, he was an originator, one of those leaders who spring up from time to time and show their power most clearly in subjugating their own generation. Under his influence the country near Cambridge was full of young men and women walking barefoot, sharing his passion for bathing and fish diet, disdaining book learning, and proclaiming that there was something deep and wonderful in the man who brought the milk and the woman who watched the cows." It was during this period that Brooke's friend, the poet Frances Darwin (later Cornford), described him, half tongue-in-cheek, as a "golden-haired Apollo, magnificently unprepared for the long littleness of life."[4]

In 1913 Brooke left England for an extended trip to America, Canada, and the South Pacific. Bruised emotionally in an unhappy love affair with a young woman he had met through the Cambridge Fabian Society, the poet turned angrily against feminism, Bloomsbury, and much that he perceived as "modern." His enthusiasm for Fabian socialism noticeably cooled; and standing before the immense grandeur of Niagara Falls, he realized that he had remained at heart a man of the Victorian age. "Please don't breathe a word of it," he wrote to one of his friends. "I want to keep such shreds of reputation as I have left. Yet it's true. For I sit and stare at the thing and have the purest Nineteenth Century grandiose thoughts, about the Destiny of Man, the Irreversibility of Fate, the Doom of Nations, the fact that Death awaits us All, and so forth. Wordsworth Redivivus. Oh dear! oh dear!"[5]

Brooke had long been fascinated by the vagabond and the wanderer as human types. The spiritual vagabond, he had observed while still at Rugby, was a rebel "against the safeties and little confines of our ordinary human life." That idea was not without representatives in the Victorian world. Now Brooke began to think and write of himself increasingly in these terms—as an adven-

turer out of Conrad and Kipling who had disappeared into the fairyland of the
South Seas. In Samoa and Tahiti he experienced deep contentment and was
captivated by the romance of living with peoples who felt rather than thought;
who were simple rather than complex; and who looked up, like children, to
their European masters. In his letters home to England Brooke claimed to have
lost all knowledge of art and literature, as well as what remained of his "frag-
mentary manners." To Edward Marsh, his literary sponsor, he insisted that he
would never write again, and that what he wanted was "to talk and talk and talk
. . . and in the intervals, have extraordinary adventures." He remembered
London as a cesspool of vice thronged with "lean and vicious people." Yet at
the same time he longed for love and marriage—or so he said—and envied his
friends who were pairing off and settling down. He also wondered, half romantically perhaps, but also half seriously, if it were not too late for him, if something inside him were not broken.[6]

Brooke returned to England in June 1914. It was clear that he was suffering
from a dilemma. He wanted to marry and have a family—or at least one side of
him did. He was afraid of wandering, no doubt because he enjoyed it so much.
To Cathleen Nesbitt, the actress who loved him and toward whom he felt enormously attracted, he wrote plaintively, "I don't want to be washed about on
these doubtful currents and black waves or drift into some dingy corner of the
tide." But the other side of him felt inadequate and "dirty," equated marriage
with surrender to convention, feared getting old, and sought outlet in adventure. For two months he struggled with, and savored, the dilemma, until the
outbreak of the war came to provide him with a solution. He would marry England and flee into the fellowship of men and the waiting embrace of death.[7]

Brooke did not immediately see the war as a solution to his personal problems. In the short run, "this damned war business" merely interfered with his
vacation plans for August and presented him with another unpleasant set of
choices. "If fighting starts," he wrote to a friend on July 31, "I shall have to
enlist, or go as a correspondent. I don't know. It will be Hell to be in it; and
Hell to be out of it. At present I'm so depressed about the war, that I can't talk,
think, or write coherently." As war became a certainly rather than a possibility
and as the first reports of combat arrived from France, Brooke agonized over his
situation and treated his friends to instant replays of his internal struggles. The
inevitable two sides of Brooke's character reappeared, as they normally did
when he was presented with a problem. The "straight," "honorable," and "English" half wanted to fight for his country; the wanderer half, which was "solitary, selfish, unbound, and undoubtful," wanted to watch the war from the
sidelines and to write about it as a correspondent. By the middle of August
1914 Brooke had decided that going to France as a correspondent to satisfy his
curiosity would be a "rotten trade" when decent people were laying down their
lives for their country. The only honorable thing to do was to enlist and fight.[8]

But getting into a combat unit, Brooke found, was no easy matter. Unlike the continental countries, England had no tradition of a mass, conscript army, and the professionals were in no hurry to create one. It was generally expected that volunteers without previous military affiliation or training would get stuck in territorial units and either spend the entire war standing guard over the English coast or get to France too late to take part in the fighting. This delay did not appeal to the adventurer in Brooke, and he took steps to ensure that it did not occur. By September Edward Marsh, who was Winston Churchill's private secretary when he was not playing the patron to promising young poets, had pulled strings with his boss, then First Lord of the Admiralty; and Brooke had become a junior officer in a Royal Naval Volunteer Division that was being formed for immediate service in France.

Brooke saw action briefly in early October 1914 when his division was shipped suddenly to Belgium in a last-minute attempt to save Antwerp from the German advance. The sight of the city in flames and refugees fleeing, the thunder and wailing of artillery fire through the night as he stood guard while his troops slept in the courtyard of an abandoned chateau, the smell of smoke and burning petrol, and the discovery of his own coolness under fire excited Brooke and gave him the purpose for which he had so long been seeking. The thing God wants of me, he wrote to Cathleen Nesbitt in November, "is to get good at beating Germans." Back in England to train with his men before going overseas again, Brooke worked at some sonnets that expressed his feelings about the war. These sonnets proclaimed his sense of cleanness and resolution, his thankfulness and gladness, as well as his conviction that the old virtues of holiness, honor, and nobleness—the very virtues that he had felt he lacked—had been revived. "And we have come into our heritage," he ended his sonnet "The Dead." [9]

This metaphor of the patrimony is helpful for understanding Brooke's attitude toward the war. The war had arrived unexpectedly, like a legacy from an unknown relative, to save Brooke from a fate he had long feared. It provided an escape from the dreary sleep of middle age and conventional living. Now, thanks to God's intervention, he and other young men like him could turn "as swimmers into cleanness leaping, glad from a world grown old and cold and weary." They could "leave the sick hearts that honour could not move, and half-men, and their dirty songs and dreary, and all the little emptiness of love." They could offer up the gifts that fortune had bestowed upon them—the "red, sweet wine of youth," the "years to be of work and joy," their carefully refined artistic sensibility, their friends, their future issue, their serene old age—and devote themselves to the task of winning the war. They could redeem the sins of their past and achieve at least a temporary resurrection. "Oh! we who have known shame, we have found release there." It was true that they might die. But death on the battlefield was not to be feared, for there was "nothing to shake the laughing heart's long peace there but only agony, and that has ending." Once dead all evil would be "shed away" and the dead soldier would take his place as "a pulse in the eternal mind," which would give "somewhere back the thoughts by England given."[10]

These sonnets were the public form in which Brooke chose to communicate his feelings about the war. In private he was more down-to-earth and less optimistic. War, he explained in January 1915 to his friend the poet John Drinkwater, was

rather exhilarating and rather terrible . . . Still, it's the only life for me, just now. The training is a bloody bore. But on service one has a great feeling of fellowship, and a fine thrill, like nothing else in the world. And I'd not be able to exist, for torment, if I weren't doing it. Not a bad place and time to die, Belgium, 1915? I want to kill my Prussian first. Better than coughing out a civilian soul amid bed-clothes and disinfectant and gulping medicines in 1950. The world'll be tame enough after the war, for those that see it. I had hopes that England'ld get on her legs again, achieve youth and merriment, and slough the things I loathe—capitalism and feminism and hermaphroditism and the rest. But on maturer consideration, pursued over muddy miles of Dorset [where Brooke was training], I think there'll not be much change. What there is for the better, though. Certain sleepers have awoken in the heart. Come and die. It'll be great fun. And there's great health in the preparation. The theatre's no place, now. If you stay there you'll not be able to start afresh with us when we come back. Péguy and Duhamel; and I don't know what others. I want to mix a few sacred and Apollonian English ashes with theirs, lest England be shamed.[11]

This letter is full of contradictions. Like all Brooke's letters, it contains a certain measure of stiff-upper-lipped bravura and cannot be taken as an exact transcription of his feelings. Just as Brooke had earlier assumed the persona of the *poète maudit*, the social reformer, and the South Seas adventurer out of Conrad and Kipling, he now presented himself in the guise of the happy warrior, eager for combat and determined to kill his Prussian before "going West" himself. There is also the obligatory trace of self-irony in the reference to the "sacred and Apollonian English ashes" that he wanted to mix with those of the French writers and poets who had already died in the war. But beneath the devil-may-care attitude and the light-hearted braggadocio of "come and die," the central message is clear and quite seriously meant. The war would not accomplish all the things that were being claimed for it. It would be horrible. It would be terrifying. It would also be a bore. Some men would die. But along with the horror and the terror and the tedium, it would provide good fellowship, excitement, adventure, and honor at least for some. And the alternative—not fighting—would be dishonorable, hence unacceptable.

Brooke did not live long enough to question these assumptions—or to see them called into question by others. He died of blood poisoning in April 1915 en route for Gallipoli, where many young Englishmen would fall, leaving in Brooke's phrase "in that rich earth a richer dust concealed." He was given a hero's funeral by his fellow officers and men and buried on the Greek island of Skyros in a grove of olive trees that he had visited and admired a few days before. Five of his closest friends stayed behind, as the others departed, and made a cairn over the grave from tiny bits of pink and white marble they found lying about on the ground. All had the feeling that they were participating in some extraordinary moment of English history; and one confided to his diary that evening that "it was as though one were involved in the origin of some classical myth." Inspired perhaps by the secret thoughts of the English officers who had gathered there to pay Brooke homage, the party's interpreter inscribed in Greek on the back of a simple wooden cross some lines that captured the romance of the occasion and established the connection, felt by all those present, between the Gallipoli expedition and the Crusades:

> Here lies
> the servant of God
> Sub-lieutenant in the
> English Navy
> Who died for the
> deliverance of Constantinople from
> the Turks. [12]

Back in England, meanwhile, Brooke's 1914 sonnets had been published and cited with approval by the dean of St. Paul's Cathedral, who observed that "the enthusiasm of a pure and elevated patriotism had never found a nobler expression." The mythical power of the poems was enhanced by a highly stylized photograph of Brooke taken in profile and heavily touched up, with his chestnut locks gracefully flowing, his neck arched delicately forward like a swan's, and his shoulders unaccountably nude. It conveyed no feeling for the young poet's ruddy complexion or his casual and distinctly masculine good looks. His friends declared it obscene. It was certainly no good likeness. [13]

When news of Brooke's death reached London, Churchill himself stepped forward to eulogize him in words that transformed this tormented and extraordinarily complex young man into a patriotic monument of marble. For Churchill, Brooke was the epitome of the upper-class volunteer in a country where conscription was still regarded as an institution both unnecessary to its security and out of keeping with its insular traditions—something that continental countries did. "Joyous, fearless, versatile, deeply instructed, with classical symmetry of mind and body," the First Lord of the Admiralty wrote, "he was all that one would wish England's noblest sons to be in days when no sacrifice but the most precious is acceptable, and the most precious is that which is most freely proffered." The country needed consolation and heroes in this time of crisis, and Brooke's life, along with his poetry, became an icon in which an entire class could recognize itself and by means of which it could justify the sacrifice of its sons, whose slaughter was assuming alarming proportions. By a strange irony, the man who had wanted to serve his country in order to escape from himself, and who had been deprived of the honor of dying in battle by a particularly virulent infection, now rendered a posthumous service by sanctifying as holy a war that many of the country's keenest minds had begun to call into question. [14]

PROPERLY speaking, Rupert Brooke was not a war poet. His 1914 sonnets do not derive from personal experience of trench warfare on the Western Front. They expressed Brooke's feelings about the coming of the war, the possibilities for release and renovation that it brought, and the likelihood of dying in it. Much of the imagery of these poems stems from Brooke's hesitations about marriage and the sense of shame he had taken away from his entanglements with women. Hence the strong emphasis on escape, liberation, purification. Nonetheless, these highly personal verses soon achieved a collective significance For they captured a feeling or complex of feelings that was widespread among young men of Brooke's class and education. That feeling, as Robert Nichols, himself a poet and a volunteer, wrote much later in defense of Brooke's sonnets, was one of exhilaration and "being gathered up." It was, Nichols said, as if a great beam of light had suddenly descended and illuminated an entire generation with its resplendence. "About that beam of light there was something mysterious, as there is something mysterious about such a beam in a cathedral, since, passing within its clustered shafts, the individual becomes invisible." Nichols warned against the mistaken impression that he and his coevals felt themselves to be victims. "On the contrary we felt we were in some way privileged. 'Bliss was it in that dawn to be alive, but to be young was very heaven!' " Nichols was right. More than one young man went to France convinced that "we cannot but be thankful that we were chosen, and not another generation, to do this work and pay this price." [15]

This emotion could not survive the reality of the Western Front, a nightmarish moonscape where men lived underground like rats and died collectively like hordes of swatted flies; where death was impersonal and wounds unpretty; a desolate hell surpassing Dante's worst imaginings. What seems surprising today is that the emotion surived as long as it did. For two and a half years the war was represented as exciting, fulfilling, glorious, holy, noble, beautiful, gay, and, all in all, great fun. Death in battle was, for the British soldier, "the greatest of all adventures; the journeying, by a long, long trail of which no sure chart exists, into a land more wonderful and remote than that on the unseen side of the Moon." British troops died "gaily" with songs on their lips or at the least after expressing the regret that they could not join their fellows in storming the enemy trenches. They died with their dream of glory and knightly adventure fulfilled, as they departed "to join the men of Agincourt." As Julian Grenfell phrased it in his famous poem "Into Battle," "he is dead who will not fight; and who dies fighting has increase." And all the British troops asked of the civilian population back home in case they should fall, Ian Hay told them in one of the most widely read books of the war,

> Is this. Within their hearts be writ
> This single-line memorial:—
> He did his duty—and his bit! [16]

We smile when we read these lines today. Yet they were written by a soldier, and the representations of the war that flourished on the home front could not have survived the contradiction of returning combatants if they had not corresponded in some way to the experience and feelings of many soldiers—or, to be more accurate, of many officers, for it was above all line officers and war correspondents who interpreted the war to the English public. [17]

What did young English officers find upon arriving at the front? To be sure, it was hell. Officers, fresh from schools and universities, suffered from the isolation of the trenches, the deafening noise of persistent artillery fire, the fatigue brought on by nights without continuous sleep, the filth of the living conditions, the undivided attention of lice, the stench of decaying corpses, the scurrying of rats grown fat on human flesh, and the boredom of trench routine. But there were compensations. The troops were not always in the trenches. Some sectors were relatively quiet. The chances of getting killed in 1915–1916, the period when the first volunteers began to arrive at the front, were relatively slight. One lived outdoors, and though Flanders could be wet and cold there were also moments, like those described by Julian Grenfell, when "the naked earth is warm with Spring, and with green grass and bursting trees" and life was "colour and warmth and light, and a striving evermore for these." Most important of all, there was the glowing feeling produced by the thought that one was doing what was right. Few young English officers doubted that Germany had broken the code of European nations and deserved to be punished. [18]

Another factor colored the first representations of the war made by young officers. They had all been trained in a literary tradition that translated quotidian and unpleasant reality into elevated sentiment and diction. Avid readers of the *Oxford Anthology of English Verse*, they arrived in France with a ready-made store of images and metaphors with which to interpret their experience. Death was a crossing of the bar, a kiss, or an embrace. It was an awakening from the dream of life. They knew from their Horace that it was sweet to die for one's country and from their Homer that it was in battle that one demonstrated one's virtue and worth. Landscapes, whatever their actual appearance, were supposed to be idyllically pastoral and filled with larks and nightingales. Officers were shepherds guiding their flocks. The ugly aspects of life one never talked about, not even to one's parents and most intimate friends. The needs of the body, for example, were not to be mentioned. Sex could be discussed only after it had been rarefied into love. Fear was such a disgrace that it had to be disguised beneath bluff humor, and pain had always to be understated if talked about at all. Since the front was filled with ugliness, since death was seldom noble, since bodily functions—sexual and otherwise—could not be hidden and provided one of the main sources of imagery in conversation among the other ranks, and since fear and the struggle against it were uppermost in the thoughts of all men at the front, educated Englishmen found it impossible, or undesirable, to describe in simple and direct language what they were seeing and feeling. Experience, even when unpleasant, was quickly transformed into "literature," and in the process of transformation was distorted and rendered palatable to those at home. This processing and repackaging of experience occurred not merely in poetry designed for a public audience, but also in private letters written to friends and loved ones who, it was believed, would and could not understand. Thus the death-ridden world of the trenches was described in the same words that had formerly been used to qualify fox hunts and cricket matches: "ripping" and "great fun."[19]

The parents, teachers, and rulers of these young men collaborated gratefully and wholeheartedly in this distortion of experience and this idealization of mass slaughter. It was natural, perhaps inevitable, that they should. Innocent of all experience of the front, they imagined the deaths of their sons and pupils in terms that bestowed upon those brutal moments a resplendent beauty. Death in battle, they liked to think, was a magnificent culmination of those splendid short lives. They said, and they believed, that the young men who were dying on the field were lucky and they, who were compelled to stay behind and honor the dead, had the hard and tragic fate. "I am sorry for us, but not for him," the novelist Maurice Baring wrote to console the mother of Julian Grenfell, after hearing that the son of a mutual friend had been killed. "For him it is a privilege and a prize beyond anything he can have dreamed before the war. To say it is a waste is to me like saying the frankincense, gold and myrrh of the Three Kings was a waste—or a waste to give an engagement ring to someone you are going to marry whom you love."[20]

Not until the winter of 1916–1917 did a new image of the war and the generation who were fighting it begin to emerge, and even then it remained the disputed image of a minority, angrily rejected by the English establishment and the great majority of the English public. This new image was born in the trenches of the Western Front among some of the more sensitive officers and men, who had begun to feel a sense of identification with the enemy and a skepticism about the aims for which the war was being fought. It received its confirmation during the battle of the Somme in the summer and fall of 1916, when more than four hundred thousand British soldiers fell in a vain and badly planned attempt to pierce the German defenses. On those churned-up and blood-drenched fields the dream of an imminent victory died. So did faith in the wisdom of the General Staff. The fact of mass and meaningless death seared itself on the consciousness of the survivors and was never to be removed. Even final victory could not heal the scar. Yet at home the stalling of the offensive was presented as a temporary setback, and the government instructed the army command to prepare for new attacks. After the Somme morale among the troops deteriorated. Undersized and unenthusiastic conscripts took the place of fallen volunteers; new weapons were introduced; and the final illusions about the knightly character of the war began to vanish. The men in the trenches felt deceived, abandoned, betrayed. France was no longer a place to which one went in search of glory, but a place one went to die and to disappear into mass and unmarked graves. England had become a strange land where business went on as usual and where people were incapable of understanding what life was like at the front. Why bother, then, to tell them? Embittered silence broadened the rift between the civilians and the soldiers. And out of the trauma produced by the shattering of the dream of victory and this estrangement from the civilian population arose a new poetry, and ultimately a new literature, which represented the fate of the English generation of 1914 in radically different terms.[21]

The leading exponent of this new poetry was Siegfried Sassoon. In *The Old Huntsman* and *Counter-Attack*, collections published in 1917 and 1918 respectively, Sassoon broke through the gossamer veils of rhetoric and sentiment that had surrounded even the best of the early war poetry to portray the war as it was actually experienced by an infantry officer on the Western Front in 1916–1917. In his world nothing was beautiful; heroism was a virtue reserved for conversations with civilians; and the enemy was at home in Parliament and on the General Staff. Sassoon's soldiers floundered, blundered, slid, tripped, and lurched blindly through slimy, sludge-filled trenches. They were denizens of "death's gray land" and dwelled in a place "rotten with death" where all was ruin "and nothing blossoms but the sky." They were disconsolate, haggard, and hopeless. Their faces were dulled and sunken. They raved at the "bleeding war" and moaned, sobbed, and choked with "rampant grief" when they heard of a brother's death. They committed suicide out of despair in "winter trenches, cowed and glum with crumps and lice and lack of rum." They attacked with "muttering faces, masked with fear" and defended their trenches "dizzy with galloping fear, sick for escape,—loathing the strangled horror and butchered, frantic gestures of the dead." They died slowly in isolated shell-holes moaning for water or "flapping above the fire-step like a fish." When they returned to England on leave, they were "driven stark, staring mad" by memories of the "whispering guns" and by "dreams that drip with murder." They were pursued by images of "green-faced Germans" running and screaming while British troops stuck them like pigs. And in their fantasies they imagined their troops and war machines being turned against the "Yellow Press-men," the "Junkers in Parliament," and the crowds that thronged music halls and cackled at patriotic jokes:

> I'd like to see a Tank come down the stalls,
> Lurching to ragtime tunes, or 'Home, sweet Home,'—
> And there'd be no more jokes in Music-halls
> To mock the riddled corpses round Bapaume.[22]

Sassoon was ill suited by temperament and social background to play the role that fate unkindly thrust upon him. Related through his father to a family of wealthy financiers of Jewish and Persian origin who were said to associate with the fun-loving Prince of Wales, and through his mother to a family that included a well-patronized sculptor (Sir Hamo Thornycroft), a leading man of letters (Edmund Gosse), and a shipbuilder who specialized in torpedo boats and destroyers, Sassoon (1886) grew up in the Kent countryside surrounded by untouched natural beauty, unquestioned deference, and great quantities of maternal love. Not even the separation of his father from his mother and his father's early death in 1895 could trouble the well-insulated country paradise in which Sassoon spent his first years and which he later evoked with unrepentant nostalgia in *Memoirs of a Fox-Hunting Man.* [23]

Sassoon's earliest passions were for music, poetry, and country sports—especially riding, cricket, tennis, and golf. His mother was convinced that her son would be a great poet. Sassoon was inclined to agree, and at the age of eleven he produced his first volume of poems, which he proudly bestowed upon his mother for Christmas. Sassoon's ambition was, and remained for many years, to portray lofty and noble states of soul, like those rendered by the painter G. F. Watts, a photograph of whose painting *Love and Death* was prominently displayed in Sassoon's home. What he did not want to do was to go to university or to pursue a career in law, as the family solicitor urged. Thus he seized the first opportunity to come down from Cambridge without his degree; and at the age of twenty-one devoted himself, on his comfortable income of £600 a year, to a life of fox hunting in the autumn and winter, cricket and tennis in the summer, and the writing of high-minded verse, some of which he published privately in the years before the war. In July 1914 Sassoon was twenty-eight with little to show for himself other than a quickly mounting overdraft, some racing trophies, a good seat on a horse, and a few poems that testified to his feeling for the music of language—and to his lack of a topic about which to write. [24]

Sassoon volunteered for military service on August 1, three days before England entered the war. He made this decision for a variety of motives, of which the most important, aside from the emotional stimulation derived from yielding to the *force majeure* of a great collective cause, was his belief that it was the right and noble thing to do. The first phase of Sassoon's war experience gave him no cause to regret his enlistment. He spent the beautiful fall of 1914 training beneath cloudless English skies as a trooper with the Sussex Yeomanry. He was once more on horseback, and inevitably he saw a comforting continuity between this life and his earlier existence as a fox hunter. Later Sassoon remembered these days as idyllic. "Never before had I looked at the living world with any degree of intensity. It seemed almost as if I had been waiting for this thing to happen, although my own part in it was so obscure and submissive." In January 1915 he broke his arm in a riding accident and was sent home for two months' convalescence. This was one in a series of lucky accidents, illnesses, and nonfatal wounds between 1915 and 1918 that kept Sassoon from the front and thus helped to save his life. While on leave, he arranged through one of his family's friends, a retired army captain, to be transferred to the Royal Welch Fusiliers, where he was given a commission. Becoming an infantry officer required further training, and it was not until November 1915 that Sassoon, now a junior subaltern, arrived in France. He was not displeased with what he found. Though poor fox-hunting country, northern France had moments of beauty; and it was a healthy outdoor life "saturated by the external senses" and free of responsibility. It was true that he could get killed—and that was a bad thing—but "for somebody who allowed himself to think things over, the only way out of it was to try and feel secretly heroic, and to look back on the old life as pointless and trivial." There were even times when Sassoon could glory in the idea of the supreme sacrifice. A training course behind the lines in the spring of 1916 helped to extend this feeling of an idyll. "There was nothing wrong with life on those fine mornings when the air smelt so fresh and my body was young and vigorous, and I hurried down the white road, along the empty street, and up the hill to our training ground. I was like a boy going to early school, except that no bell was ringing, and instead of Thucydides or Virgil, I carried a gun. Forgetting for the moment that I was at the Front to be shot at, I could almost congratulate myself on having a holiday in France without paying for it." When he returned to his battalion in June, after a short leave in England, he had been in France eight months and had yet to see a dead German. [25]

Sassoon saw plenty of dead soldiers, both German and British, during the next month. In late June he won the Military Cross, at that time still a relatively rare and highly sought after decoration, for risking his life to bring back wounded after an unsuccessful raid opposite the Mametz sector. During the Big Push on the Somme he won a reputation as an officer of awesome and slightly mad courage who enjoyed patrolling no-man's-land alone and who would enter enemy trenches for the fun of it. Sassoon enjoyed fighting, as long as he could go about it his own way, as a sportsman. On one occasion he ignored a written order from his commanding officer in order to occupy and hold a German trench—alone. Sassoon had wanted badly to kill a German at close quarters. But once out of the line, the introspective poet took over from the warrior. Watching his men as they slept at night rolled up in their blankets with the battle raging in the distance and the guns "shaking the hills and making lurid flashes along the valleys," he tried to understand the meaning of their suffering and sacrifice, and failed. "Armageddon," he concluded, "was too immense for my solitary understanding." All he could do was to accept the destruction as part of some hidden purpose. [26]

Sassoon was more fortunate than most officers who participated in the first day of the attack on the Somme. Three out of four of them were killed. Sassoon survived long enough to come down with gastric fever in late July, when he was invalided back to England. It was at this point, during the enforced leisure of his convalescence, that Sassoon began to revise his attitude toward the war. He was annoyed by what the newspapers wrote about the brave and noble boys doing their bit for England on the Somme. He was unable to talk with his mother, for whom England was St. George and Germany the dragon. And he was shocked when his uncle Hamo Thornycroft, whom he much admired, referred to his military service as "a thing well and truly accomplished" and compared it to an early seventeenth-century water clock. Sassoon came away from these encounters feeling that "no explanation of mine could ever reach my elders—that they weren't capable of wanting to know the truth. Their attitude was to insist that it was splendid to be in the front-line. So it was—if one came out of it safely." [27]

At the same time, Sassoon came into contact with the group of pacifists and conscientious objectors that had gathered around Lady Ottoline Morrell at her country house in Garsington, near Oxford. In September 1916 he spent a week at Garsington and for the first time heard arguments by well-informed people against the war and in favor of a negotiated peace. These experiences left their imprint on Sassoon's war poetry, for he had discovered, after an early period in 1915 of composing verses inspired by Brooke's 1914 sonnets in which he described British soldiers as a "happy legion" who were fortunate to fight, that he had "a hitherto unpredictable talent for satirical epigram." This talent he now applied to the realistic description of a world that was as yet unknown to most English civilians. The change in Sassoon's poetry, according to his own account, had begun in early 1916 when he had determined to record his surroundings with photographic accuracy. He may also have been inspired by his friend and fellow Royal Welch Fusilier Robert Graves, whose temperament led him, then as later, to dwell on the war's gorier details. But the savage satires in the volume of poems published by Sassoon in May 1917 went beyond realistic description. They gave voice to the alienation Sassoon had felt upon coming home from the Somme and finding the contrast between life as it was being lived and died at the front and the distorted representation of that life that was being manufactured and retailed at home. It was the atmosphere in England, as much as conditions at the front, that fueled Sassoon's anger and gave bite to his fierce epigrams. [28]

Sassoon returned to France in February 1917, in time for the spring offensive at Arras. He had ceased to believe in the justice of the war, which he now perceived as "a hopeless, never-shifting burden," and he felt little joy in rejoining his battalion, for too many familiar faces were missing and those few that remained were now depressed and dispirited. Nor was there much incentive to develop new friendships, for the friends one made merry with today might well be dead and gone tomorrow. "A single machine-gun or a few shells might wipe out the whole picture within a week." The one thing that kept Sassoon going and gave him the courage to return was the need to gain further material for his war poems. He was now a man with a mission. "My strength of mind thus consisted mainly in a ferocious and defiant resolve to tell the truth about the War in every possible way. For that purpose the more I could see of it the better my opportunities would be for discharging sardonic epigrams on those on 'the Home Front' whose behavior was arousing my resentment." One of the fruits of his return to the front was this savage poem, published the following year in *Counter-Attack*:

> "Good morning; good morning!" the General said
> When we met him last week on our way to the line.
> Now the soldiers he smiled at are most of 'em dead,
> And we're cursing his staff for incompetent swine.
> "He's a cheery old card," grunted Harry to Jack
> As they slogged up to Arras with rifle and pack.
>   *   *   *   *   *   *   *   *   *   *   *
> But he did for them both by his plan of attack. [29]

Fifteen weeks after arriving in France, Sassoon was hit in the shoulder by a bullet while peeping over a parapet. He was again sent back to England, where he convalesced in the luxury of Lord and Lady Brassey's beautiful Sussex country house, Chapelwood Manor. Oppressed by the comfort of his surroundings, haunted by memories of the dead and by guilt toward the living whom he had left behind to die, disgusted by the hypocritical and class-conscious spiritualism of Lady Brassey, Sassoon determined to protest the continuation of the war.* This protest, he believed, would have greater impact because it came from a member of the fighting forces who had proved his courage more than once in battle. Upon leaving Chapelwood Manor in June 1917, he sought out H. W. Massingham, the editor of the pacifist review, *The Nation*, who encouraged him to pursue his opposition to the war and who put him in contact with Bertrand Russell. Russell helped Sassoon compose an antiwar statement, which Sassoon presented to his commanding officer at the regimental base at Litherland and which Russell arranged to have read in the House of Commons. [30]

Sassoon now became something of a celebrity. His poems were read and discussed in London literary salons. Glyn Philpot's "Byronic" portrait of him, done about this time, promised to do for Sassoon what Sherill Schell's half-nude photograph had done for Rupert Brooke. And Lady Ottoline Morrell, much taken by Sassoon's Levantine good looks, was clearly interested in promoting the young officer's career, both as a pacifist and as a poet. Yet Sassoon remained a soldier on active service and thus under the jurisdiction of military law. The situation was potentially serious: in 1917, as the will to fight weakened and talk of a negotiated peace spread, civil liberties were being restricted

---

* Lady Brassey had been so untactful as to point out to Sassoon that he had nothing to lose in going back to France as he was not the bearer of a great name.

everywhere, and England was no exception. Only the intervention of Robert Graves spared Sassoon from the unpleasant consequences that his rash act might otherwise have caused him. Graves pulled strings with the authorities, arguing that Sassoon was not responsible for his actions because he was shell-shocked. The upshot was that Sassoon was pronounced "neurasthenic" and packed off to the military hospital at Craiglockhart near Edinburgh for treatment, thereby giving him further chances for survival and a chance to perfect his ever improving poetic technique.[31]

S ASSOON'S achievement was to provide in poetic form a precious, almost documentary record of what the English war was like and what it was like to be in it. At his best, Sassoon was without peer in his ability to evoke the soul-wrenching terror with which troops stumbled over the top "clumsily bowed with bombs and guns and shovels and battle-gear"; the "galloping fear" with which they awaited a counter-attack; the chilling impersonality with which death reduced men to lumps of insensible meat "beyond all need of tenderness and care"; and the angry feeling of isolation from government, army staff, country, and family that English soldiers developed after the Somme.[32]

Nonetheless, Sassoon's war poetry has one outstanding limitation: It is not "true" in that it does not express the complexity of his feeings about the war. The anger of the prophet drowned out the internal contradictions of the warrior. For Sassoon was powerfully attracted toward the front—so powerfully attracted that he was never happy when away from it. There was something in him that courted death, that craved annihilation, that derived a drug-like satisfaction from facing danger unafraid, that drove him back to France time and again until chance provided him with the wounds and ailments that saved him. And "that sense of immolation to some vague aspiration," which Sassoon was unable to throw off, never shines through clearly in the poems. This, I think, is the most damaging criticism that one can make of Sassoon's war poetry. In its own way, it is as distorted as Rupert Brooke's. It is aimed too single-mindedly against the noncombatant population. Sassoon fires away against the general, the staff officer, the bishop, the journalist, the mother, the father, and the sweetheart for not understanding the nature of a war they had supposedly wanted and allowed to happen, while he portrays the soldier as a victim of a dirty trick played by the older generation. His is a poetry of compassion—and this compassion is what raises it above mere polemic and makes it great. But it is also a poetry of self-indulgence, which conceals the positive values Sassoon found in the war.[33]

In this respect, Wilfred Owen, the shyly handsome and velvet-voiced young poet and fellow victim of shell-shock whom Sassoon met at Craiglockhart, was truer to himself. Perhaps this is one reason why Owen's war poetry has been judged greater and of more enduring significance than Sassoon's. Owen hated

Top: Rupert Brooke in 1913; Scherill Schell photograph of Rupert Brooke in 1913. Bottom: Rupert Brooke's grave on the island of Skyros.

Joyous, fearless, versatile, deeply instructed, with classical symmetry of mind and body, he was all that one would wish England's noblest sons to be in days when no sacrifice but the most precious is acceptable, and the most precious is that which is most freely proffered.

Winston Churchill, 1914

Love and Death by G. F. Watts.

And the worst friend and enemy is but Death.
Rupert Brooke, "Peace," 1914

We Are Making a New World by Paul Nash.

No pen or drawing can convey this country . . . Sunset and sunrise are blasphemous, they are mockeries to man, only the black rain out of the bruised and swollen clouds all through the bitter black of night is fit atmosphere in such a land. The rain drives on, the stinking mud becomes more evilly yellow, the shell holes fill up with green-white water, the roads and tracks are covered in inches of slime, the black dying trees ooze and sweat and the shells never cease . . . It is unspeakable, godless, hopeless.

   Paul Nash to his wife, 1917

Top: Siegfried Sassoon in the early 1920s, by William Rothenstein. Bottom: Wilfred Owen (front row, second from right) with fellow officers in 1916.

On all the officers' faces there is a harassed look that I have never seen before, and which in England, never will be seen out of jails.
   Wilfred Owen to his mother, 1916

Top: Erich Maria Remarque in the early 1930s; Henry Williamson at a meeting of the British Union of Fascists in the late 1930s. Bottom: Vera Brittain at a meeting of the P.E.N. Club in the 1930s.

Ghosts of a time no future can restore,
We desolately roam forevermore
An empty shore.

Vera Brittain, 1933

Top: T. E. Lawrence (left) with his brothers when Lawrence was an undergraduate at Oxford. Bottom: Sir Oswald Mosley addressing a meeting of the British Union of Fascists in the late 1930s.

What an uncertain, disappointed, barbarous generation we war-timers have been. They said the best ones were killed. There's far too much talent still alive.

T. E. Lawrence to William Rothenstein, 1928

the war from the beginning with undivided feeling and devoted himself to celebrating its victims rather than to exposing and satirizing the supposed authors of their sufferings.

Background, as well as temperament, may have been important in shaping the contrast in poetic approach between Sassoon and Owen. The son of a minor railway official and a fiercely religious mother whose once well-to-do father had broken the most inviolate of Victorian commandments by squandering his capital, Owen (1893) was condemned by his family's straitened circumstances to work for a living. This stern sentence brought him into contact with the outside world at an age when Sassoon's horizons were still bounded by the territory of the Atherstone Hunt. Owen's first employment was as an assistant to a vicar in Oxfordshire. These two years were critical in the young poet's development. They weakened to the breaking point his faith in organized Christianity and stimulated his natural sympathy for the underdogs of English society. They may also have revealed to him his latent homosexuality. Eager to escape from an existence that he regarded as restrictive and uninspiring, and equipped with the handy excuse of faltering health, Owen secured a job in Bordeaux as a language instructor for Berlitz and then extended his stay abroad by agreeing to serve for a year as tutor to the sons of a local family. He was in France when war broke out, and even though he was safely removed from the combat zone, he experienced at first hand some of the panic and fear that gripped the French as they stood face to face with defeat during the first six weeks of the war.

There is no reason to believe that Owen perceived the war at first as anything but a disruption of his private life and a threat to poetry and progress. His poem "1914" speaks ominously of the coming of "the Winter of the world," evokes the image of a "foul tornado, centered at Berlin," and predicts that the war will bring "famines of thought and feeling." Any illusions the poet might have had about the effects of lead and steel on human flesh were brutally dispelled when he visited a Bordeaux hospital in September 1914 and saw operations being performed on mangled bodies without the aid of anesthetics. Still, the greatness and the collective madness of the event were such that even men of pacifist temperament were swept up in its maelstrom; by July 1915 Owen felt *"traitorously* idle: if not to England, then to France." He played, half-seriously, with the alternatives of serving as a stretcher-bearer in the French army or joining the Italian cavalry. After fulfilling his contract in Bordeaux, he returned to England in September 1915 with the intention of joining the Artists' Rifles.[34]

Owen was commissioned into the Manchester Regiment in June 1916 and sailed for France in late December. He arrived at the front a little over a year after Sassoon had first come over. What changes had taken place during that year! It was the moment when British morale had reached its nadir. The winter, the coldest in the century, was bone-chilling; and the troops went thirsty in the trenches because they could not unfreeze their water cans. The new drafts arriving from England consisted of inexperienced and unenthusiastic soldiers who, in their great majority, had been conscripted and lacked the élan of their predecessors. And the fighting along the Somme was still fierce, despite the icy winter weather. Among veterans of the original Somme attacks, the feeling that the war would never end had begun to make its way.

Unlike Sassoon, Owen was introduced almost immediately to the worst the war had to offer. His letters to his mother during his first three months of front-line service read like a catalog of horrors. Upon arriving in France, he was startled by sudden change of the soldiers' faces. "On all the officers' faces there is a harassed look that I have never seen before, and which in England, never will be seen out of jails." Owen was assigned to the Beaumont-Hamel sector, where British troops were within sight of the important city of St. Quentin. Within two weeks of arriving there he had spent fifty consecutive hours holed up in no-man's land, had undergone a tremendous bombardment in a dugout filled with water that rose above his knees, and had found his sentry knocked down and blinded by a shell just outside the dugout. Worse even than the cold and the fatigue and the threat of hand-to-hand death, Owen reported to his mother, was the all-pervasive ugliness. "Hideous landscapes, vile noises, foul language and nothing but foul, even from one's own mouth (for all are devil-ridden), everything unnatural, broken, blasted; the distortion of the dead, whose unburiable bodies sit outside the dug-outs all day, all night, the most execrable sights on earth." It was not long before Owen felt death's hand brush over him. In April he was whacked on the calf by a spent fragment of shrapnel, and not long afterward he watched with horror as his trench coat, which he had just hung on a bush, was pierced through by a shrapnel splinter. On April 25 he described a tour of twelve days in the line.

For twelve days I did not wash my face, nor take off my boots, nor sleep a deep sleep. For twelve days we lay in holes, where at any moment a shell might put us out. I think the worst incident was one wet night when we lay up against a railway embankment. A big shell lit on the top of the bank, just 2 yards from my head. Before I awoke, I was blown in the air right away from the bank! I passed most of the following days in a railway Cutting, in a hole just big enough to lie in, and covered with corrugated iron. My brother officer . . . lay opposite in a similar hole. But he was covered with earth, and no relief will ever relieve him, nor will his Rest be a 9 days-Rest. I think that the terribly long time we stayed unrelieved was unavoidable; yet it makes us feel bitterly towards those in England who might relieve us, and will not.[35]

Owen's bitter thoughts would not go away. Given his intensely religious background and training, it was natural that the young poet would try to relate his sufferings and those of his fellow soldiers to the doctrines of Christianity; but the relationship came out to be the reverse of that being preached in England by English bishops. On May 16 Owen confided to his mother that he had "comprehended a light which never will filter into the dogma of any national church: namely that one of Christ's essential commands was: Passivity at any price! Suffer dishonour and disgrace; but never resort to arms. Be bullied, be outraged, be killed; but do not kill. . . . Christ is literally in no man's land. There men often hear His voice; Greater love hath no man than this, that a man lay down his life—for a friend. Is it spoken in English only and French? I do not believe so." [36]

Suffering from neurasthenia and trench fever, Owen was shipped home to England and transferred to the Craiglockhart War Hospital in June 1917. Sassoon arrived in early August. After two weeks Owen finally worked up the courage to visit Sassoon and show him some of his poems. In the meantime, he had read *The Old Huntsman*, Sassoon's first collection of war poems, and had concluded that "nothing like his trench life sketches has ever been written or ever will be written. Shakespeare reads vapid after these." Sassoon, a shy man not easily given to enthusiasms, was less impressed by Owen. Indeed, he may have been embarrassed by what was clearly hero worship expressed in terms reminiscent of a schoolboy crush. But by October he had read enough of Owen's work to realize that he was a poet of rare power and real originality.

The meeting with Sassoon was providential for Owen in several respects. Sassoon confirmed the younger man's intuition that he was a gifted poet who was capable of doing important work. He encouraged him to simplify his verse, to introduce coloquialisms into it, and to purge it of the high diction and sickly sentimentalism that were a lingering legacy of his earlier admiration for Keats and Tennyson. He provided Owen with all-important introductions to writers and poets in London who could get his poems published and his career launched. And he put into his hands Henri Barbusse's antiwar novel *Under Fire*, which was later to inspire some of Owen's most impressive poetic images. Four months after meeting Sassoon, Owen could write to his mother, "I am started. The tugs have left me; I feel the swelling of the open sea taking my galleon." But in the same letter he recalled the strange dead looks on those faces in France and said, "It will never be painted, and no actor will ever seize it. And to describe it, I think I must go back and be with them. We are sending seven officers straight out tomorrow." [37]

Owen left Craiglockhart in late October 1917 and was assigned to light duties as majordomo of an officers' hotel in Scarborough in November. He returned to France in September 1918 and died on the morning of November 4, after winning the Military Cross and fighting with exemplary valor. These twelve months were the most creative period of Owen's short career. During them, largely because of the lightness of his duties and the encouragement of his newly found literary friends, he was able to express his own distinctive poetic vision of the war. The essence of that vision was the conviction "that England one by one had fled to France." The best of England's sons were in the fighting forces. The plight of the trench soldiers might be terrible. They might move like caterpillars and die like worms. Those few who would "creep back, silent" would be "disabled," "insensitive," or "mental cases" "whose minds the Dead have ravished." But on those battlefields in France they had "dropped off fear," "witnessed exultation," "made fellowships untold of happy lovers in old song," "perceived much beauty," and known real love, in comparison to which the "kindness of wooed and wooer seems shame to their love pure." Only those who had shared their world of flares and shells, only those who had known their "sorrowful dark" hell, could ever understand their contentment and their mirth. "These men are worth your tears. You are not worth their merriment." [38]

But though Owen could sing proudly of the combatants' deep contentment and marvel at the merriment and unsullied beauty of their comradeship, he was at his most powerful and most typical when mourning the vanity and futility of their sacrifice and the terrible loss of the idealism and glee that they might have shared with the world. For these, in Owen's vision, were men who would have poured out their "spirit without stint" in order to see the reign of truth prevail. Now they were dead or disabled; their years were "undone"; their hopes had been squandered; and none of the poetry or the possibilities of progress they had had within them were ever going to come to be. The loss of all this human potential made the outlook for the future bleak.

> Now men will go content with what we spoiled,
> Or discontent, boil bloody, and be spilled.
> They will be swift with swiftness of the tigress.
> None will break ranks, though nations trek from progress. [39]

Owen had no time or opportunity to reflect on the deeper reasons for the war. Like Sassoon, he lacked the background in history and international politics that would have been necessary to understand them. He was typical of his age-group and his class in that he was more at home with Keats than with Clausewitz or Marx. But myths do not depend upon detached or even well-informed reflection. They arise and derive their purchase over the collective mind from the way people *feel* about their history *as they live it*. This was Owen's great contribution to the myth of the war generation. From the beginning he felt that the coming of the war represented a disaster and that its price was going to be paid by the young men of his generation. His experience at the front confirmed this intuition. Steeped in the imagery of the Bible and still deeply Christian in his patterns of thought, he came quite naturally to view the combatants as a generation of innocent youth being led to the slaughter, with himself as both the agent of their suffering and the celebrant of their sacrifice. Many war poets wrote verses on this theme, but none expressed the central idea so powerfully or related it so effectively to Christian tradition as Owen did in his poem "The Parable of the Old Man and the Young."

So Abram rose, and clave the wood, and went,
And took the fire with him, and a knife,
And as they sojourned both of them together,
Isaac the first-born spake and said, My Father,
Behold the preparations, fire and iron,
But where the lamb for this burnt-offering?
Then Abram bound the youth with belts and straps,
And builded parapets and trenches there,
And stretched forth the knife to slay his son.
When lo! an angel called him out of heaven,
Saying, Lay not thy hand upon the lad,
Neither do anything to him. Behold,
A ram, caught in a thicket by its horns;
Offer the Ram of Pride instead of him.
But the old man would not so, but slew his son,
And half the seed of Europe, one by one.[40]

THE war poets had provided the theme: doomed youth led blindly to the slaughter by cruel age. But a decade passed before this theme was developed in prose in a systematic or sustained fashion. Then came a rash of books about the generation of 1914 and their war experiences, many of which became runaway best-sellers. These books were pessimistic, cynical, and sometimes very bitter and brutal. All seemed like an extended gloss on the epigraph from Barbusse's *Under Fire* that Sassoon had placed at the beginning of his 1918 collection of poems, wherein Barbusse asserted that war brought in its wake everything that was basest in man: "wickedness to the point of sadism, egoism to the point of ferocity, the need for pleasure to the point of madness." Most of these books were by people born in the 1890s, who had been just out of school when the war began. Though sometimes cleverly written, they did not come easily to their authors, many of whom had tried to write about their experiences soon after the war ended, had failed or been too discouraged to continue, and had resumed the effort only when the public again appeared ready to hear about the war. Then manuscripts were fetched from trunks and the presses began to groan with dozens and eventually hundreds of war books, until the critics cried out for mercy and respite. While focused on the period of the war, most of these books tried to encompass the prewar and postwar periods as well, thus putting back together, at least in memory, worlds and compartments of life that the war had torn asunder. Some were written as novels; more often they abandoned all claim to fiction and were called memoirs, autobiography, or testaments; all were meant to provide a record of personal experience that would throw light on the collective experience and fate of an entire age-group.[41]

First, in 1928, came Edmund Blunden's *Undertones of War* and Sassoon's *Memoirs of a Fox-Hunting Man*. Blunden (1896) anticipated and helped to shape the approach of later war books by abandoning any attempt to describe the general context of warfare within which his personal experience took place. He chose to concentrate on "the little things" that filled the foreground of life at the front, and he was at his best when evoking, in prose that was often heavily literary and self-consciously mannered, "the bitterness of waste" that developed in 1917 among the survivors of the Somme attacks. "The uselessness of the offensive, the contrast in the quality of ourselves with the quality of the year before, the conviction that the civilian population realized nothing of our state, the rarity of thought, the growing intensity and sweep of destructive forces—these views brought on a mood of selfishness. We shall all die, presumably, round Ypres." Sassoon's memoir, lightly fictionalized and at first published anonymously in a small edition, was notable chiefly for the understated and patrician irony with which the now famous poet contrasted the world in which he had grown up—a world of Elysian air, "green hedgerows that had been drenched by early morning sunlight," untroubled downs, gentle horses, loving aunts, deferential servants, and "merry" hop-pickers from the slums of London—with the dim, grey, ugly world of the Western Front. His protagonist George Sherston is plunged in 1916 into a world of warfare and ugliness that his prior life has not prepared him to understand. As the book ends on Easter Sunday 1916, Sherston's groom has died at the front from pneumonia and his friend Dick Tiltwood, "a shining epitome of his embittered generation," has been killed mending wire. Sherston realizes with regret that the war is going to destroy his past; and standing in a "dismal ditch," he can "find no consolation in the thought that Christ has risen."[42]

The big year for war books in England was 1929. Some twenty-nine were published, as compared with twenty-one in 1928 and only six in 1926. Of these the most important were the translation of Erich Maria Remarque's *All Quiet on the Western Front*, Robert Graves's *Good-bye to All That*, and Richard Aldington's *Death of a Hero*. These books bore the same relationship to Blunden and Sassoon's genteel memoirs that a soldier's conversation bore to a Brooke sonnet. *All Quiet on the Western Front*, which enjoyed an immense success in England, selling more than 250,000 copies in its first year after being serialized in the Sunday papers, was an inspired exercise in neogothic Grand Guignol. Remarque's soldiers die like flies, splattered across the wall of the trench so that "you could scrape them off . . . with a spoon and bury them in a mess-tin." Before they die, they desert, refuse to attack out of cowardice, steal the watches of their wounded comrades, haggle over the boots of a dying friend, and show concern for no cause larger than their basest bodily needs. At the heart of his book, Remarque later explained in a letter to General Sir Ian Hamilton, commander of the Dardenelles expedition, was "the intention of presenting the fate of a generation of young men who, at the critical age when they were just beginning to feel the pulse of life, were set face to face with death."[43]

Good-bye to All That was more distanced, less bitter, more in the stiff-upper-lipped tradition of the British public school. As such, it was more to the taste of the London critics who found it a "gay book and a gallant one" because of its "attempt to be detached and to maintain a saving sense of humour." But Graves's book too made nonsense of civilian ideas of patriotically inspired courage among the troops by pointing out that an infantry officer's effectiveness in the line was largely a function of how long he had been there. "The unfortunates were officers who had endured two years or more of continuous trench service. In many cases they became dipsomaniacs." This apparently innocent remark will shock no one today; it did shock in 1929 when the pretense was still maintained that drink was a malady of the lower orders and not a source of courage for officers and gentlemen. Graves's soldiers fight not for king, country, or God, but for their regiment's honor, or for their friends, or sometimes because they enjoy it. They are not especially gallant. Indeed, they show a deplorable insensitivity to their comrades' fate and do not always remember to take prisoners. It was true that Graves's anecdotes were meant to shock and that the book occasionally struck a note that came close to sounding comic. But if the text left any doubt about the author's attitude toward the war, he clarified it by writing a typically irreverent letter to the editor of the *Times Literary Supplement* in which he explained that "the average British soldier of 1914–18, unlike his predecessors, the scum of the gaols who sacked Badajoz, had to be duped into the toughness and immorality that made a successful civilized fighter, by lying propaganda and a campaign of organized blood lust. This was the peculiar dirtiness of the Great War." There was nothing comic about this.[44]

Aldington's *Death of a Hero* was by far the shrillest of these books. Critics generally do not recommend it today, but anyone trying to understand the attitudes of English survivors of the war would be well advised to read it. Written in the form of a novel, it was an angry indictment of the generation of late Victorians who had lightheartedly sent their sons to die on the battlefields of France and Flanders. Aldington (1892) attempted to establish a connection between the sexual hypocrisy of the Victorians and the jingoistic mood that prevailed in England between 1914 and 1918. "It was the regime of Cant *before* the War," he cried, "which made the Cant *during* the War so damnably possible and easy. On our coming of age the Victorians generously handed us a charming little check for fifty guineas—fifty-one months of hell, and the results." Aldington's protagonist George Winterbourne goes "heroically" to his death in November 1918, "a wrecked man, swept along in the swirling cataracts of the War." His wife and his mother will not miss him, for they have already found consolation in lovers; and his father will justify it all in the name of the mysterious ways of God. No other war book drew such a stinging contrast between those who stayed at home or safely behind the lines—especially the women—and those at the front who inured themselves to hardship without becoming cruel and who fought and died for a cause in which they no longer believed. The reviewer of the *Times Literary Supplement*, himself an ex-combatant, wrote admiringly of Aldington: "We do not wish him in this 'Death of a Hero' other than he is—a man appalled by the inhumanities suddenly concentrated upon those who were in their hopeful youth at the outbreak of the War, and assailing with inspired intensity those who seem responsible for and apathetic towards the sacrifice."[45]

More war books followed in 1930, chief among them Sassoon's *Memoirs of an Infantry Officer*, Frederick Manning's *Her Privates We*, and Henry Williamson's *The Patriot's Progress*. This last book narrated in a blunt, tough, machine-gun prose the adventures of private John Bullock, a London clerk who volunteers for service in August 1914 and who is invalided home in 1917 after being stripped of every illusion about a war that at one point he perceives as "slavery." In a text of fewer than two hundred pages, profusely illustrated with line drawings, Williamson (1895) presents a gallery of inglorious episodes meant to expose the iniquity and degradation of war as it was lived by the men in the ranks. The reader is told in quick succession about a soldier who blows his brains out because he cannot bear the pressure of life at the front; a mutiny of British troops, which is sternly repressed; an attack in which six hundred out of seven hundred men failed to return; an attempt by the hero to induce fever by chewing cordite in order to stay out of the line; a visit to a prostitute followed by drunkenness and a failure to report for parade; two weeks of field punishment imposed by an unfeeling colonel; and the third battle of Ypres, where John Bullock loses his best friend and his leg. By 1917 "John Bullock took no heed of the dead men, nor of the wounded on the stretchers. He was just kept going by one hope: the hope of getting a wound which would put him out of the war . . . Every time the brutal droning of shells increased into the deep, savage, sudden buzzing which told they were going to burst near, he crouched and sweated and cringed." Shaking with fear, John Bullock attacks when ordered, only to be blown into a shell crater. He returns home without ever having seen a German, to the disgust and disbelief of his father, who hoped that his son would bag at least one Hun. As the book ends with the one-legged John Bullock taking the air in a London park on Armistice Day, it is clear that "the patriot" is now a superfluous man whose sacrifice will soon be forgotten.[46]

Efforts were made to counter this view of the war and the reaction of the war generation to it. Douglas Jerrold (1893) wrote an indignant pamphlet exposing "the lie about the War" and arguing that the war books of 1929–1930 were statistically false in representing as frequent what in fact was rare and historically inaccurate in claiming that the men who fought the war lost all faith in what they were doing. Jerrold insisted that "no honest, dispassionate, and *really* frank retrospect of war, no crystallisation in words of its full store of memories and ultimate meaning by decently humble and conscientious men, will reflect anything but a mixture of good and bad, intensified above the *tempo* of peace but in proportions fundamentally the same." Jerrold also pointed out shrewdly that the new war books achieved their literary effect by focusing on the sufferings of the individual soldier and separating him from the larger units of which he was a part. They obscured the fact that the war was a collective struggle and that important collective issues were at stake. In his book *A Subaltern's War*, published in 1929 and reissued in 1930, Charles Carrington (1897) also claimed that the legend of disenchantment was false. "Disillusion," he submitted, "came in with peace, not with war; peace at first was the futile state." Still another ex-combatant felt after reading this literature that the war had not been as the new books described it.

One was not always attacking or under fire. And one's friends were not always being killed. One had friends in those days, and one has hardly any now. And friendship was good in brief rests in some French village behind the line where it was sometimes spring, and there were still fruit trees to bloom, and young cornfields, and birds singing. And even after the first great disillusionment, that followed the Somme, reached England through men coming home, young subalterns still went out from school full of enthusiasm. One wanted to get there oneself and see what it was like, even though one knew.[47]

These lonely and uninfluential voices failed, however, to dissuade the majority of the English literary establishment from what had now become an *idée fixe*. They continued to assert, with Sassoon, that the war had been a dirty trick played by the older generation on the younger, that it had been a "crime against humanity," and that it was responsible for most, if not everything, that was wrong with England. In retrospect, it is easy enough to understand why they did so. By the end of the 1920s most English intellectuals believed that the war had been a general and unmitigated disaster, that England's victory was in reality a defeat, and hence that the men who had caused England to enter the war and to fight it through to the bloody end were either mercenary blackguards or blundering old fools. Such ideas could rally radicals as well as reactionaries.

From a conservative point of view, it seemed evident that the war had demolished the old world beyond all hope of restoration. Upper-class people found their actions increasingly limited by the state, their inherited rights threatened by the Labour party and the unions, and their economic superiority undermined by a diminished and fluctuating pound. Some members of the landed aristocracy had been forced by death duties to subdivide their estates and sell them off to profiteers, who had made their money (or added substantially to it) while the sons of the former owners had been dying in the field. It was also true that English might and prestige in the world had slipped, to the point that no one could delude himself into thinking that Britannia ruled the waves or that England was *primus inter pares* in the club of global powers. Who would have dared to write in 1929, as a well-known journalist had done so confidently just a decade before, that "the British Empire is sure of at least as long a lease of life as the Roman *Imperium*"? In short, the England of Victoria and Edward was dead and gone forever.[48]

Viewed from the Left, things looked little better. The war had not made possible a breakthrough into some new and more dynamic future. The old elites, led by Stanley Baldwin, had proved themselves incapable of putting the country back on its feet. But neither were they willing to give up the reins of power. They plodded along, tediously, from concession to concession, a tired and defeated army making an agonizingly slow retreat. The Labour party appeared briefly to carry the standard of the future. But by 1931 Labour had disappointed most of its intellectual supporters. Voted into power by a large majority in 1929, Labour's leaders quickly pledged their allegiance to the doctrine of fiscal conservatism and demonstrated an appalling dearth of new ideas. The Socialist Ramsay MacDonald emerged as the Baldwin of the Left. Nor had the war brought Europe peace. The persistence of tension among the continental countries and the mounting tide of German nationalism were additional reminders that the "war to end all wars" had been fought in vain. What was more natural than to blame this dreadful situation on the Victorians and the hard-hearted old men who lacked courage, compassion, and imagination. Thus intellectuals old enough to remember the prewar world but young enough to equate it with innocence and untested youth bemoaned the fate of their "depleted" generation and reflected on the absence of really "first-rate" men. They predicted that England, like Europe, was heading for a terrible disaster, though few were willing to go as far as Sir Oswald Mosley (1896), who bolted the Labour party in 1930 and declared war against the old men "who muddled my generation into the crisis of 1914, who muddled us into the crisis of 1931—the old men who have laid waste to the power and glory of the land."[49]

Mosley slipped toward Fascism. Henry Williamson and a handful of intellectuals followed him. Mosley described the British Union of Fascists, which he founded in October 1932, as an alliance of the war generation and English youth directed against an aging and incompetent establishment. Yet in England, unlike in Germany, the generational idea was even more popular among intellectuals of the Left than it was among intellectuals of the Right. The classic example of English lost generation literature, Vera Brittain's *Testament of Youth*, was written by a woman of strong socialist and feminist convictions. A student at Oxford when the war broke out, Brittain (1895) volunteered for overseas service as a nurse after her finacé was killed in action in France. Before the war ended, she had lost her brother and two close male friends to whom she was devoted. Brittain decided in 1925 to write a novel based on her experiences. Not until November 1929, however, did she begin to draft the book. In the meantime, seeing the hit play *Journey's End** and reading the war books of 1928–1929 had convinced her that her story was worth telling and that she should cast it in the form of a generational memoir. "After reading these books, I began to ask: 'Why should these young men have the war to themselves? Didn't women have their war as well?' . . . With scientific precision I studied the memoirs of Blunden, Sassoon, and Graves. Surely, I thought, my story is as interesting as theirs? Besides, I see things other than they have seen, and some of the things they perceive I see differently." [50]

Testament of Youth was too self-indulgent, too self-pitying, and too lacking in self-irony to be good literature. But it sold well and gained its author considerable notoriety when it was published in 1933. It owed this success to the fact that it made explicit, as no other war book had, the narrative sequence within which many English survivors of the war had come to perceive their past. This form was an adaptation of the medieval romance. First came a phase of innocence identified with the years before 1914. As Vera Brittain's talented young heroes graduate from their public school in July 1914, they have no premonition of "the threatening woe" that their "adventurous feet" will "starkly meet." Then followed the ordeal of war service in France. Full of enthusiasm when they volunteer, they lose their heroic illusions before dying in a war that they have come to regard as evil and futile. The third stage in the narrative was the return to England. Battered by "storm winds," a few survivors make their way home, only to discover that they are "ghosts of a time no future can restore." They are condemned by their fate to "desolately roam for evermore an empty shore." The final disillusionment was the survivors' discovery that the sacrifice of the dead had been in vain. The so-called victory had in fact been a setback for civilization; war would come again; another idealistic generation would be destroyed.

It was on this doom-filled note that *Testament of Youth* ended. The war generation had failed in its mission. The survivors had been too few in numbers and too dispirited by their experience to remove the old men from power. "Perhaps, after all, the best that we who were left could do was to refuse to forget, and to teach our successors what we remembered in the hope that they, when their day came, would have more power to change the state of the world than this bankrupt, shattered generation." Vera Brittain's lament seems to have touched some deep emotions in the English reading public; within six years, *Testament of Youth* sold 120,000 copies. It was reissued in 1978. [51]

---

* R. C. Sherriff's *Journey's End* described life in a dugout on the Western Front and starred Laurence Olivier in the role of Stanhope, a gallant officer and public school graduate who had survived at the front by bucking up his courage with drink. After being refused by several producers, it became the smash success of the 1929 theatrical season in London.

BY the outbreak of the Second World War in 1939 the idea of a lost generation had installed itself securely in English minds and was on the verge of
hardening into a generally accepted interpretation of recent English history. To
be sure, it appeared most frequently on the pens of journalists and memoir
writers, in obituaries, and in conversations among academics at high table; but
it sometimes crept obliquely into the books and articles of serious historians.
Meanwhile, an interesting shift in usage had begun to occur. "Lost" generation
was increasingly being equated with "missing" generation; the idea of disorientation and discontinuity was being subordinated to the suggestion of physical
absence, so much so that the term was sometimes used as if there had been no
survivors worth mentioning at all.

This strange idea made its way like a rumor passed on and further distorted
in each retelling. Already in 1930 a leading English magazine, *The Nation*,
had published an article whose author had asserted, without contradiction from
the editors, that "if you look you will not find in England in politics, in business, in the professions any young men of that generation occupying the higher
and better paid posts." The lost generation had few survivors, he added paren-
thetically, and the few there were had been "hustled out of England in the
years immediately after the War as if their survival had indeed been a mistake
and they were something to be hidden so that the War might be done with and
forgotten." In 1942 the historian E. L. Woodward expressed bitter disappointment with the treatment meted out to the war generation by their elders and
remarked hyperbolically that "The men who came back from the war have
counted for less, perhaps, in the political life of their country than any generation during the last two or three centuries." Assessing this interpretation of
recent English history in 1964, Reginald Pound, a well-known biographer and
himself a volunteer in 1914, concluded in a book entitled *The Lost Generation*
that the real losses in the Great War were losses of cultural potential and of
character. "There was no estimating the extent to which creative thought was
depleted, or the cost to learning, literature and science of the destruction of so
many strong and cultivated intelligences." Pound wondered if those missing
would have "resisted the Satanic forces that have invaded the arts? Could they
have seen to it that their second-rate would not become our first-rate, or have
arrested the decline of moral indignation into unheroic tolerance?" In Pound's
view, British national life presented "as never before the embarrassing spectacle
of men of minor powers wrestling with major responsibilities. There is impoverishment at all levels." The publishers of this volume were so impressed by
these reflections that they placed them on the flyleaf of the book and repeated
them in a short description of the book's contents placed just inside the cover.
The legend is so hallowed that even an historian determined to be revisionist
can fall prey to it. Recently, Robert Skidelsky asked if Mosley might not have
pulled off his revolt against the established parties in 1930 if only so many men
of his age-group had not been killed in the war. On reflection, Skidelsky

believed that there were not enough young Tories, Liberals, and Labourites to rally to Mosley's cause when he embarked upon the creation of the New party. "But for the 'missing generation' there may have been many more of them, and the history of England might have been very different."[52]

An historian determined to rewrite British history from the point of view of the subordinate classes would have little trouble demolishing the myth of the missing generation. British losses were proportionately less than those of the other major European countries that went to war in 1914. With an approximately equal population, France had twice as many dead: and if Britain's losses had been at the same rate as Germany's in relation to population, they would have totaled 1,200,000 instead of 700,000. True, the number of males aged twenty to forty, per thousand of the population, dropped between 1911 and 1921—but only from 155 to 141, hardly a devastating or radical change so long as one remains on the level of statistics. Three years after the war ended, the population included more than five million men born between 1882 and 1901. These age-groups had borne the brunt of front-line war service. Losses among them had been terrible. But not sufficient to destroy a generation—if one defines a generation in mass terms as a group of people of roughly similar age bound together by a common historical experience and a common fate.[53]

Yet figures like those just cited do not get at the kernel of the lost generation myth. For the myth holds that the best men died. Supposedly, the purest and noblest, the strongest and most cultivated had fallen; the weakest and least courageous had survived. This process of reverse selection had meant "failure and calamity in every department of human life" and was held responsible by some for the decline of England and the coming of the Second World War.[54]

One is inclined to dismiss this idea as elitist nonsense. First of all, one of the main characteristics of trench warfare during the First World War was its impersonality and the fact that death was meted out at random to brave and cowardly alike. The chances were far greater that one would be killed by an unseen machine gun, a bomb projected blindly from an enemy trench, or an accidental artillery hit than by a soldier's rifle or a bayonet in anything resembling direct combat. Many soldiers died without ever glimpsing the enemy. Survival had little to do with purity or nobility, though one could argue that stronger and better-nourished men from the more affluent sectors of society had a greater chance of withstanding the rigors of the climate, the danger of infection, and the fatigue brought on by hard physical labor and irregular sleep. Many were killed because they were too tired to take cover or too wet and miserable to care whether they lived or died. Intelligence also helped in staying alive: Some soldiers stubbornly refused to wear gas masks or neglected to inform themselves about snipers when entering new sectors. Robert Graves may have had these facts in mind when he shocked the local rector and his parishioners at a memorial service held soon after the war had ended by telling them that "the men who had fallen, destroyed as it were by the fall of the Tower of

Siloam, were not particularly virtuous or particularly wicked, but just average soldiers." His advice to the survivors was that they "should thank God that they were alive, and do their best to avoid wars in the future."[55]

There is no reason, therefore, to believe that the age-groups who fought the war were too reduced in numbers to play a role in postwar England, or to think that the survivors were any worse—or better—than the men who died. Why then did the notion of a missing generation take such deep root in England? Primarily, no doubt, because of the small and well-defined nature of the English elite and its unprecedented involvement in the actual fighting of the war. It is easy to forget that Britain differed from other continental powers in that before 1914 military service was not a sacred obligation incumbent upon all able-bodied male citizens, but a profession practiced by a privileged few— generally the less talented sons of the upper classes—and a refuge and dead end for members of the lower orders who had been unable or unwilling to make their way in civilian life. Between 1914 and 1918 this changed: The army became a fate that the majority of men born between 1880 and 1899 shared. This fate embraced men of all social categories. In the records left for posterity and in the annals of the higher culture, however, it was associated almost exclusively with members of the middle and upper classes.[56]

In retrospect, it is clear enough how and why this happened. Though men of all social backgrounds rushed to volunteer during the early stages of the war, those from the upper and middle classes were healthier, larger, and more easily spared from their peacetime occupations (if they had one); thus they were more likely to be passed for active service and sent to France or Flanders where five of every nine who fought were killed, wounded, or missing. Losses among university and public school graduates were especially high, because they were preferred as junior officers. Junior officers suffered heavier losses than the men who served under them. It was the job of junior officers to lead attacks, conduct raids, and see to it that the wire in front of their trenches was mended. They risked their lives when asked to, knowing that it was their function to set an example to their men. The younger the junior officer and the more privileged his education, the more likely he was to be killed.[57]

Heavy and unprecedented losses within the younger age-groups of the upper and middle classes created a collective trauma that intensified with every year of the conflict. One way that those at home coped with these losses was by directing their rage against the German enemy and denouncing presumed spies and slackers who were not doing their bit; another was by celebrating the dead and pretending that their death was glorious and lucky. Obituaries were published in the *Times;* memoirs by parents, friends, and teachers were written and circulated; plaques, busts, and memorials were installed in schools and universities. In many cases, the fallen officer's poems and correspondence were collected and published. Everything was done to keep the memory of *these* dead—that is, the dead of the elite—alive. Later when the war had ended and its fruits appeared so meager, these losses became a popular way of explaining British decline.[57]

There was nothing mythical about these losses—only about the uses to which they were later put. The "firstborn" of England's sons fell in dismaying numbers during the Great War. Figures to illustrate this can be taken almost at random. Of the 5,588 Etonians who served in the war, 1,159 were killed and 1,469 were wounded. Robert Nichols calculated that among the 136 members of his college at Oxford from the classes of 1911, 1912, and 1913 who served, 31 were killed in action or died of wounds. Two hundred and twenty-eight members of Guy Chapman's Oxford college, Christ Church, died in the war, a number that represented three years' intake of students in that college. Several eminent families lost their eldest sons; some lost two or three sons in the space of a year.[58]

Still, the fact remains that most men who served, even from within the elite, came back. Two—Anthony Eden and Harold Macmillan—became prime ministers of England. Countless others served in Parliament and occupied less exalted but still important positions in public life. They ran ministries, political parties, and publishing companies; they wrote newspapers, books, and book reviews; they administered businesses and universities; they directed scientific institutes and laboratories; they represented their nation abroad; and they shaped the mentality of their countrymen in many and varied ways. Their momoirs would now stock several library shelves, and few of them fail to pay homage in those books to the better and more brilliant men from their age-group who died. This raises a perplexing question, more elusive than the one concerning origins with which we have just dealt: Why did survivors of the Great War perpetuate the myth? What stake could they have had in keeping alive the idea of a lost or missing generation?

The answer is that the myth of the missing generation provided an important self-image for the survivors from within the educated elite and a psychologically satisfying and perhaps even necessary explanation of what happened to them after they returned from the war. The cult of the dead became a means of ac- counting for the disappointments of the present. To be sure, this cult had its origins in the war experience itself. It reflected the natural guilt of the survivors who knew they had no right to live when those around them had died, as well as their angry feeling, stronger in England than anywhere else, that they had been the victims of a dirty trick played by History incarnated in the evil form of the Older Generation. Owen's war poetry had already sounded most of the es- sential themes: the grandeur of the fighting forces; the betrayal of Youth by Age; and the tragic nature of his generation's fate. But the sentiments his poetry expressed might have faded with time and renewed activity, if it were not for the fact that the return to England and the experience of life during the twen- ties and early thirties confirmed them. What the survivors found upon re- turning was not a home fit for heroes, but a "long weekend" in which life was experienced as being "downhill all the way" and a "contrary experience." In this atmosphere of decline, nostalgia for the past, and persistently postponed crisis that was England between the wars, the myth of the lost generation with all its references and meanings performed an important function for the survivors. It evoked the childhood world they had lost; the friends and acquaintances who had perished in the war; the disorientation and estrangement they had experienced upon returning home; the battles they had fought and lost during the two decades that followed 1918. And at the same time, it explained their inability to achieve the greatness that they had been brought up to believe would be theirs and that many of them felt they had achieved, even if only fleetingly, on the fields and in the trenches of the Great War. By focusing on the extraordinary virtues of those who fell, by pointing to the gaps in their ranks, and by blaming their defeats on the resistance of the older generation, the survivors from within the privileged classes accounted for the depressing disparity between their dreams and their accomplishments.[59]

Among the more famous and articulate English war survivors, T. E. Lawrence was alone to understand and to denounce the dangerous uses of the myth of the lost generation. This is all the more surprising because Lawrence himself, by his actions and writings, had contributed to the articulation and credibility of the myth during the immediate postwar period. Like Rupert Brooke, Lawrence had already created a legend around himself before the war began. But in Lawrence's case, there was a good deal more substance to the legend and more authentic mystery surrounding the circumstances of his life. His father, Thomas Chapman, an Irish nobleman of Protestant background, had abandoned a wife, four daughters, and a position of eminence and financial solidity to run off with the family's Scottish governess. The couple changed their name to Lawrence and had five sons, the second of whom, Thomas Edward, was born in 1888. Eventually, the family settled in Oxford, where they lived modestly and to themselves on an income of £300 a year. Such economy precluded the style of life that Thomas Chapman had known in Ireland and forced the Lawrences to tighten ranks and to substitute spiritual for financial resources. Everything indicates that these spiritual resources were great. Sarah Lawrence was a Calvinist of strict observance and deep belief who sought to compensate for the terrible sin of carrying off another woman's husband by living an otherwise pure, blameless, and abstemious life. A woman of iron will and unflagging determination, she successfully imposed her values on her husband and her sons. Of the five, one became a missionary, only one married, and all took away from their mother the conviction that the spirit must stand stern guard over the vile and ever-present appetites of the body. Sarah also taught her boys that they must settle for nothing less than high achievement. In T.E.'s case, this feeling took the form of a yearning for adventure, an ambition he fired and kept alive, both as a boy and as an adult, by the reading of medieval romances.[60]

Looking at the early photographs of Lawrence, one finds it hard to reconcile the image with the legend. Yet those who knew Lawrence when he was young remembered him as an extraordinary boy in a band of extraordinary brothers—"a nest of young eagles," the Oxford don Ernest Barker called them, with T.E. the fastest and most free-flying of them all. From early youth, he demonstrated a knack for learning languages, a capacity for physical endurance, and a memory for archaeological detail. He was especially fascinated by the military architecture of the Middle Ages, and by the age of eighteen he had acquired an expert's knowledge of the field. He was also a great traveler—and, unlike Brooke, an authentic adventurer. Between 1906 and 1909 he explored French castles and churches on bicycle, sometimes doing as many as 250 kilometers in a single day and living on milk, bread, cheese, and fruit when he could find and afford them. These trips, however, were a mere preparation for the real adventures of the next few years. In 1909 Lawrence went to the Middle East for the first time on a walking tour of Syria to gather information for his Oxford thesis on Crusaders' castles. Despite the illness, adversity, and harassment he encountered on his journey, he was so captivated by the country and its inhabitants that he returned in December 1910 to undertake excavations at Carchemish, an ancient Mesopotamian site on the Euphrates River. While at Carchemish Lawrence worked on his Arabic and showed himself adept at winning the respect and confidence of the local population. Although he could have looked forward to a career as an archaeologist, he preferred to think of himself during this period as "an artist of sorts and a wanderer after sensations." He had just returned to Oxford for a brief vacation when the war began.[61]

Three Lawrence brothers—T.E., Frank, and Will—volunteered for service and were commissioned. By September 1915 two of them had died in France. T.E.'s war was luckier and much more glamorous. After a year and a half of relatively undangerous service with military intelligence in Cairo, he got himself transferred to the newly constituted Arab Bureau and, despite his young age, low rank, and lack of seniority, became a central figure in the planning and execution of the Arab revolt against Turkey. In October 1916 he made his first trip to Arabia to establish contact with Abdullah and Faisal, the sons of King Hussein, Sheriff of Mecca; and in 1917–1918 he became the effective commander and strategist of Faisal's forces, with whom he entered Damascus triumphantly in October 1918. The story of Lawrence's campaigns in the desert—what he did, what he failed to do, what he claimed to have done—is still in dispute and probably always will be. What matters from the point of view of our theme is that Lawrence was able to act out in the real world the romantic dreams that so many young men entertained when they went off to war in 1914. He blew up bridges, scouted behind the Turkish lines, engaged in guerrilla raids, and never knew the immobility and impersonality of trench warfare that so afflicted Sassoon, Graves, Owen, and others. He became a full-fledged hero and was acknowledged by the world as such.[62]

Yet in the end Lawrence too was transformed by his war experience: The patriotic and stiff-upper-lipped volunteer of 1914–1915 became an unhappy, self-doubting Hamlet who symbolized better than anyone else the postwar disorientation of the men who had fought the war. Lawrence himself has given bountiful clues as to how and why this change came about. Eighteen months of continual exertion and deprivation, he said, weakened his body. A brief episode in Turkish captivity, which culminated in a savage beating and perhaps in Lawrence's rape, degraded his spirit and his image of himself. This image of purity was further undermined when he discovered within himself the capacity for bloodlust and reprisal that he had formerly associated with primitive and non-European peoples. Any of these experiences could have triggered the change that took place in Lawrence's personality; but the chances are that the real origin of his psychic wound lay elsewhere. An extraordinarily complex man, Lawrence could not bear the burden of his own success. The illegitimate son of Thomas Chapman could never shake the feeling that he was a hypocrite and a trickster. Deep within himself he felt unworthy. He suffered from the realization that he was playing out his childhood ambitions and fantasies at the expense of individuals who were dying and peoples whose destinies were being trifled with in the pursuit of aims that had little to do with their desires or well-being. He was unable to reconcile his double role as an agent of British national interests in the Middle East and the liberator of the Arabs from foreign domination, for he knew, or suspected, that the one was not compatible with the other. The growing awareness that he could not make good on his promises to the Arabs merged with the pain deriving from his soiled image of himself to create a tremendous wave of disgust and self-hate. By July 1918 Lawrence had concluded that his job was "too big" for him. Everything had begun to feel unreal. It was as if he were a daydreamer, a player on a foreign stage, "in fancy dress, in a strange language, with the price of failure on one's head if the part is not well filled." "Achievement, if it comes, will be a great disillusionment, but not great enough to wake one up." [63]

Achievement came, but not easily. Back in London and then in Paris during the Versailles Peace Conference, Lawrence fought for the interests of Faisal and the Arabs. A lieutenant-colonel covered with decorations, the interpreter and advisor of Prince Faisal, and thanks to the efforts of Lowell Thomas a world-famous figure, he was able to move, for a brief moment, at the pinnacle of world politics. He had the ear and admiration of Lloyd George, Clemenceau, Wilson, and Colonel House. He was one of the few ex-combatants to see the peace conference from the inside. What he saw did not please him. He watched in misery and growing frustration as the possibilities for change opened up by the victory were thrown away. In the case of the Middle East, the cause of the Arabs was sacrificed to the fears and ambitions of the French. The Syrian Kingdom, for which Faisal had fought and which the British had pledged to attain for him, was entrusted to France in the form of a protectorate.

Lawrence's dream of three Arab kingdoms freely associated with Great Britain vanished in the smoke of unfulfilled promises. Lawrence expressed his feeling of betrayal and defeat in a strange and beautiful preface to an early version of *Seven Pillars of Wisdom*, his history of the Arab revolt. Though full of special references to the Arabian campaigns and understandably more positive in its presentation of the war experience itself, it falls exactly into the narrative pattern that characterizes the English prose works of the late 1920s and early 1930s: innocence, followed by betrayal and defeat at the hands of the older generation.

We were fond together, and there are here memories of the sweep of the open places, the taste of wild winds, the sunlight, and the hopes in which we worked. It felt like morning, and the freshness of the world-to-be intoxicated us. We were wrought up with ideas inexpressible and vaporous, but to be fought for. We lived many lives in those whirling campaigns, never sparing ourselves any good or evil; yet when we achieved and the new world dawned, the old men came out again and took from us our victory, and remade it in the likeness of the former world they knew. Youth could win, but had not learned how to keep, and was pitiably weak against age. We stammered that we had worked for a new heaven and a new earth, and they thanked us kindly and made their peace. When we are their age no doubt we shall serve our children so. [64]

Lawrence sought to make his own peace. He fled from the glare of his fame; but his reputation followed him as inexorably as his shadow. Briefly drawn back into politics in 1921–1922 by Churchill when the Middle Eastern settlement devised at Versailles collapsed, he helped to install Faisal on the throne of Iraq, secured the kingdom of Trans-Jordan for Faisal's brother Abdullah, then seized the first available opportunity to withdraw from public life. To the surprise and consternation of his friends, who by then included a sampling of the leading minds and statesmen of England, he gave up a fellowship at All Souls College, Oxford, changed his name to Ross, and joined the Royal Air Force as a simple enlisted man. This decision was not as irrational as it seemed to his friends at the time. Lawrence loved engines and fast vehicles and felt strongly that conquering "the air . . . [is] the only first-class thing that our generation has to do." Sick of leading other men and being invested by them with qualities he did not believe he possessed, he wanted to experience the air force from the ranks. Most of all, he longed to escape from his self and his past, which had become intolerable to him. Perhaps he hoped that the R.A.F. would restore to him the sense of purpose, close comradeship, and self-discipline that he had missed ever since leaving the army. [65]

Meanwhile, Lawrence completed his history of the Arab revolt, which he hoped would be a masterpiece of the magnitude of *The Brothers Karamazov*, *Zarathustra*, and *Moby Dick*, his favorite classics. He had begun to feel that his future might lie in writing, and he set out, with his usual thoroughness, to learn the trade. Again he was disappointed. Though his writer friends were full of admiration and generous with their praise when they read it, *Seven Pillars of*

Wisdom was seriously flawed, and Lawrence knew it. The book was too personal and too limited to the perceptions and experiences of the author to be a satisfactory account of the war against the Turks; and at the same time, it hid too much and was too cryptic to be a truly great psychological portrait of the man who led the Arab revolt. It was neither history nor fiction, but a strange combination of the two that left out all the links that would have been necessary for a real understanding of the story. Lawrence himself came to feel that his vision of the war had been distorted by the mood of disillusionment in which he had written his account. If the book had been written later, he told Frederick Manning, it might have been happier—and more objective.[66]

Lawrence's dissatisfaction with his own war book led him to approach with skepticism the war writings of his contemporaries. In 1929, when the war-book boom was getting underway and self-pity among the survivors had become a respectable and financially profitable attitude, Lawrence warned his friends against blaming all their current problems on the war. The war, he noted, seemed more horrible in retrospect than it had seemed when they were in it. It was a change in the survivors and their situation, he thought, that had produced this blurring of perspective. When the translation of *All Quiet on the Western Front* appeared in England, Lawrence dismissed it as "postwar nostalgia shoved into the war period" and "the screaming of a feeble man." "The worst thing about the war generation of introspects," he complained to Henry Williamson, "is that they can't keep off their blooming selves." The war, he repeated again and again, was something that had to be overcome, for it had been an "overwrought time, in which we had lost our normal footing." Lawrence seems to have feared that the legend of a lost generation was becoming an excuse for inaction and self-indulgence on the part of many men like himself who had fought and distinguished themselves during the war. It was not true, he protested, that no first-rate men were left among the war survivors. "What an uncertain, disappointed, barbarous generation we war-timers have been," he wrote to the painter William Rothenstein in 1928. "They said the best ones were killed. There's far too much talent still alive."[67]

Today we can distance ourselves from the myth in a way that even Lawrence could not, and sort out fact from fiction. Like most myths, the English myth of a lost generation did correspond to a reality. It referred simultaneously to the severe losses suffered within a small and clearly defined ruling class and to the difficulties that survivors from this class (and others below it) had in adjusting to the political and social realities of postwar England. Families from all social strata suffered; but elder sons from the dominant political and cultural elites died in disproportionate numbers, and their loss was publicized in what now appears to have been a disproportionate (if understandable) way. The term "missing generation" in England meant "missing elite." "Missing elite" meant the decimation, partial destruction, and psychological disorientation of the graduates of public schools and universities who had ruled England during the previous half-century. Reading the literature on the lost generation, one seldom has reason to remember that of the 700,000 British combatants who died during the war, only 37,452 were officers—and yet it is these 37,000 and not the troops they commanded who are enshrined in the myth.[68]

Many sons of the elite, certainly, were missing from the postwar scene. Even if they had survived, however, they would have discovered, as Siegfried Sassoon did, that their world had died, for the war accelerated already firmly entrenched and irreversible tendencies toward the broadening of access to political power, the growth of government bureaucracy and the welfare state, the emergence of organized business and labor as a challenge to the rule of the gentlemen-scholars and the landed gentry, and the decline of British power throughout the world. They had been brought up to rule a country and an empire; in midlife they discovered that they were going to have to preside over the transformation of the country, the phasing out of their values, and the dissolution of the empire. Small wonder, then, that they felt "fallen in a gap wide between two worlds."[69]

What was missing in England during the interwar period, therefore, was not merely men of ability and character who had fallen in the war. It was the conditions necessary for the realization of the dreams of the "firstborn" among those who survived—fantasies of power and greatness with which the privileged members of the generation of 1914 had been brought into the world. These dreams, as Lawrence came to understand, had to be abandoned and replaced by others, more suited to the circumstances in which the English and other Europeans now found themselves. This was a demanding and unpleasant task, which most members of this generation were unable or unwilling to undertake and carry through to its conclusion, as Lawrence did in giving up his own fantasy of power and joining the Royal Air Force as a simple airman. The English generation of 1914 blamed the loss of their world on the war; but the truth was that Ithaca had begun to change long before they had embarked for Troy.

CHAPTER FOUR

Spain:
The Theme of Our Time

There exist, in effect, many reasons for presuming that European man is lifting his tents off that modern soil where he has camped for three centuries and is beginning a new exodus toward another historic ambit, toward another mode of existence.

   José Ortega y Gasset, 1933

"I am I and my circumstance." This idea, first formulated by Ortega in 1914, became the leitmotif of all his thought. The "I" was a prematurely balding thirty-year-old metaphysician with a flair for "general and deliciously empty phrases," who had the good fortune to come from the family that controlled Madrid's leading liberal newspaper, *El Imparcial*. The circumstance was Spain—the Spain of 1900 that had just suffered a humiliating defeat at the hands of the United States. A country, Ortega complained in his youthful writings, without physicists or mathematicians, without ideas or ideologues, without libraries or science: a fantasy rather than a nation. A people composed of failures, cripples, blind men, paralytics, and discontented individualists who mistook the absence of a tradition for tradition and who confused Mediterranean pathos with Greek profundity. A land where incompetence reigned and theory was considered incompatible with intelligence. An Augean stable. A nation at the crossroads of its destiny. A shipwrecked race. A Spain in crisis.[1]

These intemperate accusations—some might call them cries of anguish—issued from an angry young man who was determined to rescue his country from decline but fearful that the disease he sought to cure was terminal. Today historians would put the matter more prosaically. As the century turned, Spain was suffering the birth pangs of modernity. A society that had missed to a considerable degree the social and economic transformation experienced by its Western European neighbors, it was straining beneath a burden of change made heavier by the poverty and inequitable distribution of its land, the inflexibility of its old elites, the fears of its new ones, and the demands of its awakening masses. Islands within the country, like Bilbao, Barcelona, and Valencia, were experiencing a burst of rapid growth marked by increases in population and prosperity, while the majority of Spain remained a "chain of deserts without a bird, a tree, a drop of water or a flower, a heap of *pueblos* without roads, telegraphs, sewers, hospitals, slaughter-houses, lighting, police, fire-brigades, morals, or hygiene."[2]

Today it is clear that Ortega exaggerated the uniqueness, if not the gravity, of his nation's plight. Spain shared its uneven development with much of Europe, as it did the system of government known as the Restoration, a constitutional monarchy in which a narrowly based oligarchy composed of liberals and conservatives had agreed to alternate peacefully in power. Spain's politicians were no more corrupt or incompetent than Italy's. In Italy too politics was an express train that stopped in most towns and villages only at election times. There too the elections were "made," that is, their results were prearranged by local agents of the central power. There too the commercial and industrial middle classes had reached an understanding with the landholding aristocracy. There too the modern periphery was married unhappily to an "African" core. There too national unity was a myth and a project rather than a reality. And there too men of sensibility who knew life in England, France, and Germany suffered from a feeling of what Miguel de Unamuno called "maddening stagnation."[3]

What set Spain apart from Italy and other European countries was the wound of its lost empire, the unrelenting obscurantism of its reactionary Catholics, the equally dogmatic anticlericalism of its progressives, the tradition of military intervention in public affairs, and the bizarre fact that it was the most dynamic and industrialized sectors of the country that were questioning the doctrine of the unitary and indivisible nation. In such circumstances, "Europe" and "Spain" appeared not as geographical names, signifying two complementary entities, but as incompatible ways of life; and the cult of learning and ideas seemed un-Spanish and fraught with untold dangers, not the least of which might be the crumbling of the country into its constituent parts. A small group of professors, led by Don Francisco Giner de los Ríos (1839) labored diligently to educate in European ways a select minority whose very education cut them off definitively from the largely illiterate masses they would have liked to lead. The isolation of these intellectuals merely dramatized the fact that most Spaniards had yet to come to terms with the ideas and aspirations that had emerged from the Anglo-French Enlightenment.[4]

For twenty-five years the Restoration system worked smoothly; then around 1900 it entered into a state of chronic crisis in which new forces such as socialism, anarcho-syndicalism, and Catalan separatism emerged to challenge the hold of the old parties. Events like the antimilitarist strikes and riots of Tragic Week in 1909 brutally shattered the sleepy peace of Spanish politics and announced the presence of discontented masses and new political leaders who were no longer willing to leave the stewardship of public affairs to the small, inbred Restoration elites.[5] Yet nothing fundamental changed for over two decades, because the forces that desired change were divided over what that change should be, and because the middle-class opponents of the oligarchy had little following among the peasantry and the tiny industrial working force. The war with the United States did not cause this breakdown of institutions, but it did bring home to concerned Spaniards that Spain had fallen from the ranks of Europe's first- or even second-rate powers and that something radical had to be done to keep the country from slipping permanently into the category of nations whose grandeur was a memory rather than a promise of achievements yet to come. The central theme of Spain's political history between 1900 and 1936, the years of Ortega's most creative activity, was the search for a solution to this crisis.

Ortega first viewed Spain's crisis through the eyes of the Regenerationists, a group of intellectuals and political leaders who called for the modernization of Spain and the raising of the level of Spanish civilization. The driving force in the Regenerationist movement in 1902, when the nineteen-year-old Ortega began his writing career, was Joaquín Costa (1846), a social and legal historian who sought, unsuccessfully, to organize the "neutral classes" of Spain—the small farmers of the North and the Levante, the businessmen and industrialists of Catalonia and the Basque provinces, and the intellectuals of Madrid—and lead them in a crusade against the oligarchy. Costa seized upon the defeat by the United States to dramatize his argument that Spain possessed only the appearance of a modern nation. "This nation that we thought cast in bronze," he wrote in 1898, "has turned out to be a hollow reed. Where we thought we saw an army, a navy, a press, schools, thinkers, justice, parliament, credit, parties, statesmen, ruling classes, there was nothing but a painted backdrop, a Potemkin-style trick, which the roar of a few cannons has caused to slide almost noiselessly to the ground." Costa called for more schools and irrigation projects, for expansion of the railroad and highway systems, and for an agricultural policy that would protect the small farmer and increase his production and his markets; but most of all he called for reform of the parliamentary system and for the training of men capable of regenerating Spain. The present system, he said, ensured that the worst ruled the best. It violated every natural law by keeping the intellectual and moral elite of the country far from the levers of power, thus causing it to be confused with the servile mass. Spain, he believed, had lost her "natural aristocracy" in the religious wars and futile colonial ventures of the sixteenth, seventeenth, and eighteenth centuries; her greatest need was the restoration of this "phosphorous, this chosen blood." Though ineffective politically, Costa had an indisputable gift for phrases. His words lived on long after his organization of national producers had died. And the message of his words, delivered with passionate conviction, was that Spain could escape from the misery of her present only by abandoning her colonial mission and by submitting herself to an "iron surgeon." She had to go to the school of Europe and put "seven locks" on "the tomb" of her past.[6]

Ortega was strongly influenced by Costa's program and style of rhetoric, as he was by that of another Regenerationist, Ricardo Macías Pacavea, who wrote in 1899, "Today we are disoriented, lost, astray as never before . . . we have lost the polestar of our history, and we do not know where we are going either from within or without . . . every Spaniard is a man lost in the desert."[7] Both Costa's intellectual elitism and Macías Pacavea's imagery of disorientation would resurface and figure prominently in Ortega's mature writings.

Ortega first identified, however, not with these middle-aged men but with the so-called generation of '98, a group of younger intellectuals born in the late 1860s and the 1870s. It is worth tracing the way this "generation," the most famous in all of Spanish history, came to be acknowledged. In 1910 the well-known novelist and essayist Azorín published an article entitled "Two Generations," in which he wrote of a group of young men with literary ambitions who had come to Madrid around 1896. Azorín (1873) identified this generation as consisting of the writers Miguel de Unamuno (1864), Ruben Dario (1867), Pío Baroja (1872), Ramón Valle-Inclán (1866), Jacinto Benevente (1866), Ramiro de Maetzu (1874), and himself, and he perceived as its outstanding traits a rejection of older formulas, a profound love of art, a sense of purity, and a desire for change and perfection. Azorín was concerned because a new generation of erotic novelists had appeared who seemed to represent the negation of everything that "the generation of 1896" had stood for; he took comfort in the work of the younger Spanish poets and in the certainty that in fifteen years there would be yet another generation of writers to redress the errors of the erotic novelists.[8]

Two years later Azorín returned to the same theme. Seizing upon a term used by the Regenerationist political leader Gabriel Maura, he rebaptized his generation "the generation of 1898," thus connecting its spiritual development with a political event, namely the Spanish defeat in the war with the United States, instead of with the writers' arrival in the capital. This generation, Azorín added in a series of articles that appeared in 1913, had continued the ideological movement of its predecessor, best represented perhaps by the novelist Pérez Galdós; and at the same time, it had been stimulated by foreign influences and by the defeat to create a new variant of Spanish sensibility.[9]

Azorín's articles set off a debate that has continued to the present day. Some writers, including Baroja, have denied the existence of a generation of '98; others have affirmed its reality and its influence; but none has questioned the fact that a group of writers, however defined and however loosely tied together, developed a critique of Spanish values and institutions between 1900 and 1914 that went beyond the bounds of aesthetics and that set them off not only from the writers who had preceded them but also from other articulate social groups contemporaneous with them. Literary genres—the novel, the essay, the poem, the drama—were only means that these writers employed in pursuing a common goal: the regeneration of Spain. The term "generation of '98" was invented to deal with this reality. It implied a unity of concern and action that no one at the time doubted, even if literary critics have since found the concept difficult to apply.[10]

The main characteristic of the group was their radical disaffection from Restoration Spain. They all loved Spain "bitterly" and had a vision of their country that did not correspond to the smug and powerless state they discovered when they came to Madrid in the last decade of the nineteenth century. They all wished for a more vital and creative nation that would regain Spain's former grandeur and reestablish her prestige among other European peoples. All distinguished between the "real Spain" and the superficial Spain of the large cities, the bureaucracy, and the political parties. All found the conflict between liberals and conservatives sterile and hoped to transcend the terms of contemporary parliamentary politics. Men of the provincial periphery, all were, or became, antidemocratic and antiurban. All felt intensely the isolation of Spain from the mainstream of European culture. All called for the regeneration of Spain through action and will, and all looked back beyond the empire to the Middle Ages as the model for the Spanish future. Influenced either directly or indirectly by the geographical determinism of the French historian Taine, all believed that beneath the surface of contemporary Spain lay an unchanging Spanish character or essence. Hence all traveled the Spanish provinces in search of the Spanish people, their language, and their folk traditions. Having learned from Taine that a great work of art may contain within it the key to the psychology of a race, all devoted themselves to the interpretation and reinterpretation of the story of don Quijote. All exalted the "free and happy youth" of medieval Castile and deplored the gloomy decadence of their own time. And all believed that they were living in the twilight of a civilization from which a new type of Spaniard was bound to emerge.[11]

These ideas were expressed most powerfully and most passionately by Miguel de Unamuno, professor of Greek philology, rector of the University of Salamanca, and Ortega's elder by nineteen years. A savage critic of every facet of fin-de-siècle Spanish existence, ranging from its oligarchic politics to its provincial intellectual life, Unamuno believed that only by "opening up the windows" and exposing Spain to the stimulus of "European winds" would it be possible to regenerate this "moral steppe" and to save it from stagnation. There was no need to fear, as the traditionalists did, that Spain would lose her character if she came into contact with foreign ideas and styles of life. For beneath the changing forms of civilization the Spanish people always remained the same; and their virtues of individualism, realism, and Quixotic longing after total knowledge would serve them well in the modern world. "Faith," Unamuno urged, "faith in our own spontaneity, faith in the fact that we will always be ourselves, and let the flood and the shower from outside come."[12]

Unamuno developed a theory of history, rife with Nietzschean overtones, to justify his critique of contemporary Spanish reality and his program of Europeanization. History, he thought, developed through cycles of expansion and contraction. Every period of contraction brought with it the end of a civilization and the birth of a "new man." Every new man, in turn, represented a stage in mankind's evolution and its ascent toward superhumanity. Unamuno believed that late nineteenth-century European culture was going through such a crisis. Modern civilization was disintegrating, and out of its ruins would arise a man capable of building a new civilization. This new man would be Spanish. He would be *el hombre quijotisado*—the Quijoticized man—sad, serious, beyond pessimism, a resigned fighter, a man of will, more spiritual than rational, far from the model of the ancient Greeks and closely related to the Christians of the Middle Ages. His life would be devoted to combat and struggle. He would be a pilgrim moved by a "hunger for universals and a longing for eternity." He would fight to give rise to a new Middle Ages, which would be "dualistic, contradictory, passionate." His philosophy would be one of will and faith. [13]

Inspired by this vision and convinced that progress depended upon the replacement of older men by their juniors, Unamuno addressed himself to the youth of Spain and called upon them to abandon "the old ground that ossifies our souls" and to seek "the virgin islands and deserts" of the future. In order to make way for the new, he said, they must contribute to the decomposition of the old; they must liberate culture—the realm of eternal spirit—from the material and ephemeral civilization that was smothering it; they must break "the cyst" that was enslaving the new man. "What a beautiful sight," Unamuno wrote in 1901, "to see a new man emerge from the ruins of a civilization!" [14]

Ortega appreciated the literary achievements of the generation of '98 and admired the passion and unflagging energy with which Unamuno struggled for the enlightenment of Spanish minds and the revival of Spanish culture. But before he had reached the age of his majority he had become critical of the way the generation of '98 had gone about the achievement of its mission. This generation, he felt, had known how to destroy but not how to create. He objected especially to the mood of nihilism and to the celebration of apocalypse that he perceived in the writings of these men, and to the strain of irrationalism that was beginning to surface more and more in Unamuno's essays. Writing to Unamuno in January 1904, the twenty-year-old Ortega chided his well-established elder for his "mysticism" and his "barbarism" and proclaimed with surprising self-assurance that he intended to take another path.

Perhaps you'll tell me that one doesn't need to know anything in order to think; but I have to confess to you that this Classical-Spanish mysticism that appears in your intellectual program from time to time doesn't convince me . . . Only someone with formidable intuition will be able, with a few facts and with a few stones, to construct a temple; if he doesn't have any facts, he will create something anachronistic and brutal . . . and if he does not possess a tremendous intuition, he will only produce nonsense. This is what the men of thirty have done, and what we twenty-year-olds *were beginning* to do. The men of thirty brought with them something fresh and antiliterary, and burst like barbarians into the field of ideas. True, better something than nothing. But I'll be frank with you and tell you that I have no intention of reducing myself to the role of a barbarian, and as much as I'm praised for the robustness of my arms and my good savage colors, I believe myself capable of being a candid, good, and just man with an air of openness about him, while at the same time being understood, dedicated, *studiosus*, cautious, and devoted to book learning." [15]

A year later, again in private correspondence with an older friend, Ortega put his criticism of the generation of '98 in the form of an educational theory. It was the duty of the older generation, he said, to provide the up-and-coming generation with one or more intellectual systems sufficiently rigorous to satisfy them, if only temporarily. Why? Because the formation of the brain presupposed a period of training during which the young person was exposed to preexisting systems of morality and values. These systems acted as catalysts for the development of the mind. When they were lacking, the new generation could not mature properly. Intellectual pressure produced density of thought; its lack produced aeriness and soggy thinking. Whoever had not believed in a system of morality and submitted himself to the straitjacket of a hierarchy of values at twenty would remain for the rest of his days "a vague and flighty being who will be incapable of putting three ideas in a row." And this, concluded Ortega contentiously, was the kind of person he and his fellow Spaniards of twenty were condemned to be, because the previous generation had not believed in education and had sown anarchy when they should have been preaching the love of science, of loyalty, and of intellectual depth. [16]

These harsh words were written from Leipzig, where Ortega had gone to study philosophy, physics, and mathematics during the winter of 1905. In 1906 he won a fellowship to study abroad and returned to Germany where he spent the academic year, first settling in Berlin and then transferring to Marburg where he enrolled in the seminars of the neo-Kantian philosophers Hermann Cohen and Paul Natorp. The German sojourn, particularly the period in Marburg, was extremely important for Ortega's intellectual development and may have played a role in the crystallization of his theory of generations. On the one hand, it offered him the model of a type of intellectual unknown to him in Spain: the academic philosopher who derived from his research "norms for public and private action, a system of morality, and principles of law," which he was able to oppose to those that "were conquering the public mind." On the other hand, it introduced him to the highest level of contemporary German thought and gave him a platform of fact and personal experience from which to judge the shortcomings and national characteristics of his own country. There is every reason to believe that the discoveries about Spain and what it meant to be a Spaniard that Ortega made while in Germany were extremely painful. Not long after returning to Madrid, Ortega wrote an article expressing his conviction that many of his generational comrades felt "at every hour, during every

minute an ethnic shame that burns their entrails and tortures their fantasy."
"The young men of my time who have traveled outside the country have
learned a terrible lesson, ominous and discouraging, that must be revealed
without fear and without equivocation: outside Spain, to be Spanish is to be an
object of ridicule."[17]

Once back in Madrid, Ortega had ample opportunity to reflect on the differences between Germany and Spain. Never the unqualified Germanophile
he was later made out to be, he did not perceive these differences as being
solely to Germany's advantage. The Germans lacked harmony and personality;
they were crude, philistine, and materialistic; and they were overly given to collective forms of social organization in which the individual lost his identity.
German liberals were faint-hearted in their liberalism, and German socialists
were sometimes "barbarous." German culture was in decline, and the Germans had no idea of literature or poetry. But in philosophy, physics, and mathematics—and above all, in the level and continuity of their civilization—the
Germans were far ahead of Spain. They were an integral part of Europe.
Spain, on the other hand, was nothing but a phantom and a fiction. It was a
world of lies and counterfeit currencies in which the political and intellectual
elites circulated antiquated ideas whose value they never troubled to examine, a
country where everything was false—"todo falso, todo falso." In Germany an
intellectual could take the organization of society for granted: He could, if the
fancy took him, spend twenty years pondering the problem of the infinite,
knowing that the Department of Health would protect him from disease, that
the libraries would supply him with books, and that his vote, once placed in
the urn, would be truthfully reported. The Spanish intellectual who tried to
flee from national problems, by contrast, would be taken prisoner by them ten
times a day. Since the instrument with which social reality was transformed
was politics, a man born between Bidassoa and Gibraltar, like it or not, had to
be "first and foremost" a politician. Upon returning to Spain, therefore, Ortega
devoted himself to politics. But what kind of politics? Much as it may surprise
readers who know Ortega primarily from *The Revolt of the Masses*, the politics
he embarked upon in 1907 was a politics of the Left, which he unhesitatingly
qualified as socialist.[18]

Ortega spelled out the nature of his political program in a series of newspaper
articles and speeches drafted between October 1907 and the spring of 1914.
These articles and speeches were directed explicitly to young men like himself
between twenty and thirty, a generation that had come into the world to find itself bankrupt, "without a home and without fathers in the spiritual order." We
shall not be surprised when we discover the reasons the young Ortega gave for
limiting himself to this youthful clientele. Like Maurice Barrès in France and
like his own Unamuno, Ortega believed fervently that the reform of the nation
required a transformation of sensibility too radical to occur in already formed
adult minds. And like so many others who thought in generational terms, Or-

tega used the word "youth" to refer to the educated elite among the middle and upper classes. The message he addressed to these shock troops of the future was the following: Spain was not a nation, but a problem and a possibility; for men of his generation, it was a source of pain and grief. Whatever their merits as individuals, the older generation of Spaniards—those around fifty—had failed in their mission, which had been to Europeanize Spain and bring her to the level of civility enjoyed by England, France, and Germany. Politics was above all education. It was the process by which the most educated sector of the population acted on the masses and provided them with ideals by which to live and to organize their common life. The ideals Spain needed were liberty, social justice, competence, and Europeanization. Regeneration was inseparable from Europeanization. Regeneration was the desire; Europeanization was the means of satisfying this desire. Spain was the problem; Europe was the solution. And by "Europe" Ortega meant science and culture, for he was persuaded that sound government was based on clear thinking. The old parties were incapable of carrying out this mission. Liberalism was still valid as an ethical ideal; but it had to be renovated and brought up to date as a political program. Today's liberalism had to be socialist. Indeed, socialism was the continuation of liberalism. But one must be careful not to confuse this socialism with the socialism of Karl Marx or of the existing workers' parties. The only way to prevent revolutionary violence—which Ortega confessed to abhor—was by organizing a revolutionary political party that would implement the social transformations that the times required. The mission of democratic radicalism and socialism was to avoid revolution by achieving the aims toward which the people blindly and violently groped. The task of the younger generation was to organize this new party of the Left. To accomplish this would not be easy. Because the younger generation labored under a terrible limitation: They had grown up without teachers, and a powerful generation could never derive from an inept one. Hence the younger generation's lack of energy and enthusiasm, and the bitterness that lay so heavily on their hearts. Ortega called upon his generation to study and to struggle. And in 1913 he announced that they had achieved the first part of their mission. By criticizing what existed, they had made possible a new life for Spain. Now their task was to institute the reign of democracy by means of "the revolution of competence"—by which he meant the replacement of rhetoric by knowledge and of ideology by technical expertise. [19]

By March 1914 Ortega was widely recognized by young men of his age as the intellectual and political leader of his generation. His leadership of others was facilitated by the stabilization and consolidation of his personal situation. He was now a married man, with one child, another about to be born, and a permanent academic position as professor of metaphysics at the University of Madrid. Foreign friends, like Hermann Cohen, Nicolai Hartmann, and Paul Scheffer, acknowledged him as a coming force in European thought and saw him as the leading representative of his country's younger generation in the field of philosophy. His intellectual talents and his growing political influence were also appreciated by the country's political and cultural leaders, and he was on the verge of being elected to membership in the Royal Academy of Moral and Political Sciences, some indication that, despite his vigorous polemics, he had won the esteem and respect of those who occupied the system's commanding heights. He had recently written the meditations on *Don Quijote* that would represent his first important philosophical work. And he had founded, in October of the preceding year, with some other young men of his age-group and political persuasion, a movement called the League for Spanish Political Education, which was loosely affiliated with the Reformist party of Melquíades Álvarez and which Ortega may have perceived as the nucleus of the new left-wing party whose organization he had for so long been urging. It must therefore have been with a feeling of considerable self-assurance and the premonition that he was living an important historical moment that the thirty-year-old Ortega stepped before the crowd that thronged into the Teatro de la Comedia in Madrid to hear him discourse on "the old and new politics." [20]

This speech was the fullest and most important version of his political program that he had given up to date. It is of special interest to us because it contains some of the first adumbrations of his generational theory, along with many of the concepts that he would later develop in a more systematic way. It was addressed, like most of his orations, to Spanish youth and especially to that generation of educated and privileged Spanish youth who had come to reflection "in the terrible year of 1898" and who now found themselves in the middle of life's path. Real politics, said Ortega, consisted in penetrating to the depths of the collective mind and in rendering clear the already existing opinions and ideas of social groups—of a generation, for example. Only when a generation knew what it wanted could its work be fertile. A generation that did not affirm its own uniqueness and its own sentiments might condemn itself to sterility. For if generations wished to serve humanity, they must begin, like individuals, by being faithful to themselves. His generation, Ortega noted, seemed reluctant to take up its task. And this reluctance was all the more serious because the hesitation of the young generation to enter national politics would entail not merely its own failure, which was bad enough, but also the definitive failure of the Spanish people as a whole and their lapse into a state of permanent and irredeemable mediocrity. Ortega therefore concluded that his generation must take up the arduous work of national renovation; it must occupy itself "in all consciousness, in a premeditated way, organically" with the national future. [21]

It is said, Ortega continued, that all epochs are epochs of transition. This, he admitted, was true. But some epochs were marked by sudden jumps and subterranean crises that produced a radical deviation in the center of gravity of the public consciousness. When this happened there arose two nations that coexisted and yet were completely foreign to each other: an official nation that obstinately repeated the gestures of a dying age, and a vital nation, blocked by the other, that was unable to push its way onto the stage of history. This coexistence of two nations, said Ortega, was the decisive fact of present-day Spain. The representatives of official Spain—the political parties, the bureaucracy, the press—had lost all contact with the vital segments of the nation and were nothing but phantoms that defended the illusion of ideas. They were in the process of dying, and the moribund needed to be put to rest definitively so that their misery would not be unduly prolonged. Vital Spain was represented by the young intellectuals who had refused to join the parties. These men of the "new generations" had come to realize that they were totally alien "to the principles, the patterns, the ideas, and even the vocabulary of those who direct the official organisms of Spanish life . . . The same word pronounced by one or the other signifies two different things." These men had a grudge against the Restoration, and some day they would demand from it an accounting, for because of its mediocrity they were only a shadow of what they otherwise might have been. Ortega had now come, he explained, to ask for the collaboration of these men, especially that of those minorities who pursued intellectual occupations. They must enter politics, but they need not, and they must not, leave their intellectual standards and abilities behind. Let the new generations enter politics, Ortega urged, as doctors and economists, as engineers and professors, as poets and industrialists; for concrete know-how, not general ideas, was what Spain needed. [22]

The new politics, Ortega warned, must not be directed exclusively toward the capture of the state. It must take the form of an historical attitude. We consider the state as one of the organs of national life, Ortega explained, but not the only or even the decisive one. We must ask for greater efficiency from the state, but we must go to the villages not just to ask for votes, but so that our propaganda will be creative of culture, of technology, of social cooperation—in short, of human life in every sense. The League for Spanish Political Education would therefore side with society against the state. And if the state and society entered into conflict, the League must serve society against the state; for Ortega and his friends placed spontaneity and national vitality above public order. The new politics would be liberal; but it would have nothing to do with the present Liberal party that had lost its vitality and proved itself unable to transcend individualism. Nor could the League cooperate with the Conservatives—who represented the past—or with the Republicans, who tended to be demagogic and doctrinally inflexible. [23] The new politics would be pragmatic on the question of the monarchy, for in the twentieth century the only possible stance was experimental and the only possible theory one of practice. The new politics would be radical in that it would cooperate with the Socialists in the extension of liberal freedoms to the lower classes, but it could not confuse its efforts with those of the Socialists, for it abhorred all dogma and doctrine and refused to separate the question of social justice from that of national resurgence. It would be national without being nationalist or imperialist. The future of Morocco (at that time occupied by Spanish troops), for example, would be decided on pragmatic grounds, not on doctrinal ones. The new politics would be extraparliamentary in being directed toward the vitality of society rather than toward the simple control of the state. The real problem, Ortega insisted, was one of vital energies; and what his movement sought was a Spain "with a backbone" that could stand on its own two feet.

How was this vitality to be generated? On this decisive question, Ortega was both eloquent and precise.

We are going to flood with our curiosity and our enthusiasm the most remote corners of Spain: we are going to get to know Spain and to sow it with our love and indignation. We are going to travel the fields like crusading apostles, to live in the villages, to listen to the desperate complaints there in the places from which they derive; we are going to begin by being the friends of those whom we shall later lead. We are going to create among them strong bonds of sociability—cooperatives, circles of mutual education; centers of observation and of protest. We are going to propel toward an imperious spiritual rising the best men of every capital who today are prisoners of the terrible burden of official Spain, heavier in the provinces than in Madrid. We are going to make these fraternal spirits, lost in provincial inertia, understand that they have in us allies and defenders. We are going to extend a network, composed of knots of effort, throughout the Spanish land, a network that will be both an organ of propaganda and an organ devoted to the study of national life; a network, in short, that forms a nervous system through which will run vital waves of sensibility and automatic and powerful currents of protest. [24]

To us today, this program and its rhetoric may sound suspiciously fascist—or as some historians would put it, in phrases that are easily abused, pre- or protofascist. And indeed Ortega's program did contain many of the themes and slogans that fascist leaders would later use to great effect. The condemnation of parliamentary politics, the affirmation that liberalism and conservatism were equally dead, the rejection of ideology in favor of pragmatism and competence, the demand for a fusion of nationalism and socialism, the concern for national renovation, the appeal to the younger generation, the affirmation of a rupture between the nineteenth and twentieth centuries, and the call for a "politics of vitality" to ward off the danger of decadence—all these would reappear in the programs and propaganda of the fascist parties of the 1920s and 1930s. But to categorize the League for Spanish Political Education or its eloquent young spokesman as prefascist would be both to commit a serious error in historical judgment and to confuse two things that, for all their apparent similarities, are fundamentally different. Perhaps we need to distinguish between a political impulse that appeared within the European middle classes around 1905 and the distortion of that impulse that developed in the very different conditions that followed the Great War.

What Ortega sought in 1914 was the mobilization of young intellectuals like

himself—men who stemmed from those same neutral classes to which Costa
had earlier appealed—toward the end of a more modern, a more dynamic, a
more liberal, and a more European Spain. Like his friend Ramiro de Maetzu,
he wanted Spain "to serve the world, to stop being a parasite in the common
work of culture, not to live on loans, to contribute to the progressive amplifica-
tion of spirit in human souls." The political program he put forward for achieving these goals was essentially reformist. He did not want a revolution; nor did
he wish to blow up a storm of resentment and hate. Where there was shouting,
Ortega always insisted, there could not be science; and science, or rational discourse, was and always remained for Ortega the central aim. "More light, more
light," he cried with Goethe, against those, like Unamuno, who felt drawn
toward murky spiritual depths. [25]

Besides, the driving motives behind fascism and Ortega's group were very different: His was not a movement inspired by fear of the workers and peasants but
rather a movement inspired by hope—hope in the possibility of raising the
Spanish to the level of other European peoples. The state for which he longed
was one in which politics played a minimal role and people could get on
with their work. True, he spoke of nationalizing socialism. But his nationalism was directed within, toward the reform of society, rather than without,
toward the aggressive expansion of the state. And his socialism had nothing to
do with collectivism or leveling but was motivated by his belief that inherited
privilege interfered with the development of competence and culture. [26]

It has been said and resaid that Ortega was an elitist. So he was. But how was
Spain to be transformed, except by elites? Ortega's error lay not in his elitism,
but in his narrow and overly intellectual definition of the existing and potential
Spanish elites. In his analysis of the Spanish crisis, he both underestimated the
determination and ability of the oligarchy to preserve its privileges and power
and overestimated the willingness of the people to subordinate their needs to
the cultural aims formulated by intellectuals like himself. He also neglected or
underestimated other areas of Spanish vitality—the army, anarcho-syndicalism,
socialism, the separatist movements—that were going to play decisive roles in
Spanish politics during the next twenty-five years. But the shortcomings of the
political analysis do not detract from the grandeur of the vision. And the heart
of more than one young man of the Spanish "generation of 1914" was moved
by Ortega's message, as a glance at the list of members of the Spanish League
for Political Education shows. [27]

THE generational idea, then, was deeply rooted in Ortega's background and
in his youthful thought and action. Like Henri Massis, the young Ortega
was an early and indefatigable practitioner of the art of generational polemic.
There is scarcely an article or a speech written by him before 1914 in which he

did not complain of the failure of the older generation or lament the lasting wound that their intellectual mediocrity had left on the minds and souls of the younger generation, a generation without teachers and masters, hence "bankrupt," sacrificed, and lost because it had not received the education and stimulation it deserved. Like Massis, Ortega appears to have "learned" or "inherited" this critique of the preceding generation from older, well-established intellectuals, in his case from Costa, Unamuno, Azorín, Baroja, and Maetzu. Ortega's generationalism, like that of Massis, first manifested itself in the context of a campaign for national revival. And it is plain that he was drawn to "youth" and the "younger generation" as a third way between the existing oligarchy on the one hand and the developing mass movements on the other, "youth" being used by Ortega, as by Massis, to mean a small, educated elite between the ages of twenty and thirty. Finally, the clientele toward which Ortega turned—what he called "la gente moza," "friends of my time," "the new generations"—was that same generation of 1912 that Massis had attempted to describe, shape, and inspire. Where Ortega differed from Massis was in the explicitly political nature of his generationalism; and Ortega's decision to enter politics derived from his conviction that in Spain, as opposed to France, Germany, and England, there existed no area of social vitality, no organ of socialization, no means of acting on the national spirit, save politics.[28]

There is another way in which Ortega differed from Massis: Unlike his French counterpart, he thought of himself primarily as a theorist. He counted himself among those for whom "it is above all important to achieve a certain decorum, cohesion, and rigor in one's ideas." Yet even the most devoted Ortegian would have to admit that Ortega's theories were badly known by the public both within Spain and abroad. His disciple Julián Marías has an ingenious way of accounting for this. Ortega's thought, he says, is like an iceberg: Only the top tenth is visible in any one of his writings. The rest—the philosophy—is "there even when not there, it is 'underneath,' underlying everything he says, literally sustaining and nourishing it." A less mystifying way of putting it might be to say that many of Ortega's ideas and insights make sense only when interpreted in the context of his entire oeuvre. And this oeuvre was not accessible, even to those who read Spanish, until well after the Second World War.[29]

Take, for example, Ortega's generational theory. If one scrutinizes Ortega's writings between 1907 and 1914 one sees that by the time the First World War came Ortega had already produced the elements of a generational theory that differed in some important particulars from the theories we have studied up to now. But these elements remained dispersed throughout his letters, newspaper articles, and speeches and were probably not known in their entirety to anybody at the time except to Ortega himself. It was not until 1921–1922, in his lectures on "the theme of our time," that Ortega sought to formulate these ideas more systematically; and even then they remained known to only a handful of disciples until they were published in Spanish in 1923 and then translated into German in 1928 as *Die Aufgabe unserer Zeit* [The Task of Our Time].[30]

The ideas propounded in Ortega's 1921–1922 lectures remained essentially the same as those explicitly or implicitly set forth in his prewar writings. But the context within which the ideas were embedded and the mood in which they were advanced had changed radically, as Spain and Ortega's own life had changed. Between 1907 and 1914 Ortega had spoken and written as one of the potential leaders of a political movement that aimed at nothing less than a realignment of Spanish parties and a reform from top to bottom of Spanish life and institutions. The lectures on "the theme of our time" were given *ex cathedra* by a theorist who was trying to formulate a new science of man in society; and Ortega's conception of that science, or at least his presentation of it, was strongly influenced by the "new biology," particularly the theories of Jacob von Uexküll, who stressed the special and reciprocal relationship between every organism and its surroundings. Moreover, the precocious young man, who had liked to begin his speeches by proclaiming that he was nothing but a youth, had become a man; and the man was widely recognized throughout the Hispanic world as Spain's most eminent philosopher and the leader of an intellectual renaissance. To organize that renaissance and to spread its gospel, Ortega had helped found in 1917 a newspaper, *El Sol*, which soon became one of Europe's most influential and respected dailies. Now, at thirty-eight, with several books behind him, a new and powerful forum at his disposal, and the wind of public acclaim in his sails, Ortega was ready to stake out his claim as a European rather than a purely Spanish thinker. A sort of Spanish Spengler, if you will, whose *Decline of the West* Ortega much admired and was soon to help translate into Spanish.[31]

Meanwhile, the Spanish political crisis deepened. Between 1917 and 1923 Ortega's country was shaken by a wave of strikes, street fighting, terrorist attacks, assassinations, and corporative rebellions against the authority of the state. "During these years," the Catalan historian Jaime Vicens Vives has written, "syndicalists, theoretical anarchists, professional terrorists, and hired gunmen mingled in one of the most explosive, destructive moments . . . of that general European social complex which emerged from World War One. They were people disposed to wrest power from the hands of the bourgeoisie and their coercive forces, to annihilate the state in one great revolutionary blow, and to initiate a life of collectivized property organized into free municipalities and based on an agrarian and patriarchal economy. An enervated utopia, with no possible counterpart in the world, it was purely the reaction of an illiterate peasant transformed into the mechanized worker of an urban enterprise."[32]

Faced with the insurgency of striking workers and the unchecked violence of hired thugs in Barcelona, the seizure of lands and entire municipalities by peasants in the South, the insubordination of ill-paid army officers, the demands of separatists spurred on by Woodrow Wilson's doctrine of self-determination, and the ongoing campaign of the parliamentary Left to wrest power from the oligarchy, the Restoration system fell into a state of permanent paralysis. The old parties could no longer govern; yet there were no new political forces capable of taking their place. For a time it appeared that Spain might follow the path of revolution traveled earlier by Russia. In both countries, "confusion and uncertainty at the top were matched by continuing unrest and disaffection in the lower levels of society." The movements of the workers, the peasants, and the nationalities threatened to coalesce. Only the loyalty of the army, after an initial period of syndicalist revendication, saved the Spanish state from chaos and collapse. But the price of order was repression. And even repression could not cut short the lengthening list of murders. In 1921, the year Ortega gave these lectures, killings averaged twenty per month, and no end of street violence was yet in sight.[33]

The events of 1917–1921 made Ortega painfully aware of the difficulties of social pedagogy and reformist politics in a backward country torn by ideological feuds and burdened by a social structure unlike that of France, England, and Germany. Though careful to distinguish between socialism and syndicalism and still inclined to blame the extremism of the workers on the failure of the oligarchy to modernize and Europeanize Spain, he moved during these years toward a more aristocratic and less optimistic analysis of the Spanish situation than the one that had underlain his 1914 speech on the old and the new politics. In the absence of more detailed biographical information than we currently possess, it is difficult to say with any assurance why and how this evolution took place. It may conceivably have had something to do with the company Ortega kept; or alternatively, it could have arisen from a profound disgust at the erosion during the years of the war and the postwar crisis of a certain way of life to which he was profoundly attached. But regardless of the cause, the direction of his development is unmistakable. Spain, he complained intemperately in a famous little book he published in 1921, was, along with Russia, the most plebian of European nations. Ever since medieval times, the elites had been weak and the masses had hated and revolted against "the best." This characteristic of the Spanish people, and not any presumed decline in the quality of men available in contemporary Spain, Ortega said, was what had caused the present crisis and brought the nation to the brink of social disintegration. Spain's history since the Middle Ages, he concluded darkly, had been a history of decadence; and that decadence was now reaching its final stages. For where the masses refused to obey their natural leaders there could be no society and no nation. "People" meant spontaneity and abandon; "aristocracy," on the other hand, meant discipline and regimen. "Well then, a nation is a people organized by an aristocracy."[34]

Ortega had long suspected that he was not cut out for politics. Now he began to wonder if his kind of politics was cut out for Spain. And who could blame

him, given his commitment to enlightenment, culture, competence, individual liberty, and good taste? For left-wing politics in Spain between 1917 and
1921 had produced pistol shots, killings, apocalyptic rhetoric, and a formidable
backlash of the middle classes that rendered impossible, at least in the short
run, a politics of reform. The members of the League for Spanish Political Education either had been drawn off toward the Socialist party or, in the case of
the more conservative, had slipped backward, toward the parties of order. The
Reformist party, for which Ortega had nourished such hopes, had become little
more than a feeble adjunct of the liberals. One can ask, of course, why Ortega
himself did not move toward the Socialists. The answer, I think, is that he was,
and always had been, inalterably opposed to any movement that identified itself
with a single corporative or class interest. Politics was the art of listening to the
nation and translating its secret desires into acts—or at least, Ortega thought it
should be. The Spanish Socialist party, by contrast, was the champion of a segment of the Spanish people: the workers. And it had never shown itself especially hospitable to intellectuals, particularly those who paraded their sense of
intellectual superiority, as Ortega did. Hence Ortega was not attracted to the official Socialist organization, though he continued to appreciate the importance
of the Socialists' role. Critical of both the Right and the Left, he found himself
without a party or a political following, and this too may have left its mark on
his theoretical writings of this period. Like most men, Ortega may have found
it difficult to distinguish between the frustration of his own political ambitions
and the failure of a period, nation, or social group. Mulling over the experience of the years between 1914 and 1921, Ortega began to wonder whether
Spain's tragedy might also be Europe's and whether the failure of the present
generation—of which he was convinced—was confined to Spain. In this disen-
chanted and pessimistic mood, he wrote the lectures that made up his book *El
tema de nuestro tiempo* [The Theme of Our Time]*.[35]

The Theme of Our Time began with a theory of social and cultural change
that was aimed explicitly against those who believed that politicians made history and implicitly against the Marxist interpretation of historical change. According to Ortega, there were two kinds of epochs: those in which people considered themselves as heirs of their predecessors and those in which people
experienced the achievements of their predecessors as something that had to be
radically reformed. His period, Ortega claimed, was of the second type. Men
were uncomfortable with past forms and felt the need to escape from them.
History was the instrument by which men understood the changes that took
place in the human spirit. But history had a hierarchical structure; it was not
the study of everything that had happened, or even the study of everything that

---

* The English translation of *El tema de nuestro tiempo* is entitled *The Modern Theme* (London,
1931); but this title is inappropriate, since Ortega's central point is that the modern period is coming to an end and giving way to a new organization of thought and feeling.

had changed. Some changes were more important than others; in fact, some changes determined others. Economic and political changes, for example, depended on changes in ideas, taste, and mores. These changes, in turn, were merely consequences of changes that took place in the way that individuals experienced their life in "its undifferentiated integrity." This way of feeling and experiencing the world—what Ortega chose to call "vital sensibility"—was the primary phenomenon in history and what one had to define in order to understand any historical epoch.[36]

Decisive changes in vital sensibility were brought about by the appearance of new generations. A generation, Ortega explained, repeating one of the major themes of his speech on old and new politics, was not a handful of unusual men, nor was it simply an undifferentiated mass. It was like "a new integrated social body, with its select minority and its multitude, which had been launched on the orbit of existence with a determined vital trajectory." Ortega acknowledged that changes in vital sensibility would have no historical significance if they occurred only within isolated individuals. But this was not the way that human life was structured. Historical life was coexistence and *convivencia* with other human beings. No one lived alone. The life of the outstanding individual took the form of action *on* the masses. There was a community between superior men and the common crowd. The man who was absolutely different from the mass of his contemporaries would have no impact on the life of his times. To study such deviates was not the historian's major task. Generation, then, conceived as a dynamic compromise between the individual and the mass, was the most important concept in history and the hinge upon which history executed its movements.[37]

It was characteristic of Ortega's style that he strove constantly for new and more extravagant metaphors with which to express an idea that he had already presented in a different form. This was especially true in the case of the concept of generation. Thus in *The Theme of Our Time* he went on to describe a generation as a "human variety," explaining that he was using the word "variety" in the sense that naturalists gave to the term. The members of a generation, he said, came into the world possessed of certain typical characteristics that gave them a common physiognomy and that differentiated them clearly from the previous generation. Within this identity of type, the members of a generation could differ from one another sufficiently so that they might become antagonists and even bitter enemies. But beneath the most violent intragenerational hostility the attentive observer could easily discover a common "filigree." All the men of a generation would be bound together by the time in which they lived, and no matter how much they differed, their similarities would be even more striking. Indeed, the most important variation within a generation was not between those who were for and those who were against a certain cause—for example, those who were liberals and those who were conservatives—but rather the contrast between the select elite and the mass of common men. Some men lived their historical time more fully than others and reached a higher level. "And, in effect, each generation represents a certain vital altitude, from which existence is determined in a determined manner."[38]

Ortega tried to make his point more precise by expressing it with two metaphors borrowed from biology. Each generation, he said, represented a moment in a nation's vitality; it was a pulsation of the nation's historical potency. And each pulsation had a unique and peculiar physiognomy. Similarly, one could think of a generation as a "biological projectile, launched into space at a precise instant, with a determined violence and direction." Both unusual and ordinary men participated in these movements, but the select minority came closer to reaching the highest level of perfection in theoretical knowledge and practical accomplishment permitted by their times.[39]

At this point in his lecture Ortega undertook to systematize the distinction between his own generation and the generations of the Restoration, a distinction he had introduced in a polemical context in his articles and speeches between 1907 and 1914. Generations, he submitted, were not born in a vacuum. Each oncoming generation encountered the forms that its predecessor had created, forms which it temporarily took for reality itself. At the same time, each generation created its own truths through the play of its spontaneity, but these truths were never experienced as complete or definitive. To live was thus a task pursued in two dimensions. The spirit of each generation depended on the equation between these two ingredients—between what was received from the previous generation and what the new generation spontaneously created. Some generations felt a continuity with the past; these generations lived in *cumulative* epochs. Other generations felt a profound break with the past; these generations lived in *eliminatory* or *polemical* epochs; and such periods produced combat generations that attacked their predecessors and defined themselves in terms of what they opposed. Cumulative epochs were dominated by old men; eliminatory epochs were times of youth. The rhythm of epochs of old age followed by epochs of youth was such an obvious phenomenon in history, Ortega remarked, that it was astonishing that it was not a commonplace in historiography. Ortega proposed the creation of a new scientific discipline called metahistory, which would have the same relationship to concrete history that physiology had to the medical clinic. One of the most interesting metahistorical investigations, he suggested, would be to discover the great historical rhythms, of which the alternation between epochs of youth and epochs of old age was only one example.[40]

Ortega began the second lecture in the series by insisting that every generation had its vocation or its historical mission. This was one of Ortega's most persistent themes. It had figured prominently in his remarks on old and new politics, and it would appear again in the lectures of the 1930s. Each successive generation, he said, lived under the severe imperative to develop the germ of its individuality, with which it had begun life, and to inform other human life around it—presumably other generations—with the model created by its spontaneity. Some generations failed to carry out their vocation and left their mission unfulfilled. There were generations, just as there were individuals, who were unfaithful to themselves. Instead of taking up their task, they preferred to remain comfortably lodged in the ideas, institutions, and amusements created by their predecessors, for which they felt no real affinity. Such generations did not escape unpunished. The delinquent generation dragged its way through life in perpetual discord with itself, a vital failure. The present generation in Europe, and particularly in Spain, was one that had deserted its cause and failed to take up its historical task. Seldom had humanity tolerated so meekly forms that did not suit it, as at the present time.

This last affirmation provided the transition into Ortega's central theme, the inauthenticity of European life. European institutions were all residues of a former age. Even "the very best" among the present generation seemed to ignore the fact that the Western sensibility was in the process of making a radical shift in direction. Ortega insinuated that his contemporaries had failed to see this because they were mired in the political categories they had inherited from the generation of 1890. They continued to debate the merits of liberal versus reactionary politics. Yet politics was secondary. What counted were biology, physics, and philosophy. A new sensibility expressed itself first in contemplative thought, then spilled over into active life. "What one will live tomorrow in the public place depends on what one begins to think today." The new science taught that "life" was replacing rationalism as a way of experiencing reality. Ortega offered himself as an interpreter of the message of the new science and as a philosopher of "life." The essential note of the new sensibility, he proclaimed, was the determination never to forget that spiritual functions were also biological functions—like digestion and movement. Pure reason was only a small island floating on a sea of primary vitality. Culture was a biological instrument and nothing more.[41]

The "theme of our time" was thus the subordination of reason to vitality and spontaneity; and the mission of the present generation was to discover spontaneity through the use of reason—to make of "life" both a principle according to which people could live and a right. This mission implied the creation of a new kind of culture that would treat art less reverently and that would be perspectivist rather than relativistic or rationalist. For every life was a point of view on the universe, and truth could only be grasped from a localized perspective. One of the prophets of this new culture was Nietzsche, who had had the genius to discover and to introduce as a cultural theme the distinction between ascending and descending life, between life that was successful and life that was a failure—between what other men of the time called vitality and decadence.

Ortega feared that *The Theme of Our Time* would not be properly understood, and his fears proved justified. It is easy to see how his meaning might be missed. He seemed to be saying that the transcendent ideals of culture should be subordinated to the immanent imperatives of life; that history was a branch of biology; and that historical life was governed by certain biologically determined rhythms that expressed themselves in individual lives, generations, and civilizations. This was certainly what Mannheim, Gründel, and others took away from the book when they read it at the end of the 1920s. Besides, who could be surprised if some misinterpreted Ortega's call for a new culture that would have the honesty to appreciate a magnificent specimen of human life like Napoleon for the sake of his grace and animal vitality? As often happened in this period, Ortega had found unfortunate words with which to convey his idea. Consequently, *The Theme of Our Time* is a hard book to understand and an even harder book to like.[42]

Yet for all its baroque indulgence in biological metaphor, *The Theme of Our Time* is one of the most revealing and important of Ortega's writings. In it he projected onto a European canvas the ideas and theories he had developed in the isolation of Spain. Generation, the primary social group with which Ortega identified and in which he saw the key to Spanish *regeneration*, was proclaimed by him to be the most important historiographical concept, the only one capable of accounting for significant historical change. The nub of the generation problem he located in the attitude taken by the intellectuals of a new generation—those who lived at the height of their times—toward what they had received from their predecessors. And the crisis in Spanish politics he now asserted to be part of a larger European crisis of values—the most radical in modern European history—a crisis that had its roots, according to Ortega, in the inability or unwillingness of intellectuals to abandon pure reason as a basis for life.

What stands out in these lectures is Ortega's grudge against ideological politics. The utopian, he said in a revealing aside, was the person who refused to accept his perspective on reality—the man who deserted his place in favor of an abstract ideal. Indeed, the central message of *The Theme of Our Time* was that utopianism was simply rationalism translated into politics; and thus the transcendence of rationalism by vital culture could be expected to bring about a new politics as well. What would this new politics be like? Ortega failed to say; but for some time he had been predicting a reaction against the leveling tendencies of democracy and the dogmatic excesses of the working-class movement. Life was essentially structure, he had warned in 1916; and a bad structure was better than none. The reformist was beginning to lose his faith in reform.[43]

The Theme of Our Time contained some intriguing and promising ideas about the generational phenomenon. Ortega broke new ground in seeking to unravel the relationship between the mass of a generation and its elite; and he was also quite original in perceiving that the attitude taken by a younger generation toward its predecessor was not always identical in all historical periods. His idea that every generation had a task or mission to perform, though elusive, was worthy of further exploration, as was his insistence that the potency of a generation depended on the education that it had received from its elders. But although Ortega asserted unequivocally that generation was the most important concept in historiography, he did little to show how the concept might be used; for he failed to specify, as François Mentré sought to do in his contemporaneous book, why generations appeared, how they differed from or were similar to other social groups, how long they were, or how they could be located. Nor did he go on to apply his generational theory to recent Spanish or European history with any rigor.[44] All he offered was the sketch of a generational theory that still needed to be fleshed out. It was therefore to be expected that Ortega would return to the generation problem to treat it more fully, and this he did in his 1933 lectures "En torno a Galileo" [On Galileo], later translated into English as *Man and Crisis* and indisputably one of Ortega's most impressive works.

In the ten-year interval between the publication of *The Theme of Our Time* and the lectures on Galileo, both Ortega's situation and that of Spain underwent changes of such magnitude that they could not help but leave their imprint on the formulation of his generational theory. From his vantage point as professor of metaphysics at the University of Madrid, as editorialist on *El Sol*, and as impresario of Spain's intellectual renaissance, Ortega watched uneasily the last agonies of the constitutional monarchy and put his mind to the task of foreseeing the outlines of Spain's future. In 1923 the tottering parliament regime collapsed and gave way to the dictatorship of Primo de Rivera, a well-meaning but heavy-handed general with a gift for alienating his most dedicated supporters. Ortega greeted the coup without surprise, perhaps even with relief. He knew that Primo de Rivera's rule could only be temporary, and he thought or deluded himself into thinking, that a period of dictatorship would be salutory, for it would teach the Spanish people that the liberal freedoms established during the nineteenth century were now inalienable rights without which European man was incapable of living.[45]

Primo de Rivera may also have understood that his dictatorship was destined to be fleeting; but, like most political saviors, he lacked the talent for making graceful exits. The result was that his regime lasted long enough to become oppressive. For six years Spain had all the disadvantages of dictatorship without the illusion of competent and efficient government that Mussolini was able to give Italy. When Primo de Rivera slipped away into exile in 1929, a broken and dying man deserted by the very groups he had come to save, the monarchy itself was seriously weakened. The only way that the king, Alfonso XIII, could have restored his prestige and ensured the continuation of his dynasty was by acting quickly to liquidate the old political system; instead he clung on to the support of the army and the old, discredited politicians from the predictatorship days and appointed another general, Dámaso Berenguer, to oversee what was currently referred to as a return to parliamentary normality. This misguided act brought into being a coalition of Neoconservatives, Left Liberals, Socialists, and Catalan separatists, which brought down the monarchy in April 1931 by electoral means. It all happened so quickly, so effortlessly, and so bloodlessly that a condition approaching euphoria swept over large sectors of the Spanish people, especially the Republican leaders, who found themselves suddenly transported from prison and exile to positions of cabinet responsibility. The Second Republic had arrived, and even the least historically minded Spaniards understood that a new era in their national life had begun.

Ortega played a minor role in these events. He was both a belated and a qualified Republican. And if one reads his political writings between 1920 and 1930 it is easy to understand why. His position throughout these years was that no purely political or institutional reform would be sufficient to solve Spain's problems. The real source of Spain's misfortune, he believed, was the hostility of the Spanish man in the street—whether of the Left or the Right—to any change in his way of life or manner of thinking. And this hostility he attributed to the fact that the tone in Spanish life was given by the petty bourgeois. There were no real "aristocrats of blood or finance," no "intellectuals of the lyre, of the idea, or of the logarithm," no "workers with hunger and hate," to counterbalance the tyranny of the average man. As long as these elements were lacking, there could be no subsantial reform. Political renovation therefore presupposed a prior reform of society. To think anything else was to fall prey to illusion. Ortega also thought it useless to embark on a political movement that had as its objective nothing but the restoration of past liberties. It was necessary, he maintained, to offer some alternative means of reforming and strengthening the state, since the demand for a stronger and more efficient state was what had given rise to the antiparliamentary dictatorships in the first place. The demand for more competent government had to be met.[46]

Ortega thus had little sympathy for the oppositionist activities of Liberals and old-fashioned Republicans—and they, in turn, may have suspected him of secret sympathy for the dictatorial regime. But eventually even Ortega was goaded into overt opposition by Primo de Rivera's blundering interference in intellectual and private life. Hence in 1929 he resigned his university chair in protest against the dictator's educational policies; and in November 1930 he jolted his readers by declaring on the front page of *El Sol* that the monarchy had lost its right to rule. In pretending to return Spain to normality after six years of unconstitutional government, he said, the monarch had encouraged the worst of Spanish political habits, namely the willingness to accept political abuses and illegalities as the normal state of affairs. By appointing another general instead of proclaiming the necessity to rebuild the state from its foundations, Alfonso had committed an act of *lèse-dignité* against the Spanish nation. "And as it is irremediably an error, it is we, and not the regime itself—we, ordinary citizens who have nothing revolutionary about us—who have to say to our fellow citizens: Spaniards, your state does not exist! Reconstitute it! *Delenda est Monarchia.*"[47]

To pursue this end of a reconstitution of the Spanish state, Ortega formed, with his friends Ramon Pérez de Ayala and Gregorio Marañon, an organization called the Group in the Service of the Republic, which issued in February 1931 an appeal to professors and magistrates, to writers and artists, to doctors, engineers, architects, and technicians of all kinds, to lawyers, notaries, and other men of the law, and especially to youth, calling upon these groups to rally behind the cause of the Republic and to mobilize opinion in its behalf. Ortega argued that the monarchy had been nothing but a mutual aid society dedicated to the defense of the interests of an oligarchy consisting of the large Spanish cities, the higher echelons of the army, the aristocracy of blood, and the church. It must now, he said, be replaced by a new state that would be truly "national." When the monarchy fell in April 1931, Ortega was temporarily carried away by the possibility of at last achieving the reform of the Spanish state that had so long been his goal; he dreamed of raising the provinces from their torpor and lack of political consciousness by means of a thorough decentralization of power and a campaign of political education conducted by the Group in the Service of the Republic, which he now headed. In June 1931 he stood successfully for election to the Constituent Cortes in the district of Leon. Thirteen other deputies from his Group were elected, and the enthusiastic response that the speeches and declarations of the Group met in the provinces authorized every hope and every ambition.[48]

What Ortega saw during the next few months, however, saddened and disconcerted him and made him wonder about the intentions of the Republican leaders and their commitment to nationalizing the Spanish state. The Republican coalition that had overthrown the monarchy included Conservatives, Left Liberals, and Socialists. But the Constituent Cortes elected in June 1931 was weighted heavily and (in Ortega's view) dangerously toward the parties of the Left, with the Republican Right too weak to act as an effective counterbalance.* The issues of religion, education, regional autonomy, and land reform soon came to divide this fragile and volatile coalition, while disorder reigned in the streets of Spain's towns and cities, essential services were brought to a standstill by striking workers, and fires burned in Spanish churches. Socialist spokesmen spoke ominously of carrying out the revolution to which they

---

* One's interpretation of the results of the elections of June 1931 depends, of course, on one's definition of the "Left." Gabriel Jackson writes that these elections resulted in a "strong victory" for the coalition of Left Republicans and Socialists. According to his calculations, the Left received about 250 seats, of which 120 were Socialist and 80 controlled by the Left Republican parties. The remainder of the left-wing coalition consisted of Catalan and Galician separatists. In the center were some 100 Radicals, led by Alejandro Lerroux. Jackson classifies only 80 deputies on the Right. Gabriel Jackson, *The Spanish Republic and the Civil War* (Princeton, 1967 ed.), p. 41.

claimed their party's parliamentary predominance entitled them; and the enemies of the Republic rallied their forces for a counterattack. Alarmed by the mounting wave of revolutionary rhetoric and by the withdrawal of the moderate and conservative elements from loyal participation in the affairs of the Republic, Ortega issued a warning to the leaders of the ruling coalition on September 9, 1931: "This isn't it, this isn't it! The Republic is one thing. 'Radicalism' is another. If not, let it [the Republic] wait."[49]

Ortega saw the crisis of the Spanish political system in connection with a larger crisis of European institutions and values—in his opinion, the greatest crisis that Europe had faced since the early modern period. Some day, he wrote in 1932, it would be clearly seen that Spain, just as she was about to launch herself on a spiritual flight after centuries of cultural sleep, had been halted by a "fierce despiritualizing wind" that blew from the continent. *La rebelión de las masas* [The Revolt of the Masses], the most widely read of Ortega's writings, represented a first attempt to analyze that crisis on a European scale. Despite its provocative title (reminiscent of Edgar Jung's *The Domination of the Inferior*) and its crude analytical categories ("mass-man" and "select-man"), the book's real theme was the vacuum of leadership in contemporary Europe. In some ways, it may be considered a response to Spengler's *Decline of the West*. Ortega rejected the idea that Europe was declining. The truth, said Ortega, was that there had been a tremendous expansion in the scale of European life and in the comforts and choices open to the average European. Why then did Europeans have the impression that they were living in a period of decline? Because the elites had failed to provide ideals for the masses. Since the masses were incapable of providing ideals for themselves, Europe was threatened by a fall into barbarism. The message of the book was that what seemed to be the new movements of the time—Communism and Fascism—were incapable of providing European man with new ideals because they were atavisms and were oriented toward the destruction of liberalism rather than toward its absorption and transcendence. History, Ortega believed, could only be lived forwards. Nineteenth-century achievements, like industrialism and liberal democracy, must be superseded; they could not be undone. And movements which sought to undo them were bound to fail in the end.[50]

These were also years of crisis in Ortega's personal life. Between 1930 and 1933 he was dogged by bad health and financial problems. Because of the stand he took against the monarchy in 1930, he was deprived of his tribune on *El Sol* and forced to found another newspaper, which had only indifferent success and which cut him off from an important segment of his reading public. Never again was he to write regularly for a major Spanish newspaper.[51] Ortega's greatest sense of personal dissatisfaction, however, undoubtedly came from the failure of his political initiatives and from his feeling—perhaps one should call it a fear—that he had wasted valuable years in an occupation that was not his authentic vocation. From late 1929 until August 1932 he devoted himself almost exclusively to political activity, with the degree of his involvement rising in direct proportion to the passions unleashed by the fall of the dictatorship and the advent of the Republic. In the fall of 1931, after criticizing the radicalism of the republican Left, he began to play with the idea of founding a new political party that would extend from the Neoconservatives on the Right to the Radicals and Left Republicans, a party that would seek to offer a viable republican and centrist alternative to revolutionary socialism. The Republic, he said in a famous speech in December 1931, must be rectified, by which he meant that it must be redirected toward moderation. The workers must recognize that they could not improve their situation unless the productive capacity of the Spanish economy increased; and the capitalists must learn to stand on their own feet and to be more enterprising. Ortega evidently had in mind a party that would find its following among intellectuals, professional people, technicians, manufacturers, and youth, presumably university students. "The new Republic needs a new party of enormous dimensions and of rigorous discipline that is capable of imposing itself and defending itself against any special-interest party." This initiative met with generous applause, but no substantial support. The Left Republicans under Azaña were moving in the direction of the Socialists, while the conservative groups to which Ortega was appealing continued to wager on the collapse of the Republic. From December 1931 on, whatever dreams of political effectiveness Ortega had harbored quickly vanished.[52]

Ortega insisted that he had no talent for politics. His mind gravitated naturally and inevitably toward what was not quotidian. Granted that this was so—and it is undoubtedly true that he sometimes showed a remarkable lack of interest in day-to-day political reality—more damaging yet was the fact that there existed no clientele for the politics he favored. The men of the Right with whom he would have liked to collaborate were unwilling to rally to the Republic and work to change it from within. The men of the Left toward whom his sympathy for economic planning and social reform seemed to draw him were bent on a course of revolution that he refused to accept. For all his talk of realism, the Spain he spoke of creating seemed to have little in common with the existing Spain of discontented peasants, unruly workers, determined separatists, and frightened Catholics. His ideal in 1931, as in 1914, was a national front of Neoliberals and Neoconservatives who would construct a strong, efficient, and prosperous state managed by men who were above any sectarian interest and free from any ideological commitment. This state would not be conservative or bourgeois, Ortega claimed; but neither would it be socialist or democratic in a narrow ideological sense. It would have as its two central principles work and the nation. In recent European history, Gaullism comes closest to what Ortega had in mind; but Ortega would have preferred a national movement without a nationalist leader, and one oriented more toward the raising of the level of the masses than toward the restoration of national power in the international arena.[53]

The dream was beautiful, and as usual, Ortega found beautiful words with which to express it. "Well then, gentlemen, the Republic means nothing less than the possibility of nationalizing the public power, of fusing it with the nation, so that our people can devote themselves freely to their destiny, so that they can be allowed to *fare da sè*, so that they can organize themselves as they wish, so that they can choose their road over the unpredictable arena of the future, so that they can live according to their own ways and according to their internal inspiration." [54]

Alas, the moment for a responsible centrist politics in Spain had not yet arrived. For by December 1931, whether out of fear, ambition, or resentment, the great mass of Spaniards had already enrolled emotionally, or were about to enroll, in parties that represented special interests, parties whose aims were intensely ideological and incompatible with the toleration of their adversaries. Spain was falling into warring factions, and the victory would go not to the most intelligent but to those with the strongest forces and the heaviest guns.

In August 1932 Ortega withdrew from all political activity. This moment was unquestionably a difficult and bitter one for him. As he neared fifty, he realized that he was in danger of dispersing his talents, of being many things brilliantly but no one thing superlatively well. The time had come "to cry out loud" the doctrine of human existence that he had "insinuated" and "whispered" in the pages of *The Revolt of the Masses*. Otherwise, like Goethe, to whom he devoted an essay in 1932, he might stand condemned for having failed to listen to the inner voice of his destiny when it called on him to take up his task. How Ortega must have trembled when he wrote that "every life is, more or less, a ruin among whose debris we have to discover what the person ought to have been." Besides, by the fall of 1932 Ortega felt that parliamentary politics was a demeaning occupation fit only for second-rate minds; and he was persuaded that Spain was heading irremediably toward a disaster from which it might not recover for many years. Perhaps he also remembered what he had written in 1915, as Spain was just beginning its descent into political chaos: "When everything in public life is false the only thing that can save us is the loyalty of every individual to himself." It was thus in flight from politics and in pursuit of his vocation as a philosopher that Ortega embarked in 1933 on a course of lectures devoted, appropriately enough, to the theme of crises in European history. [55]

Ortega began these lectures by undertaking to define the nature of "human life." He declared that he wanted to take this ordinary phrase, which like most phrases was empty, and to fill it with content, to make it good like a check at the bank. Man, he claimed, was not his body or his soul; neither was he what he thinks or what he makes: he was his life. In these lectures, unlike in those given in 1921–1922, Ortega was careful to distinguish his views from those of the vitalists. The biological metaphors had disappeared. Life, he made precise, was not a simple biological fact. Human life had to be understood in terms of history and biography. Man was a being to whom things happened and who was constantly forced to act—to do something. Or as Ortega put it in a slightly later text, "Man is what has happened to him, what he has done. Other things might have happened to him, but what did in fact happen to him and was done by him, this constitutes a relentless trajectory of experiences that he carries on his back as the vagabond his bundle of all he possesses." Life was a problem. Every man found himself shipwrecked, adrift in a mysterious element, surrounded by dark and dangerous waters. Taken unawares by his situation, buffeted by radical uncertainty, overwhelmed by the possibilities of life, man was forced to make judgments on himself, others, his surroundings, the meaning of his existence. To survive, to stay afloat, man had to interpret the world and create for himself a "vital horizon." For man was "a passion to be." "That interpretation," said Ortega, "takes form within what we call 'our convictions'— what we believe ourselves to be certain of, what we know we can depend on." This complex of certainties, which man built for himself "like a raft in the tempestuous and enigmatic sea" of his surroundings, formed a whole and was the primary phenomenon of history. Man, concluded Ortega, was above all a maker of "worlds," a creator of fictions. He was the novelist of his own life.[56]

If all men's convictions were different, then there would be as many vital horizons, as many worlds, as there were men to make them. One man's convictions would only have validity for himself. But this was not the case. Every life was submerged in a sea of collective life. This collective life or society had its own repertory of convictions with which the individual had to come to terms. And this world of collective convictions, which was commonly called "the ideas of the epoch" or "the spirit of the times" and which Ortega called "the world in force," was determining and binding on all men regardless of whether they accepted it or not. These anonymously held convictions were there in front of man, and he could no more ignore them than he could ignore a wall that separated him from the next room into which he wanted to pass. Moreover, not only were these ideas *there*, in front of man; they were also *inside* of him since most men derived the greater part of their convictions from the collective repertory and took them for granted as indisputable truths. Indeed, it was the incontrovertible and secure nature of a man's convictions that distinguished them from mere ideas. Ortega was fond of comparing life to a drama. Man, he said, was like an actor who had been carried asleep to the wings of a theater and, barely awakened, had been thrust out onto the stage before the public. He had the option of running from the stage or making up the plot as he went along. Yet the part an individual improvised would be taken from a script determined by the vital horizon of his time. And with every shift in this horizon would ensue a change in the plot of the human drama, and a transformation of the roles played by individual men.

The metaphor becomes increasingly difficult to follow; I introduce it because it provides an insight into Ortega's view of human life, and also because it leads logically to his theory of generational change. Because of the structure of human life—because some men were always dying and others were being born—the vital horizon was always in the process of change. Man lived boxed in between his predecessors and his successors; this was the most elemental fact of human life. A man was always living in a determined segment of his allotted existence. This was what it meant to be a certain age. Indeed, the dialectic of ages was what created history. Any given moment encompassed at least three presents; there were always three distinct "todays." "Or, to put it another way: The present is rich in three great vital dimensions that dwell together in it, whether they wish or not, linked with one another, and perforce, because they are different, in essential hostility to one another." For some men "today" was the stage of being sixty; for others it was being forty; for still others it was being twenty. To be a man's contemporary was not the same thing as to be his coeval. Men lived with their coevals, not with their contemporaries; that is, they lived with their generations. Generation was thus a "vital altitude" in the historical process; it was "an integrated manner of existence, or, if you prefer, a style of life, which fixes itself indelibly on the individual"; it was like "a caravan within which man moves a prisoner, but at the same time, a secretly willing and satisfied one." On the basis of this series of assumptions, Ortega concluded that in a collective sense generations were the real actors in history. Changes in convictions and in vital horizon came with every generation.[57]

Ortega thought these changes in convictions and vital sensibility came regularly, about every fifteen years.* Why? Because human existence was structured in such a way that every fifteen years one entered a new stage of life. At twenty-five a young man encountered the world created by his elders and began to meditate on its validity. Because he had grown up in a different situation than they had, he would find their set of convictions unsatisfactory at a certain point in his development and would seek to replace it with his own authentic feelings about the world in which he lived. This young man would not be alone. Together with his coevals, he would constitute a phalanx more or less as numerous as the generation of his elders, and the combined weight of their difference in point of view and their dissatisfaction with their parents' world would transform the vital horizon. Ortega brushed aside impatiently the argument

---

* To my knowledge, this is Ortega's first mention of the fifteen-year interval. Before 1914 Ortega tended to operate with a bipolar model (the old versus the young generation), though his letters to Navarro Ledesma and his correspondence with Maetzu testify to his awareness that there was an intermediary generation between the men of the Restoration and his own generation of twenty-year-olds. Beginning in 1917 with the article on the death of Don Gumersindo de Azcárate (*Obras completas*, III, 11–12), Ortega began to stress the coexistence of three generations in the same historical period. But in that article the three generations were identified as the men of 1869, those of the Restoration, and those like Ortega who had yet to make their mark in national life. Only in 1933 and then again in 1934, in the prologue to the fourth edition of *España invertebrada*, (ibid., III, 43) did Ortega assert that the interval between generations is always fifteen years because of the structure of human life.

that generation was an illusory concept because only men born the same day could legitimately be said to belong to the same generation. Age, he argued, was not a date, but a stage of life, "a certain way of living," "a task," or *quehacer*. A man was not young at twenty-one and old at twenty-two. He continued to be young or old throughout a series of years, and in the circle of his acquaintances he realized very well who were his coevals and who were not, despite the fact that he probably was ignorant of their birthdates and even of their ages. "Age, then, is not a date, but a 'zone of dates,' and it is not only those born in the same year who are the same age in life and history, but those who are born within a zone of dates." [58]

Ortega believed that life contained five ages, each fifteen years in length: childhood, youth, initiation, dominance, and old age. From an historical point of view, some ages were more important than others. At any given moment, historical reality was composed of men between the ages of thirty and sixty. This zone of dates, Ortega was careful to point out, did not constitute a single generation; it embraced two generations, one locked in struggle with the other. The men between thirty and forty-five were in the process of finding and propagandizing their ideas; the older generation, those between forty-five and sixty, had arrived and enjoyed the perquisites of power. The older men were creating and consolidating; the younger men were preparing for command. These two "historic" generations had their hands on the levers of historical action at the same time, "so much so that those hands are placed one above the other in formal or potential struggle." Taking Wilhelm Pinder to task for misunderstanding his earlier writings on the topic and conceiving of generations in terms of succession—Pinder, it will be recalled, had been tempted by the idea of generations as exclusive worlds—Ortega made it clear that he saw the relations between generations in terms of polemic, argument, and controversy. "This controversy is not necessarily negative in character; on the contrary, the essential polemic between the generations has in normal history the form of, or is formally sequence, education, collaboration, and the prolongation of the previous by the subsequent." [59] Whatever its attitude toward its elders, each generation carried within itself all previous generations. "If the image were not so baroque, we might present generations not horizontally but vertically, one on top of the other, like acrobats in the circus making a human tower. Rising one on the shoulders of another, he who is on top enjoys the sensation of dominating the rest; but he should also note that at the same time he is the prisoner of the others." Not satisfied with this metaphor, however, Ortega quickly seized on another to nail down his point. "The decisive thing in the life of generations is not that they follow each other, but that they overlap or are spliced together." There were always two generations acting at the same time and reacting to the same themes, yet acting from different standpoints of age and thus giving to the same themes different meanings. [60]

To belong to a generation it was not enough to be of a certain age; one also had to have some "vital contact" with the other members of the generation. The space within which generations lived varied in size according to the period. During the Roman Empire the circle of collective life and *convivencia* had been large; at the dawn of the Middle Ages it had been small, and the European nationalities had developed and taken different paths. Community of time and space, then, were the primary attributes of a generation. Together they signified "the sharing of an essential destiny." This identity of destiny, in turn, produced in generational coevals secondary characteristics that resulted in a unity of "vital style," or style of life. In an earlier essay Ortega had suggested that a generation's style of life expressed itself more clearly in some aspects of human activity than in others, and especially in relationships between the sexes. Each generation had its own style of love. [61]

All serious generational theorists had taken up the problem of how one establishes the series of generations; and one of the most interesting passages in the lectures on Galileo is devoted to this elusive question. Ortega proposed the following method of determining the generational sequence. One took a fairly broad slice of historical time in which a radical change in sensibility was known to have taken place. For example, in European history one chose the period that ran from the Middle Ages to the modern era. In 1300 European man had been comfortably installed in a certain kind of world. By the middle of the seventeenth century that world had disappeared, and European man was thinking radically new and different thoughts. If one asked when this modern age had begun, when European man had first thought the new thoughts clearly, one could not help answering that this had happened sometime between 1600 and 1650. One then looked for a figure who better than any other represented the new sensibility. This eponym, Ortega submitted, could only be Descartes. One next noted the year in which Descartes was thirty, which turned out to be 1626. From this date one counted seven years in each direction to determine the limits of Descartes's generation (since generations were fifteen years in length.) The central date of the previous generation would be 1611; the one before that would be 1596, according to Ortega "a good little generation." From this point on, it was a simple matter of arithmetic. Assuming that the original calculation was correct, one could now count off the series of generations using as a measure the figure of fifteen years. Ortega denied that this method was mechanical. Suppose, he suggested, that Thomas Hobbes, who fell in the generation before Descartes's, had seen things on the same level and with the same clarity as Descartes. This would mean that the series of generations was wrong, and one would begin again, looking for a new series in which Descartes and Hobbes were included in the same group. As it turned out, Hobbes had almost but not quite thought the same thoughts as Descartes. It was as if the two men were looking at the same landscape from different heights. "It is that difference in vital level," said Ortega, "which I call a generation." [62]

Top: Miguel de Unamuno in 1917; Ramiro de Maetzu in the 1920s. Bottom:
Pío Baroja around 1900; Azorín about 1920.

[The generation of '98,] an unsuspected eruption of internal barbarians.
  José Ortega y Gasset, 1914–1916

Ortega reading the news of the outbreak of war in August 1914.

History is trembling to its very roots, its flanks are torn apart convulsively, because a new reality is about to be born.
    Ortega, 1914

Ortega in 1925.

I can only be with those who are determined to reform Spanish institutions from the bottom up . . . Without this, liberty has absolutely no interest for me, because it would be only a word.
Ortega, 1925

Ortega after his speech calling for the "rectification" of the Republic in December 1931.

Every life is, more or less, a ruin among whose debris we have to discover what the person ought to have been.
Ortega, 1933

The 1933 lectures on the concept of generation were never meant to stand alone; they were designed as an introduction to Ortega's analysis of crises in civilization. Historical crises, he went on to argue, arose when a change in the vital horizon left men stranded, without convictions. To live without convictictions, said Ortega, was terrible. Men in crisis had no clear destiny. Everything they did, felt, thought, and said lacked conviction and was therefore false. They lived in lamentable disorientation, for they had no vital horizon by which to orient their acts. They were desperate; and like all desperate men, they would sometimes perform seemingly heroic acts that proceededed not from real heroism but rather from the attempt to give meaning to a life they perceived as meaningless and empty. They were subject to enthusiasms and extremisms. They were one-sided and would try to reduce the complexity of life to simple formulas, like social justice or race, that represented partial truths. They felt a tremendous need to escape from the burden of a false and overly complex culture, and they would seek to create one that was authentic, even if this entailed destroying the old one. For their only hope was to divest themselves of what was old and false, so that they could go on to what was new and true. Thus periods of crisis, Ortega noted, always brought with them barbarization, terrible simplification, and leadership by the masses, who had no real stake in the older culture. "In history, as soon as the man of action puts in an appearance and is discussed and pampered, it means that a period of rebarbarization looms. Like the albatross on the eve of a storm, the man of action appears on the scene at the dawn of every crisis." [63]

Ortega's ostensible topic was the crisis that had followed the Renaissance and that had resulted in the creation of modern science. He gave the fifteenth century as an example of disorientation and confusion, when religious forms of thought were no longer experienced as authentic yet there was nothing new to take their place. But Ortega's main concern, and the theme to which he continually returned, was the crisis that had reached its apogee at the end of the 1920s. "We do not know what is happening to us, and this is precisely what is happening to us, not to know what is happening to us: the man of today is beginning to be disoriented with respect to himself, *dépaysé*, he is outside of his country, thrown into a new circumstance that is like a *terra incognita*." This disorientation, Ortega insisted, was not a product of the war, although it was experienced differently by those who had lived part of their life in prewar times than by those younger men who had grown up after the war ended. But both groups had the sensation of finding themselves on the dividing line between two forms of life, two worlds, two epochs. And since the new form of life had not yet come into full existence, was not yet what it would one day be, they could only gain some clarity with respect to it and with respect to their future by turning their regard toward the old form of life, which they were in the process of abandoning. Ever since Descartes European man had lived for and from reason. Was it possible that the new age would live for unreason?

Could hostility to reason provide the basis for a new world view? "I have here a gigantic question within which is to be found prisoner during these hours the concrete future of every one of us here today."[64]

Ortega left no doubt that he regarded himself as one of these mature men who had grown up in known territory and had lived to experience a time of crisis. What a pity, he remarked, that he did not have the time to describe to his audience the sense of satisfaction that Europeans had possessed thirty years before. And Ortega confided to his listeners that his own political paralysis was the result of his belief that the movememts characteristic of the moment—by which he had in mind Fascism and revolutionary Socialism—were historically false and heading toward a terrible failure.

It is not hidden from me that I could have almost all the youth of Spain behind me, as one man; I would have only to pronounce a single word. But that word would be false, and I am not disposed to invite you to falsify your lives. . . . . There was a time when the refusal of any form of extremism carried with it the inevitable assumption that one was a conservative. But now it is becoming clear that this is not so, because people have seen that extremism may be either radical or reactionary. My own refusal of extremism was due not to the fact that I am a conservative, which I am not; but to the fear that in it I discovered a vital and substantive fraud. I prefer then to wait until the first genuine generation presents itself. If by chance you are it, you will not have to wait long![65]

I N his 1929 lectures on "why people are returning to philosophy" and again in his lectures on Galileo, Ortega insisted on the chronological primacy and conceptual superiority of his statements on the generation problem. On both issues he exaggerated, although, to be fair, he probably did so out of ignorance of what others had been writing. Ortega evidently did not know of Mentré's book and Mannheim's essay, and he seems to have been unaware of the extent of the contemporary German literature on the question, so far as one can determine from his references.* In any case, whatever the breadth of his reading, it is a matter of simple chronological fact that Ortega's major analysis of the generation problem came last in the series of generational theories produced during the first three decades of the twentieth century, almost fifteen years after Mentré's, seven years after Pinder's, and five years after Mannheim's. Before 1933 Ortega's ideas about the generational concept were available only in the form of a few pages devoted to the topic in *The Theme of Our Time* and fragments of newspaper articles and speeches not easily accessible to a foreign or even to a Spanish public.

More to the point, Ortega's mature generational theory had much in com-

---

* Ortega mentioned Justin Dromel, Ottokar Lorenz, Wilhelm Dilthey, and Wilhelm Pinder as generational theorists and as late as 1933 referred to Lorenz's work as "the only book up to the present time seriously dedicated to the theme of generations." *Obras completas*, V, 45.

mon with the ideas of Mentré and Mannheim, although it was articulated with infinitely greater literary flair and with a greater wealth of historical example. All three men reached the conclusion that generations had to be defined in terms of a sensibility, a fate, and a program. All three were attracted by the notion that generations possessed styles of life. All three believed that these styles were truly collective in that they extended beyond a handful of intellectuals or politicians. All three wanted history to deal with the things men took for granted and felt as well as the things they thought or thought they thought. All three realized, albeit with varying degrees of clarity, that a person's ideas and actions must be discussed in the context of his stage of life. And all three understood that age, to use Ortega's phrase, was not a date, but a "certain way of living."

Where Ortega stood out from Mentré and Mannheim and where he had a real claim to originality was in his insistence that a generation's sensibility had to be understood against the background of a certain world, in his belief that these 'vital horizons" changed collectively and substantially every fifteen years, and in his effort to relate these generational changes to long-term cultural crises. The concept of a "world" or "vital horizon" within which every generation lives is Ortega's most distinctive and at the same time his most elusive contribution to generational theory. Like most of his ideas, he left it in the form of a rough sketch for his disciples and followers to fill out. He did specify that ideology and technology were the two most important variables determining the vital horizon. Each generation encountered a set of solutions worked out by the previous generation in response to the special problems it had faced; and each generation was restricted in its action and its spontaneity by the existing level of technology. Ortega assumed that under normal circumstances the oncoming generation would bring about a slight, by no means radical, change in ideology and technology. They would reshape the world to fit their needs and leave it different than they had found it. Hence Ortega's insistence on the fact that the normal relationship between the generations was one not of warfare or polemic but of education, collaboration, and the prolongation of the work of the old by the new. [66]

Ortega did not regard his own generation as having fallen into this normal pattern. He complained repeatedly that he and his coevals had lacked teachers and that they had had to go to Europe for an education that they should have been able to receive in Spain. One of the most unlucky generations that history had ever known, according to Ortega, they had never had the sensation of floating with the current of their times. Yet Ortega's depiction of his own generation and its relationship to those which had preceded it was exaggerated. Already by the mid-1920s it was clear that Ortega's age-group of intellectuals had carried out the work of their predecessors by pursuing the critique of Spanish values and institutions with the aid of European ideas and concepts to which they had first been introduced by the writers of '98. To be sure, the experience of living outside Spain and attending foreign universities set them off from their predecessors, who had seldom abandoned the national soil. Indeed, it may have been the sojourn experience—and the acute sense of a difference in level between life in Germany and life in Spain that this experience brought with it—that gave rise to Ortega's idea of vital horizon, despite the references to phenomenology and the new biology with which he later surrounded the concept. Yet the ambition Ortega conceived for Spain—national revival—and even the means by which he pursued it—the integration of Spanish intellectual life into the mainstream of European culture—were inherited from the men of '98 and rooted in the peculiar dynamics of the Spanish situation.

Spanish reality also inspired Ortega's concept of the fifteen-year interval separating generations, despite his elaborate and logically faulty effort to derive it from "the structure of human life." It was Ortega's friend and mentor Azorín who first made reference in 1910 to the fifteen-year interval separating generations. By the mid-1920s it was widely accepted that Spanish intellectuals could be divided into three age-groups: the generation of 1898; the generation of 1914, of whom Ortega was said to be the leading exemplar; and the generation of postwar youth, who had supposedly capitulated to the charms of Primo de Rivera's dictatorship. Ortega was slow to abandon the traditional model of three coexisting familial generations separated by intervals of thirty years. But when he did, he formulated his position in the form of a universally valid historical law. Historical reality, he said, *always* consisted of two groups of men: one between the ages of forty-five and sixty, which commanded power; and another between the ages of thirty and forty-five, which sought power. This "historical law" would provoke smiles (or sneers) today. Yet as crude as it may be as an analytical instrument, it led Ortega to an interesting interpretation of contemporary history. He had long been convinced that the roots of the twentieth-century sensibility were to be found in fin-de-siècle France among the revolutionary syndicalists and Maurrassians who opposed parliamentary democracy and preached direct action. By 1933 he was willing to argue that a new type of life had begun in 1917 and ended in 1932, thus validating the measure of fifteen years. This new type of life had as its most evident expressions Fascism, Communism, Cubism, Dadaism, and Surrealism, movements characterized by a passionate desire for destruction. Curiously, in his eagerness to proclaim these movements "null and void" in the eyes of history, Ortega failed to follow the dictates of his own theory. If he had, he would have noticed that these movements were all led by men between the ages of thirty and forty-five and that, far from being finished historically, they were bound to dominate European life during the years between 1933 and 1945, as in fact they did. [67]

Ortega liked to say that every nation, every epoch, and every individual was an organ for the perception of truth. Truth was achieved through the mechanism of perspective. Indeed, Ortega believed that truth *was* perspective. In accepting the limitations inherent in one's vantage point—or as Ortega often put it, in embracing one's destiny—one gained insight into the nature of reality. As a Spaniard writing in the early twentieth century, Ortega's special contribution to an understanding of the "generation of 1914" was his analysis of the characteristics of cultural crisis, a state of interregnum in which men awaited with impatience the emergence of a new form of life. The Spanish situation facilitated this insight. Since 1900 the mood in Spain had been one of expectation. Sensibility had changed, the level of thinking had risen, industry and commerce had begun to develop, but political life seemed to continue unaffected, a mere fantasy of days now past. This mood existed everywhere in Europe; but nowhere was it stronger than in Spain, where intellectuals wavered between hope that everything was on the verge of changing and despair provoked by the failure of things to change. The description of the psychology of crisis that Ortega gave in the lectures on Galileo was based on a life-time's observation and can be applied to early twentieth-century Europe as a whole, so long as one specifies with care the social groups to which the description applies.

One does not know what new thing to think—one only knows, or thinks he knows, that the traditional norms and ideas are false and inadmissible. One feels a profound disdain for everything, or almost everything, that was believed yesterday; but the truth is that there are no new positive beliefs with which to replace the traditional ones. Since that system of convictions, that world, was the map that permitted man to move within his environment with a certain security, and since he now lacks such a map, he again feels himself lost, at loose ends, without orientation. He moves from here to there without order or arrangement; he tries this side and then the other, but without complete convictions; he pretends to himself that he is convinced of this or that. . . . Since at heart he is not convinced of anything positive and therefore is not truly decided about anything, man and indeed the masses of men will move from white to black with the greatest of ease . . . Such a structure of life opens a wide margin for very diverse emotional tonalities as a mask for life; very diverse, but all belonging to the same negative type. On feeling himself lost, man may respond with skeptical frigidity, with anguish, or with desperation and he will do many things, which though apparently heroic, do not in fact proceed from any real heroism but are deeds done in desperation. Or he will have a sense of fury, of madness, an appetite for vengeance, because of the emptiness of his life; these will drive him to enjoy brutally, cynically, whatever comes his way—flesh, luxury, power. Life takes on a bitter flavor. [68]

Ortega was quick to admit that the doctrine of perspectivism entailed the idea that one truth was won at the expense of overlooking or distorting another. Error, he admitted, was inherent in every insight. What Ortega failed to see from the vantage point of the Spanish penisnula—and what was perhaps not so easily seen—was that the generational phenomenon as he perceived it might itself be the reflection of a certain kind of social group in a certain kind of society at a certain moment in history. Ortega's "generations" were none other than age-groupings of Mannheim's "free-swinging" intellectuals, adrift, uncertain of their role, convinced that their moment had arrived, and yet nonetheless without the influence and power they felt they deserved in a society torn by discord and about to enter the age of mass politics and rapid economic development. The tragedy of Ortega and the intellectuals who followed him was their inability to establish and maintain their leadership of the Spanish people during this period of transition from one kind of society to another. And that tragedy is to be explained by the unwillingness of the oligarchy to relinquish its power and its privileges and the resulting violence of the masses, who were not so much interested in truth and reason as in justice and vengeance.

Ortega affirmed that every generation had a mission, a project, a task, a *quehacer*. He spent much of his career outlining the task of his own generation and lamenting its failure to perform it. On these topics he was as usual eloquent and unsparing in his criticism. But he was much less convincing when he spoke of the reasons for his generation's failure, and he had little of interest to say about how his generation might have realized its task. He preferred to locate the source of his generation's failure in the distant medieval past or to ascribe it to unfavorable influences from Europe. This was to flee his own responsibility as a Spaniard, an intellectual, and a member of the "generation of 1914." Some day a biographer will unravel for us the complex of factors that gave birth to Ortega's theory of history. It should be a fascinating story. Let us hope that it is soon told. In the meantime, however, we must assume that Ortega's way of thinking about history was shaped by the Spanish environment, his situation within it, and his early experience both inside and outside Spain. A disciple of the writers of '98 who had eschewed politics in favor of the search for an unchanging Spanish national character, a product of the German university system with its passion for *Geist*, a philosopher by profession, and an observer since childhood of the charade of Spanish parliamentary politics, Ortega could never rid himself of the feeling that politics was a secondary phenomenon. What happened in the philosopher's mind, he thought, was infinitely more important than proceedings in parliament—more important even than the shutting down of parliament. As for the masses, their role was to follow the lead of excellent and disinterested men like himself.

These prejudices—or better, these convictions—crippled Ortega's generational theory and reduced it to a shadow of what it might have become. They caused him to forget his own insight, proclaimed in 1914 and repeated vigorously in 1921, that a generation was not a group of outstanding individuals but a dynamic compromise between a minority and a mass. The lectures on Galileo made almost no mention of the masses, except to condemn them; the emphasis was on the decisive role of thinkers like Cicero, St. Augustine, Galileo, and Descartes. Was it because the Spanish masses had proved "indocile" and refused to heed the call of prophets like himself? In any case, not all Spanish intellectuals made the choice or reached the conclusions that Ortega did. And one of the most serious weaknesses of Ortega's generational theory is that, unlike Mannheim's, it makes no effort to take into account the divergence of responses *within* a generation to the question, What are we to do with the world in which we live? Ortega thought that these differences were likely to fade with the perspective of time; but it is just as arguable that the passage of time may make them appear more starkly.[69]

For all his brilliance, Ortega never understood the revolutionary nature of twentieth-century politics; nor did he ever grasp the mechanism by which large numbers of people could be moved and educated in the conditions of mass society. He thought the sun had set on the age of revolution; and he believed that ideas could triumph by their very excellence and truth, simply because the old ideas had lost their power to convince men like himself. It was not enough in 1933 to be right. Truth had become a luxury that was temporarily beyond the means of even the most original thinkers. The proof is that not even Ortega could escape the pounding waves of politics. In 1936 he was forced to flee Spain to avoid the savage partisanship of the Civil War. He did not return until 1945. By then the Spanish "generation of 1914" had lost their chance to regenerate their country.

CHAPTER FIVE

Italy:
Giovinezza! Giovinezza!

We have no other ambition, basically, than to be their teachers, their guides, their prophets, and we would be satisfied to die, like Moses, before the vineyards of the Promised Land.
  Giovanni Papini, 1913

T HE origin of a generation can seldom be traced to a single source. But the organizers of generational movements, the men who transform the consciousness of generational novelty into political and cultural projects, are more easily found. The Italian generation of 1914 was born on the rainy autumn day in Florence in 1899 when the seventeen-year-old Giuseppe Prezzolini met Giovanni Papini. Papini was the older by one year, the poorer by a great deal, and the more self-assured of the two. The son of an artisan and a graduate of the local normal school, he was already exploding with talents that shot off, like fireworks, in different and mutually irreconcilable directions. A poet with an irrepressible desire to philosophize and a philosopher whose philosophies were chosen less for their truth than for their ability to stimulate his imagination, Papini's deepest desire was to play the role of a prophet, a master, an intellectual guide. Sick with the "malady of grandeur," he dreamed of inaugurating a new era, of providing a new faith. Papini seems never to have hesitated in choosing the young generation as his predestined flock. "I would like really to become the spiritual guide of the young, very young, and future Italy," he confided to a friend in 1905. Yet, as a reader of the sociologists Pareto and Mosca, he understood that he must reach and educate an elite within the young generation. In culture as in politics, he believed, it was the few and not the mass who counted. One could maintain one's individuality only by opposing oneself to the plebeian crowd. Thus he set his sights on those "few hundred young men born in Italy around 1880, that is to say *a part* of that generation that has begun to think and to act with the new century." It was this elite that Papini set out to liberate and to lash into action.[1]

This goal was one with which the young Prezzolini could sympathize and associate himself. The son of a prefect with literary ambitions, Prezzolini had shocked his father and demoralized himself by dropping out of secondary school and plunging into a period of anarchistic revolt that ended in skepticism and sullen hostility to all established institutions, above all academic ones.* "Scholar of no school, student of no topic, sworn enemy of all discipline, lacking confidence in himself and extremely proud, cynical, and melancholy," the young Prezzolini was a living example of the intellectual in crisis. Papini saved him from despair by showing him how he could channel the poison and resentment gathering within him into an intellectual guerrilla war against the "older generation." From Papini, Prezzolini learned that "intelligence and culture, the affirmation of one's own creative spirit, and the winged epigram against stupidity" could console him for the loss of the richness and power of the real world, which he felt lay beyond his reach.[2]

Though far too impatient for rigorous or systematic thought, Papini came to understand the dynamics of generational thinking as well as or better than any European social theorist, including Ortega. No better guide to the psychology of generational revolt in early twentieth-century Europe exists than Papini's youthful autobiography *Un uomo finito* [A Finished Man]. Chapter 14 of that work provides a portrait of the generationalist's mentality that is unique for its honesty and insight.

Every time a generation presents itself on the terrace of life it seems that the world's symphony is going to have to attack a new tempo. Dreams, hopes, plans of attack, the ecstasy of discoveries, the scaling of heights, challenges, fits of arrogance—and a journal. Every article has the thunder and the sound of a proclamation; every polemical thrust and witty remark is written in the style of a bulletin announcing a victory; every title is a program; every criticism is a taking of the Bastille; every book is a gospel; every conversation takes on the air of a Catiline conspiracy or a club of sansculottes; and even private letters have the panting and gallop of apostolic warnings. For the twenty-year-old man, every old man is the enemy; every idea is suspect; every great man is there to be put on trial; past history seems a long night broken only by lamps, a grey and impatient waiting, an eternal dawn of that morning that emerges today finally with us. For the twenty-year-old even the sunsets seem to have the white and delicate reflections of the dawn that is late in coming, the torches that accompany the dead are joyful lanterns for the new holidays, the regrets of the bigoted bells are pearls that announce the birth and baptism of souls.[3]

The most revealing thing about these confessions of an unrepentant generationalist, aside from the insistence on the need to throw aside "the cloaks of religion, the cassocks of philosophy, the shirts of prejudice, the ties of ideals, the shoes of logic, and the underwear of morality" in order to become nude like Adam before the Fall, is the admission that this fever to transform others and become their moral guide could have no other outcome in the conditions

---

* This early skepticism about academic institutions did not prevent Prezzolini from later accepting a professorship at Columbia University.

of early twentieth-century Italy than the production of "four, eight, sixteen pages of printed paper—the usual journal." And, indeed, for the next fifteen years Papini and Prezzolini would devote themselves to the production of small reviews designed for young bourgeois elites who felt superior to the masses.[4]

Their first independent venture was a publication called *Leonardo*, which appeared irregularly from 1903 to 1907. Its title suggests the range of their ambition. In the first issue, Papini and Prezzolini identified the editorial staff as a group of young men gathered in Florence, "desirous of liberation, wanting universality, and longing after a superior intellectual life." They were, the editors stated, pagan in life-style and idealist in cultural orientation, and in art they loved the transfiguration of ordinary experience into higher forms of consciousness. The history of *Leonardo* was the story of its enthusiasms: for William James's pragmatism, for Bergson's intuitionism, for Corradini's imperialism, for Croce's philosophical idealism, for Giovanni Vailati's critique of positivist culture, for metapsychology, and finally for the occult arts. While Prezzolini announced the advent of the "Man-God," Papini insisted that philosophy should eliminate all intermediate terms between the knowing subject and the material on which he acted. To act was to know, and the test of truth was the capacity of an ideal to produce an action. Philosophy, Papini preached, should embark upon "the conquest of the world."[5]

More important, though, than the causes Papini and Prezzolini espoused—which came and went in dizzy succession—was what they opposed and how they opposed it. Their primary target was the mediocrity of Italian intellectual life, and their favorite method *la stroncatura*, a violent polemic that spilled over easily into personal abuse. It was the intellectual equivalent of the castor oil treatment that Mussolini's *squadristi* would later use to bring their rivals into line, and Papini became a master at it. As he later explained in his article "Campaign for the Forced Revival," the goal of the intellectuals grouped around *Leonardo* was "to tear people's minds from the furrows of common life and carry them on high to contemplate from afar and in liberty the possible destinies of man and the terrible stupidity of ordinary existence." The present Italians, Papini said, were vile, stupid, and cowardly. He wanted young Italians to have courage, to be bold, to throw caution to the winds, to be crazy, and to have the guts to live life for risk, adventure, dreams, and "eternal programs."[6]

As events later proved, this was dangerous rhetoric. Yet it had formidable appeal for educated middle-class Italians born in the decade of the 1880s. They found Italy mean, ugly, dull. The man who best represented what they disliked in Italy was Giovanni Giolitti. Giolitti, a dour but shrewd bureaucrat from Piedmont, came to power in 1900 and ruled Italy, both in and out of office, for the next fourteen years. Convinced after the parliamentary struggles and street riots of the late 1890s that the Italian people were "mature for liberty," he avoided ideology in favor of temporary alliances with the Socialists, the Catholics, and reactionary elements in the South—whatever was needed to maintain his electoral coalition in power and to see his programs enacted into law. When critics denounced him as a corrupter of Italian civic morals and baptized him "the minister of the underworld," he replied that the imperfections of his system simply reflected the backwardness of Italian conditions. "A tailor who has to cut a suit for a hunchback," he once said, "is obliged to make a hunchback suit." This attitude was scarcely designed to delight the nation's youth, who had been educated by Mazzini's heirs to expect greatness from the newly formed nation. Angered by the lack of ideological coherence and moral fiber in Giolitti's Italy, they overlooked the real strides the country was in the process of making during the fourteen years of his rule. The truth is that between 1900 and 1915 no major nation in Europe made swifter or more dramatic progress than Italy did in upgrading its material well-being and consolidating its international position. Per capita national income rose by 28 percent; the expectation of life at birth rose from twenty to thirty-one years; the consumption of wheat increased by 50 percent; working hours fell from a not uncommon fourteen to a maximum of ten; while the percentage of the population over six that was unable to read and write dropped from almost 50 to 37 percent. Despite the opposition of critics from both the Right and Left, Giolitti bestowed upon the Italians in 1911 a universal manhood suffrage bill, which increased the electorate from 3.3 million to 8.6 million, of whom 3 million were illiterate. In 1911–1912 he even managed to provide his country with a successful colonial war against Turkey, which resulted in the annexation of Libya. What he could not give Italy's youth, especially those trained in secondary schools and set on intellectual professions, was a sense of pride in their country. *"L'Italia come oggi è non ci piace"* [We don't like Italy as it is today], said Giovanni Amendola in 1910, summing up the attitude of the nation's intellectual vanguard.[7]

What exactly was it that they disliked? The question is more easily put than answered, in part because young Italian intellectuals formulated their complaints in a recondite language, rich with classical allusions, that had little evident relationship to the world in which they lived. They complained, for example, of living in a time when heroic leadership had given way to corrupt administration, and they looked forward to a moment when they would discover a new faith and would be able "to unfurl all our sails to the wind and abandon this muddy sea." Only then, one sighed in 1904, would they be able to regain their youth. Yet their discontent went deeper than the impatience of young men with the grey monotony of adult life, deeper even than the fear of having missed an era of romance and great events. They felt within them unused energies for which they found no ready outlet. The new nation, in whose patriotic cult they had been raised, turned out to be a fragile state with gigantic problems and limited prospects. As their young eyes scanned the future they saw rising on the horizon new social classes, like the workers of Genoa and Turin and the bankers and industrialists of Milan, whose values and interests seemed antithetical to their own. Rage at Italy's lack of national power and anxiety concerning the internal social threat mingled in their minds and became one. Their disillusionment with the present was thus in direct proportion to their dreams of civic grandeur, their feelings of frustration, and their uncertainty about the direction of social change. Stung by the discovery of Italian reality, they transformed the myth of present greatness into a hope for future revival. This made them susceptible to the nationalistic lyrics of Gabriele D'Annunzio, who sang vaguely but seductively of a new race of young Italian heroes who would supplant the old and corrupt ruling class. It also made them listen with attention and approval to the Neapolitan philosopher Benedetto Croce, whose historically oriented idealism they misinterpreted to mean that man was above all a creator of ideals who could make and unmake reality, independent of his historical and social circumstances. In the early years of the century, it was between these two poles—that of D'Annunzio's aristocratic aestheticism and Croce's critique of positivism—that Italian culture moved; and as one young Italian literary critic put it, the great mass of Italian youth was with D'Annunzio's byzantine poetry rather than with Croce's sober prose.[8]

By 1907, when Papini and Prezzolini announced the end of *Leonardo*, their policy of a "forced revival" of Italian youth was beginning to bear fruit. Critics of the dominant liberal culture had sprung up all over Italy. Croce had been joined by a young and talented disciple, Giovanni Gentile. Together they propagated the gospel of philosophical idealism and exposed the shaky theoretical foundations of positivist thought. Modernists were calling for a renewal of the Catholic church and a bringing up to date of Catholic faith. Nationalists, led by Enrico Corradini, were demanding an expansionist foreign policy and the subordination of all other values to the higher interests of the state. Syndicalists had begun to challenge the Socialist party for the support of the workers, and revolutionary Socialists like Benito Mussolini were insisting that the Socialist party end its collaboration with Giolitti and embark on a more radical course. What united all these movements—or gave the impression of uniting them—was their common opposition to the moderation of Giolitti's government, their rejection of positivist culture, and their conviction that youth held the answer to Italy's problems. This was nowhere better stated than by the newspaper of the Republican Youth Federation, *Giovine Italia* [Young Italy], which wrote in 1906 that "in the political sphere and especially in Italy only youth can bring that spirit of abnegation and self-sacrifice that the young republicans have demonstrated so ably. Our youth is our revolutionary faith— here is our salvation. The rest is lies and illusions." A few years later the Futurist Marinetti would put the same idea even more crudely: "The oldest among us are not thirty; this means that we have at least ten years to carry out our task. When we are forty, let those younger and more valiant than us kindly throw us into the wastebasket like useless manuscripts."[9]

Always alive to the latest cultural currents in Italy, Prezzolini sensed this atmosphere and saw a chance to oversee the union of the young cultural and political elites. At the same time, his personal development had led him away from the permanent revolution of Papini's individualism toward a greater concern with politics, society, and the institutions of culture. Well aware of the limitations of his own talent, anxious to escape from the disorder of his past, and haunted in a way that Papini never had been by "the incubus of clarity," Prezzolini had gravitated toward Croce's idealism, to which he publicly converted in 1908. In Croce's *Ethics* Prezzolini found the consolation that he had been unable to find in Catholicism and that he had only fleetingly enjoyed in anarchist revolt. Indeed, Prezzolini interpreted Croce's system as a secularized religion, in which History had taken the place of God and the individual had to work for his salvation by carrying out the task that History had assigned him, no matter how minor or unpleasant that task might be. Following Croce, Prezzolini concluded that what Italy needed was not genius or rhetoric, but more character, more culture, more hard work. Not more Papinis (for whose talent and originality Prezzolini always retained the greatest respect) but a Prezzolini who was willing to devote himself modestly but energetically to the pressing task of civic education and the reform of national mores. The time had come to pass from the cultivation of the individual to the transformation of society. Why not organize the opposition to Giolitti's Italy? Why not bring together the minorities in revolt against the tired and self-satisfied majorities and see if Italy's youth were not capable of giving the country a new direction and a new morality? Why not use culture to transform politics? Out of these reflections and the personal travail that lay behind them came Prezzolini's decision to launch a new journal, *La Voce* [The Voice], which first appeared in December 1908.[10]

La Voce was a great success. *Leonardo*, for all the attention it ended by getting, had never had more than two hundred subscribers at its peak; *La Voce* soon had a thousand and sometimes sold another two thousand copies on newsstands. The greater success of *La Voce* reflected the greater range of its collaborators. Mostly in their twenties, they came from every region of Italy and represented every field of contemporary Italian culture. Equally unusual was the fact that they took care to be well informed. Scipio Slataper (1888), whose promising literary career would be cut off by his death in the Great War, reported on the situation in his home town of Trieste and stood in as editor when Prezzolini was away or indisposed. Ardengo Soffici, painter, novelist, and gadfly, kept the readers of *La Voce* up to date on the progress of French art. Emilio Cecchi (1884) and Renato Serra (1884) reviewed novels, plays, and poetry, both Italian and foreign. Piero Jahier (1884) could be counted upon for reportage, sketches, and occasional poems. The educational philosophers Vito Fazio Allmayer (1885) and Giuseppe Lombardo Radice (1879) argued the need for university reform, while the historian Antonio Anzilotti (1885) reviewed contemporary Italian historiography. Giovanni Boine (1887) was always willing to polemicize against the anticlericals in the name of a modernized Catholicism. Giovanni Amendola (1882), a philosopher from Naples, reviewed developments in Italian politics and followed carefully and critically the development of the Nationalist movement; while Gaetano Salvemini (1873), the volatile ex-Socialist professor from Apulia, wrote passionately and frequently of the crisis in the secondary schools and the neglect of the South. Prezzolini himself was an indefatigable contributor, as well as an organizer of his collaborators' efforts. Papini, as usual, wrote on anything that struck his fancy—madly, irreverently, irresponsibly, but with such a combination of literary skill and insight that no one could ignore him. [11]

During its first few years, *La Voce* came close to fitting Prezzolini's description of its content as "what young [educated] Italy thinks." [12] Yet for all its brilliance and for all the range of its collaborators, *La Voce* failed to furnish a real alternative to Giolitti's Italy. Prezzolini could not make up his mind whether the journal was to be simply critical, or whether it should pass beyond the gathering of information and the assembling of talents to a committed politics, in which case the question of implementing its policies would arise. *La Voce*'s editor confronted this dilemma honestly, if ambiguously, in 1910 in an article entitled "What Is to Be Done?" Present-day democracy, he said, no longer satisfied "honest souls." All it represented was a lowering of every standard in the name of individual improvement and the triumph in reality of the interests of the greedy and the powerful. The same compromises and fuzzing of moral boundaries could be seen everywhere—in the universities, where professors diluted their courses; in the elections, which the government managed; and even in the Socialist party, where the parliamentary group renounced its principles and voted for a bourgeois ministry. "Everything is declining," Prezzolini lamented. "Every ideal is disappearing. The parties no longer exist, but only splinter groups and clienteles. . . . Everything is coming apart at the seams." The great forces of opposition, like the Socialists and the Catholics, were surrendering to a general "mushiness" and moral disintegration. Nor was Corradini's Nationalist movement an answer, because, in addition to appealing to the rhetorical inclinations of the Italians, it held the danger of a disastrous war with Austria and distracted attention away from Italy's pressing internal problems, such as the South, the reform of the educational system, the need for regional decentralization, and the relationship between church and state. "The disgust is enormous. The best no longer have confidence. The young, if they are not opportunists and spineless, no longer enter the parties." Prezzolini confessed that he himself had no clear idea of what to do, except to abstain from taking part in those present movements (like Nationalism) that were heading toward a general disaster.

On the other hand, Prezzolini recognized that abstention was no answer. Dirtying one's hands was the price one paid for the improvement of humanity. But what kind of action was worth the price and likely to be effective? Noting that the only kind of true renewal was the continuation of that which already existed, Prezzolini warned against the illusion of a revolutionary politics. This illusion, he confessed, had prevented him in the past from acting more effectively. It was necessary to give less value to protest against the system and more to action within the system. The principal objective of Italian youth should be to acquire technical competence. They should infiltrate and renew existing institutions to which they could have easy and immediate access: the municipalities; the railroads; the schools; the public libraries; the newspapers; the banks; the clergy; the state bureaucracy; the working-class organizations. Only by acquiring the necessary technical skills and eliminating his prejudices could a young man of today be of use in the world of tomorrow. The true nationalism consisted in training Italians to master technology, not in swelling heads with lies and absurdities, as Corradini's Nationalists were doing. "The task is long," he concluded. "But if our generation goes to its death without having realized at least a part of it, then we'd be better off making the sign of the cross and throwing ourselves into the Arno." [13]

Despite the call to action with which his article ended, Prezzolini's personal preference was for pedagogy rather than for politics. He wished to use his journal to clarify, from the heights of Crocean idealism, vital issues of Italian public life. Some of his closest collaborators found Prezzolini's approach too Olympian and hankered after other, less detached forms of action. The result was a split, precipitated by the coming of the Libyan war in 1911. Salvemini, a man of strongly antiimperialist convictions, felt that Prezzolini had not committed the journal fully to the struggle against Giolitti's war. The *Vociani*, he wrote Prezzolini, were not a single group or even two; they were ten or twenty groups, living on the margin of the other parties. The time had come to achieve a unity of political outlook and to pass to action. Papini, by contrast, had long been dissatisfied with the social commitment of *La Voce*. He insisted on restoring the journal to what (in his mind) it had originally been designed to be: an open forum for the furnishing of serious and reliable information and a literary organ. "Give us this day our daily poetry," he demanded in a famous article published in 1912. Enough of this obsession with sacrifice, education, and material improvement. [14]

As a result of these divisions, Prezzolini temporarily abandoned the editorship of the review, various grouplets came into being, and a series of splinter journals were founded. Salvemini created *L'Unità*, whose task he defined as the political education of a few thousand young men now dispersed throughout the various parties. Amendola withdrew and devoted himself to journalism and his philosophical review, *L'Anima*. And Papini and Soffici, bored by Prezzolini's unrelenting seriousness and eager to relive the rebelliousness of their youth, declared themselves Futurists and launched a journal called *Lacerba*, which announced in its first issue that it intended to subordinate national interests to the needs of individual genius. Discouraged by the desertion of his friends and crushed by personal problems, Prezzolini gave up his attempt to preserve the ideological heterogeneity of *La Voce* and declared it an organ of "militant idealism," by which he evidently meant that it would combine the philosophical idealism of Croce with the uncompromising combativeness of youth. The new formula failed to work. Prezzolini once more withdrew, and the journal was devoted exclusively to literature. Like all generational coalitions, the Vociani had fallen out over the question of "what to do."

SO things stood in 1914 when events came providentially to provide the formula of unity that individuals had been unable to supply. When war broke out in August, the Italian premier and foreign minister decided on a course of neutrality. Their decision was approved by the cabinet and made public on August 2, the day Germany declared war on France. With the exception of the Nationalist party, most sectors of Italian opinion applauded the decision not to enter the war on the side of the Central Powers. What interest, after all, could Italy have in strengthening Austria-Hungary's position in the Balkans? The Italian government, however, found itself faced with a delicate problem that soon became an issue of public concern. Should Italy remain neutral, in which case the Italians would have to face the displeasure of their former allies if the Central Powers won; or should it denounce its alliance with Germany and Austria-Hungary and enter the war on the side of the Entente, thus putting itself in a position to reap some territorial advantage from the Central Powers' defeat? By September 1914 a broad coalition had formed that called for intervention on the side of England, France, and Russia; and within this coalition the noisiest and most active groups were those who claimed to represent "Italian youth" and the "younger generation."

The intellectuals who led the struggle for intervention were driven by a wide variety of motives. Some, like Salvemini, saw the war as an opportunity to liquidate the last vestiges of Habsburg tyranny and to realize Mazzini's dream of a Europe of free and democratically governed peoples. Others, like Papini and Soffici, were moved by sympathy for France and an aversion to Germany and German culture. Still others, like Scipio Slataper and Prezzolini, felt that Italy had no choice, if the Italians wished their country to remain (or become) a great European power.[15]

Yet underlying all these arguments, fueling the passion with which they were advanced, creating secret bonds of sympathy among the interventionists, and rendering them immune to counter-argument, was a feverish and intoxicating feeling that the war offered a once-in-a-lifetime opportunity to destroy the Giolittian regime, to throw off the fetters of bourgeois existence, and to open the way toward some ill-defined but radically different future. The cause of intervention thus became identified with the cause of subverting the liberal regime; and it was but one short rhetorical step to present the interventionist movement as a "revolution" of youth against age. War, Marinetti declared in his manifesto to students in November 1914, would kill conservatism (*il passa-tismo*) and would exhaust the representatives of the past (*i passatisti*) because "only war knows how to rejuvenate, accelerate and sharpen human in-telligence, to make more joyful and air the nerves, to liberate us from the weight of daily burdens, to give savor to life, and talent to imbeciles." [16]

Sentiments like these were not confined to Futurists. In February 1915 one young interventionist named Paolo Marconi recorded in his diary: "This is the hour of the courageous and the strong; this is the hour of the triumph of the most worthy values; this is the hour of youth, since the new age belongs to the young men who are maturing; our age, our tomorrow—we ourselves want to create it." And a month later: "We come out of a generation of bastards who failed to make Italy and did not know how to make Italians. Down with the old men! Enough of this nonsense! The new generation enters upon the scene with a new spirit and intends to lead a new life . . . A young man today cannot help but be revolutionary. And whoever is not a revolutionary is not young. Down with the old men of twenty [who do not favor war]!" Even so calm and antirhetorical a spirit as *La Voce*'s literary critic Renato Serra yielded to the wave of enthusiasm that was engulfing Italy's educated youth. The war would not achieve the aims that young people were claiming for it, Serra wrote in his influential *Esame di coscienza di un letterato* [Examination of Conscience by a Literary Man], which was first published in *La Voce*. It would not revolu-tionize Italy; nor would it create a new and more profound literature, as many writers were claiming. Yet it had to be fought, for otherwise the young men of his generation would have missed their only opportunity to live intensely. They would have let slip by their chance to seize the absolute, to experience to the full their historical moment. Though known in advance to be useless, the sac-rifice must be made. Otherwise those Italians who were now young would have to live knowing that they had failed for the rest of their lives. "We shall have been on the verge, on the extreme limit; the wind came upon us and raised the hair on our foreheads; in our immobile feet we felt the dizziness of movement. And we did not budge. We shall get old remembering this. We, those of my generation; those who have reached the limit or just barely passed it; failures or heroes." [17]

Serra's essay was a model of ice-cold rationality in comparison to the lava-like literature that flowed from the pens of more impassioned interventionists. For them, the war was "the hour of the world." It was "the hour of renewal: of death and life laced together in a knot of bloody intoxication." It was a moment of "apocalyptic transition" that must be regarded with courage, understood with penetration, and lived in transport. It was the "superb spectacle" of humanity in the "travail of its crisis." It was a "religious rite" that no "conspiracy" could avert, no action of reasoning could exorcise. All around, "small men" took flight, "dazzled and destroyed." [18]

In retrospect, what impresses one in language like this—aside from the tendency to portray war in aesthetic terms, thus distorting and concealing its true nature—is the willingness of Italy's intellectuals to plunge their countrymen into the war for reasons that can only be called subjective and determined by group interest. The intellectuals arrogated to themselves the right and duty to interpret the destiny of their fellow citizens—the *umili* or humble ones, who would have to bear the burden and endure the sufferings of war. They equated their subjective feelings of relief and liberation with the design of providence or history, thus suggesting that what they had willed was an inevitable fact of nature. At the same time, they made it clear that they regarded the war as an opportunity to seize political leadership from the hands of the old ruling elites and to pass it on to new men like themselves, who represented contemporary culture. Papini, with his talent for expressing what large sectors of the educated middle classes felt, put the point most directly. The interventionists—whom Papini referred to as "the young generation"—intended to take the place of the "old generation" [that is, the Giolittian establishment], and the war was only a beginning. Afterward would come a total change of the ruling class. "We're here and getting ready." [19]

The interventionists had their way. They lashed Italy into war as one might whip a sleepy horse into a gallop. Or so it seemed during the "radiant days" of May 1915 when youth, spurred on by D'Annunzio and Marinetti, descended into the piazzas of Italy demanding war, and the king and his ministers appeared to yield before the threat of a potentially revolutionary mass movement. Today we know that the decison to intervene was not imposed by crowds in the piazza; just as we know that the men who made the decision in favor of war— the premier Salandra and his foreign minister Sonnino, supported by the king—were motivated by concerns of territorial advantage and national aggrandizement that had little to do with the sentiments of the younger generation. Nevertheless, interventionists took away from these events the impression that the united forces of "youth" had imposed a revolutionary war on a reluctant and hopelessly bourgeois nation. This myth would not die easily.

Thus from the beginning, Italy's war possessed some distinctive characteristics. In other European countries parliament chose freely to enter the war, or at least was united in supporting it; in Italy the choice was forced on a lukewarm parliament and an indifferent country by extraparliamentary forces with ominous and—it now seems—predictable results. The neutralist majority, composed of Giolittian liberals, Socialists, and Catholics, accepted the war, agreed to do their duty, for the most part did it, but made no secret of the fact that they resented the way in which the decision for war had been made. The interventionist minority were forced to defend the war, to justify it even after events had called its wisdom into question, and to guard zealously against any slackening of the national will. This meant that differences among the interventionists over Italy's war aims had to be subordinated for the duration to the campaign against those people who were believed to lack enthusiasm for the continuation of the war. Intervention, it turned out, was like an express train: Once on board, no one could disembark until the vehicle had reached its final destination.[20]

The political split between interventionists and neutralists was reflected in the hierarchical constitution of the army. The nonprofessional officers, most of them young and almost all of them recruited from the educated middle classes, approached the war with enthusiasm and often with selfless dedication. They could identify with the war's aims and envision themselves as completing the work begun during the Risorgimento by their grandfathers. The mass of soldiers, most of them peasants and many from the South and islands where disaffection from the central government was most acute, at best endured the war with resignation and at worst hoped for a speedy resolution (of whatever kind) that would allow them to return home and to rejoin their families. To many of them the war seemed absurd; after all, Italian territory was not occupied and evident national interests were not at stake. What could Trieste or the Trentino mean to an unschooled Calabrian peasant whose knowledge of Italian geography was probably no better than his knowledge of Italian? Why die for the greater glory of a state whose only concrete embodiments were the local *carabinieri* and the tax collector? Was not the war, like the unified state itself, another caprice of the *signori,* to be paid for by the *contadini?* These attitudes created a serious problem for interventionist officers, who quickly came to understand that their patriotic ideals were not shared by their soldiers.

Yet the shared sufferings of war eventually brought young bourgeois officers and their men together and presented them with a common enemy: the shirker or *imboscato* who lived off the blood of the trench fighter or *combattente* and avoided the perils of the front.* Since many industrial workers had been released from front-line service to work in war plants located in or near the cities, the antagonism between combattenti and imboscati became identified on the one hand with the distinction between bourgeois patriots and worker socialists and on the other with the distinction between the countryside and the corrupt, pleasure-loving town. These antagonisms would have been muted if the war had been short, or if the Italian army had been well and intelligently treated. Instead, the Italian war dragged on with little hope of victory and the Italian army was ill fed, ill clothed, and kept in the field by coercion and the threat of decimation. This dangerous situation turned into a national disaster in October 1917, when the Austro-Hungarian forces, spearheaded by German elite troops

---

* The concept of the *imboscato* varied according to the vantage point of the user. For the infantrymen the artillery corps was imboscato, and for the whole army the Italians who were not in the war zone were all imboscati. The trench fighter divided the army into four categories: (1) *i fessi* (the asses), like himself, who fought in the front lines; (2) *i fissi* (those comfortably quartered), who were attached to the command from the division level up; (3) *gli italiani* (the Italians), who were safely behind the lines; and (4) *gli italianissimi* (the most Italian of Italians), who lived in the heart of the country. Piero Melograni, *Storia politica della grande guerra (1914–1918)* (Bari, 1969), p. 111.

from the Eastern Front, penetrated the Italian lines at Caporetto and pushed the Italians back behind the Piave river, occupying Italian soil for the first time during the course of the war and threatening the city of Venice. Fearful that Italy's always fragile will to resist would collapse completely, the interventionists pushed for the further limitation of parliamentary government and the setting up of an authoritarian Committee of Public Safety committed to the vigorous prosecution of the war.[21]

It is at this point that Benito Mussolini enters our story. Mussolini (1883) is customarily portrayed as a power-hungry opportunist, a ruthless manipulator of the masses, and a cynic who lacked all conviction. Mussolini was all these things, especially after he achieved absolute power in the late 1920s; but none of these characteristics distinguishes him from numerous other European statesmen of the period nor explains the fascination he exerted over his contemporaries. The young Mussolini possessed an extraordinary sense for the mood of the masses and the revolutionary possibilities of twentieth-century politics, based on his belief that reality was not a stable structure controlled by knowable law, but a mobile, shifting, ever changing construction that could be dominated by the will of forceful men. "Great things are not achieved with protocols, but by guessing the direction of one's century," was a sentence that Mussolini copied admiringly from one of Mazzini's works and entered in his wartime diary. "The secret of power lies in will." The difference between the two leaders was that Mussolini's commitment was to the activity of domination and not to any specific end. Humanity was mere clay to be molded by Nietzschean artists, and ideals were the tools with which the great man worked. Ultimately, it was action that mattered and gave value to life's otherwise monotonous course. As a young man, Mussolini noted that "movement" was the word that gave the twentieth century its unmistakable character. "We want to act, produce, dominate matter, enjoy the kind of triumph that exasperates illusions, that multiplies life's energies, and reaches toward other ends, toward other horizons, toward other ideals." Even today one could hardly devise a sentence that better describes the arc of Mussolini's life or the essence of his political creed than this one.[22]

In 1917 Mussolini already had behind him a decade of experience as the leader of a generational revolt within the Socialist party, where during the years between 1912 and 1914 he had been the hero of the young cadres who wished to launch a more aggressive and frontal attack on the citadel of the bourgeois state. Expelled from the party in the fall of 1914 for his espousal of intervention, Mussolini had soon emerged as one of the most vigorous and active leaders of the interventionist movement. His newspaper *Il Popolo d'Italia*, with its confused mixture of Mazzinian and Marxist ideology, became the rallying point for left-wing interventionists who placed their hopes for social change in a democratic and revolutionary war. Wounded seriously and released from the army after serving as a volunteer in the Bersaglieri, he led the campaign in

1917 for the dissolution of parliament and the setting up of an authoritarian cabinet along the lines of Clemenceau's government in France. As the Italian war entered its last year, Mussolini found himself isolated and without a public for his journal or a dependable clientele for his political career. The working-class movement, which was strongly internationalist and attracted by the Bolshevik model of world revolution, could not forgive him his interventionism and his call for class collaboration. The liberals were repelled by his activism and revolutionary rhetoric; the Catholics by his anticlericalism; the monarchists by his republicanism; the Nationalists by his antimilitarist past and his commitment to social reform. With the world veering left and his credit in working-class circles exhausted, there seemed to be no outlet for his energy and his driving ambition.

A violent man of sudden moods and irrepressible urges, Mussolini talked of abandoning his country and emigrating to America. But never seriously and not for long. For he had faith—in himself, in the incapacity of his opponents, and in the certitude that the war was going to result in a radical political reorientation. He believed that the old ideological labels—"democracy," "radicalism," "republicanism," "liberalism," and even "socialism"—would take on new meanings in the postwar world, or else lose their meanings altogether. New hierarchies and new values would emerge. The music of tomorrow would be played to a new tempo. And the "old men" who clung on to the "old mental schemes" and remained in the "old parties" would be swept aside. They would miss the train and be left gaping on the platform, with their faces twisted into grimaces somewhere "between idiocy and spite." [23]

Mussolini himself had changed drastically during the war. He was more resolute, more hardened, more reconciled to the use of violence, more conscious of the infinite pliability of the masses with whom he had lived at the front, and at the same time more open to nationalist and imperialist ideas. He had seen and felt that class had less power as a moving myth than the nation. Thus, foraging about for a new clientele with which to pursue his vocation as a public man and a leader of masses, Mussolini turned to the one group to which he felt bound and with which he had maintained good relations: the men of the front, the combattenti. On August 1, 1918, he changed the subtitle of his paper from "socialist daily" to "daily of the combatants and producers," taking care to point out that "not all the soldiers are combatants and not all the combatants are soldiers." By the end of the year he had made it clear that among the mass of the combatants, it was above all the young reserve officers—a group he christened "the trenchocracy"—that he intended to represent. The reserve officers, he said, had been the real "authors of victory." "The soldier is the mass, the stupid mass, powerful but inert, without a propulsive force that gives direction to his effort and establishes the objectives to be attained. The officers have been this force . . . They are the elite of the new aristocracy, of the Italian trenchocracy." [24]

The social group toward which Mussolini turned represented a force of uncertain but potentially important proportions. Not a class in itself but an amalgam of classes, it was bound together by a mentality. This mentality, known as *combattentismo*, combined nationalist and socialist motifs in a general and often naive demand for a purification of politics and a renewal of national mores. The call for reform went hand in hand with the charge that civilian Italy had betrayed fighting Italy. As one interventionist put it shortly after Caporetto, a dichotomy existed between the Italy of the past and that of the future, between the "prejudiced, bureaucratic, timid, flaccid, unaware Italy" and the "new Italy." Under special accusation was the parliamentary institution, "considered the center of every civic malady, of every maneuver against the nation, the receptacle of defeatists and incompetents." "Down with the old parties! Let us have new talents! Let us have new energy!" these disaffected veterans cried. "We recognize no other parties than that of the motherland, than that of those who have done their duty, than that of those who have spilled their blood."[25]

This cluster of attitudes was widely diffused throughout the mass of veterans who made their way home during the nine months between the end of the war and the summer of 1919; but it found its most enthusiastic adherents among young reserve officers from the professional and bureaucratic classes, who had no previous political experience and who regarded the war idealistically and unrealistically as a "revolution" against the established order. Devoid, for the most part, of political ideas but full of resentment and anger, they were quick to transform their war experience—the only intellectual capital most of them had—into a political myth. Not all of these veterans were reactionary; many had democratic inclinations; and some were favorable, at least at the beginning, to the Wilsonian program of national self-determination and a just peace. But others, more uprooted, more politically ambitious, and more attracted by a Bohemian existence, gathered in the large cities and forged alliances with partisans of existing radical movements, like the Republicans, the Syndicalists, and the Futurists—alliances that were aimed vaguely but alluringly at the renovation of politics *and* culture. Prominent among these urban veterans were the Arditi, the Italian equivalents of the German storm troopers, whose leaders had taken up residence in Milan and fallen under the influence of Marinetti. The leaders of this group would urge D'Annunzio to march on Fiume and, once the city had been seized, would flock to join his legions.[26]

These uprooted Bohemian intellectuals, especially the Arditi, were the people toward whom Mussolini moved in the last months of the war and the first months of 1919. He sought out their leaders, surrounded himself with their symbols and their weapons, opened his journal to their manifestos and their letters, turned himself into a mirror reflecting their conception of the world, used images that would appeal to their anger and their pride, and presented himself as a champion of their rights against the "other Italy." Addressing the

Bersaglieri of Trieste in December 1918, for example, he promised that no one would be allowed to steal what was rightfully theirs. "I promise you solemnly that I will defend with my pen and with every other means what belongs to you. First you, then the others." The decision to form the Fasci di combattimento in March 1919 represented a further milestone in Mussolini's journey from the proletariat to the elite of the producers and combatants. By calling for the organization of loosely defined "fighting groups" open to men of all political persuasions, he sought to appeal to the antiparliamentary mood of returning veterans and at the same time to affirm the (fragile) historical link between interventionism, a movement of minorities, and the mass phenomenon of combattentismo. "Holding ourselves firmly on the ground of interventionism," he announced in his first Fascist appeal, ". . . we demand the right and proclaim the duty to transform Italian life, if necessary even with revolutionary methods." [27]

Typical of the first recruits who responded to Mussolini's summons were Italo Balbo and Giuseppe Bottai. A rabid interventionist and a volunteer, Balbo (1896) had fought as an aviator and as a member of the Arditi right up to the last two campaigns of the war, winning in the process one bronze and two silver medals. His prewar political background had been Mazzinian, and at the age of fourteen he had run off to join a prewar expedition aimed at liberating the Albanians from the Turks. In 1915, when he volunteered for military service, Balbo was, according to his own description, "a child of the century," by which he meant that he was anticlerical, democratic, republican, anti-Austrian, opposed to the German program of brute force and hegemony, and a believer in Latin fraternity and the superiority of Western culture. These values faded or at least were radically transformed between 1915 and 1919. Balbo returned from the war full of hate for the enemy in the rear and persuaded that the liberal politicians had betrayed the combatants by accepting a shameful peace. He had not fought, he later claimed, in order to return to the country of Giolitti, who made commerce of every ideal. No. Better to deny everything, to destroy everything, so that everything could be renovated from the foundations up. If it had not been for Mussolini, Balbo asserted, three-quarters of Italian youth returning from the trenches would have become Bolsheviks, for they wanted a revolution at any cost. But Mussolini changed the course of events. He gave fighting youth the program of radical negation they sought; and beyond the overthrow of the existing system, he offered them a positive vision: the regime of the young, a nation of victors, the Fascist state. Taking a dagger and a sack of hand grenades from a deserted garrison, Balbo joined the Fascist movement and became one of Mussolini's most reliable lieutenants. Balbo "intuited that in order to make their way the young had to fight to the end, without remission against the decrepit Italy of the parliamentary government. He was ready. The war had taught him to command and to obey." In 1922 Balbo was in charge of the Fascist military command that organized the march on

Rome. No Fascist leader had a greater reputation for ruthlessness or personal heroism. *"Tutto osare"* (dare everything) was his motto. Destruction and intimidation were his favored methods. Action for action's sake was his only code. [28]

Giuseppe Bottai's path to Fascism was similar to Balbo's. A machinegunner and Ardito who spent two years in the trenches before being invalided out of the army, he came home to find that he had no country. At first, Bottai (1895) turned to poetry to express his disillusionment. His postwar poems were full of the twilight tones of the Italian Decadent poets, whose cadences and sentiments he had long admired. But unlike the poetry of the Decadents, Bottai's was transparently political. "One returns from those parts [the front] with the soul deeply absorbed in thought. Men press themselves upon you with their brawls and disputes. The congested cities cry at you their lies . . . One walks as in the shadows, guided by an obscure sense of the good, toward a faraway country, and all the ways of the world heighten one's desire for this destination that, perhaps, does not exist . . . A country—where? . . . At which crossroads, from which ridge, on which beach will the country appear before us, tidy and serene? . . . Someone looks and smiles: 'there is no country.' " In the midst of this despair and confusion, the young Bottai met Mussolini and became convinced that literature must be sacrificed to concrete political activity, in which Bottai now saw a new and higher synthesis of thought and action. From this point on, he had nothing but scorn for moral or aesthetic neutralism. Socialism was bad because it generated cowardice and did away with risk and creative tension; Fascism was good because it elevated the human spirit and appealed to what was noble in man. In May 1921 Bottai became the youngest deputy elected to the Italian parliament, running on a platform that subordinated political, social, and economic reform to "moral regeneration." During the march on Rome he led a column of blackshirts into the city through a working-class quarter at the expense of thirteen lives. [29]

It is easy to see how Fascism attracted young men like Balbo and Bottai. It was subversive in its attitude toward the officially constituted government; it was nationalist in its defense of the war against the internationalists who insisted on its uselessness; it was violent and pitiless in its methods; it affirmed the superiority of spirit over matter, of action and instinct over thought, and of the impetuousness of youth over the vacillation and corruption of age; it offered a means of carrying over into peacetime the attitudes and relationships typical of the front; and it provided employment for youthful energies and abilities in the name of ideals that young men could respect. Mussolini manipulated his young clientele with the faultless movements of a master showman. Here from his pen is a description of an early Fascist meeting in Milan.

From seven on—the meeting was called for nine—the piazza was reconnoitered by our advance patrols, but little by little, a crowd of citizens filtered across the police lines and grouped themselves around the truck that was going to serve as tribune. Silence. An explosion. A meeting of trench soldiers opens in a trench soldier's way. A 'Very' pistol launches a magnificent white rocket-burst that streaks the sky and falls on the acclaiming crowd. A crowd that becomes silent, withdrawn, almost meditative. The impetuous youth of the Arditi pass in vibrant waves, as they sing their immortal song, Giovinezza! Giovinezza! Suddenly the crowd becomes immobile. It listens. In the dim light of the streetlamps and the smoky glow of the torches blown in the wind, the brown faces, cut on the good old Roman and Italian model, emerge clearly from the play of shadow and light. The orators take their turn at the tribune and the crowd shows no sign of impatience.

What did these speakers say? Mussolini does not tell us, be we can be sure that somewhere in his own speech he inserted this line or its equivalent, "Life is warfare and battle: yesterday against the foreign enemy . . . today against the domestic enemy nested in the trenches of politics." This was what the Balbos and Bottais had come to hear and what they believed to be the truth.[30]

Mussolini was much too clever and ambitious to remain trapped within the veterans' perspective. Fascism, he insisted from the beginning, was above all a state of mind: It was a "movement of reality, of truth, of life that adheres to life." As a man who adhered to the lessons of life and a former Bersagliere who adjusted his fire to the moving target of reality, Mussolini understood before long that the Fascist state of mind was beginning to appeal to larger sectors of the middle classes, especially to students too young to have served in the war. This discovery elicited a subtle but decisive change in his rhetoric. He deemphasized (without entirely dropping) the subversive and Bohemian elements of the first Fascist program, and he increasingly portrayed the Fascist movement as a movement of "youth." "Youth" became a social category and a political slogan that made it possible to merge the aspirations of the combattenti with the aspirations of a larger social coalition. The members of this larger social coalition were seeking a third way between what they perceived to be the equally blind alleys of socialism and liberalism. They longed for a "revolution" that would eliminate class conflict without calling into question the priority of property rights and production over social justice or the superiority of mental over physical labor. In July 1919 Mussolini explained that Fascism was attracting the sympathies of "the Youth of the trenches and the schools" because "in the *fasci* there is not the mildew of the old ideas, the venerable beard of the old men, the hierarchy of conventional values, but there is youth, there is impetousness and faith." On July 3, 1920, he made it clear that one did not have to be a combatant to join the Fascist movement. "We are also ᵔccepting those who for legitimate reasons were unable to participate in the war." To be a Fascist, he added, all that was required was to be completely flexible, to know how to move "elastically" in reality, and to feel in one's blood the aristocracy of minorities who do not seek popularity. "Fascism is a movement. It is continuous battle, not barren wait." These were requirements that youth, and especially the bourgeois youth of the schools and universities, felt that they could satisfy. In April 1921 Mussolini could exult that the Fascist electoral list gave "the impression of a wave of youth that breaks against the old ramparts, which seem destined to collapse."[31]

Thus between 1917 and 1921 Mussolini used the term "youth" to signify a social coalition of ever broadening dimensions whose mobilization and whose leadership he sought; after October 1922, when the Fascists came to power, "youth" became a prominent and distinguishing characteristic of the regime's style, an element in its political program, and an essential aspect of its myth. This institutionalization of youth ideology in Italy was to a great extent a consequence of the Fascist movement's doctrinal poverty. Mussolini reached and retained power by exploiting the mistakes of the Socialists, the fears of the possessing classes, and the ambitions of people within the middle class who saw the opportunity to assume the leadership of the country in the name of an antimaterialist and nationalist revolution. Yet as Mussolini himself acknowledged on more than one occasion, he came to power without a program—other than the loosely defined aim of defending and giving substance to the Italian victory. This flexibility was Fascism's strength; because of it, Mussolini was able to confound and ultimately to defeat his rivals. But the lack of ideology was also a potential weakness. Once in power, the movement might disintegrate into contending cliques and be absorbed by the old elites. An admirer of Georges Sorel, Mussolini knew that myths were necessary to get large masses to act. As a Socialist and later during the war, Mussolini believed that he had verified Sorel's affirmation that men acted not out of reason, but out of faith. Thus after being named premier, he acted to achieve legitimacy for his government and to provide it, if not with a doctrine, at least with a program, a style, and a myth. One source to which he turned was generationalism.

Youth imagery was widely diffused throughout early twentieth-century Italian culture. It could be found in the novels and plays of D'Annunzio, in the pages of *La Voce*, and in the rhetoric of the interventionist movement and the struggle against the traitors in the rear. But it seems indisputable that the chief mediation between this cultural matrix and Fascism was Marinetti and the Futurist movement. The Futurists, both before and after the war, had made youth into one of their fundamental myths. "Tomorrow belongs to the young," one Roman Futurist wrote ecstatically in 1919. "Let us kneel before the daring military formation that is returning. Their dynamism will dictate the laws that will discipline the world. The world belongs in their hands!" With reason, Marinetti later claimed that Fascism was a fulfillment of Futurism—or at least of Futurism's minimum program, which included, among other things, "the coming to power of youth against the parliamentary, bureaucratic, academic, and pessimistic spirit." Once in power, Mussolini encouraged the identification of Fascism with Futurism, pronouncing his regime to be one in which "daring" youth would always be preferred to "cowardly" age. "Giovinezza! Giovinezza!" with its portrayal of youth as a superior and more beautiful form of existence, became the official Fascist hymn; and in 1923, soon after the march on Rome, the historian Giocchino Volpe write in the pages of Mussolini's monthly *Gerarchia* that Fascism could best be understood as a "rejuvenation of the Italian spirit." The Fascists were "a phalanx of men who if not actually synonymous with Italy . . . were still a conspicuous part of its most energetic and active youth." Then, comparing Fascism favorably with Mazzini's more limited conspiratorial group Young Italy, Volpe went on to observe, "For the first time the history of our country registers the fact of a robust minority, of a 'young Italy' of vast proportions, such as Mazzini never imagined even in his moments of greatest enthusiasm, arisen from one end to the other of Italy with a unanimous, willful, and disciplined thought."[32]

BY the end of the twenties it had become a truism, though a frequently discussed one, that Fascism was a creation of the war generation and that Mussolini's regime was a regime of youth. No one took more readily to this rhetoric or did more to promote these ideas than Curzio Suckert, also known as Malaparte. A dashing figure whose genius for self-advertisement and display was equal to if not greater than his gift for literature, Malaparte (1897) launched his literary career and achieved considerable notoriety during the first years of the regime with a series of books interpreting Fascism as the consequence of a revolt of the Italian masses led by war heroes, to whose "legitimate tyranny" the masses had learned to submit. This revolt, he argued further, was comparable in its causes and significance to the Bolshevik revolution, to which it represented an Italian and Catholic alternative. To those who wondered how it was possible to interpret a movement so resolutely antidemocratic and antiegalitarian as a populist revolution, Malaparte replied nonchalantly, "The vile bourgeois and proletarian world against which we fought had few defenders among the people, but many among the intellectuals. Our revolution, please note, was and is more against [the liberal philosopher] Benedetto Croce than against [the trade union leader Bruno] Buozzi or [the Socialist Emanuele] Modigliani." A volunteer who had abandoned secondary school in order to fight with Garibaldi's Italian legion in France and who had returned from his years of front-line service full of anger and pride, Malaparte was fond of presenting himself as the spokesman (and after Mussolini, one of the leading representatives) of a generation moved by a "spirit of intolerance, revolt, and heroic unrest." This generation, he never tired of repeating, had discovered for the first time "the value of earth, of grass, of light, of human life, of immortality, of sacrifice, and of individual egotism" and had surpassed for all time in patient and unacknowledged heroism "all generations, including those which gave us our myths, our heroes, and our laws."[33]

Shortly after these words were written—that is, toward the end of 1928—a debate erupted in the Fascist press about what was called "the problem of the young." The basic issue was the relationship between the rhetoric of the regime and the reality of its political and social policies. Was Fascism favoring youth over age? If so, was this a good idea? And what in general was the attitude of young people toward Fascism, as the regime neared the end of its first decade in power? The discussion took place in an atmosphere strongly colored by the publication of Alberto Moravia's first novel, which described Italian youth as "indifferent" and "apathetic." Some young people took advantage of the debate to complain that youth were not being given positions of command; that, on the contrary, they were having trouble finding employment. Older Fascists questioned the wisdom of equating Fascist virtue and wisdom with an absence of experience and grey hair. The essence of Fascist orthodoxy, one older commentator pointed out, was to have been an interventionist in 1914. How then could young Fascists claim to be more Fascist than their elders? The debate raged throughout 1929 and 1930 in the pages of Bottai's journal *Critica Fascista* and showed little sign of abating until Mussolini brought it to a halt in 1931 by announcing that Fascism was indeed a regime of youth and that whenever possible men of thirty would be favored over those of forty or above.[34]

In the absence of a detailed quantitative study comparing the age compositions of the basic hierarchies of Italian society with those of pre-Fascist Italy and of other European countries during the 1920s, it is difficult to know and hazardous to speculate about the reality behind these charges and countercharges. The Fascist regime was in general like a baroque church: The ideological facade bore but a faint relationship to the main political and social structure. "Debates" like this one were used to screen the struggle of opposing factions for power and influence within the framework of the regime. Besides, the world economic crisis hit all sectors of Italian society after 1929, and young middle-class intellectuals were in a better position than others to vent their grievances, under the guise of debating the ideological orientation of the regime. One thing, however, can be said with certainty: Mussolini was acutely aware of the problem of integrating young people into a regime founded on the heroism of their fathers, and he took steps to solve it by a policy of organizing youth into Fascist leagues, encouraging youthful criticism of older Fascists, and placing young men, like Balbo and Bottai, in prominent political positions.* Mussolini used the generational idea, just as he used the idea of revolution, to threaten the established elites in Italian society and to keep them permanently off balance. Indeed, the two ideas were connected, for the official doctrine of the regime was that the Fascist revolution could be carried through to its completion only by coming generations. The new man, modeled on Mussolini, would be a man of the future, hence a young man not corrupted by the bourgeois and liberal past. Moreover, if Mussolini's purpose was to appeal to

---

* In September 1929 Mussolini appointed a new cabinet that included the thirty-three-year-old Balbo as air minister and the thirty-four-year-old Bottai as minister of corporations.

the ambition and idealism of youth and to play on the latent hostility that always exists between young men and their fathers, then one cannot deny that in the late 1920s and early 1930s he achieved a brilliant and unequivocal success. The main complaint voiced by Fascist youth in their journals during the early thirties was that the old generation was not and never could become wholeheartedly Fascist. The youthful editors of one Roman journal, for example, deplored the sentimental nostalgia nourished by older Fascists for ideologies of the past like liberal democracy and bourgeois individualism and warned that the Fascist revolution was only just beginning. "The time has come," they concluded, "to be vigilant and armed in every respect in order to prevent such dissolving forces from harming our future in some way."[35]

It is easy to understand why the rhetoric of Fascist leaders and intellectuals like Malaparte and the aggressive posturing of Fascist youth with its pretence to superior virtue would be painful for men who still adhered to the superannuated doctrine of individual freedom and who had themselves fought in the war. One such disgruntled veteran was the distinguished historian Adolfo Omodeo, who had been an occasional contributor to *La Voce* in the years before the war. Deeply alienated from the regime, Omodeo set out in the late 1920s to compile a memorial to his fallen comrades, which was published in installments in *La Critica* between 1929 and 1933 and later issued as a book entitled *Momenti della vita di guerra* [Moments in Wartime Life]. A lonely and ambitious man, Omodeo intended his work to be a "moral history of the Italian war." He wished to penetrate behind fact, behind mere chronicle and anecdote, in order to single out those vital forces and heroic individuals who, in his view, were the true creators of history. His premise, frankly stated in the opening pages, was that "at a certain point, classes, social groups, and nations express themselves and see themselves reflected in men of rich vitality; without these men, these vast social bodies would remain mere unrealized potential." Unformulated, but unmistakably present as an underlying motivation, was Omodeo's determination to rescue his generations's memory from Fascist distortion by returning to the wellsprings of its motives and ideals. To guarantee the historical veracity of his undertaking, he decided to use as sources only materials that had been written during the war by soldiers who had fallen. The result was a tortured and self-contradictory work that exposed an unresolved and perhaps unconscious difference of perspective between Omodeo the veteran and generational witness and Omodeo the historian and critic of the Fascist regime: a work whose fascination derives from its inner tension between participation in history and the attempt to comprehend history after it has failed to correspond to the ideals in whose name men have acted, fought, and died. If not the best book on the war generation written in Europe, *Moments in Wartime Life* is the most complex and many-layered.[36]

Omodeo (1889) was born in Palermo, the son of a Lombard railroad engineer whose work had taken him to Sicily. A student and later friend of Giovanni Gentile, Omodeo early became converted to his master's brand of philosophical idealism, which set forth as one of its essential principles the identity between states of consciousness and the transformation of the world. For Omodeo, every spiritual movement was an action; consciousness did not merely reflect the world, it changed it; thinking, understanding, knowing were the forms of activity with which the historian should be concerned. Like Gentile, Omodeo believed that the writing of history was itself a form of historical action. Indeed, the young Omodeo went even further. Historiography was for him "the most elevated moment of the spirit," a state of consciousness in which the soul, having absorbed the past, became master of the future, a free creator like God himself. Omodeo therefore believed, with a faith that verged on the religious, that the study of the past was bound to lead him to political action. A letter written to his fiancée Eva Zona in November 1911 spelled out in remarkable detail the way he viewed his future. "I see my life clearly. First I must make my mark in the world of thought and, after having mastered the past, I must confront the present with all its problems." For the time being, Omodeo was satisfied to devote himself to teaching and the study of the origins of Christianity, a moment in their history that Omodeo felt the Italians had almost totally forgotten. Later he would turn to the Risorgimento because, as he explained, "to become conscious of the entire historical movement that has created us means also to master intellectually the present: The study of history will lead me directly to the political problems of our time."[37]

Though living in Sicily and drawn toward Gentile's intellectual orbit, Omodeo had much in common with the men of *La Voce*. For one thing, he shared their disdain for the Giolittian regime. The Italians, he complained, did not know how to rule themselves and so they let themselves be governed by scoundrels. Like the Vociani, Omodeo was alternately attracted by the task of national revival and discouraged by the obstacles that such a program of renovation had to face. A self-proclaimed "son of Mazzini" who dreamed of carrying out some great work for Italy, he taught secondary school in Catania and conceived of himself as an intellectual aristocrat surrounded by recalcitrant masses who refused to learn. When the European war broke out, he naturally espoused the cause of intervention. Hostile to German imperialism and critical of German scholarship, he hoped to see Italy affirm itself as a great power and avenge its earlier humiliations and defeats. Better to die in the field, he wrote to one of his former professors in May 1915, than to live with one's tail between one's legs as an Italian under the conditions of a Giolittian compromise peace.[38]

The war shook the twenty-six-year-old Omodeo to the depths of his being. Commissioned as a lieutenant in the artillery, he arrived at the front in March 1916 in time to witness firsthand one of Italy's most spectacular advances of the Great War, the capture of Gorizia in August. In October 1917 he was caught up in the retreat after the defeat at Caporetto and found himself in the thick of action when the front was re-established on the Piave. His most glorious and risk-filled moment came in June 1918, when he helped to organize the defense against a massive Austrian-German attack and won a bronze medal for his valor. Throughout his years at the front Omodeo marveled at the self-abnegation and the endurance of the young bourgeois reserve officers, whose dedication to their country seemed to bear up under every blow and disappointment. He learned to regard with compassion the ordinary peasant soldiers, who were unable to understand the reasons for the war and who sometimes had to be disciplined harshly and driven into battle. He also came to share many of his soldiers' passions: their disdain for the imboscati behind the lines; their hate for the "Austrian and German dogs"; and their distrust of the "political canaille" who were ruining Italy. When he returned, he vowed to his wife, he would make the politicians pay. At the same time, he worried over the decline of his intellectual powers and the waste of his youth. And he strove unsuccessfully to find a deeper, historical meaning in the war that would go beyond the "reasons" that his soldiers failed to grasp. To Gentile he confessed that his effort at understanding had been futile. It was as if he had been "swept away by a tidal wave." He felt strongly that Italy was justified in entering the war on the side of the Entente, but he was unable to provide historical or ethical grounds for his belief. "For other days this more serene speculation about our war: Now I must move shells up to the new positions." [39]

Omodeo returned from the war in January 1919 drained of energy, arid of intellect, and overwhelmed by a feeling of disorientation. He looked in vain for his "combat post" in civilian life. The combination of the influenza epidemic and Italy's political troubles made it seem as if a curse prevented his generation from having a moment of breath and rest. The educated class, who should have been in command, were letting "the reins" slip through their fingers, and the ineptitude of "the riders" was inviting "the horses" (the undisciplined masses) to cut up and buck. Giolitti he dismissed as an unqualified national disaster who lacked the love and passion that were the secret of moral force. The Socialists were not worthy or capable of leading the nation because they refused to defend legitimate Italian interests. England and France had stabbed their Italian ally in the back and deserved retaliation. These grim thoughts on Italy's political situation were paralleled, if not generated, by Omodeo's difficulties in adjusting to civilian life. In the spring of 1919 his brain felt impoverished and he wondered if he would ever again be himself. His main concern was to escape from secondary school teaching by winning a university chair; but he feared (rightly, as it turned out) that getting a professorship would be "an arduous business." It was easy for him to see a connection between his own problems and those of Italy. "At certain moments," he complained to his wife, "I seem to be living in a world that has lost all moral conscience, whether in the international, the national, or the private realm. There's the most bestial explosion of all forms of egotism, and I don't know if this is the eve of revolution or the revolution itself." And yet in the midst of his despair, Omodeo continued to believe that if "the youth" that had won against the Austrians could understand the reasons for this new reversal in their country's fortunes, they would find the solution and the remedy, just as they had done so heroically after the defeat at Caporetto. Salvation, he argued in a series of essays published in 1920, could only come from the young reserve officers who had "educated" their soldiers under fire and won the war. [40]

Omodeo's published letters contain nothing about his attitude toward the early Fascist movement. Perhaps living in Sicily he did not have one, for Fascism was a northern movement that entrenched itself on the island only after it had achieved power on a national scale. Omodeo's hostility to the revolutionary Left could have made him sympathetic to some of the early Fascist movement's aims. But if Omodeo ever vacillated in his attitude toward Fascism, the moment of vacillation was brief. A man for whom action had always to be coupled with ethical ideals and for whom "duty" was no empty word but a near obsession, Omodeo came quickly to despise the Machiavellian amoralism and saber-rattling militarism of Mussolini's regime. He perceived that Fascism had no moral principles, that it nourished a cult of action for action's sake, and that it represented "a radical subversivism that undermined the foundations of the nation," thus infinitely more dangerous than the subversivism of prewar revolutionary Syndicalism or postwar Bolshevism. By October 1924, as the waves caused by the Matteotti affair broke over the regime and battered its leader,* Omodeo was writing to Gentile pleading with him to break with Mussolini and to organize a movement aimed at destroying Fascism. "In short, the liquidation of the revolution, or of that which resembles it, is urgent." [41]

From this point on, Omodeo's course was set. He had found his combat post. He would become a defender of liberty and an opponent of the regime. He would use his historiography to defend the legacy of the Risorgimento and to prevent the subversion of its ideals. The study of history, as he had foreseen, had led to the problems of the present day. One implication of his opposition to Fascism was that he broke off relations with Gentile, who had agreed to serve as Minister of Education in the Duce's cabinet, and moved toward Croce, who after 1924 became the rallying point for intellectuals who opposed the regime from within Italy. *Moments in Wartime Life,* which was first published in installments in Croce's journal, has to be seen in this context. It was on the one hand an attempt to repay the debt Omodeo felt toward his fallen comrades and on the other a veiled blow against the regime's claim to

---

* The murder of the Socialist deputy Giacomo Matteotti in June 1924 was a decisive turning point in the destruction of the liberal regime. Deeply shocked by the news of Matteotti's assassination, many liberals who had been favorable to Fascism up to this date withdrew their support from Mussolini and sought to force him to resign from the premiership. Instead, in January 1925 Mussolini took responsibility for Matteotti's death and embarked upon the creation of an authoritarian and corporatist state.

represent the war generation. It was also an effort to recapture what in retrospect seemed to have been the grandest moment in Omodeo's life. As he moved into the work in February 1929, he confessed to his close friend Lombardo-Radice, another combatant and former Vociano, that he was overcome with a feeling of nostaglia for those "difficult and great days that perhaps were the noblest of my life. And with the help of the dead I seem to have come to understand the true soul of our war above the chatter and the disgusting rhetoric of the journalists, and of the heroes of the Armistice. But who knows if the voice of the dead will succeed in making itself heard over the sad passions of the living." [42]

Omodeo was unrealistic to think that the voices of his dead, now almost two decades gone, would drown out the strident voices of the living. By the time his book was finished Italy was sliding toward war with Abyssinia, and a new generation of young Italians was showing itself eager for an opportunity to fight and die. Bitterly disappointed with the reception his work received among the young, Omodeo compared himself to "an Anchorite who comes down from his retreat to preach penitence and renunciation." But, unknown to its author, the book did reach some young anti-Fascists and offered them a different view of Italy's war generation than the one they had been given in school and were getting in the Fascist press; and today it constitutes a monument to what one might call the liberal-democratic self-image of the Italian generation of 1914. [43]

The core of Omodeo's book was his contention, not set forth fully until the fifth chapter, that "the best" of the Italian combatants had been moved not by hate, desire for glory, or an orgiastic enjoyment of war, but by a noble sense of duty and a commitment to the Mazzinian dream of a Europe of free peoples. Returning to the "serene" examination of the Italian war that he had promised Gentile to undertake at some more propitious moment, Omodeo sought to distinguish between the motives that had brought Germany and Italy into the war. The rise of German militarism and the limitless ambition of German *Machtpolitik*, he said, had threatened the spiritual ideals of the Italian nation. The conflict had been between German nationalism, which was aggressive and imperialistic, and Italian patriotism, which recognized the rights of other peoples. Between material force and the force of spirit. Between brute power and lawful right. The Italians had gone to war to defend a civilization, "something deeply ingrained in the soul, for which it is beautiful to suffer and die." Devotion to these spiritual values, Omodeo insisted, was what had led the best of the Italian officers and volunteers to lay down their lives. [44]

Omodeo's prime exemplars of self-sacrifice and Mazzinian idealism were the Garrone brothers, Giuseppe (1886) and Eugenio (1888), officers in the Alpini Corps, who had both died heroically in the war. In the Garrone correspondence Omodeo found the closest counterpart to what he had felt during the war. At the same time he recognized in the "heroic ascent" of the Garrones and their almost superhuman devotion to duty at the cost of their own survival

a higher stage of idealism than the one that he, an artillery officer and an imboscato for several months in 1917, had been able to attain. Defending his
decision to make the Garrones the archetype of Italy's war generation, Omodeo
insisted that social groups should be judged by the heights of idealism which
they reach, not by their depths of selfishness and cowardice. Just as the historian was right to represent Egypt by the pyramids and the Renaissance by St.
Peter's, so was he, Omodeo, justified in representing the Italian army of the
First World War by its most heroic combatants. [45]

The sons of a secondary school teacher, the Garrones had so internalized the
values of duty and responsibility that they incarnated in its fullest form the late
nineteenth-century concept of a "man of character." Both saw the war as a
moral revolution. Both faced death with equanimity, though neither seemed
eager to give up life. Both longed after medals, in which they saw a precious
recognition of civic virtue by their fellow countrymen. Both thought that self,
events, and others were there to be dominated by men of energy and will. Both
considered the war a positive event in the history of Europe and their country.
After the ordeal was over, they believed, life would be better, purer, more
worth living. Both had faith in the utility of the sacrifice of their lives. Both
used in their letters a vocabulary heavy with words like "will," "energy," "domination," "duty," "sacrifice," "spirit," "ideal," "conscience," "faith," "purity,"
"action," "force," "justice," "health," "youth," and "evil." Both, in Omodeo's
phrase, had shown the tenderness of "good pastors" toward their men, though
both suffered from the ordinary soldier's lack of dedication to the war. Both
were eager to prove their manhood and to demonstrate their ability to live up to
the standards set for them by their family. Both were explicit about their hatred
for the German enemy. In short, both represented that unresolved contradiction between national expansion and international harmony that characterized Omodeo himself and that made it possible for him to write that the
conflict of compassion and fighting spirit within the Italian combatant was a
sign of his moral superiority and certified his right to subject lower civilizations
to his rule. [46]

Omodeo insisted that the Garrones' sacrifice had not been in vain, for they
had left as a legacy to their country a more assured sense of national unity.
Thus the war had been, as the interventionists had claimed, a fortunate opportunity and one that Italy could not afford to let slip by. On the other hand, it
became increasingly clear as the book progressed that Omodeo also regarded
the war as his generation's curse. He and his coevals had been "overwhelmed
by events," and they ran the risk of "being barred from every comfort, of being
treated by history as the reprobate mass is treated by the God of grace, according to the theology of predestination." [47] One got the feeling that Omodeo
envied those of his generation who had not lived to see the fruits of their
struggle. Together they had done their duty; they had left behind a splendid example of self-sacrifice and patriotism; but they had not been able to regenerate

Italy. Instead the Garrones had been followed by the Mussolinis and the Malapartes. Why?

As further installments of Omodeo's book appeared, this question came more
and more to the fore, although Omodeo never confronted it directly. For one
thing, said Omodeo, the war had carried out a "reverse selection." The best,
the bravest, the soundest, the most generous, those who felt most acutely the
stimulus of civic duty and the love of country, those most aware of international problems—in short, those who had the most to give and who were most
ready to give it—had been killed in greater numbers than those who lacked
these virtues. Omodeo used this idea, as others were using it, to explain the absence of an "elitist aristocracy" capable of resolving the problems left by the
war. The war, he claimed, had mutilated humanity and damaged the European peoples in their "cerebral center"—in their educated and politically conscious middle-class elites. "An entire generation had been done away with
before it had fulfilled its function of continuing and correcting the work of the
preceding generations. A gap had been created." And there was no doubt in
Omodeo's mind that this gap accounted in great part for the crisis in European
civilization, which he described, in terms reminiscent of Ortega's, as characterized by "spiritual confusion, a lack of directives and convictions, a loss of tradition and historical experience."[48]

Thus those who should have been there to give direction and values to the
masses after the war were missing; and those lesser men who had survived (like
Omodeo himself) were not up to carrying on their task, in great part because of
the toll that the war had taken on their body and their spirit. The later chapters
of Omodeo's book chronicled, with grim objectivity often verging on despair,
the waning of convictions and the dulling of sensibility among officers at the
front, particularly those born in the second half of the 1890s. Cynicism, nihilism, emptiness, activism for activism's own sake, and love of violence came to
replace the idealism of the Garrones. Enthusiasm gave way to apathy, indifference, and resignation. The faith in a common enterprise disappeared. Unwit-
tingly, the officers transmitted to their troops their own lack of confidence in
the high command. "In the officer there fermented a bitter desire for death; in
the troops—and often among the best—a Spartacist frenzy." Seeing no prospect
of victory and having lost faith in their leaders, the troops deserted and mutinied. The result was Caporetto. Omodeo did not conceal the difficulty of
maintaining patriotic convictions in the demoralizing circumstances of the
front. Even Eugenio Garrone had gone through periods of terrible doubt and
gloom. Speaking of an officer who had gone into battle in June 1918 no longer
believing in anything, not even in himself, Omodeo observed, "His entire generation experienced, to a greater or lesser extent, something similar. In the
clash and exhausting attrition of war, they saw the ruin of the faiths, beliefs,
and institutions for whose salvation they had offered their lives." The present
generation of younger men, Omodeo added, thus had no choice but to de-

scend, like a battalion that found itself among the ruins of a destroyed city, into the depths of nihilism in order to revive their hopes and faith and to rediscover direction and strength. They—and one assumes that he had in mind the Balbos and the Malapartes—sought to conceal their emptiness by means of activism and cynicism, but deep down they longed for the inspiration of religious intimacy and sincerity. Their "indifference" was a necessary pose with which they adjusted to life among the ruins. [49]

Clearly, Omodeo wished to establish a link between the combatants of the Great War and the heroes sung in epic poetry from the ancient Greeks to the leaders of the Italian risorgimento. The epigraph to his book, taken from Sophocles' *Antigone*, the classical allusions, the metaphors, and what we know of his personality all testify to this ambition.* The pathos of the book and its ultimate truth arise from Omodeo's inability to forge that link.

Emblematic of this failure is an extraordinary passage at the beginning of the fourth installment in which Omodeo evokes with a shower of metaphors and visual images the horror and squalor of the Carso front. Omodeo comments that anyone who had viewed (as he had from his artilleryman's observation post) that wretched mass of humanity dug down into its holes and enveloped by "a vast carnation of grey smoke in which grenades seemed to bloom silently" was bound to ask himself what had happened to that "note of poetry" that once made combat beautiful even in the horror of death and that once gave the warrior the feeling of having been raised onto a solitary peak where "he exulted in a more intense joy, the model of a humanity that has transcended its limits." [50]

This was the lament of a man whose dreams of heroism had been shattered. Yet the historian and the witness recorded what he had seen, not what he believed he would find or what others wanted to believe about the war now that it was over. During the Great War, he said, the sense of accomplishing great deeds had been lost. Suffering had become separated from action. Men of great valor who would have been accounted heroes in other times had died alone, unnoticed by the great mass of their comrades and unrecorded by posterity.

Even more demoralizing, the youth who fought the war after having desired it and longed for it possessed no intellectual categories with which to understand its meaning. The postulates and concepts they had been given by their teachers, which dated from the second half of the nineteenth century, proved inadequate. Thus physical suffering and obscure death were rendered even less bearable by intellectual confusion. The combatants found themselves in terra incognita. They had been overwhelmed by events which they had welcomed, but which, once upon them, they were unable to fathom or understand. Tragedy was simply tragedy; death was simply death. There was no catharsis. The

---

* The epigraph reads, "[I shall do this] since longer the time in which to please the dead than for those up here."

war had become a meaningless struggle with "inexorable forces." Whoever had hoped to make history and bask momentarily in the war's glory found himself "lost in the unnumerable multitudes, without a means of singling himself out, similar in every respect to the cartridges and shells that the machine guns and the cannons consumed with insatiable hunger." [51]

This last sentence must have been difficult for Omodeo to write. It reduced humanity to the level of mere matter and conflicted with his view of history as the story of ethical ideals overcoming the "sluggish resistance" of nature. Hence as he neared the end of his long examination of "the legacy of the dead" it became all the more important for him to discover some grandeur in this, his war, which had cost so many lives and destroyed so many promising leaders. He found it in the moral virtues that had permitted the combatants to endure their suffering and the destruction of their hopes. Perhaps, Omodeo reflected as he reached the end of his penultimate chapter, the survivors were blind to the real greatness and beauty produced by the war. What the war demanded was not ardor and enthusiasm—the nineteenth-century virtues of the warrior that he and his coevals had been taught to admire—but obscure abnegation, humblest dedication, austere performance of duty, pertinacity capable of surviving every disillusionment, and the faith that makes up for the failure of those who despair. And these virtues, he added, existed above all in those who "like active and directing will" inspired and permeated with their faith the immense mass of the army. Now "we"—and it was clear that by "we" Omodeo meant the Fascists—distorted these virtues by decorating them with heroic-epic elements of the old tradition and did violence to what the war really meant, thus missing the real grandeur of the war, the spectacle of an entire nation fighting to keep alive an ideal of civilization. "All that," Omodeo concluded, "is well worth Murat's cavalry charges and the sacrifice of the Old Guard." [52]

Looking for the common denominator underlying the various war experiences he had studied, Omodeo located it in a Kantian sense of duty. The Italian combatants, he claimed, had felt spontaneously that the ideal for which they fought transcended the life they sacrificed so freely. In the fragments of writing they had left behind survived something of the ancient classical ideal that was embodied in the Parthenon sculptures. The letters of the dead were a form of poetry produced by "gentle Latin blood." This "autonomous concept of duty" had made possible the second wave of "sacred enthusiasm" that had followed Caporetto, when for the first time the country seemed in danger of defeat. Would the war turn out to have a meaning? Would it result in moral progress for humanity? Would it someday become clear why and for what cause so many had given their lives? Omodeo's answer to these questions was tortured and grounded more on hope and sentiment than on historical analysis. The historian and the embittered anti-Fascist had to concede that the recovery after Caporetto had only been temporary and that the Mazzinian vision of "the best" of Italy's officers had not been realized. Aggressive nationalism and economic and political autarchy had been the most evident fruits of the war. It seemed as if "the Niebelungen delirium" of the vanquished had infected the victors. The effort required to win the war almost seemed to have clouded over the vision of the ends and aspirations for which the war had been fought. But the "son of Mazzini" and interventionist in Omodeo could not shake the feeling that the war had been fought for a purpose that had not yet been revealed to its protagonists. What was necessary, he concluded, was to abandon the false path taken after the war and to return to the legacy of the Garrones. The secret the dead had yielded up to Omodeo during his long journey through their most intimate thoughts was that the war would not be over until the peoples who had won it returned to the principles for which it had been fought. The ideal of a more just world and a "more human" life had allowed the Western peoples to triumph over "German furor" and the "Niebelungen instinct." Only by living in and for that ideal would the victory acquire "sense and value."[53]

Omodeo's book is more than a great work of history. It is one of those rare documents that reflect the contradictory nature of a vast human experience while at the same time salvaging it in its details and reflecting the author's efforts to grasp it as a whole. It was the kind of work that could only have arisen out of wrenching personal torment and that probably was possible only in Italy, where the tension between the ideals of the interventionist movement and the tawdry reality of Fascism posed a problem which Italian intellectuals—whether Fascist or anti-Fascist—had to face. *Moments of Wartime Life* is a remarkable achievement, the product of a sensitive and unusual historical mind. Yet in its analysis and even in its selection of materials, Omodeo's book has to be judged and has been judged unsatisfactory. Omodeo formulates the central problem, assembles a mass of fascinating documents, deploys them with considerable literary skill, brings to bear on them the apparatus of his own experience, probes and ponders them with a powerful historical imagination; but for all this he is unable to provide a convincing answer to the question with which his book began. The series of explanations his fertile mind provides for the failure of the combatants' vision—the action of reverse selection, the curse of a merciless fate, the fathomless ways of history, the enervating effects of prolonged exposure to the war, the destruction of hopes, the spread of indifference, the infection of the Italian troops by "Niebelungen delirium"—though some are important and worthy of consideration, merely screen off a more fundamental issue, which even his own highly selected materials raise: To what extent was Fascism implicit or potentially present in the literary and political consciousness of his generation before the war?

This question could not be answered or even squarely faced by Omodeo because to do so would have involved recognizing the extent to which he shared or had shared certain convictions that had given rise to the Fascist mentality, among them the belief that "the sluggish mass" was merely the resistant nature that "lively and active personalities" sought to mold. He would have had to break with Gentile's idealism and appreciate the role that economic and social circumstances played in determining the development of "spirit." He would have had to understand individual ideals in the context of social interests. He would have had to admit that "Niebelungen instinct" was not confined to Germany and that activism was not peripheral among Italian interventionists and combatants. And he would have had to acknowledge that, to a great extent, Fascism was the creation of forces within his own generation.[54] In short, he would have had to carry out a thorough critique of his own world view. This he was (like most men) unwilling or unable to do. Thus when Omodeo's question was confronted and answered it was by another generation of historians, less wedded to elitist and liberal conceptions, who were inspired by the thought of the Marxist and Communist leader Antonio Gramsci.

BY background and by initial cultural orientation, Antonio Gramsci had a good deal in common with Omodeo. Almost his coeval and like him an islander and the son of a solidly bourgeois family engaged in minor state service, Gramsci (1891) too was drawn toward the study of letters and history and hoped through good grades to climb the social ladder that led toward the superior status of a university professorship. He too was caught up at an early age in the movement of moral and intellectual reform associated with Croce, Gentile, and Salvemini. Like Omodeo, he too began as an idealist who believed that history could replace religion as the faith of modern men. But there the resemblance ended. For whereas Omodeo remained a liberal, Gramsci became a revolutionary who viewed the world in terms of an eternal struggle between oppressors and oppressed.

A classic example of the outsider, Gramsci grew up in a small town on the remote island of Sardinia, where he knew poverty and illiteracy at first hand. While still a child, he imbibed the local population's mistrust and hatred of the mainland. Thus the liberal regime was from the beginning identified in his mind with the oppressive rule of what Sardinians called "the continentals," and the young Gramsci's first political emotion was his desire to see them thrown into the sea. Even more important than his provenance was the physical deformity that would always mark him off from other men. Gramsci was hunchbacked. A face that many found beautiful was attached incongruously to a twisted and sickly body. Gramsci's childhood appears to have been unhappy. One of seven sisters and brothers, he grew up feeling neglected by his parents and unworthy of their or anyone else's love. When at the age of eleven he was taken from school despite excellent grades and put to work to help support the family, he interpreted this interruption of his studies as the aggression of a fundamentally hostile world.[55]

These experiences turned the young Gramsci into a rebel; but his rebelliousness might well have assumed a more literary and less political form had the pursuit of a higher education not taken him to Turin. In Turin he discovered a lively university of European stature and the most self-consciously modern working class in Italy. This working class was highly organized, combative, and deeply penetrated by socialist ideas. It exercised a powerful attraction on both the faculty and students of the university; with its meeting halls, strikes, processions, and newspapers, it was a prominent feature of the fog-enveloped urban scene. Within three years of arriving in the Piedmontese capital, Gramsci had become a Socialist. Adhering to Socialism was the young Sardinian's way of indicating his allegiance to the modern world and at the same time affirming his faith in a brighter future for humanity than the one he enjoyed himself. More concretely, membership in the Socialist party put Gramsci into contact with a tightly knit and clearly demarcated community in which he could take refuge from his loneliness, and it soon provided him with employment as a journalist, thus rescuing him from poverty and opening up a new and unexpected career.[56]

Deferred from military service because of his deformity, Gramsci used the war years to develop a vision of socialism that was heavily encrusted with idealism and voluntarism. A reader of *La Voce* before 1914, he believed that the task of the new generation of Socialists was to effect a synthesis between the materialism of Marx and the idealism of Croce and Gentile, in his view the most advanced philosophies of twentieth-century Europe. The critical element in this synthesis, as Gramsci worked it out, was the emphasis on consciousness and will. Man, he wrote in one of his earliest articles, was above all spirit: He created history. Otherwise, given the fact that there had always been exploiters and exploited, it was impossible to explain why the socialist ideal had not yet been realized. History was the story of human liberation. Step by step and social stratum by social stratum, humanity had acquired consciousness of its value and freed itself from dominating minorities. According to Gramsci, this consciousness of freedom had not been formed under "the whip of physiological necessities"; it was the result of "intelligent reflection," first by individuals, then by entire social classes. Every revolution had been preceded by an intense campaign of criticism, of cultural penetration, and of the forceful permeation of ideas through groups of men who at first resisted these ideas out of narrow self-interest. The key to the creation of a socialist society, Gramsci therefore concluded, was education and the transformation of consciousness. Revolutions came about when heroic elites succeeded in imposing new values and habits on amorphous and indifferent masses. "To wait to become the majority plus one is the program of timid souls who expect socialism from a royal decree countersigned by two ministers." Given this view of history, it is not surprising that the contemporary figures whom Gramsci most admired during this period were men whose "red hot" souls gave out "myriads of sparks." Men of "intense faith" and "will" like Ernest Psichari, Charles Péguy, Romain Rolland, Renato Serra, and Mussolini, whose enthusiastic supporter he had been before the impatient editor of *Avanti* had bolted the Socialist party in November 1914.[57]

Top: Giovanni Papini. Bottom: Giuseppe Prezzolini.

We are determined to live not only as individuals but as a generation.
  Giuseppe Prezzolini, 1911

The first number of the Florentine journal *Leonardo*.

Every time a generation presents itself on the terrace of life it seems that the world's symphony is going to have to attack a new tempo. Dreams, hopes, plans of attack, the ecstasy of discoveries, the scaling of heights, challenges, fits of arrogance—and a journal.
Giovanni Papini, 1913

Benito Mussolini leading the march on Rome in October 1922.

Life is warfare and battle: yesterday against the foreign enemy . . . today against the domestic enemy nested in the trenches of politics.

Benito Mussolini, 1919

The union of older and younger generations in the Fascist militia.

Giovinezza! Giovinezza!
Primavera di bellezza!
Youth! Youth!
Beautiful spring of life!

Fascist anthem

Adolfo Omodeo during the Great War.

Studying the writings of the dead surprises me by inspiring a sense of melancholy and . . . quasi-nostalgia for those difficult and great days that were perhaps the noblest of my life.

  Adolfo Omodeo to Giuseppe Lombardo Radice, 1929

Antonio Gramsci shortly before his arrest in 1926.

Antonio Gramsci has the head of a revolutionary; his portrait seems constructed by his will . . . the brain has overwhelmed the body.

  Piero Gobetti, 1924

Primo quaderno (8 febbraio 1929)

Note e appunti.

Argomenti principali : —

1) Teoria della storia e della storiografia.

2) Sviluppo della borghesia italiana fino al 1870.

3) Formazione dei gruppi intellettuali italiani: — svolgimento, atteggiamenti.

4) La letteratura popolare dei «romanzi d'appendice» e le ragioni della sua persistente fortuna.

5) Cavalcante Cavalcanti : la sua posizione nella struttura e nell'arte della Divina Commedia.

6) Origini e svolgimento dell'Azione Cattolica in Italia e in Europa.

7) Il concetto di folklore.

8) Esperienze della vita in carcere.

9) La «quistione meridionale» e la quistione delle isole.

10) Osservazioni sulla popolazione italiana: sua composizione, funzione dell'emigrazione.

11) Americanismo e fordismo.

12) La quistione della lingua in Italia: Manzoni e G. I. Ascoli.

The first page of Gramsci's *Prison Notebooks.*

My life [in prison] is as monotonous as ever. Even studying is more difficult than one would think . . . . I'm pursued . . . by this idea: that I must do something "für ewig."
    Antonio Gramsci to Tania Schucht, 1927

Gramsci responded enthusiastically to the news of the Russian Revolution, letting his imagination far outrun his information. Seizing upon a report that the Russian revolutionaries had opened the jails and that in one case common criminals had refused their freedom and elected their own guards, he exulted that the Revolution was "the most grandiose phenomenon that human effort has produced . . . It is the liberation of minds and the establishment of a new moral consciousness . . . It is the advent of a new order that coincides with everything our masters have taught us." By July 1917 Gramsci had become a champion of the Bolsheviks. Lenin and his followers were real revolutionaries, he argued, because they understood that it was necessary to whip people out of their lethargy and to conquer minds. They realized that true revolutionary thought rejected the idea that progress was somehow dependent on the passing of time. When the October Revolution occurred, Gramsci greeted it provocatively as "the revolution against *Das Kapital.*" The Bolsheviks, he said, had denied Karl Marx and affirmed through concrete action and real achievement that "the canons of historical materialism are not as iron as one would think and as one has thought." They had shown that revolution was possible where the will to revolution existed. Moreover, though not dogmatic followers of a sacred and unvarying text, the Bolsheviks had nonetheless remained true to the spirit of Marxism, "that which never dies, which is the continuation of Italian and German idealistic thought, and which in Marx had been contaminated by positivist and naturalistic incrustations." This thought was based on the central insight that the course of human history was not determined by brute economic facts, but that men were capable of understanding their economic circumstances and adjusting them to their will. Objective reality was like "bubbling volcanic lava" that could be channeled "where the will wishes and as the will wishes." A few months later Gramsci stated his heresy even more overtly. Marx, he announced, represented "the entrance of intelligence into human history . . ." He was a "master of spiritual and moral life, not a shepherd armed with a crook."[58]

When the war ended Gramsci threw himself into the struggle to radicalize the Socialist party and to push it toward revolution. With his friends and former classmates from the University of Turin, Angelo Tasca, Palmiro Togliatti, and Umberto Terracini, he founded a weekly of socialist culture entitled *Ordine Nuovo* [The New Order]. *Ordine Nuovo* defended the Bolsheviks and claimed to find in the burgeoning movement of factory councils in Turin and Milan an indigenous variant of the Russian soviets. For the first time, Gramsci became a working-class leader as well as a journalist and party intellectual. He addressed workers' meetings and was present when the workers occupied the Fiat factories in September 1920. His effort, as always, was to educate a proletarian elite, to call into being a collective will, and to prepare the intellectual and cultural basis for a future workers' state. His model remained the Bolsheviks, whose ruthless repression of their enemies he had come to accept as "the tithe" that revolutionaries had to pay to history.[59]

When the Italian Socialist party split in January 1921 at Livorno, in part as a result of the activities of the *Ordine Nuovo* faction, Gramsci became one of the leaders of the newly formed Communist party. In May 1922 he was selected to represent the party at Moscow, where he remained for almost two years. During this period, several months of which he spent in a provincial sanitorium recovering from exhaustion, overwork, and malnutrition, he fell in love with a Russian woman, who returned his affection. He was also introduced to the realities of Soviet life and the Machiavellian intricacies of Comintern politics. Meanwhile, in Italy the Fascists had come to power and Gramsci's party had become a semi-clandestine organization living on the edges of illegality, with its leaders and militants in constant danger of arrest and Fascist aggression. These events left their mark on the man and the thinker. In some ways, to be sure, they pulled in opposite directions. The private man opened himself to another human being and bared his deepest feelings. But the public man deemphasized consciousness and culture and showed an unsuspected talent for intraparty politics. The educator became an organizer, the intellectual a Comintern agent.[60] The common denominator of his two selves—the lover and the politician—was the commitment to the Soviet Union. His ideological infatuation with Russia had been consolidated by his love for Giulia Schucht. To judge by the experience of his friend Togliatti, it is unlikely that Gramsci would have returned to his early interest in culture and history until late in life, had he not been arrested by the Fascist government in November 1926 and spent almost all the remaining years of his short life in a Fascist prison.

Gramsci thus came to the generation problem from a quite different perspective than Omodeo. He had not fought in the war. He had no psychological stake in the victory. He had no medals and felt no nostalgia for the front. Years spent abroad living in the Soviet Union had reinforced his Marxism and allowed him to achieve a certain distance from his earlier Crocean beliefs. He now assigned a greater weight to economic and material factors. He knew that moral and intellectual reform could only be achieved by powerful and disciplined organizations. Yet at the same time, he was fully aware that the creation of the Italian Communist party was to a great extent the result of a generational revolt.[61] Forced to suspend his political activity, determined to keep his mind alert by use, Gramsci returned to a problem that had interested him since his earliest days as a Socialist: How was thought translated into action? How was the collective consciousness of large social groups transformed? And how did a minority—such as the Communist party—succeed in imposing its way of viewing the world on the normally conservative and indifferent masses? The *Quaderni del carcere* [Prison Notebooks] contain Gramsci's answers to these questions; reaching these answers required him to reexamine the history of the Italian generation of 1914.[62]

The originality of the *Prison Notebooks* lies in Gramsci's use of the terms "historical bloc" and "hegemony." Gramsci believed that before becoming politically dominant and capturing the state a social coalition or historical bloc establishes cultural hegemony over the masses by means of the action of its intellectual elite. By intellectuals he meant all those engaged in maintaining the social hegemony and political power of the dominant social groups. Thus he extended the concept to include civil servants, judges, newspaper editors, architects, and lawyers as well as the categories traditionally regarded as forming the intellectual class, like novelists, poets, literary critics, philosophers, and scientists. Indeed, he used the term in much the same way as Ortega had used "select minority," to refer to an elite or an aristocracy, with the difference that Gramsci saw these intellectuals not as independent and autonomous but rather as the "clerks" or "errand boys" of the dominant social and political groups. Gransci also differed from Ortega in emphasizing the critical role of the intermediary cadres within the intellectual class. These intermediaries, Gramsci held, transformed "the philosophy" of great intellectuals like Croce into "the common sense" of the masses and thus helped to maintain a social and cultural consensus. [63]

This theory of the intellectuals as a social group determined Gramsci's approach to revolutionary politics. Revolutions, he believed, were always preceded by a transfer of cultural hegemony from one social coalition to another. The taking over of the state, though necessary, was a later event. Politics thus consisted above all of "social pedagogy" and education; and the essential *political* problem in Italian history had been the inability or the unwillingness of Italian intellectuals to break with a cosmopolitan and elitist view of culture (a legacy of the papacy and the Renaissance) and to forge organic and democratic links between themselves and the people by means of a "national-popular" culture with which the masses could identify. The most egregious example of the failure of the intellectuals in modern Italian history, Gramsci thought, had been the Risorgimento, when even the most radical Italian revolutionaries like Mazzini had been unable to engage the masses in the struggle for national unity. The role of the Communist party was therefore to lead and to organize an "intellectual and moral reform" that alone could make it possible for the Italians to achieve a higher and more socially integrated form of modern civilization. [64]

With this approach to revolutionary politics, it is not surprising that Gramsci was interested in the problem of generational conflict. Gramsci's notes on the generational problem were all recorded between 1929 and 1933. Although sometimes formulated as universal propositions of the Ortegian type, they represent his reaction to the discussion in the Italian press of the so-called problem of the young and of the alleged alienation of the younger from the older generation. Summarized and restated in more accessible language, Gramsci's thoughts on the generational question were the following: (1) The older generation always educates its successor, and the younger generation always stands in a position of subordination to its predecessor. (2) Generational conflict arises when the older generation gives up its pedagogical responsibilities and fails to prepare the young for the tasks that the existing state of historical development thrusts upon them. (3) This generational conflict remains superficial—unless the youth of the dominant historical bloc are moved to transfer their loyalties to an antagonistic social class. (4) Any attempt on a national scale to prevent the transfer of generational loyalties from a socially retrogressive class to a socially advanced one is bound to lead to a crisis of authority and to produce disaffection and morbose behavior among the young. (5) This crisis of authority occurs because the old conception of the world has lost its power to attract the young, while the new conception is prevented by force from winning hegemony. (6) An old generation with antiquated ideas may be followed by a young generation with infantile ideas, if the intermediary generation that should correct the old and educate the new is missing or quantitatively weak. (7) This pattern is more likely and of graver consequence among the subordinate classes because their intellectual elites lack a cultural tradition and because the few individuals in these groups who are at the height of their historical epoch have a difficult time organizing an intellectual center that can effectively counter the hegemony of the dominant social coalition. [65]

These notes on the generation problem mean little unless they are placed in the context of Gramsci's interpretation of the history of his own generation. This interpretation goes something like this. Toward the end of the nineteenth century the dominant historical bloc—composed of northern industrialists and southern landed interests, and headed politically by Giolitti—lost the allegiance of their sons because their political solutions and social policies were reactionary and not up to the possibilities of development offered by the times. In reaction against these policies, the intellectuals or elite of the young bourgeois generation moved collectively toward the working class and its organizations, unconsciously seeking to realize the hegemony of their own class over the workers. Other groups of young bourgeois intellectuals on the periphery of the workers' movement sought (like Papini and the Futurists) to undermine the old liberal culture and (like Prezzolini and the Vociani) to create a truly national culture that would include wider strata of the population. Prezzolini, for instance, undertook to diffuse Croce's idealism to the intermediary layers or "lieutenants" of the bourgeois intelligentsia and thus to lay the basis for an "intellectual and moral reform." Almost all these intellectuals stemmed from the rural petty bourgeoisie and were attracted by ideas of adventure and escape. They often used the rhetoric of revolution. But they were linked by social and economic interest to the reactionary and parasitic classes concentrated in the rural areas and the nonindustrial cities of southern and central Italy. No matter how much they might attack these classes in print and talk of revolution, they owed to these groups their relative well-being and their superiority over the illiterate, ill-fed, and overworked masses. This debt, in Gramsci's view, explained the otherwise puzzling fact that the prewar journals founded by these intellectuals, though radical in words and program, had never been willing to identify themselves consistently with the only potential revolutionary classes in Italian society, the southern peasants and the northern workers. They had never been willing to appeal to a class clientele and had instead sought to speak for and to "the best" of all classes, thus predetermining their failure to achieve their stated goals. [66]

Between 1917 and 1920, when it appeared that the hegemony of the ruling groups were threatened by a lower-class revolution inspired by events in Russia, bourgeois youth had abandoned the working-class movement and had, like the Futurist Marinetti, the syndicalist Michele Bianchi, and the ex-Socialist Mussolini, returned to the "womb" of their own class. And those who did not desert the working-class movement either were not at the height of their times, like the leadership of the Socialist party or, like the *Ordine Nuovo* group, were too few in number to organize a successful revolution around their own "brain trust." Thus no guiding center existed to lead and direct the spontaneous feelings of the oppressed workers and peasants, or to mobilize the disaffected *combattenti* toward democratic and socialist ends. The Fascists thus were able to maintain the dominance of the former historical bloc by organizing a militant counterrevolution, using violence and the habits of command and attack learned during the war when, as young officers, they had been in charge of troops. [67]

But the Fascists were soon confronted by a rebellion of their own youth, caused by a gap between the regime's revolutionary pretenses and its reactionary practice. Mussolini and his lieutenants sang hymns to youth and claimed youth led; but in fact the old generation continued to dominate, and the regime created no outlets for the employment of youth's energies. Young intellectuals soon discovered that the Fascists had provided neither revolution nor jobs. Hence their indifference, their cynicism, their restlessness, and their discontent—all "chaotic" expressions of rebellion, which, in Gramsci's view, were unjust in their form but not in their substance. [68] The only possible long-term solution to the crisis was the passage of middle-class youth from the former historical bloc to the side of the working class, a social revolution, and the opening of new "horizons" (and new jobs) for both bourgeois and working-class youth. This solution the regime refused to permit and worked actively to prevent. The function of Fascism was therefore primarily negative and obstructionist: It could prevent others, like the Communists, from resolving the crisis, but it could not resolve the crisis itself. Gramsci drew three conclusions from this analysis: the weakness of the Fascist regime; the need for a corps of working-class intellectuals grouped around a political party and bound by "organic" links to the lower orders of society; and the likelihood of a long war of attrition for the cultural hegemony of Italian society and the political domination of the Italian state, a war in which the progressive coalition led by the Communist party was bound to triumph.

Gramsci had no sympathy for the Fascists' generational rhetoric, whether in-dulged in by older or by younger men. A generation that sought to downgrade its predecessors, as the Fascist generation was systematically doing, could not help being "petty" and lacking self-confidence, he thought, even if it assumed "gladiatorial poses" and put on airs of greatness. "A vital and strong generation that has the intention of working and making its mark tends rather to exaggerate the value of the preceding generation because its own energy gives it con-fidence that it will go beyond its predecessor." For the opportunism, vanity, snobbery, superficiality, and verbal radicalism of Malaparte, Gramsci had nothing but contempt. One of the first entries in the *Quaderni* compares Malaparte's generation unfavorably with that of Papini and Prezzolini. "The old generation of the intellectuals has failed, but it had a youth . . . The gen-eration of those now young hasn't even had this age of brilliant promises: ugly asses even when little." The generational manifesto of a group of younger Fas-cists four years later elicited an even more negative response. It was not true, Gramsci mused, that the younger generation had no ideals. It was just that their ideals were all contained in the Fascist penal code, which they seemed to consider eternally binding.[69]

Gramsci's judgment of Omodeo (and the liberal intellectuals in general) was almost equally harsh. In Gramsci's view, Omodeo was an organizer of the repression of the southern peasants and an agent of the Sicilian landowners. Gramsci took sharp issue with the central thesis of *Moments in Wartime Life*, which he read as it appeared in *La Critica*. Omodeo, he noted irascibly, had sought to show that a robust sense of national unity, formed by the liberal dem-ocratic tradition, had already existed in 1915 and that it had manifested itself during the torment of the war in the letters and diaries of his fallen officers. Omodeo's ideological aim, he said, like that of Croce in his history of Italy, was to demonstrate that the unfairly maligned Giolittian period contained within it an "insuperable treasure of idealism and heroism" and thus to con-demn as absurd any tendency toward revolution once the war had ended. For Gramsci, Omodeo's concept of national consciousness and national unity was too narrow and class-bound to be convincing. Omodeo, he felt, had reduced the protagonists of national consciousness to a small group of noble individuals who in the intimacy of their consciences had achieved a certain level of patri-otic feeling and spirit of sacrifice. To put the matter this way, Gramsci con-cluded, was to exalt "moral voluntarism" at the expense of collective conscious-ness and to overlook the real problem of how elites succeeded in establishing an "organic bond" between themselves and the masses.[70]

THERE is no mention of Ortega or of any of his writings in the 2,848 pages of the new edition of the *Quaderni*. This omission is surprising because Gramsci was interested in the special problems of Spanish intellectuals, read

Spanish well enough to follow the Spanish press and make his way through *Don Quijote*, and furthermore shared many of Ortega's concerns.[71] Both men were interested in the conditions under which consciousness is transformed and culture is renewed. Both felt that destiny had called them to educate their respective countries. Both were "European," in their wish to deprovincialize their country's culture, just as they had earlier deprovincialized themselves. Both were unwilling to equate "thought" with philosophy and wanted to extend the definition of thought to include the ideas about the world that ordinary men took for granted. In their study of cultural innovation, both emphasized the process by which elites succeed or fail in asserting their leadership over masses. Both provided diagnoses of the cultural crisis. And, under the pressure of events, both became painfully aware of the power of traditions and consensus in slowing social and cultural change.

Yet there the similarity ends, and it is easy to reconstruct the critique that Gramsci might have made of Ortega's generational theories, had he known them. To begin with, although Gramsci might have agreed that the fifteen-year interval described accurately enough the generational ruptures that had occurred in Italy during his own lifetime, he would have taken issue with Ortega's belief that generational changes occur regularly because of the biological structure of human life. To Gramsci, this idea would have smacked suspiciously of positivism and of Spencerian social laws and furthermore would have conflicted with his conviction that shifts in collective consciousness always correspond to shifts in the social and economic structure, which themselves are never subject to exact prediction because they result from the action (or inaction) of human will embodied in social groups. Significant generational changes, Gramsci would have countered, were responses to or symptoms of deeper changes in the social process, and thus by their very nature were bound to be irregular in occurrence.[72]

Gramsci would have located the weak point of Ortega's sociology in his failure to identify concretely the protagonists of change and the process by which changes in consciousness are transformed into social reality. Gramsci deviated from Ortega in insisting that the intellectual elites capable of making history—those select minorities whose absence in contemporary Europe Ortega so deplored—are never independent, but are always related to larger social groups, which are themselves defined in terms of their relationship to a mode of production and a style of life and thought. Gramsci claimed that to be effective these elites must consist not just of great intellectuals (like Croce and Ortega) who think new thoughts, but also of intermediary elements and purveyors of culture who translate these thoughts into common sense and integrate them into popular culture. The League for Spanish Political Education, *El Sol*, and the *Revista de Occidente* were Ortega's efforts to organize, educate, and broaden the cadres of Spain's intellectual class. But Gramsci would have leveled against these enterprises the same criticism he directed at Prezzolini's *La*

Voce and Salvemini's *L'Unità*: namely, that such undertakings were condemned to impotence because they were directed toward social groups that had little or no incentive to transform society. Indeed, Gramsci might even have seen in Ortega's philosophy, with its emphasis on sensibility rather than social and economic structures, a Spanish equivalent of Croce's idealism, which he identified from 1926 on as one of the ideological bulwarks of the Italian status quo. If he had read Ortega's lectures on Galileo, Gramsci might have reiterated his conviction that in twentieth-century Europe a revolutionary politics directed toward the elevation of the subordinate classes was the only effective means of moral and intellectual reform; and he might have gone on to argue that men who rejected politics in favor of detached thought were, whether they realized it or not, ideological agents of the dominant social groups. Thus Gramsci would have been likely to dismiss Ortega's generational theory as an interesting but ultimately confused and confusing mystification, a reflection of the social situation of Spanish intellectuals who aspired toward a higher and richer culture but were unable to perceive in the overcoming of their country's backwardness and industrial underdevelopment the means by which this revival might be achieved.

Gramsci might have suspected that Ortega's background had determined the conservative direction of his social thought, leading him increasingly away from his early sympathy for socialism and inspiring him to fear and disdain the masses. To Gramsci, Ortega would have appeared the quintessential example of the "aristocracy of the toga": the intellectual who perceives himself, erroneously, as a member of an autonomous corporation, free of any social interest, whose traditions reach back to Plato and Aristotle.[73]

One can think what one likes of Gramsci's view of the bourgeois intellectual as an agent of the dominant elite; but it is indisputable that his observations in the *Prison Notebooks* provide a much needed corrective to Ortega's ambitious generational theory. The virtue of Gramsci's social thought is its historical specificity. He saw and pointed out that the generation that complained of having to live through a cultural crisis was in its great majority a group of middle-class intellectuals with small but comfortable incomes, strong ties to rural ways of life, and a commitment to the elitist and humanistic culture that had flourished in this preindustrial social setting. Just as Ortega was becoming famous as the author of *The Revolt of the Masses*, Gramsci provided his own interpretation of the European cultural crisis:

The old intellectual and moral leaders of the society feel the ground begin to move under their feet, they realize that their 'sermons' have become 'sermons' and nothing more, that is, things extraneous to reality, pure form without content, skeletons without spirit; hence their desperation and their reactionary and conservative tendencies: Since the particular form of civilization, of culture, and of morality that they represent is decomposing, they proclaim the death of all civilization, of all culture, of all morality and demand from the state repressive measures and constitute themselves into groups of resistance cut off from the real historical process, augmenting in this way the duration of the crisis, since the waning of one style of life and way of thinking cannot take place without a crisis.

Gramsci added almost as an afterthought, "the representatives of the new order in gestation propagate utopias and unrealistic programs, out of 'rationalistic' hate for the old." [74]

This passage, though possessing none of Ortega's stylistic brilliance, contains an important insight: Gramsci understood that what intellectuals perceived as a crisis of "culture" and "civilization" was in fact the crisis of their own leadership of that civilization. What Gramsci either did not see or chose not to mention was that, in most cases, the intellectuals who turned toward reaction came from the same social groups as those who propagated unrealistic programs out of hate for the old. Indeed, the distinctive characteristic of the Italian intellectual of the generation of 1914 was his combination of revolutionary yearnings with profoundly elitist and reactionary values. Squeezed between a working class that he feared and a bourgeois elite that he despised, the Italian intellectual of this generation wavered between a desire to destroy culture and a determination to defend it against the encroachment of the masses, if necessary by authoritarian means. He talked of revolution, yet regarded the hegemony of his own class as God-given and eternal and secretly longed for discipline and order. He wanted to be a teacher, prophet, and spiritual guide of a docile peasant-people whose primary virtue was their willingness to follow those educated to rule. He lacked the imagination to conceive of a society in which culture was an acquisition open to all and not the birthright of a privileged few, and in this failure of imagination he reflected the prejudices of the provincial social setting from which he was likely to have come. He suffered; but his agony derived from his inability to reconcile his concept of civilization with the new social forces that were pressing in upon him. Thus he dreamed of a spiritual revolution that would avoid the leveling objectives of socialism and the equally threatening tendencies of corporate capitalism. He was sincerely anticapitalist; but, paradoxically, his radicalism contributed to the maintenance of the status quo. While he nervously fiddled the tunes of apocalypse and crisis, the parade of modern industry and corporate organization nonchalantly passed him by. [75]

Not even Gramsci himself entirely escaped from the contradictions bedeviling the intellectual caste into whose ranks he had once aspired to ascend. After all, no one carried further than he the elevation of the intellectual's station in the hierarchies of Italian life. In his system, the intellectuals were to be the captains and shock troops of the proletarian revolution. The exalted role ascribed to intellectuals in Gramsci's system no doubt provides a clue as to why Italian intellectuals found it easy to convert en masse to Gramsci's interpretation of Marxism once the Fascist regime had fallen. But Gramsci understood— and it is easy to underestimate his achievement in a culture permeated by philosophical idealism—that the only lasting solution to the cultural crisis was not a new set of ideas, but the augmentation of production and the transformation of class relations. Not a new philosophy, but wider social horizons, new civic habits, and more and better-paid jobs. Gramsci was not alone to understand this; but such "materialistic" views were rare among the generation of 1914.

CHAPTER SIX

Wanderers between Two Worlds

*I was born wandering between two worlds, one dead, the
other powerless to be born, and have made, in a curious
way, the worst of both.*
  Aldous Huxley, 1942

T HE "generation of 1914" is best approached as a specific instance of a general idea, that of social or historical generations. This idea should not be
confused with the traditional (and still often used) notion of generations as
thirty-year intervals of genealogical time. Like so many other ideas taken up
and popularized by the nineteenth century, that of historical generations provides a way of understanding society. It directs the mind to the unity within age-
groups and the discontinuities among them. Date of birth, it suggests, is destiny. The truest community to which one can belong is that defined by age and
experience. Communication across generational boundaries will always be illusory. The young man, as Unamuno put it, can no more understand his elder
than the sick man can comprehend what his robust neighbor means by health.

Once grasped, the dynamics of the generational idea make it easy to understand why all generationalists have a tendency to represent their generations as
unique, sacrificed, and lost. The notion at the heart of the generational idea—
the discontinuity of age-groups—demands it. Barrès and others had pronounced their generations lost and sacrificed long before the Great War came.
So too Erich Maria Remarque and Ernest Hemingway were marching in the
line of a long-established tradition when they put this idea at the heart of their
books in the 1920s. Nothing suggests that the idea is dead today. All historical
generations are "lost."

The generational idea was gaining in popularity and winning enthusiasts
around 1900. More people were using it and in a greater variety of ways. One
can trace its progress in dictionaries. During the early nineteenth century the
term "generation" was used primarily to signify either the relationship between
fathers and their sons or contemporaneity. The French lexicographer Emile
Littré defined a generation in 1863 as "all men living more or less in the same

time." In the second half of the nineteenth century the term was employed increasingly to connote coevals, and especially to evoke the dichotomy between the older generation and "youth." Hence the widespread use of terms like "the rising generation," "the new generation," and "the young generation." This shift in usage is critical. It implies that society is divided into compartments or worlds defined by age, and it suggests the existence of a significant group called "youth." Consciously or unconsciously, Henri Massis was responding to this shift in usage when he published his famous enquête in 1912. Though Massis was inspired by the ideas of a small group of Parisian intellectuals, most of whom he personally knew, he had the happy intuition of presenting these ideas as the expression of French "youth." Without knowing it, he had slipped from the nineteenth- to the twentieth-century definition of generation. [1]

Several long-term trends encouraged the spread of generational thinking. Though by no means identical or reducible to one, all were related to the process of modernization that swept over Western and Central Europe after 1750. Generational consciousness had its deepest roots and its first stimulus in the new concept of time and attitude toward change that developed in the late eighteenth century; and the people to whom the generational idea first appealed were relatively small groups of intellectuals dedicated to the cause of cultural and political renewal. The Enlightenment had taught that the future could be better than the present if men learned to tap the rich reserves of reason that lay within them. First, though, the obstacles to a life of reason must be removed. According to the reaching of the philosophes, these obstacles took the form of superstition and tradition; they were the remnants in the present of a less liberated past. The French Revolution and its aftermath showed how liberation from the past could be achieved—through political rebellion. At the same time, the French events of 1789–1871 taught a powerful lesson in the discontinuity of historical development; for revolutions and restorations went by in dizzy succession, suggesting that every era had its distinctive and authentic quality that walled it off from what had come before and what would come later. Both these ideas—the rooting out of the past for the sake of the future and the discontinuous nature of human existence—encouraged the equation of youth with cultural renewal. If the future was going to be fundamentally different from and better than the past, then the young represented the new. They were the standardbearers of the future in the present; whereas their fathers, the adults, were the incarnation of the past in the present and thus a pernicious obstacle to progress and change. To struggle against the older generation, therefore, became the duty of all men who identified themselves with the cause of the future. The cultural and political history of the nineteenth century shows a steady escalation in the rhetorical violence and determination with which this struggle was waged. The writers of the Sturm und Drang, the French Romantics of 1830, young Italy, young Germany, the Russian revolutionary youth described by Turgenev and Dostoyevsky, and Nietzsche and his followers had prepared and prefigured the system of discourse with which the generation of 1914 would discover and describe itself. Hence in 1900 there was a ready-made language of political and cultural combat that predisposed European intellectuals to think in generational terms. The young generation had become a tradition.[2]

Around the end of the nineteenth century the idea of generational rebellion began to crystallize into a cluster of attitudes that can be called the ideology of youth. This ideology was a by-product of the century-long pursuit of social liberation. The liberation of the bourgeoisie had been followed by the liberation of the peasants; the liberation of the peasants, by movements aimed at the liberation of workers, national minorities, and women; now, around 1900, it seemed natural to liberate youth.* During the two decades before the Great War youth began to organize and to challenge collectively adult authority. Indeed, the organization of youth and the challenging of adult values by younger men and women is one of the most striking aspects of the prewar period. Although young people were organized by adults in most cases out of fear of delinquency or concern for social discipline, the organizations created by adults sometimes escaped from their control and gave rise to revolts against the older generation in the name of youth. The Jugendbewegung in Germany and Austria, the nationalist revival in France, the revolt of young Socialists against the party leadership in Italy, and the mobilization of young intellectuals in Spain against the existing parties were all manifestations of the desire of young people to broaden their personal feelings of generational uniqueness into social movements and to gain greater control over their own fate. In this sense, the German Youth Movement was especially significant (though not as unique as many German historians have claimed) because it was organized by youthful leaders and directed toward ends that appealed to youth. Its goal was both to save youth from corruption by adult values and to transform the society at large by infusing it with youthful ardor and enthusiasm for noble, noncommercial tasks. It operated with the premise that youth was a superior and privileged stage of life, beyond which lay degeneration. Its enemies were adulthood and adults, who were connected with a crass and decadent society. It did not stop at

---

* The surprising thing is not that this occurred, but that it took so long to occur. As early as the beginning of the nineteenth century, Hannah More foresaw the impact that the doctrines of the French Revolution would have on relations between parents and their children. In a work published in 1801 she wrote, "Not only sons but daughters have adopted something of that spirit of independence and disdain of control, which characterizes the time . . . The rights of man have been discussed till we are sometimes wearied with the discussion. To these have been opposed, as the next stage in the progress of illumination, and with more presumption and prudence, the rights of women. It follows, according to the actual progression of human things, that the next influx of that irradiation which our enlighteners are pouring in upon us, will illuminate the world with grave descants on the rights of youth, the rights of children, the rights of babies." Quoted by F. Musgrove in *Youth and the Social Order* (London, 1964), p. 61.

asserting the values of childhood and youth as stages in the life cycle, to be enjoyed for their own sake, but went on to claim that youth was a higher form of human existence. Some of its more extreme leaders went so far as to declare a war of youth against the adult world.[3]

These movements of generational revolt on the surface of society, so prominent during the decade before 1914, were called forth and made possible by even deeper shifts in society's structure. One of these was a change in the relationship between fathers and sons in the industrialized and industrializing countries of Europe. Young men began to feel the dominance of their fathers as oppressive and to denounce it as illegitimate, not because their fathers were harsher or less affectionate than before but because fathers could no longer guarantee their sons a smooth entry into the society outside home. In a period of rapid social and economic change the skills and patterns of behavior that had served the father well often appeared useless to the son, especially if he belonged to the middle strata of society most caught up in the maelstrom of modernization. Once the father had ceased to be a bank of wisdom and traditional skills on which the son could draw for his future success, the father's stern demands for obedience, respect, discipline, and achievement in a fiercely competitive capitalist society were perceived by sons as expressions of an unbearable tyranny that justified every revolt. Moreover, this revolt was all the easier to undertake and carry to a successful conclusion because it need not have devastating material consequences for the son. Greater possibilities for social and geographical mobility liberated sons from economic dependence on their fathers. Only then, when traditional social structures had begun to crack and give way, could the biological urge for autonomy that arises in every human being between the ages of fifteen and twenty produce a full-fledged generational revolt that recognized and proclaimed itself as such.[4]

Yet conflict between fathers and their sons is by no means a sufficient explanation of the rise of generational consciousness in late nineteenth-century Europe. Critical to this development were the growing numbers of youth and their segregation from the adult world of life and labor. Throughout the nineteenth century "youth" referred to the stage of life intervening between the end of childhood and the assumption of the adult roles of work and marriage. In most countries this stage of life was spent in secondary schools and universities. Before 1880 youth was a luxury restricted to the aristocracy and those sectors of the bourgeoisie with land and incomes. In the late nineteenth century, as the needs of industrial society transformed and enlarged the middle classes, swelling the ranks of the white-collar class of salaried workers and civil servants, youth became a necessary step along the way to a well-paying and socially respectable job. At the same time, youth grew longer as more and more graduates of secondary schools went to universities and as governments intervened to limit youthful labor and to require periods of military service of all young men. Hence, although the relative number of young people in the population was stable or decreasing in most industrialized Western European countries as the result of extensions in the average length of life, the number of youths (defined in terms of those able to afford the luxury of an uncompensated moratorium between the years of childhood and the years of marriage and work) was increasing, thus giving older people the impression that youth was on the march and also giving young people the unpleasant feeling that competition for a shrinking number of places was likely to render the way to fame and fortune more difficult for them than it had been for their elders.[5]

The final element contributing to the development of generational consciousness was the weakening of traditional forms of social identification and a growing sense of collective (as opposed to individual or local) destiny. Regional and religious differences faded between 1870 and 1914 throughout Western Europe. Politics ceased to be the private business of a club-like elite and was opened up almost everywhere in Europe to some degree of mass participation. Social barriers were assaulted, and some fell. National languages undermined regional dialects. Dress became increasingly uniform. Cities were rebuilt on the model of Haussmann's Paris and began to resemble one another in the amenities and security they provided their inhabitants. Newspapers reached a larger public, linking their readers together and creating a feeling among them that they possessed a common fund of information. Schoolmasters indoctrinated their elementary school students in the cult of the nation; and the number of students available for indoctrination increased with every year as a result of the spread of schools to rural areas and the raising of the age of obligatory education. Men of all social classes were confounded in the common duty of universal military service.

All these developments contributed to the sense of nationality; they also encouraged the tendency to think in generational terms. Both Mannheim and Ortega concluded that membership in a generation implied above all the sharing of a common destiny. Modern historians have seldom operated happily with the concept of fate, whether collective or individual. But we can give this idea some empirical substance if we amend Mannheim and Ortega's assertion to read that the greater the sense of collective destiny, the greater the inclination to think of oneself as belonging to a historical generation. To this extent, we can say that the rise of generational consciousness was one of the side effects of the coming of mass society. It was, like the concept of class, a form of collectivism and determinism, but one that emphasized temporal rather than socioeconomic location.[6]

THE nineteenth-century tradition of the young generation as the vanguard of cultural and political change, the emergence of youth as a clearly defined and demographically significant social group, its organization, and a growing sense of collective historical destiny all converged to create a formida-

ble wave of generational thinking during the first few decades of the twentieth
century. This swell of generationalism reached its peak between 1928 and
1933, then slowly ebbed, leaving its main traces in literature and memoirs. But
during the years of flow the generational idea appeared on the pens and lips of
men and women of all camps and countries. All these people were struck, as
Ortega and T. E. Lawrence were, by the discovery that one's generation was a
destiny whose iron shackles permitted no escape. "The fateful act of living in
and with one's generation," Martin Heidegger wrote in 1929, "completes the
drama of human existence."[7]

The appearance of the "generation of 1914" as a theme in the discourse of
the period coincided with this wave of generational thinking. So did the formulation of the most original and significant twentieth-century generational
theories of social and cultural change. Stripped of their pretensions to universality, the theories of Mentré, Mannheim, and Ortega were attempts to make
sense of generational consciousness and the movements it inspired. The
Achilles heel of generational theory, and a weakness acknowledged by many of
its exponents, was the inability of generational theorists to specify with any
degree of precision the object of their inquiry. Most generational theorists hesitated, as Mentré did, between defining generations in terms of small elites and
defining them in terms of larger masses. Yet the contradiction that generational
theorists perceived between these two formulations reflected an underlying
social and political reality characteristic of the period between 1900 and 1933.
For the essential feature of the generational concept, as Ortega perceived, was
that it represented a mediation or "dynamic compromise" between outstanding
individuals and a mass. In an age when men of the European elite had come to
understand their need for followers, the generational idea held out the tantaliz-
ing possibility of a new kind of mass formation that would be defined by age,
mentality, and experience as opposed to income, status, and interest. It posited
a potential connection between privileged individuals capable of shaping attitudes and masses capable of implementing these attitudes through political action. This possibility of a new kind of political coalition explains the fascination
the generational idea exerted on Europeans seeking an alternative to the determinism of class.

Although the concept of a "generation of 1914" suggested the possibility of a
mass formation that would cut across classes, it is also true that this idea was
the creation of, and had its most direct reference to, a specific social group: literary intellectuals. Not a social class in their own right, these intellectuals were
distinguished by their possession of a secondary education and their activity as
the creators of the symbols and images with which members of other social
groups interpreted and gave meaning to their lives. Since the number of students attending secondary schools during this period in most European countries was extremely small—in some countries, no more than 2 or 3 percent of
the eligible population—their possession of a secondary education placed intel-

lectuals automatically into a well-defined and privileged elite. Early twentieth-century intellectuals were seldom rich. Most depended upon newspapers for the support of their families and the cultivation of their talent. But whether they were comfortably well-off, like Siegfried Sassoon, or scrambling for money, like Giovanni Papini, they distinguished themselves carefully from the "people" and those who worked for a living with their hands. They thought of themselves as the bearers and embodiment of culture—and when they used the word "culture," they were inclined to write it with a capital "C." These people articulated the concept of a generation of 1914 and provided the images of it with which members of other social classes later came to identify.[8]

Critics of the generational concept often went so far as to suggest that generationalists represented no one but themselves. This was not so; and, indeed, to propose it is to run the risk of seriously misunderstanding the nature and significance of the generational phenomenon. Early twentieth-century intellectuals were not alone in feeling and responding to a sense of discontinuity in the Europe of their time. On the contrary, they drew their ideas from members of other social groups with whom they were in contact—from aristocrats, entrepreneurs, engineers, doctors, lawyers, peasants, artisans, shopkeepers and salesmen, civil servants, and in some cases (but more rarely) even workers. In this sense, intellectuals reflected the mentalities of the society at large. But because the majority of intellectuals tended to come from the middle strata of society, the ways in which they articulated their feeling of discontinuity and the representations they provided of the past, the present, and the future were colored by the special anxieties and aspirations of the classes to which they belonged. In most Western and Central European countries during this period the middle classes were torn between their desire to wrest power from the former elites and their fear of a "rebellion of the masses." Intellectuals from these classes dreamed of a spiritual revolution that would eliminate the exploiters and the exploited and fuse all sectors of society into a unified and conflict-free community. The generational idea appealed to them because it pointed to one way in which this spiritual revolution could be accomplished.[9]

The "generation of 1914" was therefore first of all a self-image produced by a clearly defined group within the educated classes at a particular moment in the evolution of European society. It was both an attempt at self-description by intellectuals and a project of hegemony over other social classes that derived its credibility and its force from circumstances that were unique to European men born during the last two decades of the nineteenth century.

GENERATIONAL theorists worked hard to devise a reliable and scientifically respectable method of determining the chronological limits of generations. Their goal was a periodic table that would set forth the history of modern Europe in a succession of quantifiably delimited generations.[10] These efforts were in vain because they rested on a misconception of the generational phenomenon. A historical generation is not defined by its chronological limits or its borders. It is not a zone of dates; nor is it an army of contemporaries making its way across a territory of time. It is more like a magnetic field at the center of which lies an experience or a series of experiences. It is a system of references and identifications that gives priority to some kinds of experiences and devalues others—hence it is relatively independent of age. The chronological center of this experiential field need not be stable; it may shift with time. What is essential to the formation of a generational consciousness is some common frame of reference that provides a sense of rupture with the past and that will later distinguish the members of the generation from those who follow them in time. This frame of reference is always derived from great historical events like wars, revolutions, plagues, famines, and economic crises, because it is great historical events like these that supply the markers and signposts with which people impose order on their past and link their individual fates with those of the communities in which they live.

What allowed European intellectuals born between 1880 and 1900 to view themselves as a distinct generation was that their youth coincided with the opening of the twentieth century and their lives were then bifurcated by the Great War. Those who survived into the decade of the 1920s perceived their lives as being neatly divided into a *before*, a *during*, and an *after*, categories most of them equated with the stages of life known as youth, young manhood, and maturity. What bound the generation of 1914 together was not just their experiences during the war, as many of them later came to believe, but the fact that they grew up and formulated their first ideas in the world from which the war issued, a world framed by two dates, 1900 and 1914. This world was the "vital horizon" within which they began conscious historical life.[11]

The primary fact of this world—and the first thing that young people noticed about it—was that it was being rapidly transformed by technology. Europeans were being freed increasingly from the traditional constraints imposed on mankind by nature. Life was becoming safer, cleaner, more comfortable, and longer for most sectors of the population. Death had not been vanquished (though many death-bearing diseases had), but its arrival was now more predictable, and the physician, along with the engineer, had been elevated to the priesthood of the new civilization.

At the same time that life was becoming more secure, its pace quickened and the sense of distance among people shrank. Even rest became recreation. Instead of picnicking *sur l'herbe* or strolling on resort boardwalks, Europeans began to pedal, swim, ski, and scramble up the sides of mountains. The great events of the era, from a technological point of view, were the invention and diffusion of the automobile, the motorcycle, and the airplane. Speed still implied romance and adventure and had yet to be connected with traffic fatalities, tedium, and pollution. It is difficult to determine the precise effects that these changes of velocity had on the sensibility of intellectuals growing up in early twentieth-century Europe. Certainly, though, the acceleration of movement enhanced the feeling of novelty and encouraged the conviction that the twentieth century would be fundamentally different from its predecessor, if only because it would be faster. [12]

The second characteristic of the prewar world, prominently featured on the front page of every daily newspaper, was that it was undergoing a revolutionary change in political and social structures. Old empires were under attack in Central and Eastern Europe. Oppressed peoples were clamoring for statehood. Workers were insisting on higher wages and shorter hours. Peasants were demanding land or more favorable sharecropping arrangements. Everywhere in Europe there was a movement to open political participation to larger groups of people. The old systems of deference were under attack, and the old elites were being pressed to make concessions. Authority, whether exercised by landlords, factory owners, clergymen, or fathers within their own families, was being angrily disputed. As Ortega was later to complain, people were no longer content to occupy the place that destiny had assigned them. And since the number of people in Europe was increasing at a rapid rate, there was much talk about "the masses" and what they were likely to do. The great political and social movement of the day was Socialism. It seemed certain that Socialism would play as important a role in the twentieth century as liberalism had played in the nineteenth. In 1900, though, it was far from clear what that role would be. The still unsatisfied ambitions of the subordinate classes and their organization into groups that challenged the forces of public order on the streets of Europe's capitals meant that the threat of revolution hovered menacingly on the horizon of the middle- and upper-class mind. But the commitment of the most prominent Socialist leaders to democracy and peace and their often professed abhorrence of violence kept alive the hope that the transition to a new society could be made painlessly and with benefit to all.

A third characteristic of this world—one that is especially difficult to grasp today—is that while it stood under the cloud of threatening war, its inhabitants viewed the possibility of this war from the perspective of a century in which warfare in Europe had been kept within such narrowly circumscribed limits that it had never interfered with improvements in the quality of life. War among the major European powers seemed both inevitable (because of Germany's determination to dominate the continent and challenge England's control of the world's seas and markets) and impossible (because of the complex economic interrelationships that bound the great powers to each other and made the prosperity of one dependent on the prosperity of all). This was the paradox that defined European international relations between 1900 and 1914. There was no lack of signs that conflict was coming. Major European crises erupted with regularity almost every year after 1895. The Boer War, Faschoda, the Russo-Japanese War, Agadir, the Balkan wars—these were the events with which the generation of 1914 grew up. But somehow the final breakdown of the system was averted, and war became in people's minds a dangerous sport, like big game hunting, that some particularly adventurous Europeans practiced outside or on the periphery of Europe. These conditions of increasing ease of life, along with increasing sources of domestic and international conflict, explain how among Europeans of the ruling classes optimism about the future could be "allied insanely" with the expectation of Armageddon.[13]

This was the world that young people growing up between 1900 and 1914 encountered; this was the vital horizon within which they had to act. To understand what they thought about that world, we must look at the prevailing state of culture. Toward the end of the nineteenth century, European high culture began to split into two related but mutually antagonistic camps. On the one hand, there was the official bourgeois culture; on the other hand, there was the culture of the trailblazing vanguard. Middle-class intellectuals born during the last two decades of the nineteenth century reacted fiercely and self-consciously against the first and gave their allegiance to the second. It was from the leaders of the avant-garde that young intellectuals learned how to interpret their world; and it was from them that they took their criticism of contemporary society and their visions of the future. These cultural innovators were in the process of redefining and restructuring European culture. Men like Bergson, Poincaré, Sorel, Freud, Weber, James, Blondel, Mosca, Pareto, and Croce had brought about a radical change in the way European intellectuals thought and the way they viewed the products of thought. The very possibility of achieving sure knowledge had been called into question. Philosophers of science and society showed that the laws linking subject and object were fictions, thus not really laws at all, unless legislated into fleeting reality by human will. Time was redefined in subjective terms to free experience from the determinism of sequence. The standard of truth was abandoned in favor of the idea of efficacity. The bridges between the individual consciousness and the outside world were blown up. Even the unity of the self was thrown into doubt. Descartes's *Discourse on Method* became a favored example of faulty thinking, the product of an age now disappeared.

The new culture was, in one of its most important aspects, a "culture of Anti-Necessity."[14] Varieties of neoidealism competed for the allegiance of the European intellectual elite, and the prophets of these systems of belief dedicated the major part of their energies to demonstrating that no self-respecting intellectual could assume a materialistic outlook on the world. Reality, they said, was a perspective and a construction rather than a verifiable fact or a thing. Man was not the executor of natural and historical laws, but a creator of his life with no limits on him but those imposed by lack of imagination and weakness of will. Scientific analysis was considered to be a mental instrument of severely limited validity; intuition into the multiplicity of human realities took its place; and action rather than contemplation was recommended as a source of knowledge. With organized religion in retreat and reason exposed as the greatest of illusions, it became essential to find new bases for life and new systems of morality by which to judge men's actions. No longer was it possible to count on the beneficence of history or to rely on receiving steady dividends handed out by progress. The mind became an instrument with which intellectuals dominated and took possession of the world; civilization, a precarious achievement of the spirit that must constantly be renewed through the process of destruction and re-creation. [15]

These attitudes represented a break with the main tradition of European rationalism. Yet the very intellectuals who prided themselves on being liberated from the illusions of progress and the mystique of science remained strangely indentured to determinisms of various kinds, determinisms, furthermore, that were themselves inspired by scientific theories. For some, it was the determinism of biology; for others, the determinism of geography; for still others, the determinism of history or race. Whatever the determinism chosen, however, it led toward the acknowledgment of a painful contradiction: that man was free to create his own life, as the novelist creates a fiction; and yet was a slave to the material conditions of his existence. Most European intellectuals of the late nineteenth century sought escape from this dilemma by asserting that man could master the determinisms that bound him only by raising them to consciousness, accepting them, and living life with vitality and passion.

Some intellectuals were quick to perceive the political implications of these attitudes and to push them to their most extreme consequences. Democracy and socialism, they noted not unhappily, were based on faulty premises. All societies were dominated by aristocracies and all civilizations were doomed to collapse. Why, then, get concerned about the misery of the masses? Suffering was the price that peoples paid for culture. Progress, insofar as it existed, took place in individual minds. Better, then, the cultivation of one truly successful human being than the futile, life-destroying pursuit of an impossible egalitarian utopia. Since life was struggle, truth was a matter of perspective, and annihilation awaited us at the end, we ought to endeavor, as Unamuno put it, "to stamp others with our seal, to perpetuate ourselves in them and in their children by dominating them, to leave on all things the imperishable impress of our signature." War was the seedbed of culture, the foundation of morality, and the form of social intercourse that brought men closest together. Peace came at a cultural price too high to pay. This was the message that many people derived from Nietzsche's teachings; and if, for some reason, they were put off by the mists of Teutonic terminology that surrounded Nietzsche's aphorisms or the intimations of derangement with which the message was relayed, they could get the same complex of ideas from a dozen other sources, for the notions of an aristocracy of intellect and a tragic sense of life were everywhere in the air. [16]

Naturally, the new culture was not taught in schools. It remained the possession of a small elite: that literary and artistic vanguard living in the great capitals of Europe that Hugo von Hofsmannthal called the "conscience" of the young generation. But it was discovered and disseminated among young intellectuals during the years immediately preceding the war. The spiritual guides and mentors acknowledged by the members of the generation of 1914—Barrès, Péguy, Sorel, and Romain Rolland in France; Nietzsche, Langbehn, and Moeller van den Bruck in Germany; Shaw, Wells, and Hardy in England; Unamuno, Azorín, and Baroja in Spain; D'Annunzio, Croce, Gentile, and Pareto in Italy; Ibsen and Strindberg in Scandinavia—were all proponents of the new culture. Their syntheses of neoidealism and biological determinism, their elitism, their pessimism about the future of Western culture, and their critiques of democracy and socialism were the ideas that seemed most up-to-date between 1900 and 1914. The existence of this new culture, and the excitement it produced, contributed to the consciousness of a generational rupture among people born between 1880 and 1900; yet, paradoxically, the generational idea concealed the extent to which the new culture was a creation of the intellectuals of the preceding generation. "I could not have defined what all this was about that had laid so strong a spell on me," Carl Zuckmayer (1896) later wrote, "but it was *our* time, *our* world, *our* sense of life that came rushing upon me, falling upon me, and suddenly I awakened to a consciousness of a new generation, a consciousness that even the most intelligent, most aware and unbiased parents could not share." What Zuckmayer and other young intellectuals like him did not realize was that the intellectuals in the generation of their parents had created that new art and those new ideas which his generation experienced as a "revelation" and an "illumination."[17]

Thus it was from intellectuals among the age-group of their fathers that men born between 1880 and 1900 learned to think of themselves as a generation. Massis inherited the idea from Barrès; Ortega took it from Unamuno and Azorín; Prezzolini and Papini found it in Croce and D'Annunzio. Moreover, it was these same intellectuals who taught their disciples what to think about the society in which they lived.* Prewar European intellectual youth grew up in revolt against the comfort, coziness, and predictability of modern life. They feared that they had been born into a declining world, and they longed after risk, danger, and brutal contact with the elemental realities of life, as they

---

* I am aware that I am sidestepping here the important question of the role played by natural parents in the education and formation of the generation of 1914. Unfortunately, the evidential foundation upon which to generalize about the relationship between intellectuals born in the late nineteenth century and their parents is not yet available; and unfounded speculations in this area would be futile and misleading. One question worthy of investigation would be the influence of mothers on their sons and the degree to which they instilled within them dissatisfaction with the existing society and the dream of heroic achievement. For first steps in this direction, see Nicholas Mosley, *Julian Grenfell* (London, 1976), and John Mack, *A Prince of Our Disorder* (Boston and Toronto, 1976).

imagined that life was lived outside of European cities. The first images of the generation of 1914, devised during the decade or so before the outbreak of the war, were nothing but a reversal of the qualities that young intellectuals disliked or feared in the generation of their parents. The previous generation had been thinkers; they would be doers. The previous generation had floundered in moral relativism; they would seek assurance in calm faith. The previous generation had been weak and indecisive; they would be strong and vital. This supposed change in character was rendered superficially plausible by the spread of team sports, the quickening of the pace of life, greater possibilities for travel, and the weakening of the authority of fathers over their sons as society became more complex and opportunities for employment and careers became more varied.

The sentiment of generational unity grows out of and is nourished by an even deeper feeling. What draws young people together and ignites the sparks that join them is a sense of common grievance. This does not happen regularly, as some generational theorists assumed. But when it does, groups of coevals will form to set the world aright. The complaint voiced most often by young intellectuals during the period before 1914 was that they had the misfortune to be born into a dying world that lacked energy, vitality, and moral fiber. It was characteristic of this age-group of European intellectuals that they perceived the problem of decadence in connection with a crisis of the nation. The nation was perceived as being weak, morally flabby, a shaky structure that might at any time collapse into its constituent parts. The desire for a reform of the nation and a renewal of its spiritual resources was ordinarily allied with a profound ignorance of the realities of national life. Young intellectuals generally knew little about the people or their problems. But their longing for regeneration was nonetheless strong, and it was a feeling capable of inspiring action. Hence the prevalence of national revivals and the popularity of nationalist movements during the decade preceding the Great War. The nation, they believed, must somehow be whipped into action; its classes and contending factions must be reconciled; its citizens must learn to subordinate their corporatist and selfish interests to the spiritual interests of the national community conceived as a whole. This was what Ortega meant in 1914 when he said that Spanish society must be nationalized; but his program for backward Spain was an ideal shared by Massis and Prezzolini and others like them all over Europe.

Partisans of national revival perceived two ways by which their goal of national regeneration could be accomplished. One was to implement the Socialist program, which called for the democratization of political institutions, the extension of political participation, the elimination of social inequities, and the defense of international peace. Between 1900 and 1914 most young intellectuals felt some attraction toward this program; many called themselves Socialists and even joined their country's Socialist party. Among these converts to Socialism were Brooke, Ortega, and Gramsci. But most middle-class intellectuals of this generation withheld their adherence from Socialist parties, or withdrew soon after joining, because of their feeling that Socialism was a plebeian movement in which intellectuals had no place and their fear that Socialism's victory would destroy elitist values and undermine the cohesion of the nation. Socialism, Henri Franck confided to a friend in 1908, could be the salvation of life, sensibility, and art. It could create new values and bring about the renewal of civilization. But if the Socialists remained bound to a "sterile Marxism" and a "base materialism," if their movement resulted only in "appetite, envy, and hate," and if they were not willing to give their lives to defend "that ensemble of feelings of veneration that is called France," then everything would be finished. "There is something more important yet than the success of the working class; it's the preservation of France." [18]

The other way the nation could be rejuvenated and civilization saved from decadence was through a sudden trauma or blow of fate. The only deliverance from the languor of bourgeois complacency that most young Europeans could imagine was the outbreak of a general war. Hence some leaped to the treacherous assumption that it was on the field of battle and in the stress of national emergency that a sense of national consciousness would develop and that a new, more ethical, less commercial man would emerge to replace the bourgeois and the proletarian, both products of the hateful and selfish society into which young intellectuals cursed themselves for having been born. This idea may seem strange and even demented; but it will appear less so when we remember that all European wars since 1815 had been short, progressive in their effects, and, in memory at least, heroic. One did not have to be a reactionary like Walter Flex to believe that war offered a means of breaking the impasse of prewar politics, of creating a sense of national unity where none existed, and of nourishing "those virtues of sacrifice, fortitude, and boldness that constitute the essence of the combatant and that make of the fighting man, with all his excesses and brutality, a type infinitely superior to that shrewd sybarite who finds in the cult of peace the best expression of his sensual concept of life." [19]

Attitudes like these explain the feverish enthusiasm with which large sectors of European intellectual youth greeted the outbreak of war in 1914. European youth did not actively want war; but many young European intellectuals desperately wanted change and were willing to risk their lives (and those of others) to achieve it. More than one prewar intellectual had gazed into the future and sensed that something new and wonderful was coming. "It is brooding heavily in the air as a storm does, and soon, oh, very soon, it will thunder upon the world. Flashes of lightning have appeared on the horizon, the echoes of thunder have been heard in the air, but the great reckless storm, the storm that will make us abandon mediocrity and will set us free from pettiness, has not yet come—yet soon it will break over us." When war did break over Europe, it was interpreted by intellectuals as an hour of redemption, a rite of purification, and a chance, perhaps the last, to escape from a sinking and declining civilization. This is why Rupert Brooke could sing "Now, God be thanked Who has matched us with His hour"; why the German poet Bruno Frank could shout "Rejoice, friends! that we are alive"; why the Italian writer Giani Stuparich was so happy that he wept with joy; why Drieu la Rochelle remembered the outbreak of the war as a marvelous surprise and the unexpected fulfillment of his youth; and why Ortega immediately interpreted the news of war on August 5, 1914, as the end of one world and the birth of another. "History," he wrote, "is trembling to its very roots, its flanks are torn apart convulsively, because a new reality is about to be born." [20]

SOME great historical events may sweep the various age-groups within a society together and confound them in a common struggle. Young and old may find themselves suffering side by side. But this was not the case with the Great War, which caused a deterioration in the relationship between young and older age-groups and which intensified the feeling of a break between the generations that was already strong before 1914. This is not to suggest that men born between 1880 and 1900 alone experienced the effects of the war. All inhabitants of Europe were exposed to the militarization of life and language, the erosion of individual freedom and social differences, the disruption of economic life, the drain of wealth, the hardships caused by food shortages, the growth of collectivism and bureaucracies, the collapse of the international system, and the release of huge reservoirs of aggressivity and violence. The case of Spain shows that not even nonbelligerent countries could escape the tornado of destruction let loose on the world from Vienna and Berlin. It is nonetheless true that these global developments were experienced by different age-groups in different ways, at different times in their life cycles, and hence from different perspectives. For someone born between 1885 and 1895, the war came just as he was advancing from adolescence and youth to young manhood—that is, to follow Mentré, just as he was beginning to perceive the deficiencies of the education he had received from his parents and teachers and was about to create his own hierarchy of values and ideals. Moreover, intellectuals in this age group differed from their predecessors and successors in that large numbers of them had experienced the war at the front, many as junior officers. Among intellectuals, therefore, they alone had had the front experience. But just how important was this experience, and what were its effects on the intellectuals who underwent it?

Reading some of the more famous war books, it easy to take away the impression that the war was experienced exclusively as an irretrievable disaster. In *Under Fire*, Barbusse asserted that war degraded every great idea, commanded every crime, and gave bent to every evil instinct, including "wickedness to the point of sadism, egoism to the point of ferocity, the need for pleasure to the point of madness." Remarque developed the same theme in *All Quiet on the Western Front*, but he related the evil effects of the war specifically to his own age-group. The war, he claimed, had destroyed his generation morally as well as physically. At the front, he explained, one learned to live with death. All the things that had mattered before—distinctions, breeding, education—were blotted out and replaced with a concern for sheer survival. This had transformed front soldiers into creatures lower than Bushmen. For Bushmen could still develop their inner forces, while the front soldier exerted every effort to become primitive so that he could survive. Richard Aldington agreed with Remarque's somber view of the war's effects and the war generation's postwar prospects. The war, he lamented, had been a curse and a "knock-out blow" to the sensibility of those who had fought it. Even Omodeo was forced to acknowledge that whereas the war had "carried to sublime heights superior spirits" like the Garrone brothers, it had also "fearfully extended the range of cruelty and cowardice." In killing the best and most generous, in destroying hopes, in spreading cynicism and "Niebelungen delirium" among the very young, it had driven a whole generation into the depths of nihilism and brought about an unquestionable retrogression of civilization. [21]

What intellectuals found most difficult to accept about the war was its mechanical and impersonal quality. Death and wounds were not ordinarily doled out in hand-to-hand combat, but in the whizzing and hissing and booming of shells fired by an unseen foe. Soldiers lay huddled like animals in craters and dugouts for hours and sometimes for days expecting death and praying for survival. The pounding and seething noise of artillery barrages was the instrument with which the soldier's will and mental health were undermined and finally broken; attacks, when they came, were an almost welcome release from the prison of emplacements and the agony of waiting. The real challenge in this kind of war, as Omodeo observed, was to survive the terrible monotony and the psychological strain of seeing one's friends and companions die with no end or noticeable advance in sight. Soldiers soon learned that the war was not something one fought; it was something one endured or suffered. The men of the front came to view themselves as lepers who had been struck down by fate, cordoned off from the healthy population, and consigned to caves to die. Conceptions of heroism had to be abandoned, then refashioned out of new materials. "Instead of heroes, there were only victims; conscripts instead of volunteers . . . We were all of us cogs in a great machine which sometimes rolled forward, nobody knew where, sometimes backward, nobody knew why. We had lost our enthusiasm, our courage, the very sense of our identity." The instinct to survive made cowards of the bravest men, and "shriveling fear" was the most persistent enemy the soldier had to face. Sensitivity to beauty was dulled by omnipresent ugliness, the mind lost its capacity to concentrate and think, youthful innocence was covered over by the hard cast of a soldier's remorseless face, and the boy of twenty crammed into weeks a range of experiences that most men of his era never underwent in a lifetime. Eventually, soldiers even lost their ability to react to death.[22]

But if the war was experienced by intellectuals as unrelieved horror, catastrophe, brutalization, subjection to matter, fear, loss of innocence and sensitivity, and a graveyard of dearly held prewar illusions, it was also experienced by many of those same men as an opportunity, a privilege, and a revelation. Ambivalence toward the war is the main characteristic of the best and most honest of the war literature. The same men who cried out at the inhumanity of the war often confessed that they had loved it with a passion and wondered if they would ever be able to free themselves from the front's magical spell.

What of value could intellectuals have found in the ugliness and the senseless slaughter of European trench warfare? What secret charms drew them to it? Pierre Teilhard de Chardin (1881), priest, stretcher-bearer, and intellectual, who spent four years under arms, sought to explain the front's appeal in a letter to a female cousin in September 1917:

> The front cannot but attract us, because it is, in one way, the *extreme boundary* between what you are already aware of, and what is still in the process of formation. Not only do you see there things that you experience nowhere else, but you also see emerge from within yourself an underlying stream of clarity, energy, and freedom that is to be found hardly anywhere else in ordinary life—and the new form that the soul then takes on is that of the individual living the quasi-collective life of all men, fulfilling a function far higher than that of the individual, and becoming fully conscious of this new state. It goes without saying that at the front you no longer look at things in the same way as you do in the rear; if you did, the sights you see and the life you lead would be more than you could bear. This exhaltation is accompanied by a certain pain. Nevertheless it is indeed an exhaltation. And that's why one likes the front in spite of everything, and misses it.[23]

This passage could be read as a commentary on the eternal appeal of war; and indeed, some combatant intellectuals were inclined to explain their fascination for the front from this perspective. "War," Montherlant wrote, "will always exist because there will always be boys of twenty to bring it into existence, by dint of love." Frederick Manning, author of one of the best of the English war novels, made a similar observation. "Life," he said, "was a hazard enveloped in mystery, and war quickened the sense of both in men." War offered the possibility of adventure, of leaving behind parents, friends, examinations, responsibilities, fiancées, and careers, and sailing out into unlimited and uncharted waters. It gave young men a chance to test their courage and prove their manhood. It offered freedom from peacetime authorities and, for middle- and upper-class men, the chance for power over the fate of others. All these things had been true of wars before the Great War of 1914-1918, and would be true of others after it. But it would be a mistake to consider the war's fascination simply as an eternal human temptation to triumph over everything that is petty in life and to reach out for the absolute, even though these elements were surely present. The war possessed a special value for intellectuals born in the late nineteenth century, and this value can be understood only in terms of a particular historical moment and a particular society. [24]

The theme that comes back most frequently in the literature of the war is the discovery of comradeship. Comradeship was not the same thing as friendship. Noel Coward called it "a sort of splendid carelessness . . . holding us together." It was, he claimed, "beyond even what love you have, something intangible and desolately beautiful." Comradeship arose out of the sharing of a common danger and a common disillusion that was "beyond all hope." It was sharpened by the enjoyment of common pleasures and by a sense of alienation from those behind—those who had not been there, who had not seen the horrors, who had not experienced the fear of dying and the relief of survival, and who therefore would never understand the looks on the survivors' faces. Comradeship rested on an awareness of mutual egotism: wanting one's comrades to live, regretting them if they died, but knowing that even if they did die life would go on without them; and realizing further that they felt the same way with regard to you. [25]

The acuteness of the pleasure that comradeship gave and its ability to live on as an ideal long after the war ended can be properly appreciated only when placed against the background of a society that divided people by putting up unbreachable ramparts of language, dress, and education. Many middle- and upper-class soldiers had had little previous contact with people from the classes beneath them. Peasants, workers, and even artisans had been perceived not as individual human beings but as creatures deliberately designed to serve those above them—or alternatively, as members of a grey mass whose growing demands were to be feared and resisted, if necessary by force. Now men of the upper and lower classes lived and died together in holes and dugouts; they swore the same oaths; they looked forward to the same pleasures; and their lives were equally expendable, or at least equally expended. Individuality and class distinctions were difficult to maintain in the face of artillery and machine-gun fire that was blind to social hierarchies. One person melted into another in the mud of the trenches, and the drab colors of the new uniforms that were introduced after the first battles of the war—khaki, horizon blue, field grey—reinforced the impression of an undifferentiated mass. Most intellectuals experienced the sense of belonging to this mass as a gain and a breakthrough. Like Teilhard, they felt that they had been liberated from their individuality and elevated to a higher state of being. Those who experienced these feelings of solidarity most intensely found it difficult to believe that things would ever again be the same. And it was not uncommon for young soldiers to say—and to believe—that they had come to know the meaning of the nation for the first time in the communion of the front-line trenches. [26]

A second aspect of the war that was experienced as a gain was closely related to the aspect of barbarism and primitivism that Barbusse and Remarque denounced as encouraging the expression of men's baser instincts. That was an enormous simplification of life, a throwing off of forms, and a going down to bare essentials. Many intellectuals were surprised to discover that they could live—and live more fully—without the comforts they had been taught to believe were essential aspects of a civilized existence. They learned to appreciate the simplest kinds of food, drink, talk, and sex in the company of their comrades and found, to their amazement, that life had more savor than it had had in prewar times. They no longer hid the facts of life and death, but lived with them on firsthand terms. They recognized their own egotism, and at the same time discovered themselves to be capable of sacrifices that they would never before have contemplated as within their reach or power. They lived in close companionship with nature and learned "to suffer, to bless blood, torment, wounds, hunger, thirst, blows . . . to know the exact value of things, the changes of the seasons, natural phenomena, to measure and to weigh the elements that have a mysterious meaning of fatality in the life of men." They felt that they had seen behind the screen of civilization, and they spoke of having returned to basics, or "last things." This impression of a return to fundamentals would only have been conceivable in a society where conventions had developed to the point where they were experienced as a burden and failed to express what people felt. The dissatisfaction with existing forms had appeared before the war, especially in artistic movements that sought to revolt against bourgeois culture. The breach in taste and values had already been made in culture, but only within a small elite that conceived of itself as an avant-garde. The war diffused this revolt against convention throughout the mass of men who had known the front-line trenches. It was a school in what was essential and what was not; and even those who hated it insisted that it left a lasting mark on them by changing their system of priorities and putting their prewar cultural attitudes to the test of facts.[27]

Many a young soldier therefore came home from the war convinced, like Ernst Jünger, that he had become a different and better man. Those who survived, many returning combatants believed, would be purer and more sincere; they would experience life more intensely; they would have more pity and more love for their fellow human beings; they would possess a deeper sense for the community and be more sensitive to the needs of the nation. And beyond that, they would be marked forever by "a certain grandeur" that derived from the adventures of their youth and from having risked their lives in useless causes. "We have been, and above all, after the war is over, we shall be . . . what you dreamed of being," the young Drieu la Rochelle immodestly wrote the aging essayist André Suarez in November 1917, summing up the attitude of more than one of his returning comrades.[28]

The historian might wish to credit these extravagant visions of future achievement and moral renewal; unfortunately, the evidence does not permit him to do so. Looking at the lives of the survivors, it is difficult to generalize about the impact of the war. The front experience appears to have weakened some and strengthened others; to have driven some toward the Right and others toward the Left; to have given some the taste for war and violence and to have persuaded others to preserve peace at any cost; to have led some to identify with the dead and others to throw themselves into the enjoyment of life; to have made some more compassionate and others crueler. No unitary pattern of response emerges.

But one thing does seem clear: The front taught an unforgettable lesson in generationalism to those who came to know it. For those risking their lives at the front were in great majority young, and those directing the war from the rear and providing reasons for the slaughter tended to be older. Hence the dichotomy of young versus old was invested with a new and powerful emotional charge and became a synonym for the distinction between the victims of the front and the heartless warmongers and profiteers of the rear. [29]

Not that the war gave birth to the idea of a "new generation." That notion was a product of the decade before 1914 and a reflection of the atmosphere of novelty created by technological change, shifts in the structure of society, the threat of a general European war, and the appearance of a new culture. But the war did fortify and diffuse the consciousness of a new generation and gave plausibility to the idea of its unity by creating an overwhelming sense of rupture with the past. Those who lived through the war could never rid themselves of the belief that one world had ended and another begun in August 1914. And part of the appeal of the front derived precisely from the feeling that it was there amid the fire and flame that the new world was coming into being. [30]

At the same time, the war transformed the way that people thought about the new generation. Before the war the model for a generation had been a small group of cultural innovators, usually men of letters; after the war it became common to think of a generation in terms of an army with its officer corps and its mass of common soldiers. The war also internationalized the generational idea by giving rise to an experience shared by millions of young Europeans. Before 1914 the community of age to which most generationalists referred, either implicitly or explicitly, was the nation; after 1918 it became "European youth" or the pan-European "generation of survivors." Finally, the war shifted the chronological center of the young generation away from men born in the 1880s, like Massis and Prezzolini, to those born in the 1890s, like Jünger, Graves, Montherlant, and Malaparte; for it was these younger men who tended to identify themselves with the war. Older men were able to return to the homes, professions, and wives they had left in 1914. But the younger men had nothing to return to and were haunted by the memory of an experience that would overshadow everything that would happen to them during the rest of their lives. It was these younger men who would seek to turn the trench experience into a metaphor and a model for life in general, just as it was they who would take over and cultivate the idea of the "lost generation." [31]

W HEN we think of the army of returning veterans during the 1920s, we see them through the eyes of Remarque and Hemingway as a genera- tion of men crippled, both physically and morally, by their service in the war. Many no doubt were. Yet it is a fact that the famed cynicism and disillusion- ment of the survivors were, to a great extent, a product of the first few years of peace. To understand this mood of disillusionment we must recall the attitudes and expectations that soldiers brought home with them, attitudes and expecta- tions that were also widespread among the younger population as a whole.

Many soldiers had, like Omodeo, come to think that the war must have a secret meaning that only the future would reveal; they found it necessary to believe that their sacrifice and suffering would not be in vain; and they clung to the hope that the war would turn out to have been a rite of purification with positive results. Sensing this feeling and realizing its importance, political leaders in all countries encouraged the fighting and civilian sectors of the popu- lation to expect from peace not merely an end to bloodshed but a real alteration and improvement in the tenor and quality of life. It was said, and widely believed, that class barriers would fall; that selfishness would give way to coop- eration; that harmony would reign; that conflict among nations would cease; and that everyone's sacrifice and suffering would somehow be compensated.

These expectations were often encapsulated in the word "revolution," but peo- ple of different social backgrounds assigned very different meanings to the term. Governments encouraged these hopes with their propaganda, and in 1918 Wil- son came to incarnate the dream of renovation. The Wilsonian vision of a world safe for democracy merged with the equally vague idea of a revolution carried out by returning soldiers in the name of the values of manhood and self-sacrifice they had discovered on the battlefield. If the war had been a rite of regeneration and if it had fostered the development of new values, as many soldiers had come to believe, then it was logical that the men who had been closest to it should play an important and privileged role in postwar affairs. Von Unruh's soldiers at Verdun were not alone in thinking that they should bring home with them the light of revelation. The veterans' movements established all over Europe in the last year of the war were inspired by these hopes and were meant to make the survivors' weight felt in national politics.[32]

The expectations of the returning combatants were almost invariably disap- pointed during the first few years that followed the war. From the point of view of generational theory, it is clear why they were and why they had to be. One explanation given for the "defeat" of the survivors was that the "old men" had come back and deprived the young men of their victory. This was nonsense. The old men had not come back. They had never left. Nor were the men who wielded power in most European countries during the 1920s all that old. What took place after 1919 was the normal renewal of personnel in the commanding heights of politics and culture, a process of generational turnover that was much less affected by the gigantic losses of the war than everyone thought. The leaders of postwar Europe had all served their apprenticeship before 1914. The strange thing was to expect them to yield their places to younger men who had little more to recommend them than their medals and their ambitions.[33] The truth was that most returning veterans, especially the younger ones, lacked the skills necessary for postwar reconstruction. They had to be educated in the techniques of peace. They were also tired and eager for pleasure after years of suffering and renunciation. And they had to liberate themselves from their memories of death and war before they could be useful or happy in the civilian world. It would be hard enough for most of them to save themselves, not to mention to redeem the problem-saddled world to which they were returning. Some degree of disillusionment was thus implicit in their situation. It always has been and always will be difficult for young warriors to come home, and it was especially difficult in 1919 because the armistice did not immediately bring with it a cessation of conflict among nations or within them.[34]

Disillusionment comes in many forms. The special form it took in Europe in the 1920s had to do with the development of the political situation and the frustration of apocalyptic hopes. Between 1917 and 1920 a revolutionary wave broke over every European country. Armies grew restive and mutinied; urban populations staged riots and insurrections over dwindling food supplies and rising prices; unions swelled in membership far beyond their prewar size; and workers began to challenge factory owners for the control of production. In March 1917 the Russian autocracy was overthrown and replaced by a democratic republic. This republic moved leftward quickly, and in November Lenin and his party seized power in the name of a socialist revolution. When the war ended in the following year all Europe was in seething turmoil. In 1919 soviets were set up in Turin, Fiume, Berlin, Munich, Vienna, Budapest, and Glasgow. The Austro-Hungarian and Ottoman empires collapsed under the burden of defeat. To the west, peasants occupied estates in Italy and Spain. Hordes of angry demonstrators thronged over the Champs-Elysées in Paris. Anything and everything seemed possible. Even such a conservative spirit as Siegfried Sassoon thought that Europe had entered the "antechamber to the millennium."

But the doors to the future were suddenly slammed shut. The old class barriers sprang up with remarkable rapidity. The spirit of gain reasserted itself over the spirit of sacrifice. Employers reneged, when they could, on the concessions they had made in fear to their employees. The peace signed at Versailles in the spring of 1919 was a peace of interests and imperialism rather than one that would reconcile peoples or lead to international harmony. By the end of 1920 the socialist revolution was defeated in the western and central regions of Europe; and where it was not defeated, as in Russia, its leaders were thrown on the defensive and forced to adopt measures that seemed to run counter to the spirit of socialist doctrine. Radical change and the much touted revolution in values turned out to be yet one more illusion. Thus there was nothing for young soldiers to come back to, and many fled in disgust into a spiritual exile or a "flight without end." As Sassoon said, 1919 had "laboured under a pervasive disadvantage. Too much was expected of it. It was a year of rootless rebeginnings and steadily developing disillusionments."[35]

This disillusionment was felt by men and women of all age-groups in all parts of Europe; but the feeling of betrayal and defeat was especially strong among returning veterans born in the 1890s. They suffered from a tremendous sense of anticlimax, and the younger they were the more disoriented they felt. Charles Carrington (1897) sought to recall the nature of these feelings in 1930 when they were beginning to be buried beneath a layer of myth. "The spell which had bound us for so long a time was broken; the charm failed; an illusion came crashing down upon our ears and left us in an unfamiliar world—our fairy gold turned to dust and ashes." It was long, Carrington said, before demobilized soldiers could resume a civilian's sense of time. During the war combatants had lived only for the moment. "The future had for so long meant only a series of trips up the line, punctuated by short paradisal intervals of rest in each of which you laughed and drank in a company of whom some would probably be dead in a month, and the others in a year, that to survive the next tour in the trenches, to enjoy one more spell in rest-billets, perhaps to get one more week's leave in England, were all the ambitions and hopes that life could offer, the farthest rim of the horizon being bounded by 'next spring offensive.' " The future, insofar as soldiers thought about it, was "as vague as heaven and much more remote." Then when the end of the war came, soldiers hardly knew what to make of it. "Friends were parted. Life seemed large and empty. You had to earn a living. It was not easy to begin again, to take thought for the morrow when you had not expected to be alive for it." False prophets appeared who bid for your attention. "Some told you that you were the savior of your country, which must immediately be converted into a utopia for your benefit. Others said that you were a rotter who had acquired habits of idleness and insobriety in the King's service. All this was very confusing for a soldier lad who had picked up his education in a strange school, who had borne burdens which these prophets would not touch with their little fingers, and whose moral fibre was strained and tired. Disillusion came in with peace, not with war; peace at first was the futile state."[36]

The developments of 1917–1920 engendered disappointment and frustration; they gave rise to bitterness and cynicism; but among young war veterans, the dream of cultural and political renewal did not die. Brought up in a crepuscular atmosphere of cultural crisis, subjected while still young to the ordeal of the war, witnesses during the immediate postwar years to a wave of revolution that swept away century-old empires and shook to its foundations every European institution, intellectuals born in the last two decades of the nineteenth century could not divest themselves of the feeling that the apocalypse had only been postponed and that any restoration of the postwar era would be temporary. The survival of the revolutionary regime in Russia, the creation of Communist parties throughout Europe, the victory of the Fascist movement in Italy, the collapse of parliamentary government in Spain, the difficulties that Great Britain and France experienced in regaining their prewar dynamism, and the onset of the worldwide economic crisis in 1929 confirmed these intellectuals in their belief that the world of their childhood was dead and that a new postwar world was being born.

This sense of living through an interregnum, though shared by large numbers of people, did not create a new world view or a new philosophy. Nor did it launch a new school of thought that expressed the ideals and aspirations of an entire generation. It did bring into being and keep alive a mentality, a collective state of mind, that left its imprint on the language and literature of the 1920s. The intellectuals of the war generation were fascinated by the image of the traveler. They viewed themselves as wanderers and vagabonds who traveled without itineraries because timetables were undependable and "tour guides gave false information." They were "never tiring analysts of the verb 'depart' " who, like Henry de Montherlant, were "always wandering, always pursuing something, always fleeing something . . . at the prey of all temptations." They were people, like Nikos Kazantzakis, who "longed for flight." They were always ready "to leave everything" and "to take off on the highways." They carried within themselves "the unsatisfied desire for great departures." They suffered from and enjoyed the vice of evasion, "this desire to flee every place in search of I don't know what." They delighted in the wanderings and adventures of Charlot, "the tramp," "the vagabond," "the emigrant," and "the gold prospector," whose vocation it was to leave behind everything he treasured and whose youth was "the discovery of the world." And they were fascinated by the story of Ulysses, whose *Odyssey* they translated (like T. E. Lawrence) or rewrote and brought up to date (like James Joyce and Nikos Kazantzakis). Like Ulysses, they wandered without real hope that they would ever again find the shores from which they had departed.[37]

The passion for traveling and for departures can be explained to a great extent by the ready availability of new and faster means of transport. Men and women born after 1880 inherited a fully developed transportation system, which was new enough to be exciting and efficient enough to get them almost any place they cared to go. They could explore the European countryside on their bicycles, as T. E. Lawrence did when gathering information for his thesis on Crusaders' castles before the war. Or they could flit from one European capital to another on an elegant and rapid train that would very likely be on time.*

* It is not completely frivolous in this connection to recall that Mussolini and Italian Fascism were credited with having made the trains run on time. Speed, movement, and mastery of the air were all important elements in Fascist ideology; and Fascist ideology was formulated by men from the generation of 1914.

Steamships and the new canals made it possible to reach the most exotic or foreign lands in a fraction of the time that had been required fifty years before. Mysterious ports of call like Bombay, Singapore, Saigon, Rio, and San Francisco were now within reach of the reasonably adventurous European—yet still exotic enough when visited to compensate the traveler for his effort. By the time the soldiers marched off to war in August 1914 there were over two million automobiles functioning in Europe; men from the generation of 1914 were in the first age-group to have grown up with them and to have taken them for granted as the natural means for getting from one place to another. In the early 1920s automobiles were still expensive and within reach of only the relatively well-to-do; but the motorcycle, which was faster and more exciting, could be bought, and was, by impoverished veterans and young men without private means. During the 1920s airports were built, airplanes entered into general use for the transportation of civilian passengers, and Lindbergh succeeded in flying the Atlantic. Transatlantic telephone calls, oceanic cables, and radio broadcasts had ceased to be extraordinary and were accepted as everyday facts of life. And the fast-moving and jerky cinema had already overtaken the more static theater and opera house as the most popular form of entertainment—for intellectuals as well as workers—bringing with it a new rhythm of movement and a new, more discontinuous and disjointed sense of space and time.

The intellectuals of the war generation were elated by these opportunities and made a religion out of speed and movement. They loved the feeling of domination and power that came with driving a car. They marveled at the way that the airplane deprived them of all sense of time and space and left them with a feeling of suspension. They were persuaded that the pace of life was picking up. Some complained that they were losing their sense of distance. But for most the excitement of new worlds to be discovered more than made up for the loss of the security of living in small and clearly delimited territories. In the 1920s the open road became a symbol of freedom and escape (for those who could afford it) from the cramped quarters of the city. "To leave," cried one enthusiastic partisan of velocity. "To take off down the road. To cruise with the top down on the highway . . . at 160 [kilometers] an hour, to push on straight ahead, from one road marker to the other, to tear the world in two, as one tears a prospectus 'in following the dotted line.' "38

Some of the most popular literary works of the period were written in the form of travel reportage, and many authors from the war generation capitalized on the interest in foreign settings to get their careers underway. Hemingway described the cafés of Paris, the bullrings and trout streams of Spain, and the green hills of Africa. Paul Morand rhapsodized over New York and Shanghai. T. E. Lawrence recounted his adventures in Arabia. Saint-Exupéry brought to life the perils of flying in Patagonia. Céline took a protagonist of *Voyage au bout de la nuit* [Journey to the End of the Night] from the battlefields of the Great War to Africa and then to Detroit before returning him to his dreary lower-middle-class existence in a Parisian suburb. Montherlant chose Spain and North Africa as the settings for his novels and essays in the 1920s. Jünger wrote of the Dalmatian coast, Sicily, Rhodes, and the Greek Islands.

But the novelist of evasion par excellence was Blaise Cendrars. Cendrars (1887), who usually wrote about himself and mixed truth with liberal doses of fantasy, was always on the way either to or from some other exotic country. His motto was "drive to the bottom of the abyss, to the bottom of the unknown in order to find something new." His only truth was action, "the kind of action that obeys a million different motives, ephemeral action, action which submits to every possible and imaginable contingency, antagonistic action, Life." And for Cendrars, Life was not books or theories or sweetness and light. It was "crime, theft, jealousy, hunger, lies, screwing, stupidity, volcanic eruptions, earthquakes, heaps of corpses." Action alone liberated. It resolved everything, and anything it could not resolve was unworthy of Cendrars's consideration. "That's why I always participate and take a side, although I no longer believe in anything." "I am a kind of Brahman in reverse, who contemplates himself in the midst of agitation." And the kind of agitation, after waging war, that appealed most to Cendrars was traveling around the world, for he claimed to know all languages and every variety of people.[39]

Why this fascination with movement? To begin with, traveling offered nourishment to a spiritual life that was unable to sustain itself on its own resources and that was constantly on the verge of dissolving into suicidal despair. It was a liberation from the self for young men overwhelmed by the weight of their egos and the hopelessness of their time. If one kept going, one could forever be in flux. There was no need to fix oneself or to make any commitment—to a woman, to a friend, to a career, or to a cause. For men who had lost their personal equilibrium and who were persuaded that their time was out of joint, one solution was to place themselves in a situation of universal disequilibrium. "As you move, you pass before a moving backdrop without ever having to stay in any one place too long." To depart meant "to confront one's dreams with the world." It was "the never satisfied desire constantly to know something new." It was "tomorrow, eternally tomorrow." It was a way of fleeing from decisions and from oneself. The essential thing about this kind of travel was not the destination, but the fact of the departure. " 'Where are you going,' people sometimes ask those who are about to embark. Where? Does that really matter? . . . For me, traveling is not arriving: It's departing."[40]

Yet none of these explanations provided by writers of the period takes us beyond the surface of the issue. As Teilhard de Chardin perceived when trying to explain his nostalgia for the front, spatial and geographical exoticism was nothing but a metaphor for something deeper and more universal: the longing for renewal. The equation of traveling with spiritual rebirth was an old theme in Western culture. It was the desire to be reborn and to shed their civilized selves that took Ernest Psichari to Africa, Rupert Brooke to Tahiti, and T. E.

Lawrence to the Middle East; this same desire impelled Ernst Jünger to run off to Marseilles to join the Foreign Legion during the years just before the war. What was more novel in the 1920s, however, was the widespread belief, diffused by men like these, that an entire world or culture was about to be renewed. The intellectuals of the war generation found themselves irresistibly attracted toward the imagery of travel because they conceived of themselves as "wanderers between two worlds." They felt, like the Austrian Communist Ernst Fischer (1897), that they were living in "the abyss between two times." This is one of the reasons why they took so eagerly to T. S. Eliot's difficult poem "The Waste Land" and chose it as a metaphor for their times.[41]

From this conviction of being fated to wander between two worlds, "one dead, the other powerless to be born," flowed a whole series of assumptions that ran through the books and poems of the 1920s: that a new system of values would one day arise; that "new men" would appear who incarnated these new values; that the old world should be aided in its demise; that destruction was a means of creation; that activism was always preferable to passivity; that the war generation might never live to see "the unknown promised land" toward whose banks they were marching "enveloped by the obscure and thundering cloud of history in the making"; and that the main virtue, perhaps the only virtue possible in such a time of smoke and flame, lay in searching and experimenting and in having the courage to accept and affirm one's fate, no matter how unpleasant. For the only thing a man had, the only thing he could be certain of, was his epoch; tomorrow new generations would emerge who understood him no better than he had understood those who had preceded him; and "the first, the only nobility of thought and life" was to wander like Ulysses, "to go, without knowing where."[42]

This vision of a Europe torn between the old and the new underlay and nourished the generational utopias of the 1920s and early 1930s. Once one assumed that the old world was dying and that another was coming into being, it stood to reason that the agents of this cultural parturition would be the young, for only they possessed the necessary energy and freedom from the fetters of the past. By 1920 the word "youth" had only a tenuous connection with chronological age. To be "young" meant only to possess a receptivity to the new and the vitality required to meet and master the ordeal of the crisis. To be "old," by contrast, was to be attached to the forms of a dying world, to be a nineteenth-century man.[43] This equation between youth and cultural renewal was both inspired and confirmed by the promotion of spectator sports, the passion for records in athletics, driving, and flying, the taking up of youthful fashions in clothes by older age groups, and the vitality manifested by the "young" country across the Atlantic and the "young" regime in Italy. Youth had become a state of mind, a style of life, and—because it was not strictly limited to age—a potential political force that might rescue Europe from the sterile conflict between the parties of the bourgeoisie and the movements of the proletariat.

THE idea of a generational coalition remained a chimera, pursued by intellectuals of weak political instincts like Ortega, Gründel, and Luchaire. But it was not without its practical and political consequences. Partisans of the Bolshevik revolution used it to undermine the leadership of the Socialist parties and to bring about a split of the European working-class movement that has persisted down to our day. Mussolini found it indispensable in attracting followers to his Fascist movement and later made it one of the ideological cornerstones of his Fascist state. Leaders of veterans' movements exploited it to maintain their organizations and to win privileges for their members. In France the leaders of the Vichy government deployed it to win support for their regime. And in England the partisans of appeasement and peace at any cost found it useful to present themselves as the authentic representatives and heirs of the men who manned the trenches. Indeed, the history of Europe during the interwar period would be incomprehensible without the omnipresent myth of a politically unified generation of 1914.[44]

But did that myth correspond to any reality? Even the most daring of generational theorists hesitated to identify age-groups with a given type of politics. Social and geographical origin is more important than age in determining political behavior. Political traditions and political parties, in order to become significant, must attract people of many age-groups, both old and young. Political preoccupations, like that of the relationship of the individual to the community or of the nation to some form of larger political organization, command the attention of several successive generations. Moreover, the appearance of political unity that is strong when the members of a generation are young soon gives way to a reality of political fragmentation as the generation grows older. Within the generation of 1914, we find communists like Gramsci, socialists like Brooke, liberals like Ortega, conservatives like Massis, extreme nationalists like Jünger, fascists like Drieu la Rochelle, and a host of others like Montherlant and Lawrence who seem to have no politics at all.

Nonetheless, it does appear that one political *tendency* may dominate within specified social sectors of an age-group, even if that tendency may lead in the direction of more than one political party or movement. In the case of the intellectuals who identified themselves with the generation of 1914, the belief in an interregnum created an openness to radical political ideologies and a skepticism about all nineteenth-century political movements, including social democracy.

Theoretically, this inclination toward antiliberal politics could have resulted in adherence to parties of either the extreme Right or the extreme Left. This was indeed the case. Men and women born during the last two decades of the nineteenth century played a critical role in the founding of both the Fascist and the Communist parties. Both movements were initiated in 1919 when people of these age-groups first began to enter political life in large numbers. Both Fascist and Communist parties exploited feelings given rise to by the war. And the mentality of the generation of 1914, with its activism, its pragmatism, its belief in the power of will to reshape reality, its pessimism about the past, and its dedication to the creation of a new world and a new man, was what gave radicals of the Right and radicals of the Left the feeling that they were somehow secretly related and what made it possible for them to pass from one camp to another, as so many of them did.[45]

But though individual intellectuals from the generation of 1914 could be attracted toward political movements of the extreme Left or the extreme Right, most found it difficult to make, and more difficult yet to sustain, a commitment to Communism. Why this was so can be readily explained. As interpreted by the Russians, Communism was avowedly a class ideology with deep roots in the nineteenth century and superficial similarities to liberalism. It aspired toward the elimination of the state and the abolition of hierarchies and elites. Fiercely egalitarian in theory if not always in practice, it proclaimed the essential perfectibility of man and held out the possibility of a society without conflict. It claimed, furthermore, that its basic propositions were based on verifiable scientific truth, and it subordinated the interests of the nation to the interests of the international working class embodied in the Soviet Union.

These principles of official Communist ideology all ran counter to the prejudices, ideals, and experience of intellectuals from the generation of 1914. The intellectuals of this age group had been brought up to revere the nation and to believe that the interests of the national community stood above the interests of classes or any international body. Their ambition, conceived in youth, had been to overcome the ideologies of the nineteenth century, to revive the spirit of adventure and risk, to live for the values of the spirit rather than for material advantage, and to combine the virtues of the warrior and the man of faith. They were radical in their dislike of the industrial and commerical civilization of the present, but deeply ambivalent about the values of the preindustrial past. Many of them aspired toward a hierarchical and stratified society, loosely and romantically modeled on the Middle Ages, in which intellectuals would replace the former landed and business elites in their leadership of the masses.

The events of 1914–1920 confirmed and reinforced these prejudices and ideals. Many intellectuals from this age-group interpreted the war as having shown that the nation was a more binding ideal than the class, that reason was weaker than instinct and feeling, that action was superior to and relatively independent of thought, that spirit was stronger than flesh, that nothing great could be accomplished without suffering and sacrifice, that men were equal in their vulnerability to fear but unequal in their ability to transcend it, that daring elites would always triumph over daunted masses, that conflict was endemic to mankind, that life could not be divorced from death, and that it was in trying to annihilate each other that men displayed the highest qualities of selflessness and love. They had learned, in short, that strife was the midwife of virtue and that combat was the ladder by which men of merit raised themselves above the mediocrity of the masses. Those from this age-group who had fought at the front were most attached to these beliefs. They could not throw off their memories of warfare, for the war was the moment in their lives that seemed most noble and most real. Their model of a community was the comradeship of soldiers and the relationship of officers to their men. Fascism appealed to many members of this age-group because Fascist ideology seemed to incorporate these values and because Fascism held out the promise of a revo-lution in which both money (capitalism) and the mob (the working classes) would be subjected to the rule of spirit (interpreted by intellectuals of the middle and upper classes). To this extent, it is fair to say that Fascism was the great temptation of the generation of 1914.[46]

Yet relatively few intellectuals from this age-group adhered to Fascist move-ments, so long as they retained a free choice. Drieu la Rochelle was an excep-tion. Most intellectuals, like Ortega, longed after a third way that would pre-serve the best in liberalism while at the same time transcending it. They were put off by the demagoguery and the plebeian leadership of Fascist parties, by the violence of their methods, and by the vulgarity of their propaganda. A neocon-servative, but not a Fascist, revolution was their aim.*

Nonetheless, the neoconservative revolution failed, the Fascist movement came to power in Italy and Germany, and even where it did not come to power, it constituted a serious threat to existing governments, whether demo-cratic or authoritarian. Many intellectuals from the generation of 1914 dis-played a sympathy for Fascism or an unwillingness to resist its claims to power. Why? Because Fascism offered embattled elites a means of defense against those social forces that threatened their political hegemony, their social privi-leges, and their way of life. For natural reasons, intellectuals were inclined to represent this threat to the social and political dominance of existing upper-and middle-class elites as a menace to "culture" and "civilization." Moreover, they were right to do so insofar as they identified culture and civilization with the *forms* of culture that were espoused and enshrined by the Western and Central European bourgeoisie during its climb to power in the eighteenth and nineteenth centuries. It was precisely those forms that were in danger, and it was paradoxically to preserve them that the intellectuals conceived the vision of a cultural rebirth.

Intellectuals from the generation of 1914 were not alone in creating the Fas-cist movements; nor were they the social group that contributed most impor-tantly to the success of these movements in Italy and Germany. But these intel-lectuals did create a cultural climate, and hence a political climate, in which

---

* I am aware that many consider the idea of a neoconservative revolution a contradiction in terms. I suspect that they are right. But I am trying to describe as accurately as possible what Euro-pean intellectuals born during the last two decades of the nineteenth century desired.

Fascism could attract members by withdrawing their support from doctrines like liberalism and socialism that sought to continue nineteenth-century trends. In retrospect, this appears to have been the most important contribution of the generation of 1914 to the politics of the interwar period.

A sense of defeat runs through most of the memoirs written by members of the generation of 1914 about the period from 1933 to 1948. "The contrary experience," the title that Herbert Read gave to his autobiography (published in 1948), might well serve as a one-line description of this phase of the generation of 1914's history. By any standard and from the perspective of any age-group, these were grim years for Europe. In January 1933 Hitler came to power. Within a few years, millions of Central Europeans had been forced to abandon their homes and seek refuge in countries to the east or west. Austrian Social Democracy, the strongest socialist movement in continental Europe, was crushed in 1934. In that same year right- and left-wing extremists roamed the boulevards of Paris and came within a bridge's width of destroying Europe's oldest democratic regime. In July 1936 the Spanish Civil War erupted, bringing to an end the hopeful years of the Second Republic. Politics everywhere became polarized between extremes of Right and Left, except where one tendency had succeeded in annihilating or imprisoning the other. Europe slid inexorably toward another major war, as England and France proved powerless to check the ruthless thrust of Hitler's power. Austria fell; Czechoslovakia fell; Poland fell; Norway fell. Republican Spain fell to Franco. By June 1940, when France surrendered, Europe's fate had been decided. England could not defeat Germany unaided; it could only seek to hold on and frustrate Hitler's ambitions at European hegemony. To accomplish this England would have to seek financial and military support from the United States. But this meant that even if England won, it would lose, for the great powers of Europe were bound to become dependencies of an extra-European state. This is what happened. By 1948 Europe had been humbled, defeated, devastated, impoverished, and taken under the control and protection of the two growing empires of the United States and the Soviet Union.

The most representative members of the generation of 1914 were in their forties in 1933 when Hitler came to power and were nearing or past sixty in 1948 when Eastern Europe was integrated into the Soviet bloc. Between forty and sixty most people implement the ideas and dreams they have developed during the previous fifteen or twenty years of their lives. This is the time of realization of projects and plans—especially for those who pursue careers in public life. Many people during these years experience a feeling of disappointment and defeat. There is always a tendency, as T. S. Eliot (1887) put it, for a shadow to fall between the idea and its realization. But in the case of the generation of

1914 the ever present gap between intention and achievement became an abyss. This was no illusion, produced by mounting age. The great causes for which the generation of 1914 had fought were all lost.[47]

They had come home from the trenches in 1919 determined that there should not be another war, and they had lost the peace. The French and British had lost it out of weakness; the Germans and Italians had lost it out of wounded pride and reckless national ambition. But the fact remains that both the policy of appeasement supported by the Left in England and the policy of aggressive expansion adopted by Fascist Germany and Italy were expressions, in their own ways, of the generation of 1914 and of the lessons learned on the battlefields of the Great War. Fascism and Communism were the great political adventures of the generation of 1914. Fascism had been in its origins an attempt to provide a middle-class alternative to the Marxist scenario of social transformation. At the beginning it had aimed at a spiritual revolution and the creation of a new man. By 1943 it was clear to all but the most doggedly reactionary and antisemitic members of the generation of 1914 that Fascism had been a colossal failure. It had provided a means for checking social change rather than for advancing it; it had failed to deliver on its promises of creating a new type of human being and a new system of values; it had released a flood of violence and aggression; it had committed crimes of unprecedented horror; and it had resulted in a disastrous civil war of European nation-states that had left Europe impoverished and powerless. Communism emerged from the Second World War less discredited, if only because Communists had shown themselves (after some initial hesitation) to be fearless fighters against Fascism. But for those who had lived the Communist adventure from within and who had experienced the purge trials of the 1930s, the terror exercised by Comintern agents in Spain during the Civil War, and the shock of the Nazi-Soviet Pact, it was clear that the Communist parties had been perverted and had become, at least for the time being, instruments of Soviet foreign policy to be used in the game for imperial influence and power rather than independent agents of social revolution. The great beneficiary of the era between 1933 and 1948 had been, without question, the United States. The United States had gained in wealth, power, and prestige and had paid only slightly in loss of life. But the United States represented the triumph of industrial capitalism, the dominance of quantity over quality, the subjection of spirit to matter, and the reign of money and the mob. These were precisely the putatively nineteenth-century values that many intellectuals born in the late nineteenth century had pledged themselves in their youth to overcome. In short, the years of realization for the generation of 1914 were years during which their youthful dreams were defeated and their worst fears about the future were confirmed. Small wonder, then, that so many intellectuals of this age-group were haunted by a sense of defeat and despair as they entered the seventh decade of life. Small wonder that they accounted for their failure by myths like the "missing generation," the destruction of "the best," or the surrender of their juniors to the superficial values of the "old men."

What had gone wrong? Was it a terrible punishment meted out by a relentless fate, as Omodeo feared?* Or was it rather the collective failure of a generation to grasp the opportunities offered by fate? Ortega insisted that some generations fail to carry out the tasks with which history presents them. They are then condemned, he claimed, to drag out their allotted time on earth in dreadful disharmony with themselves and with their most authentic urges. The contemporary reader will rightfully regard this formulation of the question with skepticism, thinking that he perceives in it more than a trace of Hegelian hocuspocus. History does not hand out tasks; nor does history punish people for having failed to perform their duties. It is people who make history, not the other way around. But it is also true that people make history within limits, of which one of the most important is their date of birth. Everyone is born into a given historical world whose structure permits certain kinds of action and forecloses others. Moreover, it is possible for the members of an age-group to develop or be instilled with ideals or desires that cannot be realized because of the historical world in which they are condemned by the accident of their birth to live their lives. When this happens, large numbers of people may indeed develop the feeling that they are living in disharmony with themselves, their time, and their most authentic urges.

Upper- and middle-class men born in the major European countries between 1880 and 1900 found themselves placed before a difficult set of tasks. They had to oversee the transition from an elitist to a mass and bureaucratic society, while at the same time resigning themselves to the relative shrinkage of the power both of their own nation in particular and of Europe in general. Upon reaching manhood, they were required to fight a war for hegemony in Europe, a war whose multifaceted consequences would overshadow and render infinitely more difficult any action they undertook. Witnesses of the breakup of the predominantly bourgeois world into which they had been born, the most perceptive among them realized at an early age the necessity of developing new forms of collective life.

Alas, neither the education nor the experience of these men prepared them to meet these challenges and accomplish these tasks. This was especially true of the literary intellectuals from this age group. Most remained obsessed by the fantasy of heroic action. Though themselves prisoners of positivism in their approach to history and society, they had little sympathy for the "materialistic" ambitions of workers and peasants to better their lives and to achieve greater self-esteem. They resented, or at best were ambivalent about, industrial society.

---

* The generation that underwent the war runs the risk of being barred from every comfort, of being treated by history as the reprobate mass is treated by the God of grace, according to the theology of predestination." Adolfo Omodeo, *Momenti della vita di guerra*, p. 124.

They placed "spirit" and "culture" above dignity and need. Moreover, they remained under the spell of the experience they had undergone during the critical decade between 1910 and 1920. They were never able to free themselves from the conviction, given lasting shape by the war, that they were living through an apocalypse from whose smoke and flame a new cultural style must necessarily emerge. This obsession with cultural renewal betrayed their nineteen-century origins. They had yet to absorb what it meant to live in a society characterized by persistent rather than occasional change. This led them to exaggerate the elements of weakness in bourgeois society and to misread the direction of development. Quick to grasp the novelty of their situation, they were much less adept at perceiving the outlines of the egalitarian and bureaucratic society that was coming. Few considered the social and economic organization of society worthy of analysis. Intellectual and moral values, they thought, were infinitely more important than social or economic facts. This attitude gave their social thought a utopian, quixotic, and, ultimately, a reactionary quality. They wavered uncertainly and unpredictably between a desire to spring forward into the future and a longing to return to the hierarchies and faith of the past. Gramsci was no doubt right in arguing that the intellectuals of the generation of 1914 were too firmly anchored in the bourgeois order and too attached to its traditions, its rituals, and its privileges to overthrow it. The real revolutionaries of this period were seldom found among their ranks.

Paradoxically, the generational idea turned out to be one of the most negative items in the ensemble of ill-assorted attitudes, prejudices, and beliefs with which the generation of 1914 embarked on life. For the generational idea, as developed by intellectuals of the late nineteenth century like Barrès and Unamuno, suggested a biological determinism that had no basis in social fact; it implied that stage of life was a prison from which there was no escape and that communication across the chasm of age was impossible; it postulated that the differences between age-groups were more important than the differences within them; it demoted the mind and called into question its autonomy by explaining ideas as the direct and unmediated product of experience; it obscured the importance of social divisions by subordinating class interests to generational values; it vastly exaggerated the importance of literary intellectuals by locating in them the conscience and dynamic vanguard of society at large; and it prevented those who fell under its spell from seeing that all lasting historical action takes the form of the transformation of that which already exists and results from the collaboration (as well as the conflict) of different age-groups.

This is why in the end the term "generation of 1914" must remain confined within the quotation marks from which I had originally hoped to liberate it. An exercise in self-portrayal that never described more than a minority within the elite of the European educated classes, a project of social and political domination that was realized only in Italy and there but for a brief historical moment, the "generation of 1914" also proved inadequate when used as a conceptual device by men and women born in the late nineteenth century to explain their history. The intellecutal foundations on which the generational interpretation was raised were too faulty to support the interpretative structure. The strange mixture of idealism and biological determinism on which the generational interpretation was based obscures our understanding of the major movements of the period more than it enlightens it.

Yet this failure of interpretation in no way annuls the importance that this idea had in the history and consciousness of Europeans who lived during the first third of the twentieth century. Ortega believed that men in periods of historical crisis were condemned to live without convictions as they crossed the inhospitable no-man's-land between styles of thought. How agonizing it was, he sighed, to have to go through life without firm beliefs. Strange that Ortega did not take his argument one step further and consider the possibility, consistent with his own line of reasoning, that the belief in generational ruptures and cultural crises was itself a form of conviction so deeply installed in the vital horizon of the early twentieth century that most social theorists never paused to examine it. The attitudes of an age-group, no matter how delimited, can never be reduced to a single idea, principle, or theme. This was as true of Europeans born between 1880 and 1900 as it is of us today. But no one who has studied the writings and followed the careers of European intellectuals born during this period can doubt that generationalism was one of the most widespread and deeply enrooted convictions of the "generation of 1914."[48]

Notes

Introduction: In Search of the Lost Generation

1. Ezra Pound, "Hugh Selwyn Mauberley" in *Poems 1918–21* (New York, 1921), p. 56.

2. "All representation—whether in the arts or in politics—contains an element of fiction which, exploited for its political effects, becomes a myth, a lie." J. P. Stern, *The Führer and the People* (Berkeley and Los Angeles, 1975), p. 20.

3. When I began work on this book, there were four well-established models for writing the history of a generation. One was the method of literary generations; the second, the method of political generations; the third, the method of youth generations; and the fourth, cohort theory. For the method of literary generations, see Julius Petersen, "Die literarischen Generationen," in *Philosophie der Literaturwissenschaft*, ed. E. Ermatinger (1930); Jean Pommier, "L'idée de génération," in *Conférences de Franz Cumont, Jean Pommier* (Paris, 1945); Henry Peyre, *Les générations littéraires* (Paris, 1947); and the more recent reconsideration by Malcolm Cowley, *And I Worked at the Writer's Trade* (New York, 1978), pp. 1–20, which brings together in a few pages his life-long reflections on the question. For examples of the application of this method to the study of literary history, see Julius Petersen, *Die Wesenbestimmung des deutschen Romantik* (Leipzig, 1926); Malcolm Cowley, *Exile's Return* (New York, 1951 ed.); Pedro Laín Entralgo, *La generación del noventayocho* (Madrid, 1945); and Claude Digeon, *La Crise allemande de la pensée française* (Paris, 1959). The method of political generations is set forth by Marvin Rintala in "A Generation in Politics: A Definition," *Review of Politics* 25 (1963): 509–522, and in "Political Generations," *International Encyclopedia of the Social Sciences* (New York, 1968), VI, 92–95. Rintala has put the method into practice with mixed results in "The Problem of Generations in Finnish Communism," *American Slavic and East European Review* 17 (1958): 190–202, and *Three Generations: The Extreme Right in Finnish Politics* (Bloomington, Ind., 1962). For other examples of the use of the method of political generations, see Rudolf Heberle, *Social Movements: An Introduction to Political Sociology* (New York, 1951); Alex Inkeles, Claude Kluckhohn, and Raymond Bauer, *How the Soviet System Works* (Cambridge, Mass., 1956); Seymour Martin Lipset, *Political Man* (Garden City, N.Y., 1963), pp. 279–286; and Victor T. Le Vine, "Generational Conflict and Politics in Africa: A Paradigm," *Civilisations* 18 (1968): 399–418. The pioneering work in the method of youth generations was Helmut Schelsky's *Die skeptische Generation* (Düsseldorf and Cologne, 1963), an analysis of the attitudes of post–Second World War German youth. See also Ludwig von Friedeburg, ed., *Jugend in der modernen Gesellschaft* (Cologne and Berlin, 1965); Viggo Graf Blücher, *Die Generation der Unbefangenen* (Düsseldorf and Cologne, 1966); Friedhelm Neihardt, *Die Junge Generation* (Opladen,

1967); and Karl H. Bönner, *Deutschlands Jugend und das Erbe ihrer Väter* (Bergisch Gladbach, 1967). In the United States work on youth generations has been inspired chiefly by the writings of Erik Erikson, especially *Childhood and Society* (New York, 1963) and *Identity: Youth and Crisis* (New York, 1968). The most successful application of Erikson's approach is Kenneth Kenniston's analysis of alienated Harvard students, *The Uncommitted* (New York, 1965). For cohort theory, see William M. Evan, "Cohort Analysis of Survey Data: A Procedure for Studying Long-Term Opinion Change," *Public Opinion Quarterly* 13 (1959): 63–72; and Norman B. Ryder, "The Cohort as a Concept in the Study of Social Change," *American Sociological Review* 30 (1965): 843–861. Peter Loewenberg has sought to explain the support of National Socialism by German youth by means of cohort theory in "The Psychohistorical Origins of the Nazi Youth Cohort," *American Historical Review* 76 (1971): 1457–1502. Lewis Feuer has applied the generational concept to the study of student political movements and scientific change in *The Conflict of Generations* (New York, 1969) and *Einstein and the Generations of Science* (New York, 1974. For a recent review of generational theory and an attempt to apply it to the present generation of West German youth, see Nerina Jansen, *Generation Theory* (Johannesburg, 1975).

In formulating my approach to the generation of 1914, I was greatly aided by Renato Treves's important article, "Il fascismo e il problema delle generazioni," *Quaderni di Sociologia* (April-June 1964): 119–147. To my knowledge, Treves was the first (and only) scholar to study the uses of generational rhetoric and to seek reasons for the generational idea's appeal. Though limited by him to Italy, his conclusions can be extended to Europe as a whole.

4. José Ortega y Gasset, *Obras completas* (Madrid, 1966), III, 38.

5. Lucien Febvre, *Le Problème de l'incroyance au 16ᵉ siècle: Le Religion de Rabelais* (Paris, 1968 ed.), p. 11.

1. France: The Young Men of Today

1. "We! We! I know very well that I am not speaking of the entire generation [that is, age-group]. I am speaking of a couple of thousand men scattered throughout the great European cities. A few of them are famous; a few write unusually arid, consciously frightening and still peculiarly moving and gripping books; a few, shy and proud, write only letters, which will be found fifty or sixty years later and preserved as moral and psychological documents; a few will leave no trace, not even a sad and malicious aphorism or a lonely note in pencil scratched on the border of a yellowed book. Nevertheless, these two or three thousand men have a certain significance: they do not necessarily have to include the geniuses or even the great talents of the epoch; they are not necessarily the head or the heart of their generation: they are only its conscience. They feel with painful clarity like men of today; they understand each other, and the privilege of belonging to this intellectual fraternity is almost the only thing that makes them superior to the others. However, it is from the secret language in which they communicate to each other their idiosyncrasies, their special aspirations, and their special sensitivity that History will learn the catchword of the epoch." From an 1893 essay on Gabriele d'Annunzio, in Hugo von Hofmannsthal, *Prosa*, I, ed. Herbert Steiner (Frankfurt, 1950), pp. 171–172.

2. Henri Massis, *La Pensée de Maurice Barrès* (Paris, 1909). Especially noteworthy

was the following passage in which Massis tried to explain why Barrès had such great appeal for the young men of his generation: "Skepticism had overcome the best among us; but one can doubt without a master. And we went in search of a mentality, imploring peace of mind, looking for a doctrine that would not degrade us in our own self-esteem and that would give us back the energy that comes from will. It was [Barrès's] *Sous l'oeil des Barbares* and *Un Homme libre* that gave us this liberating method. With what ardor we read those little books in our study rooms, books that seemed to have been written for us alone. The day on which we discovered Barrès, we discovered ourselves as well. At a time when our professors refused to talk to us about anything except universal reason, we discovered a writer who spoke to us of our soul. And then, a certain indescribable way of saying things, a certain bookish and abstract way of turning a phrase, caused us to suspect that the author of these works was a member of our spiritual family" (p. 19). In other words, Barrès had received the same philosophical and literary education as the young men whom he touched with his early books; they responded to his irony, to his literary allusions, and to his cult of sensibility. The attentive reader will note that Alfred de Tarde wrote his last name differently than his father. The Tarde family had dropped the particule after the Revolution of 1789, but Alfred restored it.

3. Henri Massis, *Evocations* (Paris, 1931), p. 131. For the campaign against the new Sorbonne, see Agathon [Henri Massis and Alfred de Tarde], *L'Esprit de la nouvelle Sorbonne* (Paris, 1911). The original articles appeared in *L'Opinion* between 23 July and 31 December 1910. For an analysis of Agathon's campaign, see Phyllis H. Stock, "Students versus the University in Pre-World War Paris," *French Historical Studies* 7 (Spring 1971): 93–110.

4. Quoted in Agathon [Henri Massis and Alfred de Tarde], *Les Jeunes Gens d'aujourd'hui* (Paris, 1913), p. 57. At about the same time Joseph Ageorge complained that such confusion as then existed in the Sorbonne had never before been seen. "Principles, programs, traditions—everything is being 'sabotaged' . . . The literary, moral, and grammatical instruction of the Sorbonne can be summed up as cacophony and confusion." *La Marche montante d'une génération (1890–1910)* (Paris, 1912), pp. 6–7. The essence of these charges was that the professors of the "new Sorbonne" had ceased to teach their students to respect tradition and were failing to provide them with a morality. The first accusation was certainly true if "tradition" meant the church and other pre-Republican institutions. The second was completely false. Most of the professors under attack conceived of themselves primarily as moralists. For contemporary sketches of this impressive array of figures, see Pierre Léguay, *Universitaires d'aujourd'hui* (Paris, 1912).

5. Massis, *L'Honneur de servir: Textes réunis pour contribuer à l'histoire d'une génération (1910–1937)* (Paris, 1937), p. 10. For Massis's original project of a novel that would be a "vast inquiry" into present-day times, see *Evocations*, p. 267.

6. The story of Massis and de Tarde's collaboration was reconstructed by Massis in detail, but with something less than convincing frankness, in *L'Honneur de servir*, pp. 3–21. This work contains many of the texts that were originally meant to go into the second volume of *Evocations*, Massis's principal memoir.

7. The number of university students in France doubled between 1891 and 1908, from 19,821 to 39,890. The increase was especially marked in the faculties of law, letters, and science. See Antoine Prost, *L'Enseignement en France 1800–1967* (Paris, 1968), p. 230.

8. *Les Jeunes Gens d'aujourd'hui*, pp. 12, 117.

9. For Massis's disenchantment with Anatole France, see *Evocations*, p. 18; for his friendship with Demange, see Massis, "Charles Demange," *Mercure de France*, September 1909, pp. 245–246. Some notion of Demange's sensibility may be gathered from a sentence he wrote shortly before he took his life: "After having slept on the carpets of infancy, we shall guarantee to our mature acts all possible space for their setting, even if subtle tissues, like dreams and mystery, mask cleverly our tenderness and weakness, our irony and passion." Quoted by Massis, ibid., p. 249.

10. For Massis's first meeting with Psichari, see *Evocations*, p. 206.

11. The quotation from Renan is in Ernest Renan, *Oeuvres complètes*, I (Paris, 1947), 557. My account of Psichari's early life and family background is based on Henriette Psichari, *Ernest Psichari, Mon Frère* (Paris, 1933), and Raïssa Maritain, *Les Grandes Amitiés*, 2 vols. (New York, 1941–1944).

12. Psichari, *Oeuvres complètes*, I (Paris, 1945), 186, 283.

13. Psichari, *Oeuvres complètes*, II (Paris, 1948), 272; and III (Paris, n.d.), 36.

14. Ibid., III, 226.

15. For Franck's fear that his personality had been destroyed by books, see *Lettres à quelques amis* (Paris, 1926), pp. 91–93, 97; for his desire to get into contact with reality, ibid., p. 272; for his acceptance of the necessity of war with Germany, ibid., pp. 127–128; for Massis's debt to Franck, *Evocations*, pp. 165–166; for the quotation from Rivière, Jacques Rivière, "Le Roman d'aventure," *Nouvelle Revue Française* 9 (1913): 762. Massis later described the published correspondence between Rivière and his friend Alain-Fournier as "the most moving testimony on this period of our life." *Evocations*, p. 158, n. 1.

16. Rivière to Alain-Fournier, 5 November 1905, in Jacques Rivière and Alain-Fournier, *Correspondance, 1905–1914*, I (Paris, 1926), 105.

17. *Les Jeunes Gens d'aujourd'hui*, p. 147.

18. The French journalist in London is quoted by Philippe Bénéton in "La Génération de 1912–1914: Image, mythe et réalité?" *Revue Française de Sciences Politiques* 21 (October 1971): 996, n. 92. For Romain Rolland, see *Jean-Christophe* (Paris, 1931 ed.), III, 429, 381; for Roger Martin du Gard, *Jean Barois* (Paris, 1921 ed.), pp. 440, 449–450. Of the relationship between the generations, Rolland wrote, "The generations that follow one another always have a more acute sense of what disunites them than of what unites them; they feel the need to affirm to themselves their own importance and right to exist, even at the cost of injustice [to their elders] or self-deception. But this feeling is, according to the period, more or less pronounced. During classic periods in which the equilibrium of a civilization's forces is briefly achieved—those high plateaus bordered by steep slopes—the difference of level from one generation to the next is less great. But in periods of renaissance or decadence, the young men who scale or descend the dizzy slope leave far behind them those who preceded them." *Jean-Christophe*, III, 424. Martin du Gard affirmed that whereas states of sensibility used to vary from one century to another, they now changed with every generation: "It's a fact, we must accept it." *Jean Barois*, pp. 438–439.

19. Barrès is quoted by Bénéton in "La Génération de 1912–1914," p. 996; Bergson by Agathon in *Les Jeunes Gens d'aujourd'hui*, pp. 285–286; Bourget by Bénéton, pp. 996–997. Emile Faguet, "La Jeunesse miraculeuse," *Revue des Deux Mondes*, 15 April 1913, p. 850.

20. *Les Jeunes Gens d'aujourd'hui*, pp. 32–33. For French opinion on the eve of

the war, see Jean-Jacques Becker, *1914: Comment les français sont entrés dans la guerre* (Paris, 1977).

21. Massis, *L'Honneur de servir*, pp. 164–165.

22. "What bothers me in the image that we traced of the Agathonian is not that it is confused or vague, but that, on the contrary, it is too clear. It sins through an excess of cohesion: it lacks the colors of life." Ibid., pp. 8–9.

23. François Mentré, *Les Générations sociales* (Paris, 1920), p. 10.

24. Justin Dromel, *La Loi des révolutions* (Paris, 1862); Giuseppe Ferrari, *Teoria dei periodi politici* (Milan and Naples, 1874). Ottokar Lorenz originally set forth his ideas in *Die Geschichtswissenschaft in Hauptrichtungen und Aufgaben kritisch erörtert* (Berlin, 1886) and then defended and reformulated them in *Leopold von Ranke: Die Generationenlehre und der Geschichtsunterricht* (Berlin, 1891), especially pp. 143–276. The second work is more restrained in its hopes for a historical science of inherited psychological characteristics.

25. Mentré, *Les Générations sociales*, pp. 299–300, 289–299, 40. Despite the reference to the struggle of children with their parents, there is no evidence that Mentré had read Freud. Nor does he consider the possibility of aggression by parents against their children. His emphasis is on the attachment of parents to their children and the inevitable ingratitude with which children repay their parents' sacrifice. "Forgetfulness is the law of familial generations" (p. 188). Mentré blamed the crisis of parental authority on the cowardice of parents and the revolt of their children and thought it was linked to the limitation of family size (p. 193).

26. Ibid., pp. 89.

27. Ibid., p. 45.

28. Ibid., pp. 41, 46.

29. Ibid., pp. 40–41.

30. Ibid., p. 317. Mentré distinguished between "institutions" and "series." The educational and judicial systems were institutions; literature and music were series. The institution was relatively fixed; the series was more fluid. Therefore, generational changes were likely to manifest themselves more clearly in series, especially in series like literature, which were structured like family dynasties and which obeyed a law of alternation rather than of progression (pp. 226–240). Mentré thought that eventually it would be possible to detect generational changes in grammar, vocabulary, and the meaning of words (pp. 304–316).

31. Ibid., pp. 47–48. In 1920, when Mentré published his book, only 2.59 percent of those between the ages of eleven and seventeen in France attended a *collège* or *lycée*. Viviane Isambert-Jamati, *Crises de la société, crises de l'enseignement* (Paris, 1970), p. 376.

32. *Les Générations sociales*, p. 246.

33. In 1953 the well-known French medievalist Yves Renouard noted, "Unfortunately, François Mentré's book has scarcely been read; people in France have not bothered to develop further the notion that he had the merit to uncover." "La Notion de génération en histoire," *Revue historique* 209 (1953): 3. For Albert Thibaudet, see "Reflexions sur la littérature: l'idée de génération," *Nouvelle Revue Française* 16 (1921): 345–346. Thibaudet (1874) left no doubt that he intended to take up the subject and that his conclusions would differ from Mentré's, if only because he intended to emphasize the diversity within generations (p. 353). Unfortunately, his *Histoire de la littérature*

française de 1789 à nos jours (Paris, 1936), published after his death, is disappointing, primarily because he used generation as a means of periodization or organization rather than as a tool for explaining similarities and conflicts within periods.

34. There are good examples of this confusion in the perception of generations in Thibaudet's *Histoire de la littérature française* and in Christian Sénéchal's *Les Grands Courants de la littérature française contemporaine* (Paris, 1934), also organized along generational lines. Both these authors had great difficulty in dealing with the relationship between the war generation and postwar generations. See Thibaudet, p. 299, and Sénéchal, p. 378.

35. André Lamandé, *Les Lions en croix* (Paris, 1923), pp. 230–231.

36. René de la Porte (1895) defined this generation as "men who entered the furnace [that is, the war] between the ages of sixteen and twenty-five." He added that fate had fused his generation with the older men of the "sacrificed generation." *Nés de la guerre* (Paris, 1928), pp. 185, 186. Presumably by "sacrificed generation" he meant the generation of Massis and Psichari.

37. Massis, *Au long d'une vie* (Paris, 1967), p. 162; *L'Honneur de servir*, p. 324.

38. For Massis's awareness that he was a man of another age, see *Au long d'une vie*, p. 88; for Montherlant's resolve to dedicate himself to his mind and soul, J. N. Faure-Biguet, *Les Enfances de Montherlant* (Paris, 1941), p. 83. Montherlant was singled out as one of the leading representatives of the war generation in the following works: Pierre Dominique, *Quatre hommes entre vingt* (Paris, 1924); Paul Archambault, *Jeunes Maîtres* (Paris, 1926); and Frédéric Empaytaz, *Essai sur Montherlant ou la génération de trente ans* (Paris, 1928).

39. Exactly how Montherlant was influenced and transformed by the war could be determined only if we had access to his large correspondence with his grandmother from this period. In the meantime, his friend and biographer Jean de Beer has offered some interesting and, for the most part, convincing speculations in *Montherlant.ou l'homme encombré de Dieu* (Paris, 1963), pp. 37–54.

40. See Montherlant's novel *Le Songe* (Paris, 1922), reprinted in Montherlant, *Romans* (Paris, 1949), pp. 110–111; and the later essay "Service inutile," reprinted in Montherlant, *Essais* (Paris, 1963), pp. 571–735. Psichari believed that "the blood of Africa's martyrs was useful." His conviction was that "nothing is lost in the world, that everything is returned and is to be rediscovered in the total picture; thus all the sublime acts of heroes formed for him [Psichari's autobiographical hero] a sort of common capital whose interest was returned obscurely to thousands of unknown souls." Psichari *Oeuvres complètes*, II, 164. Paul Archambault, Montherlant's philosophy professor in *lycée*, complained, "Thanks to Montherlant and to several others, the monstrous hypothesis of a Catholicism without Christ and the Gospels, of a Catholicism without faith, without hope, and without charity has been formulated and threatens to make its way." *Jeunes Maîtres*, p. 23, n. 1. For Montherlant's love of life at the front, and his belief that there would always be wars, see *Romans*, pp. 21, 77; for his essay on the knight of nothingness, *Essais*, pp. 595–598.

41. In June 1923 Montherlant wrote an article for the *Nouvelles Littéraires*, which appeared under the title "Une génération casquée" [A Helmeted Generation]. On 7 July 1923, a week after the article appeared, Montherlant addressed an open letter to the journal disclaiming all responsibility for the title. "I might have let myself be seduced momentarily by the expression 'a helmeted generation.' But I would have eliminated it

because to be completely truthful it probably doesn't mean anything. And even if a helmeted generation existed, I would not feel entitled to speak in its name. Besides, people overuse and abuse the word 'generation.' " For Montherlant's own abuse of the term, see *Essais*, pp. 164–166, 183, 560–562, 1251. For Drieu la Rochelle, see his *Mesure de la France* (Paris, 1922), p. 14. This curious little book contained a brief impressionistic sketch for a generational history of France. "There was the Pléiade, there were the men of 1660, there were the Romantics, there were the Symbolists in the realm of poetry. In the realm of politics there were the Encyclopedists, the men of 1848, the Action Française. Some men were twenty the same year; for them the face of the same women, at more or less the same season, has given them its youth. Among some people opinions don't count. The world has been the same surprise, a marvel never before seen. A country has melted in their arms. That's everything that I want to say, all we have left. . . We are a generation" (pp. 137–139). Note that Drieu typically confuses "the young men . . . who fought" with small literary and political elites like the Pléiade, the symbolist poets, and the Action Française.

42. This account of Drieu's prewar development is based on his autobiography *Etat-civil* (Paris, 1921), *Rêveuse bourgeoisie* (Paris, 1937), and scattered passages in his other novels and stories, particularly *Drôle de voyage* (Paris, 1933) and *La Comédie de Charleroi* (Paris, 1934). The description of Drieu as a "sniffling bourgeois" comes from *La Comédie de Charleroi*, p. 25.

43. *La Comédie de Charleroi*, pp. 54, 57, 59–60.

44. Quoted by Pierre Andreu, *Drieu: Témoin et visionnaire* (Paris, 1952), p. 43.

45. Pierre Drieu la Rochelle, *Interrogation* (Paris, 1917), pp. 86, 98, 53, 69–74.

46. For the metaphor of young soldiers as adventurers engaged in a sport, see Pierre Drieu la Rochelle, *Plainte contre l'inconnu* (Paris, 1924), pp. 118–119. Capitulation and guilt for having failed to transform civilian life were two prevalent themes in the literature of young veterans during the 1920s and 1930s. See especially Roland Dorgelès, *Le Réveil des morts* (Paris, 1923). For the young survivors as "poor children," see Drieu la Rochelle, *La Suite dans les idées* (Paris, 1927); for the improvisation of the peace, the depressing reality behind their movement, and their flight, *Plainte contre l'inconnu*, pp. 13–14, 84, 160.

47. For the sudden desire to unbend, see Frédéric Empaytaz, *Essai sur Montherlant*, pp. 122–123.

48. For Bucard, see his *Paroles d'un combattant* (Paris, 1930) and *Les Etincelles*, a journal edited by Bucard and Maurice de Barral. Jean Norton Cru gives an extraordinarily complete survey and analysis of French war literature up to 1928 in *Témoins: Essai d'analyse et de critique des souvenirs de combattants édités en français de 1915 à 1928* (Paris, 1929). The history, sociology, and ideology of the French veterans' movements is analyzed by Antoine Prost in his magisterial doctoral thesis, *Les Anciens Combattants et la société française 1914–1939*, 3 vols., (Paris, 1977). See also Robert Soucy's contribution to *The War Generation*, ed. Stephen R. Ward (Port Washington and London, 1975), pp. 59–103.

49. Henri Daniel-Rops, *Notre Inquiétude* (Paris, 1927), p. 61. Indeed, the passion for generational portraits and the interest in youth—what they thought, what they felt, what they did, what they were likely to do in the future—was such that one writer, when asked what European university youth thought, replied that if "the coming generation" had any task, it was to kill once and for all the concept of generation. Reported

by Daniel Halévy in his introduction to *Ecrits par André Chamson, André Malraux, Jean Grenier, Henri Petit* (Paris, 1927), pp. xii–xiii.

50. Marcel Arland, *La Route obscure*, 2nd ed. (Paris, 1930), p. 105, and *Essais et nouveaux essais critiques* (Paris, 1952), p. 22; Daniel-Rops, *Notre Inquiétude*, pp. 72–73; Jean Luchaire, *Une Génération réaliste* (Paris, 1929); André Malraux, "D'une jeunesse européenne," in Halévy, *Ecrits par Chamson, Malraux, Grenier, Petit*, p. 153. For further self-analyses, mostly by young men of this age group, see *Examen de conscience* (Paris, 1926).

51. Daniel-Rops, *Notre Inquiétude*, pp. 68–69. Young war veterans were well aware of this tension between themselves and the oncoming generation. "For our young twenty-year-old brothers," Empaytaz complained, "we are already old men." *Essai sur Montherlant*, p. 18.

52. The most famous and widely read example of this literature is Marcel Arland's novel, *L'Ordre* (Paris, 1929). The same theme was handled more subtly by Maurice Betz in his uncompleted trilogy, *Jeunesse de siècle*, of which only two volumes, *Le Rossignol du Japon* (Paris, 1931) and *Le Ressac* (Paris, 1932), were published. Betz (1898) wrote as a veteran and member of the young war generation.

53. Jean Prévost, *Dix-Huitième Année* (Paris, 1929), pp. 56–57.

54. André Chamson, *La Révolution de dix-neuf* (Paris, 1930).

55. For an account of Jean Luchaire's youth and early career, written by his father, see Julien Luchaire, *Confessions d'un français moyen*, II (Florence, 1965 ed.), 49–51, 237–240, 311–313.

56. For the abyss between generations, see *Notre Temps*, 20 June 1927, p. 1; for the necessity of the younger generations to preserve themselves from compromising alliances, ibid., 15 December 1929, p. 44.

57. For Crouzet, see ibid., 15 January 1930, col. 193; 15 April 1930, col. 391; and 1 May 1930, cols. 401–406. In 1924 Dominique had written; "Let us accept, let us venerate this eternal law that pits one generation against the next. All the more because it is ingeniously conceived and permits a singular revision, more or less three times a century, of values, of beliefs, of hates, and of loves." The stakes of generational conflict, Dominique affirmed, were not merely control over the "fruits of the world," but a new conception of life. "The drama of our epoch is less in the hostility than in the profound lack of resemblance of two generations." Dominique believed that generational conflict had intensified and thought that this escalation was linked to the coming of a new kind of society and civilization. "The earth is becoming a great city; a rapid, agitated, dangerous type of urban life is taking the place of the agricultural life, which was slow, calm, relatively peaceful. And the [younger and older] generations have taken the characteristics corresponding to these two types of life . . . From the two sides, [there is] an absolute lack of comprehension." *Quatre Hommes*, pp. 9–10. By 1930, however, Dominique had ceased to believe that important historical movements were generational in nature and gave as his example the Reformation, in which the leaders were separated in age by decades. See Dominique, *La Querelle des générations* (Paris, 1930).

58. *Notre Temps*, 1 May 1930, cols. 401–406.

59. Durkheim had read Mentré's work in manuscript and made "useful" observations. According to Steven Lukes, it was around 1914 that Durkheim began to accord a greater degree of autonomy and importance to collective ideas. In 1911 he wrote, "The principal social phenomena . . . are nothing more than systems of values and hence of

ideals. Sociology moves from the beginning in the field of ideals. The ideal is in fact its peculiar field of study . . . It . . . accepts them as given facts, as objects of study, and it tries to analyze and explain them." Quoted in Steven Lukes, *Emile Durkheim* (New York, 1972), p. 235. This was precisely Mentré's position, and if he did not derive it from Durkheim, he certainly found confirmation for it in Durkheim's writings and lectures.

60. For Henri Franck, see *Lettres à quelques amis*, pp. 242–243, 269–285, and his 1912 poem *La Danse devant l'arche* (Paris, 1917), especially p. 125, where he compares the members of a generation to travelers who gather at an inn toward nightfall to revel and exchange amenities before going their separate ways; for Psichari, his letter to Henri Massis, 30 September 1912, in Psichari, *Oeuvres complètes*, III, 232; for Rivière, his "Lettre ouverte à Henri Massis," *Nouvelle Revue Française* 23 (1924):425. The limited validity of Agathon's generalizations was evident to people in contact with French youth, even at the time of Agathon's enquête. As one professor at the Lycée Condorcet, Massis's old secondary school, pointed out, if Agathon had really wanted to give an accurate portrait of the younger generation, he would have tried to capture it in all of its diversity. A generation, he wrote, is composed of a variety of groups, "often very different, sometimes irreducible," which may or may not overlap. These circles have their own logic, their own field of gravitation, and sometimes the initiating tendency, the creative spark, leaps from one circle to another, causing them to merge and form a larger whole. "The political and religious groups of our present-day young men give us an idea of this curious overlapping. This is what your enquête should have captured." The group Agathon had described, this professor observed, was composed of very conservative young men, "an essentially bourgeois type." Agathon, *Les Jeunes Gens d'aujourd'hui*, p. 281. Gonzague Truc said much the same thing in 1919: "Around 1912, France was divided between the amorphous and more or less illiterate masses, who were being led toward the unknown by Socialism, and a band of young reactionaries who, without committing themselves completely, looked favorably upon Catholicism and the monarchy." *Une Crise intellectuelle* (Paris, 1919), pp. 13–14.

61. *Les Jeunes Gens d'aujourd'hui*, p. i. Thibaudet seems to have been groping toward this kind of a conception of historical generations in his criticism of Mentré's book: "In reality, a generation forms a whole of vast amplitude, a sort of debating society for the young and parliament for the old, having its right, its center, its left, and its extreme left. There is no right- or left-wing generation. And nonetheless it is true that a generation has its peculiar traits, but traits that are born from a movement and that cannot be derived from things or ideas." *Nouvelle Revue Française* 16(1921):353.

62. Maurice Barrès, *Un Homme libre*, in *Oeuvres complètes*, I, 149. I have been greatly aided in thinking about this question by Eugen Weber's unpublished essay, "Barrès: un héritier."

63. "It seems that the earth is revolving faster. To go further and faster, to nourish our activity with rapid movements and mouthfuls of salt air, to pierce the clouds and split the waters, such is the wish of our bodies cured of anguish and internal hesitation. Even physical rest has changed. It has become a brutal communion with nature: sizzling sun baths or perilous ascents of mountains, which make the old and soft generations howl." De la Porte, *Nés de la guerre*, p. 183.

64. Massis, *L'Honneur de servir*, p. 8. Emmanuel Berl, Henri Franck's cousin and a student in Paris at the time of Agathon's enquête, left an interesting piece of testimony

on the methods used by Massis and de Tarde. "Even today I see certain historical works accept as valid the famous enquête by Agathon. But I am in a good position to know what reservations it inspires. Its authors queried me as well. My answer did not suit them; therefore, they did not bother to mention it. I am nonetheless certain that I was not the only one among my friends who wished that the Trojan war would not take place; to deplore the 'three year law'; to be ashamed of the public ingratitude toward Rouvier, then toward Caillaux, who had been found guilty of having settled with great skill, and in a way that was advantageous for our country, the Franco-German dispute." *A contre-temps* (Paris, 1969), p. 155. Thibaudet also understood the political and instrumental nature of early twentieth-century French generational writings. Chiding Mentré for taking generational manifestos at face value, he noted, " 'My generation' in the mouth of a writer is often the equivalent of 'the government of the Republic' in the mouth of a minister. It's a sonorous circumlocution that designates no one but himself." *Nouvelle Revue Française* 16(1921):353.

65. For the generationalism of Balzac, de Musset, and Saint-Beuve, see Henri Peyre, *Les Générations littéraires* (Paris, 1948), pp. 53–68. Long before Peyre, Thibaudet identified generationalism as a legacy of Romanticism and traced it back to Stendahl and de Musset. *Nouvelle Revue Française* 16 (1921): 350–351. For Bourget, see *Essais de psychologie contemporaine*, 2 vols. (Paris, 1883–1885). In the 1885 preface to the second volume, Bourget explained that he had limited himself to the case studies of ten writers because they seemed most likely to demonstrate his thesis, namely "that the states of mind peculiar to a new generation were enveloped in embryo in the theories and dreams of the preceding generation. Young people inherit from their elders a way of experiencing life, which they themselves transmit, modified by their own experience, to those who follow. Works of literature and art are the most powerful means of transmitting this psychological heritage. It is therefore appropriate to study these works as educative of minds and hearts" (p. xx). For Giraud, see *Les Maîtres de l'heure*, 2 vols. (Paris, 1911–1913). Giraud consciously modeled his own book on that of Bourget, stating in his introduction that he hoped to insert the intellectual and moral history of his subjects into the history of the generation to which they belonged. "It's this collective history that I have in view, and when my enquête is finished, all I shall have to do, I hope, is to assemble the results, in order to see take shape in its principal traits the intellectual and moral history of the generation that preceded us in existence." Ibid., I, xii.

66. Barrès's first publication, *Les Taches d'encre* (Paris, 1884), alluded to the failure of "our fathers" and the need to take up the task of liberation from German hegemony, which they had dropped. In the preface to his second novel, *Un Homme libre* (Paris 1889), Barrès noted bitterly that the older generation never really understands the writings of its juniors: the gap between their sensibilities is too great (p. 10). At about the same time, he presented the movement of General Boulanger as a political expression of the younger generation and sought to rally the "princes of youth" against the parliamentary establishment. See Zeev Sternhell, *Maurice Barrès et le nationalisme français* (Paris, 1972), pp. 115–119. One of Barrès's contemporaries, Joseph Ageorge, remarked on the skill with which the author of *The Uprooted* seized the leadership of his generation. "He knew how to promote himself in society and, what is extraordinary, in making his own fortune he also made his generation's. He had the idea of modeling the sensibility of his contemporaries on his own." *La Marche montante d'une génération*, p. 101. In short, Barrès sought to call into being a new social group, of which he would be

recognized as the spokesman and leader. Ageorge was quite right in terming this an idea that Barrès had gotten and then exploited to his own advantage. In his essay on Montherlant and the young war generation, published in 1928, Frédéric Empaytaz commented perceptively on the influence of Barrès on his generation. "Our entire generation has held out its cup to the enchanted spring. Before us Jerôme and Jean Tharaud, Eugène Marsan, Henri Massis, René Benjamin, and so many others! have formed this spiritual family. Those of our age extend the chain in turn, from Montherlant to Drieu la Rochelle, from the young neoclassical enthusiasts of the Action Française to the stormy nihilists of Surrealism." *Essai sur Montherlant*, p. 37. What Empaytaz failed to see was that the tendency to think in generational terms was one of Barrès's legacies. Later, in the thirties, the chain would be further extended by Robert Brasillach (1908) and Thierry Maulnier (1909). Together they would draft a generational manifesto, and in 1939 Brasillach would write a generational memoir, *Notre Avant-Guerre*, modeled on Massis's *Evocations*.

67. As Charles Péguy did in 1913 when he explained that his generation was sacrificed because it had had to endure the mediocrity of contemporary history. *L'Argent* (Paris, 1932), pp. 46–47. And as Jean Luchaire did in 1930 when he warned his coevals that their generation would be sacrificed because its work would have an "essentially transitory character." "Its greatest mistake would consist of believing in the perennial nature of its creations, which will be more modestly soundings, sketches, but not durable masonry." *Notre Temps*, 15 Janurary 1930, p. 123. In an essay published in 1927, Daniel-Rops drew attention to the connection between the word "generation," as it was currently being used, and the sense of collective discontinuity. "Generation. This vague word has taken in common usage a precise sense; it manifests the discontinuity that presides over the evolution of historical groups." *Notre Inquiètude*, p. 61.

68. *Les Jeunes Gens d'aujourd'hui*, pp. ii–iii.

69. Gaston Riou blamed "the growing separation of literature and life" on the commercialization of the literary profession. Letters, he said, had become an industry, writers wrote what they thought the public wanted, and describing reality had ceased to be a duty. *Aux Ecoutes de la France qui vient* (Paris, 1913), p. 266. My own study of intellectuals within this generation suggests, however, that the problem was more complex. Writers both lacked a sense of what was going on in French society and despaired over their ability to represent social realities to a broader public. Thus they fell back on describing their own experience, hoping that it was somehow representative of a larger group. Drieu la Rochelle provides an excellent example of this dilemma, which was felt by many French writers. Despite occasional efforts to the contrary, he could never write successfully or happily about anybody but himself. For Barrès, see "M. le général Boulanger et la nouvelle génération," *Revue Independante* 7 (April 1888) : 55–63. "Let others address themselves to the large public; I only want to speak to my friends, to those who will follow with me the road of life . . . My complaints, my hopes, and my arguments are going to be special; for I want to reach a small public, a divine public at that: the princes of youth" (p. 57). Barrès believed there were several thousand young men like himself who could, depending on whether or not they were satisfied, "serve or disserve the commonweal" (p. 57). For numerous examples of the distortion by intellectuals of the social realities of France during this period, see Theodore Zeldin, *France 1848–1945* (Oxford, 1977), vol. II.

70. Arland, *Essais et nouveaux essais*, p. 23. Henri Peyre provides a useful sum-

mary of generational writings by French literary historians and critics in *Les Générations littéraires* (Paris, 1948). The most important of these writings is the essay by Jean Pommier, "L'Idée de génération," in *Conférences de Franz Cumont, Jean Pommier* (Paris, 1945). Pommier's emphasis on the diversity within generations appears to have had an important influence on the brilliant generational study by Claude Digeon, *La Crise allemande de la pensée française* (Paris, 1959). For the wariness of French historians and sociologists about the concept of generation, see especially the short note by Lucien Febvre, "Générations," in "Projets d'articles du vocabulaire historique," *Bulletin du Centre International de Synthèse*, no. 7, June 1929, p. 41. Febvre objected to the generational concept on the grounds that it assumed an unwarranted identity between the consciousness of intellectuals and political leaders and that of other members of society. Febvre was impressed by the difficulty of applying the generational idea to earlier periods for which no detailed documentation existed, such as the Middle Ages and the ancient world. He did not think the generational concept could provide a new means of periodization. But his main complaint went deeper. There were as many generations, he insisted, as there were classes and social categories. And generation referred to little more than a common set of influences to which a determined set of individuals was exposed at a given time. Febvre's reaction is understandable when one remembers his and Marc Bloch's effort to write the history of peasants as well as intellectuals, of artifacts and techniques as well as ideas. This effort contained an unmistakable democratic and populist note. And one can sense a political overtone in Febvre's conclusion that the generational idea was "a pretty aristocratic conception of history."

Marc Bloch apparently did not share his colleague and friend's hostility to the generational idea. He thought that generations could offer a new means of periodizing history. But he warned that generational differences do not manifest themselves with equal intensity in all milieus; that there is nothing regular about the appearance of generations; and that individuals do not necessarily react in the same way to the same events. *Apologie pour l'histoire* (Paris, 1949), p. 95. Despite Bloch's belief in its utility, the generational idea seems to have had little practical effect on the direction of French historical research since the Second World War. Yves Renouard rediscovered the generational concept after reading Julián Marías's summary of Ortega's ideas in *El método stórico de las generaciones* (Madrid, 1949). Renouard, "La notion de génération en histoire," *Revue historique* 209 (1953) : 1–23.

71. In the fall of 1925 Gertrude Stein got annoyed at Hemingway and some of his friends for dropping in on her unexpectedly in a tipsy and argumentative mood. Taking a phrase she had heard from the owner of the garage where she had her Model T Ford repaired, she told her rowdy guests that they were all a *génération perdue*. "That's what you are. That's what you all are . . . All of you young people who served in the war. You are a lost generation." Then she added, "You have no respect for anything. You drink yourselves to death." Hemingway, *A Moveable Feast* (New York, 1964), p. 29. Coming back to the incident thirty years later, Hemingway claimed that he went away unconvinced by this summary description of himself and his companions. "I thought of Miss Stein and Sherwood Anderson and egotism and mental laziness versus discipline and I thought who is calling who a lost generation? . . . I thought that all generations were lost by something and always had been and always would be." Ibid., p. 30. Nevertheless, he was impressed enough at the time to consider using the phrase as the title for his novel about American expatriates in Paris and the festival at Pamplona. Eventually,

he discarded it in favor of *The Sun Also Rises*, but he included it as one of the two epigraphs for the book. See Carlos Baker, *Ernest Hemingway: A Life Story* (New York, 1969), p. 155.

2. Germany: The Mission of the Young Generation

1. Eduard Spranger, *Psychologie des Jugendalters* (Stuttgart, 1945 ed.), p. 93.

2. For the shift in the meaning of "youth," see Manfred Marfkefka, *Der Begriff der Jugend in der deustschen Nachkriegsliteratur zum Problem der Jugend*" (Ph.D. dissertation, Cologne University, Faculty of Economics and Social Sciences, 1963), pp. 9–11. Harry Pross claims that until the twentieth century youth was always conceived of in connection with a given social class or caste. There were young peasants, young officers, and young nobles, but no "youth" in the sense of a separate social group. *Jugend, Eros, Politik* (Bern, Munich, Vienna, 1964), p. 17. Herbert Blumenthal appears to have been referring to this change in the use of the word "youth" when he wrote, "Gone is the time when youthful romanticism meant an emancipation and sickness of the individual; we are experiencing—and we are creating—the romanticism of a generation, an historical event." *Der Anfang*, September 1919, p. 136.

3. Werner Kindt, ed., *Grundschriften der deutschen Jugendbewegung* (Düsseldorf and Cologne, 1963), p. 93. Gustav Wyneken went so far as to claim in a speech in 1913 that by raising the opposition of young people to their parents from the individual to the general and by giving it an organizational form the Wandervögel had actually "discovered" youth as a stage of life. Ibid., p. 118. The best treatment in English of the Youth Movement is Walter Z. Laqueur, *Young Germany* (London, 1962). In German the literature is immense. Pross, *Jugend, Eros, Politik*, contains a useful bibliography.

4. For the quotations from Langbehn and Moeller van den Bruck, see Fritz Stern, *The Politics of Cultural Despair* (Garden City, 1965), pp. 169, 234; for Max Weber, Arthur Mitzman, *The Iron Cage* (New York, 1971), p. 141; for the summons to the meeting on the Meissner Mountain, *Der Anfang*, September 1913, p. 129.

5. Hasenclever is quoted by Walter H. Sokel, *The Writer in Extremis: Expressionism in Twentieth-Century German Literature* (Stanford, 1959), p. 100; for Roy Pascal, see *From Naturalism to Expressionism: German Literature and Society 1880–1918* (London, 1973), pp. 227–228.

6. For the quotations from Pfemfert, see *Die Aktion*, 11 December 1912 and 11 October 1913. Helmut Plessner discusses the political uses of the concept of youth in "Nachwort zum Generationsproblem," originally "Het probleem der generaties," in *Soziologisch Jahrboek* (Leiden, 1949), reprinted in *Diesseits der Utopie* (Düsseldorf and Cologne, 1966), p. 83. Walter Rüegg ascribes the identification of youth with cultural renewal to the German intellectual tradition, and especially to the influence of Herder; but he errs in claiming that youth imagery was confined to Germany. See his essay "Jugend und Gesellschaft um 1900," in Walter Rüegg, ed., *Kulturkritik und Jugendkult* (Frankfort am Main, 1974), pp. 47–59.

7. For Kornfeld's article, see *Die Aktion*, 26 March 1913; for Ernst Fischer, *Erinerungen und Reflexionen* (Reinbeck bei Hamburg, 1969), pp. 48–51; for Weber's revolt against his father, Mitzman, *The Iron Cage*.

8. For the fragility of the Reich, see Michael R. Gordon, "Domestic Conflict and the Origins of the First World War: The British and German Cases," *Journal of Modern*

History 46 (June 1974): 209–213. In 1908 Friedrich Kummer published a history of German literature in which he sought, by means of the concept of literary generations, to disprove the widespread charge that the German writers of the late nineteenth and early twentieth centuries were mere epigones who failed to measure up to the giants of the Weimar and Romantic periods. Each generation, he maintained, was worthy of respect; and it was not always the greatest writers who contributed most to the development of the national spirit. "In the up and down, in the rising and disappearing of generations, there persists . . . an eternally unchanging national core, around which the new crystallizes." Friedrich Kummer *Deutsche Literaturgeschichte des neunzehten Jahrhunderts dargestellt nach Generationen* (Dresden, 1908), p. 18. The persistence of "an eternally unchanging national core, around which the new crystallizes" had also been one of Mentré's central themes and his ultimate argument in favor of the use of the generational concept in teaching French secondary school students.

9. For Diederichs, see Kindt, *Grundschriften der deutschen Jugendbewegung*, p. 94; for Wyneken, ibid, pp. 116–128, 148–62.

10. For the quote from Binding, see ibid., p. 431; for a highly romanticized account of the "storm on Langemarck," see Hermann Thimmermann, *Der Sturm auf Langemarck* (Munich, 1933). Thimmermann emphasizes the extreme youth of the German troops, their lack of training, and the "Indian" tactics with which the British defenders routed the attackers.

11. For the quotations from Flex, see Konrad Flex, *Walter Flex* (Stuttgart, 1937), pp. 31, 68.

12. For the description of Wurche, see Walter Flex, *Der Wanderer zwischen beiden Welten* (Munich, 1917), p. 12; for Flex's dealings with his publisher, Walter Eggert-Windegg, ed., *Briefe von Walter Flex* (Munich, 1927), pp. 207–208; for the sales of *Der Wanderer*, Konrad Flex, *Walter Flex*, p. xx.

13. For Flex's view of Wurche, see *Der Wanderer*, p. 44, and Eggert-Windegg, *Briefe von Walter Flex*, pp. 181–182; for Wurche's interpretation of the war, *Der Wanderer*, pp. 40, 84.

14. For Flex's belief that moral superiority could be demonstrated in defeat, see Walter Flex, *Gesammelte Werke*, I (Munich, n.d.), xxi–xxii. In the draft of his last novel, on which he was working when he was killed in 1917, Flex affirmed that it was not enough to fight with bayonets and propaganda. It was the duty of every individual to make his nation's right to existence "the strongest right on earth" by multiplying his own intellectual and moral worth. This could only be achieved by "incessant work on oneself." Ibid., p. 241. Flex denied angrily that he was a "national fanatic." What he represented, he wrote a friend after volunteering for service on the Western Front, were moral demands. Eggert-Windegg, *Briefe von Walter Flex*, pp. 280–281. For the letter from a young volunteer, see Philipp Witkop, ed., *Kriegsbriefe gefallener Studenten* (Munich, 1928; second ed., 1933), pp. 23–24. The dramatist Carl Zuckmayer, whose later left-wing sympathies are well known, offers another confirmation of this "moral" vision of the war that motivated young German middle-class volunteers. "We saw the meaning of the war in this inner liberation of the whole nation from its obsolete conventions, in this 'breakthrough' into the unknown, into some heroic venture, no matter whom it devoured. This was what fired our enthusiasm. Aims of conquest, considerations of power—these did not matter to us." *A Part of Myself* (New York, 1970), p. 148.

15. When Unruh read *Way of Sacrifice* to a group of staff officers, General von Knobelsdorf, the chief of staff, became so furious that he gave Unruh command of a rifle company that was to take part in an assault on Fort Douaumont at Verdun. Only the intervention of the army commander saved Unruh from this murderous assignment, which was meant to bring his writing career to a hasty close. Alvin Kronacher, *Fritz von Unruh* (New York, 1946).

16. Heym's diary is quoted in Walter Z. Laqueur, *Weimar: A Cultural History 1918–1933* (New York, 1974), p. 115.

17. Unruh's description of his conversion to pacifism is quoted by Manfred Durzak in Wolfgang Rothe, ed., *Expressionismus als Literatur* (Bern and Munich, 1969), p. 496. The lessons that Unruh drew from his early war experience were embodied in the poem *Vor der Entscheidung*, written in the fall of 1914 but not published until 1919. See Sokel, *The Writer in Extremis*, pp. 178–179, and Friedrich Rasche, ed., *Fritz von Unruh: Rebell und Verkünder* (Hanover, 1960), pp. 40–42.

18. Fritz von Unruh, *Opfergang* (Frankfurt am Main, 1925), p. 126.

19. Ibid., p. 62.

20. For Unruh's plays, see Sokel, *The Writer in Extremis*, pp. 184–185, 202–205; Rothe, *Expressionismus als Literatur*, pp. 497–502; and Hanns Martin Elster's afterword to Fritz von Unruh, *Sämtliche Werke*, III (Berlin, 1973), 395–435. For Toller, see Sokel, pp. 180–183, 196–201; and Rothe, pp. 572–584. For Gropius, see Barbara Miller Lane, *Architecture and Politics in Germany, 1918–1945* (Cambridge, Mass. 1968), pp. 41–68. For the connection between German Communism and the war experience, see Hermann Weber, *Die Wandlung des deutschen Kommunismus* (Frankfurt am Main, 1969), II, 26, 57–353.

21. Of the original active officer corps, just over half were killed during the war. Even without these losses, the demand for field officers would have far exceeded the available supply. To make up the difference, more than 200,000 men were commissioned after brief periods of training. These included many young middle-class volunteers like Flex and Wurche. Still others were given temporary officer status as sergeant-major-lieutenants and deputy officers. Many of these newly commissioned officers would no doubt have stayed on in the army, if it were not for the fact that the Treaty of Versailles limited the German officer corps to only 4,000 members. Of 9,000 Bavarian officers who served in the war, 22.6 percent of all second lieutenants and 27.6 percent of all first lieutenants were active in the Freikorps. See Robert G. L. Waite, *Vanguard of Nazism: The Free Corps Movement in Postwar Germany 1918–1923* (New York, 1969 ed.), pp. 45–49. The classic account of the Freikorps operations and the men who engaged in them is Ernst von Salomon, *Die Geächteten* (Berlin, 1930). The quotation beginning "what fate is, and what man is" is from Hans Zehrer, "Die zweite Welle," *Die Tat* 21 (1929–1930): 578. Seldte is quoted by Waite in *Vanguard of Nazism*, p. 267.

22. For Jünger's love of adventure, see Ernst Jünger, *Werke*, VII (Stuttgart, 1961), 53; for his vision of Africa, ibid., p. 60.

23. For Jünger's reaction to the outbreak of war, see Hans-Peter Schwartz, *Der konservative Anarchist: Politik und Zeitkritik Ernst Jüngers* (Freiburg im Breisgau, 1962), p. 64; for his departure for the front, ibid., p. 64, and Jünger, *The Storm of Steel* (London, 1929), p. 1. The 1924 version of *In Stahlgewittern*, which was used as the basis for the English and French translations of 1929 and 1930, differs in important

ways from the text given in Jünger, *Werke*, I (Stuttgart, 1961), 11–310. It stresses much more than earlier and later versions the role of the war in the creation of a generation of new men who, "hardened as scarcely another generation ever was in fire and flame," could go "into life as though from the anvil." The imagery with which Jünger described his feelings as he marched off to war, however, remained remarkably constant. For the complex problem of Jünger's revision of his war notebooks, see Ulrich Böhme, "Fassungen bei Ernst Jünger," *Deutsche Studien* 14 (1972): 7–59. Böhme demonstrates that Jünger never treated *In Stahlgewittern* as a document, but returned to it time and again to enhance its literary effects. It is clear that the 1924 version was later reworked with political and ideological aims in mind, and it is this edition that I shall use in discussing Jünger's contribution to the myth of the front generation. For Jünger's lack of political consciousness when the war began, see Schwartz, *Der konservative Anarchist*, p. 59, and *The Storm of Steel*, p. 1.

24. The 1924 version of *In Stahlgewittern* plays down this contradiction and deliberately emphasizes Jünger's soldierly qualities and his belief in the need for Prussian discipline and unquestioning obedience to orders from above. There is every reason to believe that during this period of his life Jünger was working consciously to suppress the potential aesthete that he felt within him. Thus he presented to the world as a model for the "new man" a soldierly existence that he himself had just abandoned in favor of zoology and letters.

25. *The Storm of Steel*, pp. 235, 255. For a description of the storm trooper, "a new kind of man, a man characterized by the highest intensification of all virile qualities," see Franz Schauwecker, *Das Frontbuch: Die deutsche Seele im Weltkriege* (Halle, 1927), pp. 284–285. Both Jünger and Schauwecker neglect to mention that the storm troopers of 1918 were given special privileges, were not subjected to the same kind of discipline as other troops, and were often viewed with hostility by the soldiers who were expected to follow them into battle. See Walter Struve, *Elites against Democracy* (Princeton, 1973), p. 393. For Jünger's vision of himself as a freebooter and wandering knight, see *Werke*, V (Stuttgart, 1961), 71.

26. By 1925 *In Stahlgewittern* had sold more than 16,000 copies; by the end of the decade it had sold another 15,000, which by the standards of the period made it a good seller, if not a runaway success like Flex's *Der Wanderer* or Erich Maria Remarque's *Im Westen Nichts Neues* [All Quiet on the Western Front]. In any case, Jünger's war books and essays for journals and newspapers provided him with a continuing income and thus freed him to pursue his political and literary career. For Jünger's activities and attitudes during the immediate postwar years, see his letters to his brother Friedrich Georg, collected in Armin Mohler, ed., *Die Schleife: Dokumente zum Weg von Ernst Jünger* (Zurich, 1955), pp. 58–77.

27. Jünger's political essays are conveniently listed in Schwartz, *Der konservative Anarchist*, pp. 309–315. For his primacy among spokesmen for the war generation, see ibid., pp. 104–105, 279–280, n. 19; and Kurt Sontheimer, *Antidemokratischen Denken in der Weimarer Republik* (Munich, 1962), p. 128. For Jünger's belief that his experience was typical, see *Werke*, VII, 27–28; for the parallel between his attitude toward his public and toward the troops he had commanded, see Schwartz, p. 45. Jünger's political essays have been submitted to an elaborate quantitative analysis by Marjatta Hietala in *Der neue Nationalismus in der Publizstik Ernst Jüngers und des Kreises um ihn 1920–1933* (Helsinki, 1975). Hietala demonstrates the centrality of the war experience

in the development of Jünger's world view, shows how closely it was correlated with nationalism and elitism, and explains finally why his able and insistent interpretation of a widely shared complex of feelings and memories permitted him to become the leader of a circle and the dominant ideologue among radical conservatives in Germany during the period between 1925 and 1933. See especially pp. 175, 185, 199, 225–226.

28. *Der Krieg als inneres Erlebnis* was first published in 1922, then revised in 1926. It is quoted here from *Werke*, V, 13–22. For man as the most dangerous, the most bloodthirsty, and the most goal-conscious being, see p. 106; for the human race as a primeval forest, p. 16; for the intensity of the meeting of two peoples on the field of battle, p. 43; for war as a great school, p. 77; for war as a creative force, p. 70; for a generation destroyed in the collapse, Schwartz, *Der konservative Anarchist*, p. 265, where Jünger's 1923 novel *Sturm* is quoted.

29. For war as an eternal rite, see Jünger, *Werke*, VII, 118–119; for man as bearer and vessel of the past, ibid., V, 17.

30. For the storm troopers as the most combative men the world could bear, see ibid., V, 40. "We are—we feel every day with firmer certainty—a new generation, a race [*Geschlecht*], that has been hardened and inwardly transformed by all the darting flames and sledgehammer blows of the greatest war in history. While in all parties, the process of decomposition and dissolution leads toward its end, we think, feel, and live already in a completely different form, and it is already beyond doubt that with greater self-consciousness we will impose this form on the outside world. Therefore we are also the called-for fighters for a new state . . . The time has come at which the individual movements must align themselves in the nationalist front . . . To this end I call upon the leaders, and I shall continue these appeals within a determined circle, to do what fate wills. This is the burning demand of the hour! Acknowledge that the hour has come, put away individual concerns, and let yourselves be dazzled by the reflection of the future so that you will be proof against the personal demands that everyday life brings. We must advance, so long as the fire of youth remains in us!" Quoted in Franz Baumer, *Ernst Jünger* (Berlin, 1967), p. 36. The metaphor of the new order originating in elements of earth and fire is from Jünger, ed., *Krieg und Krieger* (Berlin, 1930), p. 30.

31. Jünger's withdrawal from political activity occurred gradually between 1929 and 1932, the date of the publication of *Der Arbeiter*. After 1932 he devoted himself entirely to his literary career and avoided contacts with all politicians, above all with the Nazis, whose rabble-rousing he abhorred. "The time of great human and manly dreams had passed" is from Erich Maria Remarque, *Drei Kameraden* (Amsterdam, 1938), p. 61. The question regarding the whereabouts of "this mighty war generation" was put by Max Ziese, quoted by Edgar Jung in "Die Tragik der Kriegsgeneration," *Süddeutsche Monatshefte* 27 (May 1930): 530.

32. The writer who sighed about youth was Jonas Lesser, *Von deutscher Jugend* (Berlin, 1932), p. 9. When pressed for a more precise definition of the realm of youth, few leaders of the Bünde could go very far. One pointed out that it was neither Luther's realm of God nor a politically unified new German Reich, although elements of both would be present in it. It was rather "the earthly representation of a God united in a new attitude and of a new generation obedient to the gods, for whose will to life the Bund was symbol and expression in microcosm." Quoted by Felix Raabe, *Die bündische Jugend* (Stuttgart, 1961), p. 121.

33. Eduard Wechssler, "Die Generation als Jugendgemeinschaft," in *Geist und Gesellschaft: Kurt Breysig zu seinem sechzigsten Geburtstag* (Breslau, 1927), I, ed. Richard Peters, 80, 91. "The crowd," Wechssler cried in despair, "is bewitched by Zeitgeist, the spirit of specialization, the spirit of foreign cultures, and all kinds of specters and has forgotten that our intellectual youth, insofar as it strives seriously and thinks honorably, is the only value in present-day Germany" (p. 96).

34. Eduard Spranger, *Psychologie des Jugendalters*, p. 93.

35. The circulation of *Die Tat* rose from less than a thousand in 1929, when Hans Zehrer was appointed editor-in-chief, to 25,000 or more in 1933. See Laqueur, *Weimar*, p. 104, and Struve, *Elites against Democracy*, p. 356. During the period 1930–1933 it probably represented better than any other weekly the attitudes of uncommitted university youth. For Zehrer, see Ebbo Demant, *Von Schleicher zu Springer: Hans Zehrer als politische Publizist* (Mainz, 1971), and Struve, pp. 353–376.

36. Hans Thomas [Hans Zehrer], "Die zweite Welle," *Die Tat* 21 (1929–1930): 577–582.

37. Hans Thomas [Hans Zehrer], "Absage an den Jahrgang 1902," *Die Tat* 21 (1929–1930): 740–748. The term "class of 1902" came from the best-selling novel by Ernst Glaeser, *Jahrgang 1902* (Potsdam, 1928), which described the adolescence of a young man born in 1902, hence too young to fight in the war. Perhaps the most quoted phrase in the book was a comment made to the German protagonist by a French friend just before the outbreak of the war: "La guerre, ce sont nos parents" [The war is our parents].

38. Edgar Jung, "Die Tragik der Kriegsgeneration." *Die Herrschaft der Minderwertigen* was first published in Berlin in 1927. A second, greatly expanded edition was published in 1929. The book was dedicated to "those who have fallen in battle" and to "those who stand in battle." In it Jung argued that the principle of equality was hostile to life, defended the right of the Gemeinschaft to be governned by the "best," and set forth in shimmering detail the faith of "the new German man," who had emerged rejuvenated from his service on the battlefields of Central Europe. Unlike the alienated survivors he described in his article, Jung had adjusted well to civilian life. He had obtained a doctorate in jurisprudence and practiced law in Zweibrücken, where he maintained excellent contacts with local business interests. See Struve, *Elites against Democracy*, pp. 319–321. Hopes for the resurgence of the war generation were expressed in four other important works published in 1929–1932: Franz Schauwecker, *Aufbruch der Nation* (Berlin, 1930); Jünger, ed., *Krieg und Krieger*; von Salomon, *Die Geächteten*; and Edwin Erich Dwinger, *Wir rufen Deutschland* (Jena, 1932). These books all emphasized the need for the front generation to analyze their feelings and experience and to produce a new interpretation of the war. As Schauwecker put it, "We must learn to be able to think what we today only feel! We are now only capable of obeying commands. And no one commands us" (p. 339). What is in the blood of the front generation, said Schauwecker (p. 402), must be brought into their consciousness. "Let us bring it into consciousness. Blood and consciousness must coincide in life. Then spirit comes into being. Everything else is secondary—intellect or reaction or mere phrases—it is dead. Let us fling it aside! It is completely worthless!"

39. Uttmann von Elterlein, "Absage an den Jahrgang 1902?" *Die Tat* 22 (1930–1931): 202–206.

40. Hans Hartmann, *Die junge Generation in Europa* (Berlin, 1933 ed.)

41. Frank Matzke, *Jugend bekennt: so sind wir!* (Berlin, 1930).

42. Leopold Dingräve [Ernst Wilhelm Eschmann], *Wo steht die junge Generation?* (Jena, 1931), pp. 7–8, 53–54.

43. Ibid., p. 11.

44. I am oversimplifying Gründel's argument for purposes of clarity. Gründel admitted in a detailed discussion of the various subgenerations' chronological limits and characteristics that to be accurate one would have to make even further distinctions within the three subgenerations. For Gründel's definition of generations as waves of humanity, see *Die Sendung der jungen Generation: Versuch einer umfassenden revolutionären Sinndeutung der Krise* (Munich, 1932), p. 14.

45. The 6,300,000 members of the war youth generation, according to Gründel, outnumbered the front youth by almost two million and the postwar youth by 1,300,000. Gründel estimated that of the 10,000 most intellectually capable men of the front youth generation, as many as 7,000 had been killed during the war, along with hundreds of thousands who would have followed their lead.

46. Gründel, *Die Sendung*, pp. 8–9, 13.

47. Ibid., p. 87.

48. Spranger, *Psychologie des Jugendalters*, p. 149.

49. For Gründel's statement about biological man as raw material and for his vision of the new social structure with its three classes, see *Die Sendung*, pp. 307–318, 414.

50. For Gründel's criticism of Communism and National Socialism, see ibid., pp. 255–263, 295–296.

51. For Hitler's reassurance of the older generation, see his speech in Berlin on 10 February 1933, excerpted in *Adolph Hitler spricht: Ein Lexikon des Nationalsozialismus* (Leipzig, 1934), p. 157.

52. For Edgar Jung's interpretation of Hitler and the Nazi movement in 1933, see Struve, *Elites against Democracy*, pp. 344–352. Jung agreed to become Fritz von Papen's secretary in 1933, but was murdered during the Röhm purge, presumably because of his lack of enthusiasm for the new Nazi government.

53. For a useful summary of some of this literature, see Detlev W. Shumann, "Cultural Age-Groups in German Thought," *Publications of the Modern Language Association* 51 (1936): 1180–1207.

54. Mannheim had shown the utility of his method the previous year in his famous essay "Das konservative Denken: Soziologische Beiträge zum Werden des politisch-historisch Denkens in Deutschland," *Archiv für Sozialwissenschaft und Sozialpolitik* 57, no. 102 (1927): 68–142, reprinted in Kurt H. Wolff, ed., *Karl Mannheim: Wissenssoziologie* (Berlin, 1934), pp. 408–508.

55. Dilthey (1833) was first drawn to the generation problem through his studies of the German Romantics. He was impressed by the way men of different origins, temperaments, and regions, who in some cases had never met, could end by having so much in common when viewed by a cultural historian like himself. The determining circumstances in which they had grown up, he concluded, bound them together and gave them their unity of style and theme. See Wilhelm Dilthey, "Novalis," first published in the *Preussicher Jahrbuch* in 1866 and later reprinted in *Das Erlebnis und die Dichtung* (Göttingen, 1965 ed.), especially pp. 187–190. Dilthey returned to the generation problem in two later essays: "Über das Studium der Geschichte der Wissenschafte vom

Menschen, der Gesellschaft und dem Staat," in *Gesammelte Schriften*, V (Leipzig and Berlin, 1924), 36–41; and "Archive der Literatur in ihrer Bedeutung für das Studium der Geschichte der Philosophie," ibid., IV (Leipzig and Berlin, 1921), 561–565.

56. Wilhelm Pinder, *Das Problem der Generationen in der Kunstgeschichte Europas* (Berlin, 1926), p. 154. Pinder's concept of entelechy parallels, to some extent, Mentré's idea of the series (see p. 243, n.30).

57. In his criticism of the German academics who explained everything in terms of spirit, Mannheim may have had in mind Wechssler, who had developed a theory of world history in which the critical concepts were *Jungendgeist, Altersgeist, Zeitgeist,* and *Ungeist.* Wechssler's 1927 essay in the Breysig *Festschrift, Geist und Gesellschaft,* was directed against the spread of *Fachgeist* (the spirit of specialization) in German universities and Anglo-Saxon-dominated Zeitgeist in German society at large. He himself favored a return to the true V*olkgeist* of the German people, which was culture, not technology, and which could be renewed periodically by Jugendgeist. These renewals, Wechssler went out of his way to point out, had nothing to do with "progress" as most people understood the term.

58. Mannheim did not refer to Freud in this essay, but he was familiar with his concept of the unconscious at this time through his wife, the psychologist Julia Láng.

59. Mannheim, "Das Problem der Generationen," first published in *Kölner Vierteljahrshefte* 7, nos. 2–3 (1928–1929): 157–185, 309–330; later reprinted in Wolff, ed., *Karl Mannheim: Wissenssoziologie,* pp. 509–565. For the discussion of generations as actualities, see ibid., pp. 542–543. Mannheim's distinction between peasant and urban youth left open the possibility that peasant youth might form different generational complexes within the same society.

60. "Grundintentionen and principles of behavior," Mannheim explained, "are the primary socializing factors in social-historical development. One must grow up in them if one really wants to participate in collective events." *Wissenssoziologie,* p. 545.

61. Ibid., pp. 550–551.

62. This remark leaves out of consideration the fact, perhaps unknown by Mannheim, that demographic development is seldom regular and may itself influence the process of generational formation.

63. The work by Petersen that engaged Mannheim's attention was *Die Wesenbestimmung der deutschen Romantik* (Berlin, 1926). For Mannheim's discussion of the connection between generations and the Zeitgeist, see *Wissensoziologie,* pp. 551–555. Mannheim defined the Zeitgeist as "the continuous dynamic concatenation of the successive generational complexes (*Generationszusammenhänge*)."

64. *Wissensoziologie,* p. 526.

65. Ibid., pp. 549–550. The work by Lukács that especially influenced Mannheim in this period was *Geschichte und Klassenbewusstein* (Berlin, 1923).

66. On other occasions, Jünger used the pronoun "we" to refer to "the youth of the land who are intellectual, full of spirit, and capable of enthusiasm." Presumably the enthusiasm Jünger referred to was for his program. The important thing was the distinction between the elite and the mass. See the final paragraph of *Im Stahlgewittern* (Berlin, 1927), p. 283, which was removed from later editions.

67. For Mannheim's essay on intellectual competition, see "Die Bedeutung der Konkurrenz im Gebiete des Gestigen," in V*erhandlungen des sechsten deutschen Soziologentages vom 17. bis 19. September 1928 in Zürich* (Tübingen, 1929), pp. 35–83,

reprinted in *Wissenssoziologie*, pp. 556–613; for his definition of ideology, Mannheim, *Ideology and Utopia* (New York, n.d.), pp. 192–194.

68. All of Mannheim's essays written in the 1920s are penetrated by the conviction that his generation was living during an exceptionally favorable time for absorbing and at the same time rising above the political conflicts of the nineteenth century. For an explicit statement of this belief, see *Wissenssoziologie*, p. 607.

3. *England: Lost Legions of Youth*

1. The phrase "scornfully detached from the common struggle" is taken from John Buchan's elegy for Raymond Asquith, quoted by Correlli Barnet in *The Collapse of British Power* (London, 1972), p. 427. For the idea that the best among the English war generation were "all scholars and sportsmen and poets—even if they did not write poetry" see E. B. Osborn, *The New Elizabethans* (London, 1919), p. 3. "They had a conviction that life ought to be lived poetically. They had the Elizabethan exuberance. They were as various and insatiate and adventurous in the art of living as were the old Elizabethans, before whom the gates of the Greek past, of a Roman future, were flung wide open."

2. Brooke's early years are reconstructed in ample, if reverent, detail by Christopher Hassall in his biography, *Rupert Brooke* (New York, 1964).

3. Ibid., p. 146. Brooke's letter of 20 September 1910 to his classmate and fellow Fabian Ben Keeling indicates that he was keenly aware of generational change and saw it in relation to political action. "Lately, when I've been reading up the Elizabethans, and one or two other periods, I've been amazed more than ever at the way things change. Even in talking to my Uncle of 70 about the Victorians, it comes out astonishingly. The whole machinery of life, and the minds of every class and kind of man, change beyond recognition every generation. I don't know that 'Progress' is certain. All I know is that change is. These solid, solemn, provincials, and old maids, and businessmen, and all the immovable system of things I see round me will vanish like smoke. All this present overwhelming reality will be as dead and odd and fantastic as crinolines or 'a dish of tay.' Something will be in its place, inevitably. And what that something will be depends on me. With such superb work to do, and with the wild adventure of it all, and with the other minutes (too many of them) given to the enchantment of being even for a moment alive in a world of real matter (not that imitation, gilt stuff, one gets in Heaven) and actual people—I have no time to be a pessimist." *The Letters of Rupert Brooke*, ed. Geoffrey Keynes (London, 1968), pp. 259–260.

4. Virginia Woolf, "Rupert Brooke," *Times Literary Supplement*, 8 August 1918, p. 371; for Frances Darwin's description of Brooke as a golden-haired Apollo and her later reassessment, see Hassall, *Brooke*, pp. 159, 277–278.

5. *Letters*, p. 491.

6. For Brooke's definition of the spiritual vagabond, see Hassall, *Brooke*, p. 122; for his loss of all knowledge of art and literature, *Letters*, p. 534; for his desire to have extraordinary adventures, ibid., p. 568; for his description of London and his fear that something in him was broken, ibid., p. 573.

7. For the letter to Cathleen Nesbitt, see Hassall, *Brooke*, p. 453. At about the same time, Brooke wrote his close friend Jacques Raverat, "You'll be relieved to know that I pray continually. Twelve hours a day, that I may, sometime, fall in love with

somebody. Twelve hours a day that I may *never* fall in love with anybody. Either alternative seems too Hellish to bear." *Letters,* p. 597. For Cathleen Nesbitt's somewhat different version of her relationship with Brooke, see A *Little Love and Good Company* (Owing Mills, Md., 1977), pp. 60–88.

8. For Brooke's depression about the war, see *Letters,* p. 601; for his decision that the only honorable thing was to enlist and fight, ibid., p. 608. Cyril Asquith, who was in Brooke's battalion, later told Cathleen Nesbitt that "they all felt almost as though they were crusaders and that they felt fulfillment and satisfaction in doing something necessary. They all had something in them of public spirit. They felt in one way or another that they owed something to society, some gratitude for the good things that life had given them, their talents and fine education." Nesbitt, A *Little Love,* p. 84.

9. For Brooke's letter to Nesbitt, see *Letters,* p. 631; his sonnets were published in *1914 and Other Poems* (London, 1915).

10. These quotations all come from the 1914 sonnets.

11. *Letters,* pp. 654–655. Brooke was mistaken in reporting that Georges Duhamel had been killed.

12. For the burial, see Hassall, *Brooke,* pp. 512–513. Charles Lister, one of Brooke's fellow officers, wrote a friend, "The grave is under an olive tree that bends over it like a weeping angel. A sad end to such dazzling purity of mind and work, clean cut, classical, and unaffected all the time like his face, unfurrowed or lined by cares. Perhaps the Island of Achilles is in some respects a suitable resting-place for those bound for the plains of Troy." Laurence Housman, ed., *War Letters of Fallen Englishmen* (London, 1930), p. 172. Of the five friends who were present at Brooke's burial, only two survived the war.

13. For the citation by the dean of St. Paul's, see Hassall, *Brooke,* p. 502; for the reaction of Brooke's friends to Sherril Schell's photograph, ibid., p. 390.

14. Churchill's tribute is quoted by Hassall, ibid., p. 515. On the day Brooke's death was reported in the *Cambridge Review,* his name was only one in a long list of sixty-six dead and forty-two wounded. Ibid., p. 514.

15. Robert Nichols, ed., *Anthology of War Poetry 1914–1918* (London, 1943), pp. 34, 25; for the young man who went to France thankful to be chosen, see Housman, *War Letters,* p. 177. Brooke's poems were bought, read, and cherished by the English. Vera Brittain recalled hearing Brooke's sonnets read to her for the first time by her Oxford tutor in May 1915, just after her fiancé had been killed in France. "These famous sonnets . . . were then only beginning to take the world's breath away . . . With my grief and anxiety then so new, I found the experience so moving that I should not have sought it had I realized how hard composure would be to maintain. Silently I struggled for it as I listened to the English tutor's grave, deliberate voice reading the sonnets, unhackneyed, courageous, and almost shattering in their passionate, relevant idealism." Vera Brittain, *Testament of Youth* (London, 1933), p. 155.

16. For death as the greatest of adventures, see Osborn, *The New Elizabethans,* pp. 64–65; for the satisfaction of their dreams of glory and knightly adventure, Herbert Asquith, "The Volunteer," in I. M. Parsons, ed., *Men Who March Away* (New York, 1965), p. 41; for Julian Grenfell's poem, ibid., p. 38; for Ian Hay, *The First Hundred Thousand* (Boston and New York, 1916), p. xi.

17. Note, however, that the British government did not allow war correspondents in the battle zones until May 1915. This fact made the testimony of returning comba-

tants all the more important. See John Terrine, *Impacts of War: 1914 and 1918* (London, 1970), p. 95.

18. Grenfell's verse is cited from Parsons, *Men Who March Away*, p. 28. Sir Osbert Sitwell's father wrote to his son that "according to the Insurance Companies it is eleven to one against an officer being killed in a *year's* fighting with the Germans, so I hope we may get you back safe and sound." Sir Osbert Sitwell, *Laughter in the Next Room* (Boston, 1948), p. 88. Robert Graves claimed that "the average life expectancy of the infantry subaltern on the Western front was, at some stages of the War, only about three months; that is to say that at the end of three months he was either wounded or killed. The proportions worked out at about four wounded to every one killed. Of the four one was wounded seriously, and the remaining three more or less lightly. The three lightly wounded returned to the front after a few weeks or months of absence, and were again subject to the same odds." *Good-bye to All That* (London, 1929), pp. 89–90. This explains, to use Wilfred Owen's phrase, why courage "leaked out" of men at the front, like sand from the best sandbags after years of rain; but it also accounts for the fact that morale remained high during the first two years, for sick and lightly wounded men sometimes stayed away from the trenches for months.

19. For the way in which literary tradition shaped the representation of experience, see Paul Fussell, *The Great War and Modern Memory* (New York and London, 1975); Bernard Bergonzi, *Heroes' Twilight* (New York, 1965); John H. Johnston, *English Poetry of the First World War* (Princeton, 1964); Vivian de Sola Pinto, *Crisis in English Poetry 1880–1940* (London, 1967); and Arthur E. Lane, *An Adequate Response* (Detroit, 1972). Even the best of early English war poets tended to interpret their experience in traditional metaphors and images. Charles Sorley is a good example. The son of a Cambridge philosophy professor, Sorley (1895) disliked Brooke's sonnets because they were too sentimental and because they emphasized what Brooke was giving up rather than the unavoidable and tragic imperatives of the occasion. *The Letters of Charles Sorley* (Cambridge, 1919), pp. 262–263. But though unwilling to see the war, as Brooke had, as a gift from God, Sorley was incapable of representing the war except as a collective adventure, which the men of his age must bear uncomplainingly and in which they would be unconscious pawns. Sorley's advice, totally in keeping with the official attitude of the English governing class, was "to cast away regret and rue" and to "think what you are marching to." "It is easy to be dead." Charles Hamilton Sorley, *Marlborough and Other Poems* (Cambridge, 1919), pp. 57, 69. Sorley did not live long enough to revise this attitude. He was killed by a sniper during the attack on Loos in October 1915.

20. Quoted by Nicholas Mosley in *Julian Grenfell* (London, 1976), p. 116.

21. The war poets of 1916–1918 recognized that their image of the war was not generally accepted. See Sir Osbert Sitwell, who wrote that his friendship with Wilfred Owen matured more rapidly because of the fact "that we were deeply in sympathy in our views concerning the war and its conduct—a link of nonconformity that in those years [1917–1918] bound together the disbelievers with almost the same force with which faith knitted together the early Christians." *Noble Essences* (Boston, 1950), pp. 101–102. For a devastating but probably not inaccurate description of the average English subaltern's attitude toward the war, see Richard Aldington, *Death of a Hero* (London, 1929), pp. 329–331.

22. Siegfried Sassoon, *The Old Huntsman* (New York, 1918), p. 31.

23. My account of Sassoon's life is based on his six volumes of memoirs: *Memoirs*

of a Fox-Hunting Man (London, 1928); *Memoirs of an Infantry Officer* (London, 1930); *Sherston's Progress,* included in *The Memoirs of George Sherston* (New York, 1937); *The Old Century and Seven More Years* (London, 1968 ed.); *The Weald of Youth* (London, 1942); and *Siegfried's Journey, 1916–1920* (London, 1946). For an excellent analysis of these autobiographical texts, as well as of Sassoon's poetry, see Michael Thorpe, *Siegfried Sassoon: A Critical Study* (London, 1967). Since the first three memoirs are written as fiction and the last three as formal autobiography, and since the two sets by no means overlap completely, it is clear that one must read all these volumes with some skepticism when trying to reconstruct Sassoon's life. It is hard not to believe, for example, that he exaggerates his innocence and naiveté before 1916 in both the fiction and the autobiography in order to emphasize the contrast between the prewar and postwar worlds.

24. For Sassoon's mood on the eve of the war, see *The Weald of Youth,* pp. 246–259.

25. For Sassoon's memory of these days as idyllic, see *Fox-Hunting Man,* p. 245; for the need to feel secretly heroic, ibid., p. 285; for a free holiday in France, *Infantry Officer,* p. 18.

26. Sassoon, *Infantry Officer,* p. 110.

27. Sassoon, *Siegfried's Journey,* pp. 13–14.

28. For Sassoon's early war poetry and the discovery of his talent for satirical epigram, see ibid., p. 29.

29. For Sassoon's loss of faith in the justice of the war, see ibid., p. 41; for the depression caused by the loss of his friends, *Infantry Officer,* pp. 190–192; for the decision to tell the truth about the war, *Siegfried's Journey,* p. 40; for "The General," *Counter-Attack* (London, 1918), p. 26.

30. Sassoon's antiwar declaration read, "I am making this statement as an act of wilful defiance of military authority, because I believe that the War is being deliberately prolonged by those who have the power to end it. I am a soldier, convinced that I am acting on behalf of soldiers. I believe that this War, upon which I entered as a war of defence and liberation, has now become a war of aggression and conquest. I believe that the purposes for which I and my fellow soldiers entered upon this War should have been so clearly stated as to have made it impossible to change them, and that, had this been done, the objects which actuated us would now be attainable by negotiation. I have seen and endured the sufferings of the troops, and I can no longer be a party to prolong these sufferings for ends which I believe to be evil and unjust. I am not protesting against the conduct of the War, but against the political errors and insincerities for which the fighting men are being sacrificed. On behalf of those who are suffering now I make this protest against the deception which is being practised on them; also I believe that I may help to destroy the callous complacency with which the majority of those at home regard the continuance of agonies which they do not share, and which they have not sufficient imagination to realize." *Infantry Officer,* pp. 284–285. Sassoon's friends at the front did not approve of this declaration. Though they admired Sassoon's courage in standing up for his convictions and shared his disgust for the politicians at home, they felt his antiwar gesture was inopportune. "No Peace now would be of any use," one friend wrote to him on 11 July 1917. "He [the Boche] is still very strong and would make the first attempt he could to pounce upon and eat up any small nation too weak to withstand him. War is hideous—and no one knows it more than you and I—but I'm

afraid fighting the swine we are—that it must go on—in the interests of our own preservation—till we are in a position to make peace which will give us a *certainty* of the war not being resumed as soon as Germany thinks she is strong enough." This friend warned Sassoon not to be misled by the intellectual "croakers" he associated with in England. "They may be pro-Germans—one never knows!" Joe Cottrill to Sassoon, 11 July 1917, in Sassoon Archives, Imperial War Museum, London.

31. Graves, *Good-bye to All That*, pp. 322–323.

32. For Sassoon's most effective images, see above all *Counter-Attack*.

33. For Sassoon's sense of immolation to some vague aspiration, see *Siegfried's Journey*, p. 42.

34. For Owen's poem "1914," see *The Collected Poems of Wilfred Owen*, ed. C. Day Lewis (London, 1963), p. 129; for the feeling of betraying England and France, *Wilfred Owen: Collected Letters*, ed. Harold Owen and John Bell (London, New York, and Toronto, 1967), p. 345; for Owen's life up to 1915, Jon Stallworthy, *Wilfred Owen* (London, 1974), pp. 1–125.

35. For Owen's impression of the officers' faces, see *Collected Letters*, p. 422; for his experience in no-man's-land, pp. 427–428; for the ugliness of the landscape, p. 431; for the piercing of his trench coat, p. 450; for the twelve days in the line, pp. 452–453.

36. Ibid., p. 461.

37. For Owen's assessment of Sassoon's war poetry, see ibid., pp. 484–485; for Sassoon's influence on Owen, *Siegfried's Journey*, pp. 58–63; for the impact of *Under Fire* on Owen's poetic imagery, Stallworthy, *Owen*, pp. 242–246; for Owen's letter to his mother, *Collected Letters*, p. 521.

38. *Collected Poems*, p. 40.

39. Ibid., p. 35.

40. For Owen's awareness of his indebtedness to Christian concepts and metaphors, see *Collected Letters*, p. 534; for his view of himself as a tormentor of the troops under his command, p. 562. For other poems on the theme of the sacrifice of youth by the older generation, see Sassoon's "The Fathers," Richard Aldington's "The Blood of Young Men," Osbert Sitwell's "Hymn to Moloch," and Ezra Pound's "Hugh Selwyn Mauberley." For "The Parable of the Old Man and the Young," see Owen, *Collected Poems*, p. 42. Poems like this understandably annoyed those who had been too old to fight. After reading Sassoon's collection of Owen's verse, which appeared in 1921, the well-known patriotic poet Sir Henry Newbolt wrote, "Owen and the rest of the broken men rail at the Old Men who sent the young to die: they have suffered cruelly, but in the nerves and not the heart—they haven't the experience or the imagination to know the extreme human agony—'Who giveth me to die for thee, Absalom my son, my son.' Paternity apart, what Englishman of fifty wouldn't far rather stop the shot himself than see the boys do it for him?" Quoted by Bergonzi in *Heroes' Twilight*, p. 122. Needless to say, the young war poets did not find this kind of argument very convincing. In 1917, Robert Graves imagined a situation in which wars were fought only by men over forty-five. " 'Well, dear father, how proud I am of you serving your country as a very gallant gentleman prepared to make even the supreme sacrifice! I only wish I were your age: how willingly would I buckle on my armour and fight those unspeakable Philistines! As it is, of course, I can't be spared; I have to stay behind at the War Office and administrate for you lucky old men. 'What sacrifices I have made!' David would sigh, when the old boys had gone off with a draft to the front, singing *Tipperary*. 'There's father and

my Uncle Salmon, and both my grandfathers, all on active service. I must put a card in the window about it.' " *Goodbye to All That,* pp. 288–289.

41. Actually, the books of 1928–1933 were anticipated by C. E. Montague's *Disenchantment* (New York, 1922), a vigorously written and penetrating inquiry into the combatant mentality. But whereas Montague tried to explain in a spirit of objectivity why disenchantment had developed among soldiers—for example, because of the sheer size of the army and the isolation of the front-line troops—many of the writers of 1928–1933 were satisfied to deplore the stupidity and bloodlust of the older generation. Barbusse is quoted in Sassoon, *Counter-Attack,* p. v.

42. For Blunden, see *Undertones of War* (Garden City, 1929), p. 236; for Dick Tiltwood as an epitome of his generation, Sassoon, *Fox-Hunting Man,* pp. 268–269; for Sherston's thoughts on Easter Sunday 1916, ibid., p. 313.

43. For Erich Maria Remarque's soldiers, see *All Quiet on the Western Front* (London, 1929), p. 143; for his letter to Sir Ian Hamilton, Douglas Jerrold, *The Lie about the War* (London, 1930), p. 26.

44. For the critics' reaction to Graves's book, see *Times Literary Supplement,* 28 November 1929, p. 991; for the effect of front-line service on officers, *Good-bye to All That,* p. 221; for Graves's letter, Graves, *But It Still Goes On* (London and Toronto, 1930), pp. 40–41.

45. For the regime of cant, see *Death of a Hero,* p. 253; for Winterbourne's heroic death, ibid., p. 429; for the review, *Times Literary Supplement,* 19 September 1929, p. 713. *Death of a Hero* has recently been reexamined sympathetically by John Morris in Holger Klein, ed., *The First World War in Fiction* (London, 1976), pp. 183–192.

46. Henry Williamson, *The Patriot's Progress* (London, 1968 ed.), pp. 151–152, 128. Another important war book of 1930 that went through several editions was Laurence Housman's *War Letters of Fallen Englishmen.* Housman was visibly embarrassed by the enthusiasm for the war shown by some of his letter writers and went out of his way to point out in the preface that war could never be "fine." "To attribute any nobility to war itself is as much a confusion of thought as to attribute nobility to cancer or leprosy, because of the skill, devotion, and self-sacrifice of those who give up their lives to its cure, or because of the patient endurance of the sufferers." This "confusion of thought," he admitted, was to be found in some of the writers of his letters (p. 6).

47. Jerrold, *The Lie about the War,* p. 38; Carrington, *A Subaltern's War,* p. 208; Paul Deane, "The Tragedy of the Survivors," *The Nation,* October 1930, p. 102.

48. For the journalist's confidence in the future of the British Empire, see Osborn, *The New Elizabethans,* p. 64.

49. For Mosley, see Robert Skidelsky, *Oswald Mosley* (London, 1975), p. 275.

50. Vera Brittain, *Testament of Experience* (London, 1957), p. 77.

51. For the tendency to structure experience in terms of the medieval romance, see Fussell, *The Great War and Modern Memory,* pp. 135–144; for the innocence of Brittain's heroes, *Testament of Youth* (London, 1933), p. 17; for the imagery of their return, ibid., p. 663; for their refusal to forget, ibid., pp. 645–646; for the sales of *Testament of Youth,* personal communication of John Bush, chairman of Victor Gollanz Ltd., to the author, 13 February 1978. Ruth Holland's novel, *The Lost Generation* (London, 1932), was structured almost exactly like Brittain's memoir and ended on a similar note. "The only thing to do [in the late 1920s] was to provide a new generation, and try and help them not to make such a mess of things." (p. 308).

52. For the hustling of the survivors out of England, see Deane, "The Tragedy of the Survivors," p. 103; for Woodward's disappointment, Stephen R. Ward, ed., *The War Generation* (Port Washington, N.Y., 1975), p. 23; Reginald Pound, *The Lost Generation*, pp. 275–276; Robert Skidelsky, *Mosley*, p. 225.

53. For British losses in comparison to those of France and Germany, see Correlli Barnett, *The Collapse of British Power*, p. 425; for the drop in the number of males per thousand of the population, Arthur Marwick, *The Deluge* (Boston and Toronto, 1965), p. 290. Curiously, the average annual death rate between 1911 and 1921 was lower than that recorded for the decade 1901–1911—1.44 percent as opposed to 1.62 percent—despite all the casualties caused by the war. Barnett, p. 426.

54. The quotation is from Brittain, *Testament of Youth*, p. 646. Note also the novelist Compton Mackenzie, who wrote in 1968, "We drifted into the Second World War because owing to the loss of the flower of our youth, there were too many careerists in politics. When I look back on so many contemporaries of mine who were killed, I know that this loss was one of the causes of the Second World War." George A. Panichas, ed., *Promise of Greatness* (London, 1968), p. 247. Reviewing Sassoon's *Memoirs of an Infantry Officer* in 1930, Herbert Read explained that its author was "a sensitive member of a generation destroyed by the greatest catastrophe in modern history; and because it was so destroyed, this generation cannot ever justify itself. A realist might object to this manner of speaking as fanciful; he would point out that, although ten million men were killed, a fair number survived, and that surely some of them had a very jolly time. But in affairs of the spirit we do not count heads, and it was the spirit or vital faith of a generation that perished, not its bare existence." Quoted by Samuel Hynes in *The Auden Generation* (London, 1976), pp. 39–40.

55. *Good-bye to All That*, pp. 397–398. Richard Aldington's account of his luck in surviving the war supports Graves's point: "It was by chance that I was given just one night off in a period of two months; and that night happened to be one when a shell dropped on a group of our officers and runners, killing or wounding all except Carl [a friend] and his officer. It was by chance that I lowered my head just as a shell burst beside me in a mine crater, so that instead of hitting my face a splinter merely crushed my tin hat. It was by chance that I shifted my foot a fraction of a second before a bullet neatly took the toe from my boot instead of smashing my ankle. It was by chance that, standing in a trench, I turned my head to speak to the man behind me exactly at the moment a large hunk of shell whizzed so close to my cheek that I felt its harsh and horrid breath. It was by chance that in the last attack of the war my field glasses shifted round over my stomach—when I went to use them I found they had been smashed and bent. And finally (though by no means completely) it was by chance that I missed the worst phase of two of the worst battles of the year." Aldington, *Life for Life's Sake* (New York, 1941), pp. 186–187. For an analysis of relative losses, among officers and men, see Samuel Dumas and K. O. Vedel-Petersen, *Losses of Life Caused by War* (Oxford, 1923), pp. 66–68.

56. For the contrast between the pre-1914 British army and the British army that fought the Great War, see John Keegan, *The Face of Battle* (New York, 1976), pp. 215–225.

57. For the relationship between social class and military service in Britain during the Great War, see J. M. Winter, "Britain's 'Lost Generation' of the First World War," *Population Studies* 31 (1977): 452–456. Winter concludes that, whereas the British

statistics do not distinguish between junior officers at risk and their superiors behind the lines, there is every reason to believe that junior officers suffered heavier casualties than the officer corps taken as a whole (pp. 456–460). We do know that the percentage of killed among officers ran well above the percentage of killed among the other ranks throughout the war, ranging from 14.2 percent to 5.8 percent in the first months to 6.9 percent to 4.0 percent in the last (p. 458). This accounts for the popular perception that losses among junior officers were two or three times as high as among common soldiers. Winter's statistics further demonstrate that deaths among Oxford and Cambridge graduates were nearly one and a half times as high as the national average for men serving in the fighting forces. The percentage of killed increased with the year of matriculation. Thirty-one percent of those who matriculated at Oxford in 1913 and served were killed, as opposed to 18 percent of those who matriculated between 1900 and 1904 (p. 463). Not even the most disillusioned postwar writers denied the devotion to duty shown by British junior officers. Richard Aldington wrote of the junior officer under whom he served: "He was exasperatingly stupid, but he was honest, he was kindly, he was conscientious, he could obey orders and command obedience in others, he took pains to look after his men. He could be implicitly relied upon to lead a hopeless attack and to maintain a desperate defence to the end. There were thousands and tens of thousands like him." *Death of a Hero*, p. 331.

58. Nichols, *Anthology of War Poetry*, pp. 53–54; Guy Chapman, *A Kind of Survivor* (London, 1975), pp. 44–45. For losses among peers and their sons, see Winter, "Britain's 'Lost Generation' of the First World War," p. 464.

59. For the guilt felt by survivors of cataclysm, see Robert Jay Lifton, *Death in Life* (New York, 1967). According to Lifton, survivors of cataclysm have a tendency to identify with those who died and to erase in their mind the distinction between life and death. They try to think, feel, and act as they imagine their dead companions might have if they had survived. There is ample evidence of this kind of identification in the literature produced by members of the war generation in all European countries, but the idea of a lost or missing generation took deeper root in England than in any other European country. The phrases describing the interwar period are taken from Robert Graves and Alan Hodges, *The Long Week-End* (London, 1940); Leonard Woolf, *Downhill All the Way* (London, 1968); and Herbert Read, *The Contrary Experience* (London, 1963).

60. T. E. Lawrence has attracted many biographers, including several well-known figures from his own generation. Robert Graves, Basil Liddell Hart, Richard Aldington, Charles Carrington, and Victoria Ocampo have all tried their hand at telling his story. More recently, Phillip Knightley and Colin Simpson have published some interesting new facts and speculations about Lawrence in *The Secret Lives of Lawrence of Arabia* (London, 1969). John E. Mack, in *A Prince of our Disorder* (Boston and Toronto, 1976), has now superseded them all from the point of view of careful documentation, especially with regard to Lawrence's family background and early years and his postwar period in the R.A.F. and the Tank Corps. But Mack's account should be corrected with Desmond Stewart's searching, if highly speculative, examination of Lawrence's legend, *T. E. Lawrence* (New York, 1977). The main primary sources for Lawrence's life, apart from *Seven Pillars of Wisdom* in the 1922 unexpurgated edition at the Bodleian Library in Oxford, are his letters, which are published in three important collections: *The Letters of T. E. Lawrence*, ed. David Garnett (London, 1938); *The Home Letters of T. E. Lawrence and His Brothers* (Oxford, 1954); and Robert Graves and Basil Liddell Hart,

T. E. Lawrence to His Biographers (Garden City, 1963). There are additional unpublished letters in the Bodleian Library at Oxford and in the British Museum. *T. E. Lawrence by His Friends*, ed. A. W. Lawrence (New York, Toronto, and London, 1963) is useful for understanding the complexity of the man and the broad range of his contacts. T. E. Lawrence, *Minorities: Good Poems by Small Poets and Small Poems by Good Poets*, ed. J. M. Wilson (New York, 1972) reveals something about his poetic sensibility. Sassoon, Sorley, and Graves are represented, but Brooke and Owen are not.

61. Ernest Barker is quoted in *The Home Letters of T. E. Lawrence*, p. 397; for Lawrence's description of himself as an artist of sorts, see ibid., p. 147.

62. For the dispute over Lawrence's desert campaigns, see Mack, *Prince of Our Disorder*, and Stewart, *T. E. Lawrence*.

63. *The Letters of T. E. Lawrence*, p. 692.

64. Quoted by David Garnett from the Oxford edition of *Seven Pillars of Wisdom*, ibid., p. 262. About the same time that Lawrence wrote the original preface to the *Seven Pillars* he published a critique of the British Middle Eastern policy and asserted that the war had had the effect on the Foreign Office, the India Office, and the War Office "of making the young men younger and the old men older. The blood thirstiness of the old men—who did not fight—towards our late enemies is sometimes curiously relieved against the tolerance of those who have fought and wish to avoid making others fight again tomorrow." Quoted in Mack, *Prince of Our Disorder*, p. 289. This statement corresponds exactly to the feelings of alienation from the older generation described by Sassoon, Graves, and Williamson in their memoirs.

65. For Lawrence's belief that conquering the air was the task of his generation, see Basil Liddell Hart, *The Liddell Hart Memoirs 1895–1938* (New York, 1965), p. 348; for Lawrence's reasons for joining the R.A.F., Mack, *Prince of Our Disorder*, pp. 319–331.

66. *The Letters of T. E. Lawrence*, p. 692.

67. For Lawrence's remark that the war seemed more terrible in retrospect, see Mack, *Prince of Our Disorder*, p. 382; for his dismissal of Remarque's novel, Henry Williamson, *Genius of Friendship: 'T. E. Lawrence'* (London, 1941), pp. 27, 32–33; for his complaint about the self-indulgence of the war generation, ibid., p. 20; for his description of the war as an overwrought time, *The Letters of T. E. Lawrence*, p. 362; for his insistence that there were still many good men from the war generation around, ibid., p. 583. Despite Lawrence's earlier criticism of the narrowness of vision of the old men in public life, his personal relations with his elders were generally good. His respect for and attendance upon figures like C. M. Doughty, D. G. Hogarth, John Buchan, and Hugh Trenchard, head of the R.A.F., are well known. Without the support of these men and others, Lawrence would not have been able to accomplish the deeds that made him a hero to the men of his age-group. He himself knew this and avoided generational rhetoric after the mid-1920s, though he continued to be interested in the problems and special characteristics of his coevals, which he recognized as also being his. Indeed, he was impressed by the power of the generational bond. Discussing Wyndham Lewis's drawings in a letter to William Rothenstein, he remarked, "Isn't it odd to like all that a man does, and to dislike, almost vehemently, all that he likes? Or is that a natural consequence of living in his generation. Your work will be exactly dateable to your epoch, in the eyes of the future: as will the work of all your contemporaries. The most academic of them, and the most fiercely revolutionary, will all be 1880–1930 . . .

isn't that odd? What are these 50 years of a man's production, if his own time takes such possession of him? I think, mainly, that it means that any search or endeavour after *difference* (as an end in itself) is wasted effort." Ibid., p. 556.

68. Correlli Barnett points out in *The Decline of British Power* that although the British Bomber Command lost 55,888 men during the Second World War, these losses did not give rise to the idea of a lost generation. The reason may be that these men came from a wider variety of social origins.

69. Henry Williamson, *The Sun in the Sands* (London, 1945), pp. 108–109.

4. Spain: The Theme of Our Time

1. For "I am I and my circumstance," see *Meditaciones del Quijote* (1914), in Ortega, *Obras completas* (Madrid, 1966), I, 322. The description of Ortega is by his close friend Ramon Pérez de Ayala, quoted by Pierre Conard, "Ortega y Gasset, écrits politiques (1910–1913)," in *Mélanges de la Casa Velásquez* 3 (1967): 417. The writer Azorin later recalled the importance of *El Imparcial:* "The height of fame in the newspaper world in those days [around 1900] was *El Imparcial.* A daily with more authority has never been published in Spain. People in government listened carefully to what *El Imparcial* said. In the parliamentary world what *El Imparcial* thought carried weight. Ministerial crises occurred because of *El Imparcial,* and a government supported by *El Imparcial* could relax. In literary matters, the influence of the daily was no less great. Each week *El Imparcial* published a literary page. There was no writer who did not aspire to write on that page." Azorín [pseudonym for Martínez Ruiz], *Madrid* (Madrid, 1941), pp. 71–72. The paper had been founded by Ortega's maternal grandfather and was directed after 1900 by Ortega's father, José Ortega Munilla. For the history of the paper, see Manuel Ortega y Gasset, *El Imparcial: Biografía de un gran periódico español* (Zaragoza, 1956). Unfortunately, no dependable biography of Ortega exists. Some anecdotal material about his boyhood and adolescence can be found in Manuel Ortega y Gasset, *Niñez y mocedad de Ortega* (Madrid, 1964). The best guide in English to Ortega's life and to the literature about him is Robert McClintock, *Man and His Circumstances: Ortega as Educator* (New York, 1971). The reader should be forewarned, however, that this is an extremely personal book, which makes no pretense to being a full biography. Like all students of Ortega, I have learned much from Julián Marías, *Ortega: Circunstancia y vocación* (Madrid, 1973), 2 vols., and from Ciriaco Morón Arroyo, *El sistema de Ortega y Gasset* (Madrid, 1968). We badly need a study that will reconstruct painstakingly and in their proper sequence Ortega's ideas and actions. Until we have such a work all writers on Ortega, and especially all writers on his political attitudes, will be forced (as I have been) to rely on considerable speculation.

2. According to J. Sendador Gómez, quoted by Ramond Carr in *Spain 1808–1939* (Oxford, 1966), p. 426. Carr adds, however, that Sendador Gómez exaggerated: "Most villages had police and morals whatever else they lacked."

3. For a judicious evaluation of the Spanish political system, see Miguel Martínez Cuadrado, *La burguesía conservadora (1874–1931)* (Madrid, 1974), p. 370. Cuadrado concludes that "the Hispanic conservative-liberal bourgeois model differed no doubt from its British and French antecedents by its lesser richness and evolution, but it was not out of harmony in any absolute sense, and even exceeded, the average model dominant in the Europe of its time."

4. For the unique characteristics of the Spanish situation around 1900, see Jaime

Vicens Vives, *Approaches to the History of Spain* (Berkeley, 1970), pp. 141–147. Giner de los Ríos's models were Eton, Oxford, and Cambridge, and his goal was the creation of "select minorities" who would constitute a new governing class similar to the one in England. Manuel Tuñón de Lara, *Medio siglo de cultura española (1885–1936)* (Madrid, 1970), pp. 55–56. For the hostility to Enlightenment ideas and aspirations, see J. B. Trend, *The Origins of Modern Spain* (New York, 1934), pp. 60–62.

5. For the intermarriage and fusion between economic and political elites, see Manuel Tuñón de Lara, *Historia y realidad del poder* (Madrid, 1967), pp. 36–40.

6. For Costa's attempt to organize the neutral classes, see Rafael Pérez de la Dehesa, *El pensamiento de Costa y su influencia en el 98* (Madrid, 1966), pp. 222–229; for his argument that Spain possessed only the appearance of a modern nation, Marías, *Ortega*, I, 61; for his belief that the government violated natural law, Enrique Tierno Galvan, *Costa y el regeneracionismo* (Barcelona, 1961), p. 233; for his feeling that Spain had lost her natural aristocracy, Pérez de la Dehesa, *El pensamiento de Costa*, p. 126.

7. Quoted by Marías, *Ortega*, I, 66.

8. Azorín, "Dos generaciones," reprinted in Azorín, *Sin perder los estribos* (Madrid, 1944–1963), IX, 1140–1143; Azorín, "La generación de 1898," reprinted in *Cla*-generational concept. In his novel *La volundad* [Will], published in 1902, he wrote of his double: "Finally Azorin decided to leave Madrid. Where would he go? *Geographically*, Azorín knew where to aim his steps; but with regard to his *intellectual and ethical* orientation, his confusion grew with every day. Azorín was almost a symbol; his perplexities, his anxieties, and his distress could very well represent an entire generation without will, without energy, indecisive, irresolute, a generation that had neither the boldness of the Romantic generation nor the affirmative faith of the Naturalist generation." Quoted by Pedro Laín Entralgo in *España como problema* (Madrid, 1956), p. 42.

9. Azorín, "Generaciones de escritores" (1912), in Azorín, *Obras completas* (Madrid, 1944–1963), IX, 1140–1143; Azorín, "La generación de 1898," reprinted in *Clasicos y modernos* (Madrid, 1913), pp. 283–314.

10. For a convenient summary of the debate over the generation of '98, see H. Ramsden, "The Spanish 'Generation of 1898': 1. The History of a Concept," *Bulletin of the John Rylands University of Manchester* 56 (1973–1974): 463–491; for the reality of the generation of '98, see also Tuñón de Lara, *Medio siglo de cultura española*, pp. 100–102.

11. See Pedro Laín Entralgo, *La generación del noventayocho* (Madrid, 1945) for a detailed discussion of these themes; for the influence of Taine, see H. Ramsden, *The 1898 Movement in Spain* (Manchester, 1974), pp. 42–95. According to Ramsden, it was from Taine that Unamuno and later Ortega learned that history was fundamentally psychology and that the Spanish problem was above all a moral problem. Speaking of works of art, Taine had written, "When this document is rich and one knows how to interpret it, one finds within it the psychology of a soul, often that of a century, and sometimes that of a race." Quoted by Ramsden, ibid., pp. 156–157.

12. Miguel de Unamuno, *En torno al casticismo*, in Unamuno, *Obras completas* (Madrid, 1950), III, 111.

13. Laín Entralgo, *España como problema*, pp. 315–326.

14. For Unamuno's conviction that progress depended upon the replacement of older men by their juniors, see "Viejos y jovenes" (1902) in Unamuno, *Obras completas*, III, 373–387; for the need to break the cyst that was enslaving the new man, ibid., III, 271–272; for the new man emerging from the ruins of a civilization, ibid., III, 271.

Azorín too believed in a coming apocalypse of civilization and the emergence of a new man. In *La volundad*, he wondered what would happen to art, science, and history when the barbarians came: "I feel sad when I think about these things, which are the highest achievements of humanity; about these things which are going to be maltreated in this palingenesis, which will be fecund in other things, also very high, and very human, and very just." Quoted by Laín Entralgo, *La generación del noventayocho*, pp. 425–426. The term "palingenesis," comes from the combination of the Greek *palin* (again) and the Latin *genesis* (birth). It was used frequently in the Latin countries during the early twentieth century to signify cultural renewal.

15. For Ortega's admiration of Unamuno, see Ortega, *Obras completas*, I, 117–118; and for Unamuno's devaluation of ideas, see "L'ideocracía" (1900), in Unamuno, *Obras completas*, III, 216–226, where he declares that "of all tyrannies, the most odious to me . . . is that of ideas"; for Ortega's letter, see ibid., III, 472.

16. Ortega to Francisco Navarro Ledesma, 28 and 30 May 1905, in Ortega, *Epistolario* (Madrid, 1974), pp. 38–45. Ortega's criticism of the generation of '98 as a group of negators and barbarians must have figured prominently in his correspondence with his older friends, for Ramiro de Maetzu replied indignantly to these accusations in a letter of 1910 written from London. Thanks to the generation of '98, Maetzu affirmed, the country had been cleaned of lies, a new kind of journalism had become possible, and younger people had been able to start from scratch with a clean slate. "But even assuming that we did nothing more, wasn't this work of ours, regardless of the fact that it may have appeared negative, profoundly positive and worthy of recognition? And don't *you* have the duty to recognize it?" Maetzu to Ortega, 1910, Ortega Archive, Revista de Occidente, Madrid. In another letter of 18 October 1911, Maetzu complained of Ortega's tendency to lump him with other writers under the collective rubric of "my generation." In 1898, he said, only Costa and himself had protested against the decadence of Spain. Maetzu's protests seem to have had some impact on Ortega, for he qualified his critique of the generation of '98 in an unpublished essay written sometime between 1914 and 1916 and now available in *Obras completas*, IX, 477–501. See especially p. 494, where Ortega calls Unamuno, Benevente, Valle-Inclán, Maetzu, Azorín, and Baroja "an unsuspected irruption of internal barbarians."

17. For the academic philosopher who derives from his research norms for public and private action, see the unsigned article on Cohen that was published in Ortega's journal *España* on 16 September 1914, which appears to have been written or inspired by Ortega; for Ortega's feeling of shame, "La cuestión moral" (1908), in *Obras completas*, X, 73.

18. For the Germans' lack of harmony and personality, see "Las dos Alemanias" (1908), in *Obras completas*, X, 22–23; for their materialism, ibid., X, 24; for their leaning toward collective forms of social organization, "La solidaridad alemana" (1908), ibid., X, 26–27; for the faint-heartedness of German liberals, "Nuevas glosas" (1908), ibid., X, 87; for the idea that German culture was in decline, Ortega to Unamuno, 27 January 1907, in *Epistolario*, pp. 76–79; for the belief that everything in Spain was false, Maetzu to Ortega, 14 July 1908, Ortega Archive; for the conviction that the Spanish intellectual had to be a politician, "La pedagogía social como programa político" (1910), in *Obras completas*, I, 507; for Ortega's espousal of socialism, Ortega to Unamuno, 1907, in *Epistolario*, pp. 76–77, and Maetzu to Ortega, 1908, Ortega Archive, in which Maetzu chides Ortega for wanting to "terrorize the bourgeois, the priest, and woman" with his socialism.

19. For the generation without fathers in the spiritual order, see "Competencia" (1913), in *Obras completas*, X, 226; for Ortega's belief that it was psychologically impossible for the older generation to change, "Los problemas nacionales y la juventud" (1909) ibid., X, 105; for Spain as a source of pain and grief, "La pedagogía social como programa político" (1910), ibid., I, 495; for the failure of the older generation to Europeanize Spain, X, 108; for the idea that politics was education, I, 503–521; for the conclusion that Europeanization was the means of regenerating Spain, I, 521; for the distinction between socialism and Marxism, "La conservación de la cultura" (1908) and "La ciencia y la religión como problemas políticos" (1909), ibid., X, 46, 119–127; for the mission of democratic radicalism and socialism to avoid revolution, X, 117; for the cause of the younger generation's lack of energy and enthusiasm, X, 107–110; for the need to bring about a revolution of competence, X, 226–227.

20. For the recognition of Ortega as the leader of his generation in Spain, see Luis Arasquistain to Ortega, 11 and 28 June 1910, and Paul Scheffer to Ortega, 26 November 1912, Ortega Archive. Scheffer invited Ortega to join himself, Nicolai Hartmann, Robert Musil, and Martin Buber in a bimonthly devoted to the thought of the younger generation in Europe. For Ortega's attitude toward the party of Melquíades Álvarez, see the notes for a communication to prospective members of the League for Spanish Political Education, *Obras completas*, X, 249, where Ortega states that the League, while not connected with any party, "views with great hope the formation of the Reformist Republic party, in whose voices it believes to have found an echo of its own longings." A letter in the Ortega Archive from Melquíades Álvarez, dated 15 April 1914 and addressed to "my dear friend and coreligionary," asks for help in raising funds for the Reformist party.

21. "Vieja y nueva política" (1914), *Obras completas*, I, 271.

22. Ibid., I, 273–274, 284.

23. Between 1908 and 1913 Ortega had been drawn toward Alejandro Lerroux's Republican party. He had joined Lerroux and other Republican leaders in the struggle against Antonio Maura, the Conservative who headed the government and organized the repression of the Left during Tragic Week in 1909. Not until February 1913 did Ortega disavow Republicanism and move toward Reformism, which conceived the state not as the instrument of a class to be destroyed or conquered but as a neutral organ that could be dominated by means of universal suffrage. From 1913 until 1930, Ortega avoided criticism of the monarchy or the monarch and instead concentrated his fire on Spanish political mores. See Conard, "Ortega y Gasset, écrits politiques."

24. *Obras completas*, I, 286.

25. For Maetzu's ambitions for Spain, see Maetzu to Ortega, 14 July 1908, Ortega Archive.

26. For Ortega's hopes for "a richer, more complex, sounder, more noble, more composed age," see his introduction to the first volume of *El Espectador*, dated 1916, in *Obras completas*, II, 20; for his conception of socialism, "La ciencia y la religión como problemas políticos" (1909) and "Socialismo y *aristocracia*" (1913), ibid., X, 119–127, 238–240. In this last article, written for *El Socialista*, the Spanish Socialist party newspaper, Ortega made the following declarations: "I am socialist out of love of aristocracy." "Socialism is nothing but the attempt to overcome, conquer, destroy capitalism. Well then, capitalism can be defined as the social state in which aristocracies are impossible." "Classes will return, who can doubt it? But they will not be economic in nature, they will not divide men into rich and poor; but rather into better and worse. Art,

science, sophistication, moral energy will once again become social values. And socialism will have been charged with the task of preparing the planet so that new aristocracies can spring forth."

27. For Ortega's elitism, see Guillermo Morón, *Historia política de José Ortega y Gasset* (Mexico City, 1960); Tierno Galvan, *Costa y el regeneracionismo*; Tuñón de Lara, *Medio siglo de cultura española*; Antoni Jutglar, *Ideologías y clases en la España contemporanea* (Madrid, 1971), vol. II; and Gonzalo Redondo, *Las empresas políticas de José Ortega y Gasset* (Madrid, 1970), 2 vols. The original members of the League for Spanish Political Education are listed in Marías, *Ortega*, I, 269–271, n. 18. They included Manuel Azaña, Pablo de Azcárate, Américo Castro, Manuel García Morente, Salvador de Madariaga, Ramiro de Maetzu, Antonio Machado, Ramon Pérez de Ayala, and Frederico de Onís.

28. Ortega, *Obras completas*, I, 307.

29. For the importance of decorum, cohesion, and rigor in one's ideas, see ibid., X, 301; for the iceberg metaphor, Marías, *Ortega*, I, 291. The Revista de Occidente began publication of Ortega's *Obras completas* in 1946, but the present eleven-volume set was not complete until 1969. Ortega's notes and university lectures have yet to be published, and one assumes that there are letters, not included in the *Epistolario* published in 1974, that will later form a separate volume of the complete works.

30. In 1909 Ortega had observed that at any given moment in history "historical reality" presented itself in the form of a generation of mature men. To understand that reality, one had to investigate the origins of their manner of thinking, desiring, and feeling. Historical reality was not a simple heap of facts. The historian had to explain why things had happened and what events meant. The historical reality of a generation resided in the fact that it was "the point of intersection with a previous generation that has educated it and a succeeding generation that emanates and derives from it: each generation is the disciple of an older one and the teacher of another that is younger. This double function of teacher and pupil is what is important, what is serious in history." *Obras completas*, X, 109. In his pre-1914 writings it is above all this emphasis on the pedagogical relationship between generations that distinguishes Ortega from other generational theorists of the period.

31. For a discussion of Uexküll's ideas and their influence on Ortega, see Marías, *Ortega*, II, 147–55. Ortega also referred frequently to the work of Hans Driesch, with whom Ernst Jünger was studying at precisely this time. For the acknowledgment of Ortega as the leader of a Hispanic renaissance, see Ricardo Baeza to Ortega, 26 November 1927, Ortega Archive. Baeza requested permission to dedicate a book to Ortega. The dedication read: "To Don José Ortega y Gasset, *Duce* of this Renaissance." For the founding of *El Sol*, see Redondo, *Las empresas políticas*, I, 11–99.

32. Vicens Vives, *Approaches to the History of Spain*, p. 147.

33. For the statement about confusion and uncertainty at the top and for the loyalty of the army, see Gerald H. Meaker, *The Revolutionary Left in Spain 1914–1923* (Stanford, 1974), p. 96; for the killings, ibid., p. 339.

34. For Spain and Russia as the most plebian of nations, see *España invertebrada* (1921) in *Obras completas*, III, 35–128; for a nation as a people organized by an aristocracy, ibid., XI, 13.

35. For Ortega's suspicion that he was not cut out for politics, see "De puerta de tierra" (1912) in *Obras completas*, X, 207–213; for the suspicion that Spain's tragedy

might be Europe's, the introduction to the second edition of *España invertebrada* (1922), ibid., III, 39–40.

36. Ibid., III, 146.

37. Ibid., III, 147.

38. Ibid., III, 148.

39. Ibid.

40. Ibid., III, 148–150.

41. For the primacy of contemplative life, see ibid., III, 146; for culture as a biological instrument, ibid., III, 177–178.

42. For what German readers took away from *The Theme of Our Time*, see Walter Scheidt, *Lebensgesetze der Kultur!* (Berlin, 1929). Readers of Ortega's essay "Biología y pedagogía," written in 1920 for *El Espectador*, would have understood that Ortega was interested primarily in intellectual and psychic vitality. "Vital phenomena begin where mechanical [that is, purely biological] phenomena finish." *Obras completas*, II, 290, n. 1; 296.

43. For the utopian as a person who refused to accept his perspective, see *Obras completas*, III, 200; for a bad structure as better than none, "Democracia morbosa" (1917), ibid., II, 137–138. "Plebianism, now triumphant all over the world, is tyrannizing Spain. And since tyranny of any kind is unbearable, it is fitting that we should be preparing the revolution against plebianism, the most insufferable of all tyrants." Ortega warned that if the program of the Left Democrats and Socialists remained purely negative and polemical and aimed merely at the destruction of the traditional structure of society, the "temperaments of delicate morality" would curse democracy and turn their hearts toward the past, which had been organized to be sure by superstition, but which in the last analysis had been organized against the threat of disorganization and social disaggregation.

44. Ortega made no effort in *The Theme of Our Time* to delineate the sequence of generations in contemporary Spain or to indicate the relationship of his own generation to the generation of '98. In an article written in 1917, however, he had affirmed that three generations coexist in every epoch: the grandfathers, the fathers, and the sons. "Thus we have inhabited the same stretch of time as the men of the [First] Republic, the men of the Restoration, and those like ourselves who still carry blank and unemblazoned shields. Well then, perhaps nothing is a better indication of the Spanish future than the fact that we men with unmarked shields feel greater affinity with the men of 1869 [those of the Republic] than with those who restored the monarchy. And certainly it was not their republic that attracted us, it was their moral sense of life, their longing for knowledge and meditation. In comparison, the men educated during the period of the Restoration appeared demoralized and frivolous, lacking in curiosity and studies. The men of the Republic were professors, writers, friends of books and ideas. Those of the Restoration were, and are, lawyers, businessmen, and lovers of trivial intrigue." "Don Gumersindo de Azcárate ha muerto" (1917), ibid., III, 12.

45. "Ideas políticas" (1924), ibid., XI, 35.

46. For the dominance of the petty bourgeois, see "Vaguedades" (1925), ibid., XI, 51–52; for the need to strengthen the state, "Entreacto polémico" (1925), ibid., XI, 58–65.

47. "El error Berenguer" (1930), ibid., XI, 278–279.

48. For the manifesto of the Group in the Service of the Republic, see ibid., XI,

126–127. There is considerable disagreement about Ortega's attitude toward the coming of the Republic. Baroja later wrote that during the months before the monarchy fell (and presumably after his article pronouncing it unfit to rule), Ortega had manifested great optimism about the possibility of regenerating Spanish political life. "He believed in a kind of magical transformation of the country." Quoted by Redondo in *Las empresas políticas*, II, 196, n. 137. Ortega's older brother Eduardo, who was part of the original Republican coalition that overthrew the monarchy, reported that Ortega admired "the elegant and simple form with which the people, in the sense of a coalition of all classes, proclaimed their Republic." But his younger brother Manuel claimed that neither he nor Ortega had wanted the Republic to come when and in the manner that it did; Ortega, he said, felt that "the thing came too fast. Spain was not ready for it." Ibid., II, 264.

49. "Un aldabonazo" (1931), ibid., XI, 387.

50. For the despiritualizing wind, see "Prólogo a una edición de sus obras" (1932), ibid., VI, 353; *La rebelión de las masas* (1930), ibid., IV, 111–278.

51. For details, see Redondo, *Las empresas políticas*, II, 203–281. The new newspaper for which Ortega wrote after 1931 was *Crisol*.

52. For the Republic's need for a new party, see "Rectificación de la República" (1931), in *Obras completas*, XI, 416.

53. For Ortega's failure to attract a following, see Redondo, *Las empresas políticas*, II, 446–447. Guillermo Morón reached a similar conclusion on the basis of much less research and an excessive degree of political passion. Ortega, he says, "showed the path and no one wanted to follow it." *Historia política de Ortega*, p. 166. Morón notes that the twenty-six points of the program of the Falange Española Tradicionalista and the Juntas de Ofensiva Nacional-Sindicalista contained many Ortegian themes and metaphors; but he is unable to demonstrate any meaningful historical connection between the founder of the Falange, José Antonio Primo de Rivera, and Ortega, other than the fact that José Antonio admired the older man. Morón is therefore reduced to the weak assertion that José Antonio would have made a good champion of Ortega's political ideas, if he had not let himself be tempted by Fascism. What exactly does this kind of assertion mean? One can choose one's enemies; but it is impossible to limit with as much precision the circle of one's admirers. In any case, Ortega's position on the question of Fascism was unambiguous. He denounced it from its very beginnings as a retrograde and reactionary movement, which was bound to fail and which the Spanish people should avoid at all costs.

54. "Rectificación de la República" (1931), in *Obras completas*, XI, 409.

55. For the remark that every life is a ruin, see "Pidiendo un Goethe desde dentro" (1932), ibid., IV, 401; for the view that parliamentary politics was fit only for second-rate minds, XI, 496–500; for the conviction that Spain was heading for disaster, XI, 522; for the advice that when everything is false in public life, the only thing that can save us is the loyalty of every individual to himself, *España*, 23 April 1915.

56. For man as what has happened to him, what he has done, see *Historia como sistema* (1941), in *Obras completas*, VI, 41; for the definition of convictions, *En torno a Galileo* (1947), ibid., V, 32.

57. Ortega first developed the idea that the dialectic of ages created history in his lectures "¿Por qué se vuelve a la filosofía?" (1930), ibid., IV, 89–93; for the present as rich in three dimensions, see ibid., V, 37; the metaphors describing generations are taken from "Para la historia del amor" (1926), ibid., III, 441.

58. For age as a zone of dates, see ibid. V, 41.

59. Ibid., V, 44. On the issue of the relations between generations, Ortega pointed justifiably to a feature of his approach to the generation problem that had figured prominently in his thought ever since 1905 and that had been formulated for the first time as early as 1909. See n. 31 above.

60. For the metaphor of the acrobats and for the idea that generations overlap and are spliced together, see ibid., V, 45, 49.

61. See "Para la historia del amor" (1926), ibid., III, 439–442. This essay contains one of the most important formulations of Ortega's generational theory between *The Theme of Our Time* and the lectures on Galileo.

62. Ibid., V, 53.

63. Ibid., V, 77.

64. For the remark that we do not know what is happening to us, see ibid., V, 93; for the gigantic question of whether European man would live for unreason, ibid., V, 89.

65. Ibid., V, 116–117. Was the one word that Ortega refused to pronounce "Fascism"? If so, a large part of the student generation he was addressing would respond to it. For a description of the uncertainty felt by that generation, see Laín Entralgo, *España como problema*, p. 435.

66. For ideology and technology as the two most important variables determining the vital horizon, see *Obras completas*, V, 26.

67. For the perception of generations in twentieth-century Spain, see Luis Olariaga, "Tres generaciones intelectuales de España," *El Sol*, 3, 5, and 25 June 1929; for a more recent discussion of Spanish generations, Juan Marichal, "Manuel Azaña and the Generation of 1914," *Ibérica*, 15 March 1961, pp. 3–7, and "La 'generación de los intelectuales' y la política (1909–1914)," in *La crisis de fin de siglo: Ideología y literatura. Estudios en memoria de R. Pérez de la Dehesa* (Barcelona, 1975), pp. 25–41.

68. *Obras completas*, V, 70–71. It is possible that Ortega's analysis of man in crisis owed something to his acquaintance through Victoria Ocampo with Pierre Drieu la Rochelle and his writings. On 5 March 1929 Ortega wrote to Ocampo that he had not yet found time to do the essay on Drieu's book *Genève ou Moscou*, which he had evidently promised her and Drieu. "Besides," he added, "it's not just a matter of 'an article' on the book, but of something more serious. I consider his [Drieu's] state of mind as representative and I have a lot of sympathy for his state of mind." *Epistolario*, p. 148. One can only assume that much of his analysis of Drieu's state of mind and its representative quality went into the lectures on man in a state of crisis. For Ortega's disapproval of Drieu's subsequent conversion to Fascism, see ibid., p. 155.

69. For an excellent summary of the different responses of Spanish intellectuals to the crisis of the late 1920s and early 1930s, see Tuñón de Lara, *Medio siglo de cultura española*, pp. 264–265.

5. Italy: Giovinezza! Giovinezza!

1. For Papini's ambition to be the guide of the future Italy, see Angelo Romanò, *La Voce (1908–1914)* (Turin, 1960), p. 19, n. 1; for the few hundred men on whom he set his sights, Delia Frigessi, *Leonardo, Hermes, Il Regno,* (Turin, 1960), p. 313.

2. For the description of Prezzolini as a scholar of no school, see Giovanni Papini,

Un uomo finito (Florence, 1952 ed.), p. 69; for the lessons Prezzolini learned from Papini, Giuseppe Prezzolini, *L'italiano inutile* (Milan, 1953), p. 59.

3. Papini, *Un uomo finito*, pp. 95–96.

4. Ibid., pp. 99–100.

5. For Leonardo's program, see "Programma sintetico" (1903), in Frigessi, *Leonardo, Hermes, Il regno*, p. 89; for Papini's belief that philosophy should embark upon the conquest of the world, "Cosa vogliamo" (1904), ibid., p. 185.

6. "Campagna per il forzato risveglio" (1906), ibid., pp. 314–315.

7. Giolitti is quoted by Christopher Seton-Watson in *Italy from Liberalism to Fascism* (London, 1967), p. 245; for Giolitti's achievements, see ibid., pp. 295–296; for Amendola's summary of the attitude of intellectual youth, Emilio Gentile, *La Voce e l'età giolittiana* (Milan, 1972), p. 20.

8. For the desire to discover a faith and regain youth, see Maffio Maffi, "Senescit iuventus" (1904), in Frigessi, *Leonardo, Hermes, Il Regno*, p. 412; for the transformation of the myth of present greatness into a hope of future revival, Giovanni Amendola, "Il convegno nazionalista" (1910), in Romanò, *La Voce*, p. 261; for the misinterpretation of Croce, Eugenio Garin, *Cronache di filosofia italiana 1900–1943* (Bari, 1966 ed.), p. 300; for the observation that the mass of Italian youth was with D'Annunzio rather than Croce, Giuseppe Borgese, quoted by Garin, ibid., p. 298.

9. *Giovine Italia* is quoted by Gary Crippin in "Pietro Nenni from Republicanism to Socialism: A Generational Approach" (Ph.D. dissc., UCLA, 1975), p. 33; Marinetti is translated by Eugen Weber in *Paths to the Present: Aspects of European Thought from Romanticism to Existentialism* (New York, 1960), p. 246.

10. For the origins of *La Voce*, see Giuseppe Prezzolini, *La Voce 1908–1913: Cronaca, antologia e fortuna di una rivista* (Milan, 1974), pp. 27–44. In 1905 Papini had complained to Prezzolini in a personal letter that he failed to understand Prezzolini's enthusiasm for Italian culture and the raising of the general level of the masses. "The respect for the individual responsibility and, what is more serious, for all personalities strikes me as having a certain democratic air that conflicts with our concept of a class that can and must transform the others, instead of simply helping them to do what feels comfortable." "It also seems to me that you're too obsessed with the teaching of philosophy in the schools . . . Why get so angry at a hundred idiots out of love for ten thousand idiots?" Giovanni Papini to Giuseppe Prezzolini, 30 September 1905, in *Storia di un'amicizia*, ed. Giuseppe Prezzolini (Florence, 1966), p. 108. The description of Prezzolini as haunted by the incubus of clarity is Scipio Slataper's, but Papini had noticed the same characteristic in a letter in March 1908. Ibid., p. 177. For the quotation from Slataper, see Gentile, *La Voce e l'età giolittiana*, p. 80; for Prezzolini's interpretation of Croce's philosophy, *see L'italiano inutile*, p. 142, and Romanò, *La Voce*, pp. 433–437.

11. For the circulation of *Leonardo* and *La Voce*, see *Storia di un'amicizia*, p. 233, and Henri Giordan, ed., *Romain Rolland et le mouvement florentin de La Voce* (Paris, 1966), p. 237, n. 1. Papini never shared Prezzolini's enthusiasm for *La Voce*, in part no doubt because it was not his creation, and even more because it coincided with a moment of crisis and disorientation in his own literary career. He did, however, contribute to it frequently from his mountain retreat in Bulciano, where he had withdrawn to live with his wife, and in 1912 he agreed to replace Prezzolini as editor-in-chief for a limited period. Relations between the two men cooled a bit during the period of *La*

Voce, as Prezzolini pushed to the forefront of Italian cultural life and Papini worried over the drying up of his talent, but their friendship became cordial again later and remained so until Papini's death in 1956.

12. Prezzolini had originally intended to call the journal "L'Italia che pensa" [Thinking Italy]. He consciously modeled La Voce on Charles Péguy's Cahiers de la Quinzaine, although some of his contributors would have liked it to be more like Charles Maurras's Action Française. See Prezzolini, Il tempo della Voce (Florence, 1960), pp. 155, 307.

13. Prezzolini, "Che fare?" (1910), in Romanò, La Voce, pp. 206, 210. Prezzolini stated his conclusion even more firmly the following year: "We are determined to live not only as individuals, but as a generation: People must see that we are a generation." Quoted by Romanò, ibid., p. 62. In other words, individual accomplishment was not sufficient; without achievement as a generation that would leave its traces in the minds of men, life and work would be worth the effort. Prezzolini's objection to a revolutionary politics appears to have been quite similar to Ortega's. Many of us, he wrote in 1914, laid our hopes in revolution. This revolution was never carried through to its completion. The state, which was supposed to be the antithesis of Catholicism, does business with and tolerates the Catholics. The church, in turn, benefits from the tolerance of a regime that it should condemn as antireligious. Socialism compromises with the state in exchange for the granting of reforms. The bourgeoisie try to insure themselves against a possible revolution by yielding important posts to the Socialists. "Italy," he concluded, "suffers from this perpetual charade, in which no one is in his rightful place." "La guerra tradita" (1914), ibid., p. 713.

14. For Prezzolini's pedagogical politics, see "La politica della Voce" (1911), ibid., pp. 393–395; for Salvemini's letter, Prezzolini, Il tempo della Voce, pp. 443–444; for Papini's article, "Dacci oggi la nostra poesia quotidiana" (1912), in Romanò, La Voce, pp. 448–452.

15. For Slataper, see his Epistolario, ed. Giani Stuparich (Milan, 1950), p. 301. Soffici set forth his position on intervention in a letter to Prezzolini on 15 August 1914: "According to us [Papini and himself], Italy has only one duty, which is to unite herself with all her forces to civilized Europe represented by France, England, and Russia (yes, even Russia) in order to crush and suffocate once and for all the German and Austrian brute, those two disgusting peoples who have always represented barbarousness, imbecility, and brutality. Italian neutrality must last as long as it takes to ready ourselves to act, and to act means to declare war against Austria as soon as possible and seize from her Trento, Trieste, Istria, and Valona." Reproduced by Prezzolini in Il tempo della Voce, p. 625. This passage brings out nicely the combination of ideological and imperialistic war aims that was characteristic of much of the interventionist movement. Most interventionists wanted to fight for civilization against German brutality and at the same time to aggrandize their own nation. It was precisely this contradiction that created the atmosphere of injured idealism and exasperated nationalism within which the early Fascist movement came into being and prospered. Soffici himself became a militant Fascist and later part of the regime's intellectual establishment.

16. Filippo Tommaso Marinetti, Futurismo e fascismo (Foligno, 1924), pp. 96–97.

17. Paolo Marconi, Io udii il comandamento (Rome, 1919), pp. 64, 66; Renato Serra, Scritti (Florence, 1958), ed. G. de Robertis and A. Grilli, p. 415. Both Marconi and Serra died in the war.

18. Quoted by Lucia Strappini in "Cultura e nazione: Analisi di un mito," in Lucia Strappini et al., *La classe dei colti: Intellettuali e società nel primo novecento italiano* (Bari, 1970), pp. 115–116.

19. Quoted by Garin in *Cronache di filosofia*, p. 313. Gramsci noted in March 1918 that, despite his unevenness and capriciousness, Papini deserved careful study because he anticipated the opinions of the average Italian bourgeois. Antonio Gransci, *2000 pagine di Gramsci*, ed. Giansiro Gerrata and Niccolo Gallo (Milan, 1964), I, 278.

20. For the contradictions of the interventionist movement, see Roberto Vivarelli, *Il dopoguerra in Italia e l'avvento del fascismo 1918–1922* (Naples, 1967), pp. 1–114.

21. The first circular issued by the Italian High Command after the declaration of war had called for absolute obedience and "inflexible and immediate repression" of all acts of indiscipline. There were 23,016 condemnations to death for military offenses of various kinds between May 1915 and May 1916; 48,296 between May 1916 and May 1917; and 82,366 between May 1917 and May 1918. During the course of the war, 128,527 acts of desertion were recorded, 55,034 of them during the third year. See Piero Melograni, *Storia politica della grande guerra* (Bari, 1969), pp. 53, 293, 305.

22. For Mussolini's citation of Mazzini, see *Opera omnia*, ed. Edoardo and Dulio Susmel (Florence, 1956–1964), XXXIV, p. 78; for his love of movement and action, Emilio Gentile, *Le origini dell'ideologia fascista (1918–1925)* (Bari, 1975), pp. 6–7.

23. Mussolini, *Opera omnia*, 140–141.

24. For the change the war wrought in Mussolini, see Da Arcangelo di Staso to Giuseppe Prezzolini, 26 February 1917, in Prezzolini, *Il tempo della Voce*, p. 719; for Mussolini's concept of trenchocracy, *Opera omnia*, XI, 243, and Vivarelli, *Il dopoguerra in Italia*, p. 279, n. 141.

25. For *combattentismo*, see Gentile, *Le origini dell'ideologia fascista*, pp. 95–109, and Michael A. Ledeen, "Italy: War as a Style of Life," in Ward, *The War Generation*, pp. 104–132. The distinction between the two Italies is made by Angelo Lanzillo in his book *La disfatta del fascismo*, published in 1918 and quoted by Gentile in *Le origini dell'ideologia fascista*, p. 80.

26. For the democratic convictions of the veterans' organizations, see Giovanni Sabbatuci, *I combattenti nel primo dopoguerra* (Bari, 1974); for the Arditi and D'Annunzio's legionnaires, Ferdinando Cordova, *Arditi e legionari dannunziani* (Padua, 1969).

27. For Mussolini's pledge to defend the Bersaglieri, see *Opera omnia*, XII, 79; the first Fascist appeal is quoted by Vivarelli, in *Il dopoguerra in Italia*, p. 293. Of the first eight demands listed in the Fascist program of March 1919, one called for putting off elections until the demobilization was complete and another for lowering the minimum age for election to parliament from thirty-one to twenty-five.

28. This paragraph is based on the self-portrait provided by Balbo in *Diario 1922* (Milan, 1932), pp. 5–8.

29. Bottai's poetry is quoted by Gentile in *Le origini dell'ideologia fascista*, p. 298; for his election to parliament and participation in the march on Rome, see Giordano Bruno Guerri, *Giuseppe Bottai: un fascista critico* (Milan, 1976), pp. 36, 43–48.

30. Mussolini, *Opera omnia*, XIV, 126, 133. Both these passages date from November 1919.

31. For Fascism as a movement of reality, see *Opera omnia*, XIII, 220; for Fascism's appeal to persons in the middle and lower-middle classes seeking a "third way," see Gentile, *Le origini dell'ideologia fascista*, pp. 204–206; for Mussolini's explanation

of Fascism's appeal to youth, *Opera omnia*, XIII, 220; for his clarification that one did not have to be a combatant in order to join the Fasci, ibid., XV, 76; for his description of the Fascist electoral list as a wave of youth, ibid., XVI, 286.

32. For the Roman Futurist who believed that tomorrow belonged to the young, see Gentile, *Le origini dell'ideologia fascista*, p. 127; for Marinetti's claim that Fascism was a fulfillment of Futurism, *Futurismo e fascismo*, p. 16; for Volpe's interpretation of Fascism as a rejuvenation of the Italian spirit, "Giovane Italia" in *Gerarchia*, January 1923, p. 689. Non-Fascists and even anti-Fascists agreed with Volpe's analysis. The most ambitious attempt to interpret Fascism as a movement of the younger generation was Alberto Cappa's series of four articles entitled "La lotta delle generazioni," published in Piero Gobetti's *La rivoluzione liberale* in September–October 1923 and then reissued as a book under the title *Le generazioni nel fascismo* (Turin, 1924) with Grildrig given as the author. Taking issue with the interpretation of Fascism as a revolt of the small and middle bourgeoisie against the masses organized by the Socialist party, Cappa sought to show that Fascism could best be understood as a collaboration between two age groups. Cappa's older Fascist generation, consisting mainly of men born in the 1880s, had been Socialists at twenty; had then rejected Socialism in favor of movements like Nationalism, Syndicalism, and Futurism; had been interventionists in 1914; and then, returning home from the war, had created Fascism. Now near forty, these older Fascists, according to Cappa, were willing to adapt to a conservative role as the dominant element in the new regime. The younger Fascist generation—those born after 1900 and hence too young to have fought in the war—had been compelled to live under the shadow of their older brothers. Haunted by the memory of a war in which they had not been able to participate, they sought, and found, outlets for their desire for action: first in the Fiume expedition, where they composed the majority of D'Annunzio's legions, then in the Fascism of the squads. Though Fascism appealed to many confused and contradictory impulses within them, the only clear and unambiguous motive drawing them to the squads was their desire to wage war: to shoot, to wear a helmet, to live a soldier's life. Now that the Fascists had arrived in power, they had been "fatally excluded" from the regime. Cappa warned that in the future these *giovannissimi* might constitute a danger to the movement they had helped to bring to power.

From a theoretical point of view, the most distinctive trait of Cappa's articles was his insistence that generational conflict was primarily instinctual and only secondarily ideological. It was in the nature of sons to try to overthrow their fathers and take their places, and it was in the nature of fathers to resist the ambition of their sons. A knowledge of the instincts, Cappa claimed, was the best possible preparation for studying and understanding history. Cappa's editor Piero Gobetti (1901) took exception to Cappa's portrait of the "youngest generation," to which he belonged. There was another younger generation, he asserted, besides that "of the [Fascist] club." This group, spared and matured by the war, had completed its education during the past five years (1918–1923) "austerely" without asking for favors or jobs. "We are interested in how Mussolini and Fascism will respond when we contrast our mystique and education to their rhetoric." *La rivoluzione liberale*, 25 September 1923. Gobetti died soon afterwards, the victim of an assault by Fascist thugs.

33. For Malaparte's generational interpretation of the Fascist revolution, see *La rivolta dei santi maledetti* (1921) and *Ritratto delle cose d'Italia, degli eroi, del popolo, degli avvenimenti, delle esperienze e inquietudini della nostra generazione* (1923), both

reprinted in Enriquo Falqui, ed., *L'Europa vivente* (Florence, 1961); for his claim that the Fascist revolution was directed against the intellectuals, see his introduction to Ardengo Soffici, *Battaglia fra due vittorie* (Florence, 1923), p. xxii; for the description of his generation as moved by a spirit of intolerance, revolt, and heroic unrest, *L'Europa vivente*, p. 152; for the assertion that his generation had surpassed all others in heroism, *La Conquista dello Stato*, 15 March 1928. Malaparte's literary career is assessed by Gianni Grana in *Malaparte* (Florence, 1968); by Giampolo Martelli in *Curzio Malaparte* (Turin, 1968); and by Malaparte himself in an autobiographical fragment he wrote for Palmiro Togliatti, reprinted after Malaparte's death in *Rinascita*, July–August 1957, pp. 373–378, and September 1957, pp. 473–479.

34. For Moravia's novel, see Alberto Moravia, *Gli indifferenti* (Rome, 1929); for the debate between old and young Fascists, Ugo d'Andrea's reply to Gherardo Casini in *Critica fascista*, 15 October 1927, p. 388. The practical result of this debate was the creation in October 1930 of the Fasci giovanili di combattimento, which enrolled young men between eighteen and twenty-one years of age.

35. For useful discussions of Fascist policy toward youth and good summaries of the ample bibliography, see Gino Germani, "La socializzazione politica dei giovani nei regimi fascisti: Italia e Spagna," *Quaderni di sociologia* 18 (January–June 1969): 11–58; and Michael A. Ledeen, "Fascism and the Generation Gap," *European Studies Review* 1 (July 1971): 275–283. For Mussolini's success and its limits, see Renzo de Felice, *Mussolini il duce: Gli anni del consenso 1929–1936* (Turin, 1974), pp. 228–246. For the Roman journal that deplored the sentimental nostalgia of older Fascists, see *Il Saggiatore*, January 1933, p. 464. This article was the conclusion of a long survey in which leading Fascist intellectuals had been asked to what extent they saw the germs of a spiritual renewal in the new generation and whether they considered the present gap between the generations, in comparison with "normal" generational discontinuities, to be "definitive and decisive." The results were published in *Il Saggiatore* between March 1932 and January 1933.

36. For Omodeo's premise, see *Momenti della vita di guerra* (Turin, 1968), p. 8.

37. For Omodeo's family background, see Eva Omodeo Zona, *Ricordi di Adolfo Omodeo* (Catania, 1968), pp. 16–17; for the influence of Gentile, ibid., pp. 13–15, and Aldo Garosci, "Adolfo Omodeo, I," *Rivista storica italiana* 77 (1965): 184; for Omodeo's belief that history was the most elevated moment of the spirit and for the view of his future, Omodeo, *Lettere 1910–1946* (Turin, 1963), pp. 14, 16.

38. For his view of himself as an intellectual aristocrat surrounded by recalcitrant masses, see Omodeo, *Lettere*, p. 62; for his interventionism, ibid., p. 100. His wife reports that in May and June 1915 he organized interventionist rallies in Cefalù. Zona, *Ricordi*, p. 18.

39. For Omodeo's bravery in June 1918, see the account by one of his fellow soldiers, quoted by Zona, *Ricordi*, pp. 22–25; for his dislike of the political canaille who were ruining Italy and for his inability to justify the war on historical or ethical grounds, see Omodeo, *Lettere*, pp. 266, 137.

40. For Omodeo's problems in adjusting to civilian life, see ibid., p. 370, and Zona, *Ricordi*, pp. 21–22, 27–28; for his belief that a curse lay over his generation, Omodeo, *Lettere*, p. 365; for his complaints about the ineptitude of Italy's rulers, pp. 344, 368; for his anxiety about the impoverishment of his brain, p. 360; for his fear that getting a professorship would be arduous, p. 364; for his feeling that the world had lost

all moral conscience, p. 371; for his conviction that youth could find the solution to Italy's problems, p. 366; for his 1920 essays, "Educazione politica," reprinted in Omodeo, *Libertà e storia: Scritti e discorsi politici* (Turin, 1960), pp. 18–30. These essays were first published in *L'Educazione Nazionale*, a journal founded by some ex-Vociani for the purpose of renovating "the consciousness of the new generations." The enterprise was based on the premise that history is made by "bold and idealistic minorities who take upon themselves a well-defined end and will its realization with unshakable decision." *L'Educazione Nazionale*, 15 January 1920. Among the signers of the journal's first appeal for the formation of a "Fascio di Educazione Nazionale" were Piero Jahier, Giani Stuparich, Giuseppe Prezzolini, Giovanni Amendola, Giuseppe Lombardo-Radice, Giovanni Gentile, and Piero Gobetti. Lombardo-Radice, editor of *L'Educazione Nazionale*, repeatedly emphasized the political aims of the journal, which he said had been founded with the aim of educating the educators of Italy.

41. There is no unambiguous evidence that Omodeo was ever attracted toward the Fascist movement. His wife reports in her memoirs that upon hearing of the naming of Mussolini as premier in October 1922, Omodeo exclaimed "poor Italy!" Zona, *Ricordi*, p. 29. For Omodeo's perception that Fascism lacked moral principles and was subversive, see *Lettere*, p. 419; for his plea to Gentile to break with Fascism, ibid., p. 418. Omodeo's presumed sympathy for the Fascist movement before 1924 is based on his use of the forms of the first person plural when discussing Gentile's attitude toward Fascism. Hence Omodeo writes to Gentile of "our" having been misled and deceived and of the need for "us" to break with Fascism. But Omodeo's wife argues that her husband used these terms tactically, so as to make it easier for his patron to withdraw from an increasingly compromising situation. More to the point, Omodeo lived in a state of virtual isolation during the early years of the Fascist movement. He does not seem to have been well-informed about national politics and operated primarily with the vague (but accurate) intuition that Italy was headed toward a disaster. Zona, *Ricordi*, pp. 27–35.

42. For Omodeo's nostalgia for the war and the ambitions he nurtured for his book, see *Lettere*, p. 445.

43. For Omodeo's disappointment with his book's reception, see ibid., p. 544; for its impact on young anti-Fascists, Leo Valiani, "Adolfo Omodeo nel trentesimo anniversario della morte," *Annali della Facoltà di lettere e filosofia dell'Università di Napoli*, 1976–1977, p. 55.

44. For Omodeo's interpretation of Italian intervention, see *Momenti*, p. 60.

45. For the Garrone correspondence, see Giuseppe and Eugenio Garrone, *Ascensione eroica: Lettere di guerra dei fratelli Giuseppe ed Eugenio Garrone*, ed. Luigi Galante (Milan, 1919); for Omodeo's belief that social groups should be judged by the heights of idealism they reach, *Momenti*, p. 83.

46. For Omodeo's use of the phrase "good pastors," see *Momenti*, p. 127; for his belief in the moral superiority of the Italian combatants and Italy's right to rule other peoples, ibid., p. 57.

47. Ibid., p. 124.

48. Ibid., pp. 124–125. Like many survivors, Omodeo was haunted by the memory of those who had died. In the last pages of his book he recalled an incident that occurred on a spring night in 1917 in a quiet sector of the front. He was strolling in a hollow beneath the mount of San Michele, the scene of some of the fiercest fighting in the Italian war. Far away the cannons grumbled angrily. The bed of the Isonzo River

bent through desolate battlefields toward the ruins of San Martino del Carso, where thousands of men had died. Down toward the river in the moonlight Omodeo could see the vast tomb of Sdraussina, which gave refuge to some of the countless dead of San Michele. Among the bushes and graves the nightingales of the Isonzo were singing. In this strangely peaceful necropolis, once the scene of violent fighting, Omodeo was overcome by fear and anxiety. "I felt a pang in my heart. I had the feeling that the best had all been killed, that they had withdrawn into a hermetic silence, taking with them the impetus and faith with which hundreds and hundreds of battalions had thrown themselves at the pitiless mount. Those white graves seemed like the froth left over from many storms. We were to be the epigones without the secret of their strength. And my spirit kneeled to ask the dead for their secret, their comfort, a liberation from the incubus of eternal war." Ibid., p. 260. In a letter of November 1916 to his wife he had described the ruins of San Martino del Carso as "the most horrible" he had ever seen. "Not an intact wall, not a stone that doesn't bear traces of a ferocious fight to the death." Zona, *Ricordi*, p. 20.

49. Eugenio Garrone's doubts about the war were not reported in the published correspondence but were alluded to in his unpublished diary, to which Omodeo had access. See *Momenti*, pp. 199–200. For the disillusionment of Garrone's generation, see ibid., p. 232.

50. Ibid., p. 45.

51. Ibid., p. 180.

52. For the virtues that the war demanded, see ibid., p. 239; for the assertion that these virtues existed above all in the officers, pp. 239–240; for Omodeo's conclusion that the Great War had equaled the Napoleonic wars in grandeur, p. 240.

53. For Omodeo's belief that the letters of the dead were a form of poetry, see ibid., p. 258; for his belief that the values of the vanquished had infected the victors and for the secret of the dead, p. 259.

54. Omodeo attempted, unconvincingly, to distinguish between the voluntarism of the best and the activism of peripheral elements within the war generation. The best, he claimed, had been inspired by a religious vision. Ibid., p. 250.

55. For Gramsci's background, see Giuseppe Fiori, *Vita di Antonio Gramsci* (Bari, 1973 ed.); Salvatore Francesco Romano, *Antonio Gramsci* (Turin, 1965); the recollections of his sister Teresina in Mimma Paulesu Quercioli, ed., *Gramsci vivo* (Milan, 1977), pp. 11–21; and Gramsci's published works, especially the letters from prison. For Gramsci's belief that history could replace religion as the faith of modern men, see *2000 pagine di Gramsci*, pp. 218–219.

56. For Gramsci's conversion to Socialism and the significance he ascribed to it in terms of his own life experience, see Romano, *Gramsci*, pp. 91–92.

57. For Gramsci's belief that Marxism and Crocean idealism were the most advanced philosophies in twentieth-century Europe, see ibid., pp. 203–204; for his conviction that every revolution had been preceded by an intense campaign of criticism, *2000 pagine di Gramsci*, p. 191; for his refusal to wait to become the majority plus one, ibid., p. 240. Gramsci's first article published in a Socialist journal was a defense of Mussolini's attack on the official Socialist position of absolute neutrality during the war. Ibid., pp. 177–180. For a discussion of Gramsci's early attraction to Mussolini, see Romano, *Gramsci*, pp. 118–119.

58. For Gramsci's interpretation of the Russian Revolution as a liberation of

minds, see *2000 pagine di Gramsci*, p. 254; for his assertion that the Bolsheviks understood that it was necessary to conquer minds and for his interpretation of the true spirit of Marxism, pp. 255–256; for Marx as a master of spiritual and moral life, p. 291.

59. Ibid., pp. 380–384.

60. On April 1, 1925, Gramsci wrote, "We are a fighting organization . . . Study and culture for us are nothing but theoretical consciousness of our immediate and supreme ends and of the way in which we will best be able to succeed in translating them into reality." Ibid., pp. 741–742.

61. A few months before his arrest, Gramsci observed in an article that it was precisely because the Communists were young and because they had no stake in the traditions and organizational unity of the Socialist party that they had been able to "perceive more distinctly [than older Socialists like Serrati] the insufficiency of the old generation to perform the tasks rendered necessary by the approach of the reactionary storm." Ibid., p. 771.

62. The *Prison Notebooks* pose formidable problems of interpretation. They consist of fragments, usually one or two paragraphs in length, some of which were reworked, recombined, or simply recopied in later notebooks. It is hard to know what Gramsci intended to do with these notes. He began them as a mental exercise to counteract the effects of inactivity. At the same time, he spoke in his letters of wanting to undertake intellectual work that would rise above the political passions of the moment, something that would be *für ewig*. Later he recognized that the notebooks contained reflections on his own political and cultural experience that might have universal or at least national value. But he warned on more than one occasion of the danger of assigning too much weight to posthumous writings that the author had never been able to rework. A finished piece of writing must never be confused with the raw material that had been assembled for its documentation. These problems of interpretation are considerably diminished as a result of the publication of a splendid new critical edition, edited by Valentino Gerratana and published under the auspices of the Gramsci Institute in Rome: *Quaderni del carcere* (Turin, 1975), 4 vols. Gerratana's brief introduction (IV, xi–xli) provides a useful history of the text.

63. For a careful study of the terms "historical bloc" and "hegemony," see Angelo Broccoli, *Antonio Gramsci e l'educazione come egemonia* (Florence, 1972). Gramsci saw common sense as a mediation between the philosophy of great intellectuals and the folklore of the masses. It was the mechanism by which ideas trickled down to the masses and became part of their conception of the world. "Common sense is not a monolithic conception, identical in time and space: It's the folklore of philosophy and like folklore it appears in innumerable forms: Its fundamental and most characteristic trait is that 'even in distinguished brains' it is a disaggregated, incoherent, and inconsistent conception that corresponds to the social and cultural position of the multitudes, whose philosophy it is." Quoted by Broccoli, p. 124, n. 46. In other words, Gramsci's "common sense" comes close to what Ortega meant by "convictions," but offers some means for determining empirically how these convictions come to be embodied in the thought patterns of different social strata.

64. *Quaderni*, III, 1560.

65. For the education of the younger generation by the older, see ibid., I, 115; for the cause of generational conflict, ibid., I, 340, and Broccoli, *Gramsci*, pp. 156–157; for the transfer of loyalties to an antagonistic social class and for the consequences of at-

tempting to block the transfer of loyalties from a socially retrogressive class to an advanced one, *Quaderni*, I, 115–116; for the origins of the crisis of authority, I, 311; for the situation when the intermediate generation is missing or weak and for the difficulty of organizing an intellectual center in the subordinate classes, III, 1829–1830.

66. For the attempt of the young bourgeois generation to win hegemony over the workers, see *Quaderni*, I, 396–397; for Prezzolini's effort to lay the basis for an intellectual and moral reform, III, 2109–2110, 2188–2189. Gramsci's polemic against the intellectuals of the rural and parasitic bourgeoisie is one of the persisting and unifying themes of the *Quaderni*. See II, 707–708; III, 2109–2110, 1880, 2204–2205; and above all, III, 1692–1693, where he writes that the Italian intellectuals have been unable to create a sense of national unity because the great majority of them belong to the rural bourgeoisie, whose economic position is only possible if the peasant masses are squeezed to the marrow of their bones. Thus for these people to pass from words to deeds would necessitate the "radical destruction" of their own economic basis.

67. For the return of bourgeois intellectuals to the womb of their own class, see ibid., I, 396–397; for the lack of a guiding center, I, 331.

68. Ibid., III, 1717–1718.

69. For the statement that a strong generation will exaggerate the value of its predecessor, see ibid., II, 947–948; for the comparison of Malaparte's generation with that of Prezzolini and Papini, I, 8; for the remark that the young generation has no ideals, III, 1812–1813.

70. For Gramsci's view of Omodeo, see ibid., II, 1010–1011, and III, 1983; for his charge that Omodeo had exalted voluntarism at the expense of collective consciousness, III, 2212–2213. Gramsci believed that in Italy voluntarism had been a surrogate for popular involvement in national affairs. Commenting on a statement by Italo Balbo praising the role of youthful volunteers in Italian history, Gramsci observed, "The volunteer solution is authoritarian, from the top down, legitimized formally by the consensus, as one is in the habit of saying, of the 'best.' But to make durable history, the 'best' are not enough; vaster and more numerous national-popular energies are required." Ibid., III, 1998–1999. In another entry Gramsci analyzed the paternalistic attitude of those Italian intellectuals (Omodeo among them) who used the term *gli umili* (the humble) when referring to the people. "For the Italian intellectual the term *umili* indicates a relationship of paternal and patriarchal protection, the 'complacent' expression of one's own indisputable superiority, the relationship between two races, one held to be superior and the other inferior, the relationship between adults and children in the old pedagogy, and worse yet, a relationship of S.P.C.A., or that exercised by the Anglo-Saxon Salvation Army toward the cannibals of New Guinea." Ibid., II, 1197.

71. In 1932 Gramsci noted that Salvador de Madariaga's book on contemporary Spain, recently translated into Italian as *Spagna: Saggio di storia contemporanea*, would be useful for understanding the function the intellectuals had performed in the fall of the monarchy. "A large literature must exist on this question in Spain these days, since the Republic presents itself as a republic of intellectuals. The Spanish phenomenon has its own peculiar characteristics, determined by the special situation of the peasant masses in Spain. Nonetheless, it is to be compared with the function of the Russian intelligentsia, with the function of the Italian intellectuals during the Risorgimento, with the German intellectuals under the French domination, and with the French intellectuals of the eighteenth century. But in Spain the function of the intellectuals in politics

has its own unmistakable character and is worth studying." Ibid., II, 1200. Apparently Gramsci did not undertake this study, perhaps for lack of material; his later comparative analysis of intellectuals in Europe and the United States (III, 1513–1540) does not include Spain.

72. The four generations Gramsci discussed in the *Quaderni*—those of Croce, Prezzolini, Malaparte, and the youth of the 1930s—were separated by intervals of roughly fifteen years. For Gramsci's view of the relationship between the economic infrastructure and historical change, see ibid., III, 1917. Significant generational changes were ruptures, as opposed to normal and healthy friction, between those who teach and those who learn. Gramsci and Ortega actually had quite similar conceptions of effective pedagogy. The good teacher, both felt, represented the best his times had to offer in such a way that the student could achieve autonomy and surpass his teacher by reacting to his challenge. The student's reaction, in turn, made possible further development on the part of the teacher. In Gramsci's opinion, this was also the desirable relationship between the generations. Mannheim had advanced a similar view in his essay on the generation problem.

73. Ibid., III, 1514–1515.

74. Ibid., II, 862–863.

75. For the Italian intellectual's combination of revolutionary yearnings with elitist and reactionary values, see Mario Isnenghi, *Il mito della grande guerra* (Bari, 1970), pp. 42, 83–85. See also his brief but penetrating essay *Giovanni Papini* (Florence, 1972). Isnenghi's argument is further developed, with specific reference to the Vociani, by Romano Luperini in *Letteratura e ideologia nel primo novecento* (Pisa, 1973), pp. 31–50, 75–78. My portrait of the Italian intellectual of the early twentieth century owes much to Luigi Salvatorelli's *Nazionalfascismo* (Turin, 1923), pp. 21–25. Taking issue with the Marxist interpretation of Fascism as an expression of the capitalistic bourgeoisie, Salvatorelli argued that Mussolini's movement derived its force and its ideological flavor from the revolt of the humanistically trained petty bourgeois intellectual against the modern scientific world represented by the proletariat and the industrial bourgeoisie. Condemning this world of productive social classes as materialistic, the petty bourgeois, Salvatorelli claimed, rallied around the countermyth of a national community in which classes would no longer exist. He identified himself not by his class—since the petty bourgeoisie did not constitute a real social stratum—but under the generic category of patriot or *combattente*. Salvatorelli's analysis suffers from a failure to define carefully the social composition of the petty bourgeoisie; but if one interprets it, as Italian scholars have recently done, to mean the educated class (*la classe dei colti*), then Salvatorelli's generalizations embrace the same diffuse social category that Gramsci described as the intermediary cadres of the intellectual class: lawyers, doctors, bureaucrats, architects, journalists, secondary school teachers, and university professors.

6. Wanderers between Two Worlds

1. For Littré's definition of a generation, see Emile Littré, *Dictionnaire de la langue française*, I, part 2 (Paris, 1863), 561.

2. For the relationship between the Enlightenment and the generational idea, see Theodor Litt, *Das Verhältnis der Generationen ehedem und heute* (Wiesbaden, 1947). Recalling the atmosphere of cultural renewal that prevailed in Italy just after the Great

War, Ugo Spirito wrote: "We had the *feeling* that we were beginning something new and, despite the anxiety of the transformation, we sensed the joy of a new road. The hymn "Giovinezza" had nothing rhetorical about it, and the reference [in the song] to *spring* and *beauty* was immediate and without reserve. The problem of the young, therefore, was for us the problem of life in its effective plenitude. We were the young and the future was our future. All the rest was secondary and debatable." Ugo Spirito, *L'avvenire dei giovani* (Florence, 1972), p. 12. (Spirito's italics.) The title of Spirito's book takes on new meaning in view of Litt's point that in the conditions of the nineteenth and twentieth centuries the future *belongs* to the young, for they are the physical incarnation of the future in the present. For an interesting case study of generationalism and the creation of a tradition of generational thinking among nineteenth-century expatriot Romanian students, see Patrick H. Griffin, *Fathers and Sons in Nineteenth-Century Romania: A Study in Generational Thinking* (Ph.D. diss., University of Southern California, 1969).

3. For the organization of youth, see John R. Gillis, *Youth and History* (New York and London, 1974), pp. 133–183; John Springhall, *Youth, Empire and Society* (London, 1977); and Thomas Nipperdey, *Gesellschaft, Kultur, Theorie* (Göttingen, 1976), pp. 338–359.

4. For the economic and social origins of generational conflict in the nineteenth century, see Friedrich H. Tenbruck, *Jugend und Gesellschaft* (Freiburg im Breisgau, 1962); Karol Szemkus, "Gesellschaftliche Bedingungen zur Entstehung der deutschen Jugendbewegung," in Walter Rüegg, ed., *Kulturkritik und Jugendkult* (Frankfurt am Main, 1974), pp. 39–46; Bruno Bettelheim, "The Problem of Generations," *Daedalus*, Winter 1962, pp. 68–96; and Fred Weinstein and Gerald M. Platt, *The Wish to Be Free* (Berkeley, 1969), pp. 146–147, 179.

5. For the exclusion of young people from the adult world of life and labor and the impact of demographic trends on attitudes toward youth, see F. Musgrove, *Youth and the Social Order* (London, 1964), pp. 58–85; for the changing concept of youth as a stage of life, Gillis, *Youth and History*, pp. 1–35, 98–105; for the increasing number of years encompassed by youth, Tenbruck, *Jugend und Gesellschaft*, p. 47; for a breakdown of European population by countries and age-groups, B. R. Mitchell, *European Historical Statistics* (New York, 1976), pp. 28–54.

6. Richard Alewyn noted the connection between the waning of particularisms of various kinds and the rise of generational consciousness in his important essay, "Das Problem der Generation in der Geschichte," *Zeitschrift für deutsche Bildung* 10 (1929): 519–527. For a case study in the fading of regional dialects and the rise of national consciousness during the period 1870–1914, see Eugen Weber, *Peasants into Frenchmen* (Stanford, 1976).

7. Martin Heidegger, *Sein und Zeit* (Halle, 1928), p. 394.

8. In my conception of the intellectual as a social type I have been primarily influenced by Gramsci's *Quaderni*, especially III, 1413–1440; but I find it necessary to distinguish not between traditional and organic intellectuals, as Gramsci does, but between intellectuals who earned their livelihood through the manipulation of the written word and those who did not. We need a descriptive typology of various types of intellectuals in early twentieth-century Europe. Theda Shapiro's analysis in *Painters and Politics: The European Avant-Garde and Society, 1900–1925* (New York, 1976) suggests that

painters may have differed in important ways from men of letters in their attitudes toward society.

9. "An intellectual class represents only itself in literary production . . . Consequently, one must determine what interests an intellectual serves through the medium of his specific profession. Such interests are the basic human ones: interests directly related to his employment and to the office he holds; the interests of the groups he belongs to; the material and moral pressures exerted by those upon whom he is dependent; psychological complexes such as routine, fear, ambition, and envy; concretely spiritual interests; and so on. Therefore, when trying to establish successive generations in the history of ideas, one must not fall into the error of generalizing by saying 'So-and-so thought in that way; everyone must have thought that way.' The history of ideas is far more capillary; in order to take full account of this, one must broaden research and consult neutral archives, that is, those archives that candidly reflect our ancestors' 'intellectual pluralism.' " Jaime Vicens Vives, *Approaches to the History of Spain*, p. xx.

10. Ortega actually prepared such a generational table for the period 1521–1611. It appears in *Obras completas*, VIII, 660–661.

11. Richard Aldington wrote of his generation: "Adult lives were cut sharply into three sections—prewar, war, and postwar. It is curious—perhaps not so curious—but many people will tell you that whole areas of their prewar lives have become obliterated from their memories. Prewar seems like prehistory. What did we do, how did we feel, what were we living for in those incredibly distant years. One feels as if the period 1900–14 has to be treated archaeologically, painfully recreated by experts from slight vestiges." Aldington, *Life of a Hero*, pp. 224–225.

12. "Up in one's brain and deep down in one's heart and one's belly, the quality of one's life is very much affected by its tempo; the tempo of living is itself enormously affected by the tempo of ordinary transport, the pace at which one normally travels from place to place. In describing my childhood I said that in those days of the eighties and nineties of the 19th century the rhythm of London traffic which one listened to as one fell asleep in one's nursery was the rhythm of horses' hooves clopclopping down London streets in broughams, hansom cabs, and four-wheelers, and the rhythm, the tempo got into one's blood and one's brain, so that in a sense I have never become entirely reconciled in London to the rhythm and tempo of the whizzing and rushing cars. And the tempo of living in 1886 was the tempo of the horses' hooves, much more leisurely than it is today when it has become the tempo of the whirring and whizzing wheels." Leonard Woolf, *Growing* (London, 1967), p. 31. Woolf was born in 1880; most intellectuals who identified themselves with the generation of 1914 grew up with the sound of automobiles and the rhythm of motorized transport. For example, Osbert Sitwell (1892) wrote in his memoirs "of that passion for speed without purpose which members of their [his mother's] and the ensuing generation—including, I may say, myself as a motor addict—were to develop to so intense a pitch that they could not be happy except at sixty miles an hour, or over." Sitwell, *The Scarlet Tree* (Boston, 1946), pp. 232–233. One suspects that this was truer of Sitwell's age-group than of his mother's.

13. Nicholas Mosley, *Julian Grenfell*, pp. 113–114.

14. The phrase "culture of Anti-Necessity" is taken from Eugen Weber's unpublished essay, "Barrès: un héritier."

15. "Man at the beginning of the twentieth century could no longer believe in his-

tory as a god, but neither could he let himself get inebriated on the narcotic of late mystical romanticism; in short, he could not be satisfied genuflecting before Napoleon or Parsifal." Giovanni Amendola, *Etica e biografia* (Milan-Naples, 1953 ed.), p. 168.

16. For the statement that we should stamp others with our seal, see Miguel de Unamuno, *Tragic Sense of Life* (New York, 1954 ed.), p. 278.

17. For Zuckmayer, see *A Part of Myself*, p. 127.

18. Henri Franck, *Lettres à quelques amis*, pp. 135–137. Franck added, "The role of us bourgeois who will never see the promised land, and who cannot associate ourselves actively with the heroic effort of the people, who cannot become part of the people, since it is so long that we ceased being it—my duty . . . is, in making way for the civilization that they will construct, to point out to them what must not be destroyed, the values that must be respected" (pp. 137–138). Yet how was a bourgeois like Franck going to react if he became convinced that the people had no intention of salvaging and respecting the values that were sacred to him? This would become the dilemma of many intellectuals of Franck's age-group.

19. This quotation is from the liberal Giovanni Amendola in "La grande illusione" (1911), in Romanò, *La Voce*, p. 304.

20. For the comparison of the war to an approaching storm, see *The Diary of Otto Braun* (London, 1924), p. 19. Images like these appear frequently. A Frenchman remembered "this kind of restlessness . . . which was not that of an animal who senses the coming of a storm and who begins to move about beneath the black sky and paws the ground, but rather that of a fighter who gathers himself for a desperate leap." Pierre Dominique, *Quatre hommes entre vingt*, p. 129. And an Italian noted in 1913, "There is hanging over us in our life and in our culture something heavy like a leaden sky." Giovanni Boine, in Romanò, *La Voce*, p. 576. For Rupert Brooke, see *1914 and Other Poems*, p. 11; for Bruno Frank, Jack J. Roth, *World War I: A Turning Point in Modern History* (New York, 1967), p. 8; for Giani Stuparich, *Il ritorno del padre* (Turin, 1961), pp. 175–176; for Drieu la Rochelle, *Interrogation*, p. 86; for Ortega, *Obras completas*, X, 251. Max Scheler was exaggerating only slightly when he wrote in 1914, "One should never forget in investigating the causes of this war that it is above all the war of a new generation—the war of European youth!" Quoted by Otto-Ernst Schüddekopf, *Linke Leute von rechts* (Stuttgart, 1960), p. 104.

21. Barbusse is quoted by Sassoon in *Counter-Attack*, p. v; for Remarque, see *All Quiet on the Western Front*, pp. 162–163; for Aldington, *Death of a Hero*, p. 227; for Omodeo, *Momenti della vita di guerra*, p. 145.

22. For the war as something one suffered rather than fought, see Emmanuel Berl, *A contretemps* (Paris, 1969), pp. 166–167; for the image of the men of the front as lepers, Carl Zuckmayer, *Als wär's ein Stück von mir* (Frankfurt and Hamburg, 1969 ed.), p. 193; for the loss of enthusiasm and identity, Ernst Toller, quoted by Hanna Hafkesbring in *Unknown Germany: An Inner Chronicle of the First World War Based on Letters and Diaries* (New Haven, 1948), p. 66.

23. Pierre Teilhard de Chardin, *The Making of a Mind: Letters from a Soldier-Priest* (New York, 1965), p. 205. See also Teilhard's essay, "La Nostalgie du front," in Teilhard de Chardin, *Ecrits du temps de la guerre* (Paris, 1965), pp. 203–214. Nostalgia for the front was of course combined with alienation from the civilians at home. Few soldiers captured the nature of this alienation as well and as objectively as Guy Chapman (1889). Chapman had returned to England in the fall of 1916 on his second leave.

"With each leave that fell to my lot now, there seemed to be a noticeable difference in England. Or was the difference only in myself? Though the weight of the war had pressed on me much more lightly than on others, it was heavy enough. I was being forced like a plant in a hot-house. The ingenuousness with which I had set out was being sweated out of me. I was growing up faster than I knew. And as this process went on, I drew further away from England. It was—I think it still is—impossible to make those who had no experience of this war understand it, as it must be understood, through all the senses. Sitting in a shelter of sandbags and corrugated iron, shivering with cold, looking out at the wrinkled frosted clay of a trench wall, hearing the sky rent by explosions and hammered by gun-fire, smelling the hundred stenches, animal and mineral, fixed in the mud, tasting a tongue sour with perpetual tobacco smoke, I let my mind retreat further and further from thoughts of home. I could find nothing to say in letters. All communication was as 'dissed' as though the lines had been broken by a shell. So on my arrival in London, I was as foreign as a Chinese, could observe the natives with unfamiliar eyes and bitterly enjoy all the prejudices of another civilization. As the war trailed its body across France, sliming the landscape, so too it tainted civilian life. London seemed poorer and yet more raffish. Its dignity was melting under the strain. It had become corrupted. There was a feeling of hostility growing up between the soldiers abroad and the civilians and soldiers at home; the good-timers, the army abroad thought them, profiteering, drinking, debauching the women. There were ugly tales of money-making in coal, wheat, wool, tea, and other necessities far above legitimate profit, stories of farmers' profits, of breweries' winnings. The 1914 values had gone bad, and instead the English were learning to respect one thing only, money, and easy money by preference. It was better in France. There a man was valued rather for what he was than what he achieved. One found germinating in one's mind the seed for a hatred for these home-keeping English. One might have recalled that it is the habit of the English from the days of Marlborough to trade with the enemy. Was not Napoleon's army shod by England? But the habitual rapacity of man seemed no excuse when it was not a dynasty but the whole nation in arms. Such gloomy thoughts entertained me as we slowly rolled through the icy dark towards the line in a train from which the windows had long since vanished." Guy Chapman, *A Passionate Prodigality*, pp. 138–139.

24. For Montherlant on the causes of war, see *Romans*, p. 77; for Manning, *Her Privates We*, p. 83; for the war as a voyage into the unknown, Teilhard de Chardin, *Ecrits du temps de la guerre*, pp. 204–206.

25. For Noel Coward on comradeship, see "Post Mortem," reprinted in *Play Parade* (London, 1934), I, 632, 617.

26. As was the case with Ernst Jünger, who returned home after four years of war to find that "almost without any thought of mine, the idea of the Fatherland had been distilled from all these afflictions in a clearer and brighter essence. That was the final winnings in a game on which so often all had been staked: the nation was no longer for me an empty thought veiled in symbols." Jünger, *The Storm of Steel*, p. 316. This passage was removed from later German editions.

27. The quotation on learning to know the exact value of things comes from Curzio Malaparte, *L'Europa vivente*, pp. 443–444. The Oxford classicist Maurice Bowra later wrote that the war had taught him to preserve his inner life against all external intrusions and had given him a sense of solidarity with men of other ranks and classes. "Before I joined the army I had lived in a very select and privileged class, knowing

nothing and caring very little about the ways of other men. The war opened my eyes to the basic similarity of human beings and the absurdity of artificial distinctions between them. Even paternal care meant very little, for though it was my task to look after my men, it was usually they who looked after me, and were more capable of dealing with a sudden crisis than I was." C. M. Bowra, *Memories 1898–1939* (London, 1966), p. 91. The French literary critic Jean Paulhan explained that the war had permitted him to realize his prewar dreams of fleeing from civilization into a world of fields and savages, but in conditions exactly contrary to those he had expected. Yet despite seeing his prewar attitudes mocked by the brutality of the war, he soon experienced a feeling of plenitude and well-being. This feeling derived not from the liberty offered by primitive existence, as he had thought before the war, but by the constraints imposed by nature and the enemy. In the few moments when he was able to escape from these constraints, his inner life was greatly enriched. "The immense earth that surrounded us participated then in my inner life. I imagined its grandeur and its variations: meadows, forests, useful fields, in exactly the same way that I would have been able to imagine my own feelings and with the same ease." The "sympathy" he developed for the war, Paulhan concluded, derived from the clarity it brought to his system of priorities. The omnipresent bullet and shell prevented one from thinking that one's well-being hinged on the accident of sun or rain. And even the most momentary escape from danger brought with it a "profound and supple sense of soul." Jean Paulhan, *Le Guérrier appliqué* (Paris, 1962), pp. 49–50.

28. Drieu la Rochelle, *Sur les écrivains* (Paris, 1964), p. 88.

29. Two quotations, one from a man of the Left and the other from someone who later adhered to Fascism, illustrate this point. The first is from Ernst Toller's autobiography. "Didn't we swear to our friends out there on the field of death, crouched together below the parapet or huddled together in the dugout, in shattered woods and villages, under the hail of shrapnel, and beneath the light of the stars—didn't we swear then by all that was most sacred that one good thing must come out of the war—an uprising of youth? Europe must be rebuilt, its foundations laid anew. Our fathers had betrayed us, and the young who had known war, hard and unsentimental, would begin the business of spring-cleaning. If we had not the right to, who had?" *I Was a German* (London, 1934), pp. 94–95. The second quotation comes from Drieu la Rochelle's fictionalized war memoir. Drieu reconstructs a conversation between himself and the mother of one of his friends, who tries to convince him to run for the Chamber of Deputies. She offers him money and the use of her connections, but he refuses. The woman persists, and the following dialogue ensues: " 'But I'm not on the Left.' 'Are you on the Right? It doesn't matter.' 'I'm not on the Right either.' 'What are you?' 'I'm against the old men.' 'I see, that's it.' 'But no, Madame, the old men are on both the Right and the Left.' " Drieu la Rochelle, *La Comédie de Charleroi*, p. 97. In 1922 Drieu had defined his generation as those young men who found themselves in a trench, "isolated from the world, from kindness and hate themselves, by an iron curtain. In the rear, the old men felt themselves to be alone with their ideas. This is all that we have left, this formidable reality: l'esprit de corps, team spirit, what shall we call it? . . . We are a generation." *Mesure de la France*, p. 139.

30. "Any intelligent European born, let us say, after 1904 reached the teens in what he or she knew to be a dangerous and cruel world. But if you were born in 1894,

as I was, you suddenly saw a great jagged crack in the looking-glass. After that your mind could not escape from the idea of a world that ended in 1914 and another one that began about 1919, with a wilderness of smoke and fury, outside sensible time, lying between them." J. B. Priestley, *Margin Released* (London, 1962), p. 88. For the belief that at the front a new world was coming into being, see Pierre Teilhard de Chardin's letter of 23 September 1917 to his cousin, where he wrote, "I think one could show that the front isn't simply the firing line, the exposed area corroded by the conflict of nations, but the 'front of the wave' carrying the world of man towards its new destiny. When you look at it during the night, lit up by flares, after a day of more than usual activity, you seem to feel that you're at the final boundary between what has already been achieved and what is striving to emerge. It's not only that activity culminates in a sort of intense but completely calm paroxysm, dilating to the scale of the vast work in which it is playing its part—but the mind, too, gets something like an over-all view of the whole forward march of the human mass, and feels not quite so lost in it." Teilhard de Chardin, *The Making of a Mind*, pp. 203–204.

31. "Had we returned home in 1916, out of the suffering and the strength of our experiences we might have unleashed a storm. Now if we go back we will be weary, broken, burnt out, rootless, and without hope. We will not be able to find our way any more. And men will not understand us—for the generation that grew up before us, though it has passed these years with us here, already had a home and a calling; now it will return to its old occupations, and the war will be forgotten—and the generation that has grown up after us will be strange to us and push us aside. We will be superfluous even to ourselves, we will grow older, a few will adapt themselves, some others will merely submit, and most will be bewildered;—the years will pass by and in the end we shall fall into ruin." Remarque, *All Quiet on the Western Front*, pp. 317–318.

32. No poet caught more accurately than Maurice Betz the hopes young veterans harbored for the future and the extent to which these hopes were underlaid with anxiety. See his poem "Nous," in *Scaferlati pour les troupes* (Paris, 1921), pp. 104–106.

33. This strange expectation explains, I think, why most of the books that were devoted to explaining the failure of the veterans to transform civilian life are so unsatisfactory. For examples, see Roland Dorgelès, *Le Réveil des morts* and *Bleu horizon* (Paris, 1944); Philippe Barrès, *Ainsi l'albatros* (Paris, 1933); and Edwin Erich Dwinger, *Wir rufen Deutschland: Heimkehr und Vermächtnis* (Jena, 1932). None of the reasons given by these authors for the "defeat" of the combatants—namely, that they were too few in numbers, betrayed by the older generation, seduced by fantasies of pleasure, deprived of their natural leadership by the process of reverse selection, or overwhelmed by their own force—will stand up to close examination. The only persuasive analysis of the survivors' situation by an ex-combatant during the 1920's that I know was made by Lucien Romier. Romier pointed out that a more or less constant historical law prevailing in France ensured that generations did not exercise a preponderant influence on public affairs until twenty or thirty years after they had completed their intellectual and moral education. All youth could do was to prepare itself for its future role. It was unrealistic, therefore, to blame youth for its passivity or to speak of the defeat of youth by the older generation. Like most survivors, Romier worried about the loss of so many potential members of the governing elite. The impact of the war on the generational mechanism, Romier said, had been triple. By destroying so many first-rate young brains, the war had

burdened, enlarged, and dispersed the task of the survivors and left them little room to innovate; it had facilitated their absorption by the preceding generation, thus breaking the homogeneity of their group; and finally, it had deprived them of the support of the multitudes who would otherwise have been present to lend their undertakings a mass following. Because of these losses, the generation of survivors might be condemned to limit their role to that of education. Perhaps all they could do was to prepare the future generation for its task. But Romier was nonetheless convinced that the time would come when this "decimated generation" would take command in every corner of society, even if only for the purpose of ensuring the continuity of the cultural heritage and providing a bridge between the generation of their elders and that of their successors. In the meantime, he advised the members of his generation to get to work. Only if they abandoned the lure of nightly pleasure could they achieve their mission, which was to institute a modern faith and to restore the basis of authority. Lucien Romier, *Explication de notre temps* (Paris, 1925), pp. 267–268.

34. The difficulties of returning to civilian life were evoked by Julian Dodd, one of Siegfried Sassoon's fellow officers, in a letter to Sassoon after Dodd had read *Memoirs of an Infantry Officer*, in which Sassoon had portrayed him as Julian Dorley. This letter is especially interesting because Dodd makes an effort to reassess the meaning of the war experience from the perspective of ten years of civilian life. "In regard to the general question of the War, although it was by far the largest experience in my life, it was mainly a wearisome and horrible one, only redeemed from utter beastliness by the spirit of the trenches which was almost entirely good, and seems far from us in everyday life. For a long time after I came back I felt like a crushed reptile that has been stamped on in the road, but has managed to wriggle through dust and filth to safety. I know now that I was simply an ordinary, rather conscientious person, faced with an abnormal emergency, who just managed to come up to the occasion, and was lucky not to have been rattled into behaving in an utterly ignominious way. I also think that as a result of it all there is a little more real striving after sincerity in our writing and thinking, and we are told it demonstrated that the more nearly civilised man is really a more tenacious fighter than the belligerent nomad. It was, I am afraid, a somewhat expensive form of demonstration, and the information not necessarily of great intrinsic value." Dodd to Sassoon, 7 January 1929, Siegfried Sassoon Correspondnce, Imperial War Museum, London. For the continuing effects of the war on the memories and sensual perception of veterans, see Richard Aldington, *Life for Life's Sake*, pp. 188–189. Aldington describes the way in which certain smells, sounds, and sights acted like "battering rams" to break through the "laboriously built wall of forgetfulness" and let memories of the war escape long after the war ended.

35. Sassoon, *Siegfried's Journey*, p. 160. *Flight without End* is a novel by Joseph Roth, published in German in 1927. It tells the story of Roth's friend and kindred spirit Franz Tunda, born like Roth in 1894, who wanders aimlessly after the war from one city to another. "He had no calling, no love, no desire, no hope, no ambition, and not even egotism. In all the world there was no one so superfluous as he." *Flight without End* (Garden City, 1930), p. 299.

36. Charles Carrington, *A Subaltern's War*, p. 208. Richard Aldington's testimony confirms Carrington's. "In a very short time I realised that the London I had come back to was a different place from the London I had left in 1914, let alone prewar London.

Everything seemed askew. The streets were dirty and shabby—there were no men to clean them and nothing had been repaired or painted for years. There were holes even in the main thoroughfares. The decent, orderly, good-natured Londoners had become as snappy and selfish as the far more sorely tried French. There was a shortage of everything except returning soldiers and debts. People fought for places in the inadequate transport system—a man who was accustomed to make way for women could not get on a bus. Food was scanty and very dear. Lodgings or apartments were almost impossible to find, because London was crowded with enormous numbers of 'war workers,' who still clung to their jobs like limpets. There was a devil-take-the-hindmost scramble for money and position in the new world, and an extravagance which seemed incredible to me who had known the old sober England. I stood aghast at this degeneration of my people, visible to me, as it was not to them, because of my long absence. I asked myself anxiously if I too had not degenerated, and it seemed to me I had." *Life for Life's Sake*, pp. 203–204.

37. For the view that tour guides were undependable, see Joseph Roth, *Romane, Erzählungen, Aufsätze* (Cologne and Berlin, 1963), p. 514; for Monterlant, *Romans*, p. 632; for Kazantzakis, *Report to Greco* (New York, 1965), p. 243; for the desire to flee, Louis-Ferdinand Céline, *Voyage au bout de la nuit* (Paris, 1952 ed.), p. 231; for the fascination with Charlot, Philippe Soupault, *Charlot* (Paris, 1957).

38. Blaise Cendrars, *L'Homme foudroyé* (Paris, 1945), p. 288.

39. For Cendrars's motto, see *Emmène-moi au bout du monde* (Paris, 1964), p. 194; for his only truth, *Moravagine* (Paris, 1956), p. 393; for his claim to be a Brahman in reverse, *Une nuit dans la forêt* (Paris, 1964), pp. 15–16.

40. For the desire to pass before a moving backdrop, see Jean Cave, *Examen de conscience* (Paris, 1926), p. 45; for the definitions of departure, Roland Dorgelès, *Partir* (Paris, 1926), p. 25. "To leave! To leave! he repeated . . . What an intoxicating word. You would almost say a door that one opens on the world." *Ibid.*, p. 155.

41. For Teilhard de Chardin, see *Ecrits du temps de la guerre*, p. 206; for Ernst Fisher, *Errinerungen und Reflexionen* (Reinbeck bei Hamburg, 1969), p. 10.

42. For the fear that the war generation might never live to see the promised land, see Adriano Tilgher, *Storia e antistoria* (Rieti, 1928); for wandering like Ulysses as the only nobility of thought and life, Emmanuel Berl, *La Mort de la pensée bourgeoise* (Paris, 1929), pp. 9–10. For an English representation of the 1920s as a wasteland between two worlds, see Ruth Holland, *The Lost Generation*, pp. 175–176, 226, and especially p. 231, where the author writes, "All the old happy state of things that should have blossomed, came to fruition, had been swept away. There was nothing to cling on to, no security in which life could take root and expand and grow. Life was all wisps and shadows drifting out of one's hungry, clutching, frustrating hands."

43. "When I say 'old' I'm not referring to a chronological relationship. I think that one is born old; that some people are old at twenty and already moribund in spirit and flesh, while there are men of seventy . . . who still have the vibration and flame of virile youth." Mussolini, *Opera omnia*, XI, 81. Mussolini wrote these lines in 1918. The next year Moeller van den Bruck, then forty-three, went even further: "Youth has nothing to do with [chronological] age. Youth has to do with attitude. Youth wants to improve. Youth is a mistrust of everything that it finds in existence and that it recognizes as having done badly. The generation of 1919 will take up again the work which

the generation of 1872 failed to acomplish. Generations live on in one another. Just as the generation of 1872 lived on in the generation of 1888, so now the outsiders of 1888 [like Moeller] rush in to join the generation of 1919." Arthur Moeller van den Bruck, "Die drei Generationen," *Der Spiegel*, 1 December 1919, pp. 9–10.

44. For the use of the generational idea by partisans of the Bolshevik revolution in France, see Robert Wohl, *French Communism in the Making* (Stanford, 1966), pp. 114–207; for the use and interpretation of the generational idea by French veterans' organizations, Antoine Prost, *Les Anciens Combattants et la société française* (Paris, 1977), especially III, 135–137; for veterans' organizations in Great Britain, the United States, France, Italy, and Germany, Ward, *The War Generation*.

45. For the references to the historical literature on the relative youth and generational community in the leadership of Communist and Fascist parties, see Juan J. Linz, "Some Notes toward a Comparative Study of Fascism in Sociological Historical Perspective," in Walter Laqueur, ed., *Fascism: A Reader's Guide* (Berkeley and Los Angeles, 1976), pp. 43–47. The ideological attraction between right- and left-wing radicals in Germany has been analyzed in detail by Schüddekopf in *Linke Leute von rechts*.

46. "Money," the "mob," and "spirit" are terms that appear frequently in the Fascist writings of Sir Oswald Mosley; they express concepts that were central to all Fascist thinking. For Fascist ideology in general, see Emilio Gentile, *Le origini dell'ideologia fascista*.

47. According to Daniel J. Levinson, all men are compelled to revise their dreams and visions of the future during the years between forty and forty-five. For someone born in 1895, like Ernst Jünger, this midlife crisis would have come betwen 1935 and 1940. Indeed, Jünger's political views did undergo radical change during this period. For the theory of the midlife transition, see Levinson et al., *The Seasons of a Man's Life* (New York, 1978), especially pp. 191–304. Levinson finds that Ortega's theory of the life cycle and the sequence of generations corresponds well to his own, based on interviews with American men born between 1923 and 1934. See pp. 28–29, 323.

48. Few members of the generation of 1914 subjected the generational idea and their own exploitation of it to a critique. One exception is Sir Oswald Mosley. An unrepentant generationalist right up into the late 1940s, Mosley devoted some interesting pages to the "youth racket" when he wrote his autobiography in 1968. Acknowledging the support he had received from established leaders in English politics when he embarked on his career, the former Fascist leader commented, "The war of generations is more foolish than the war of class, for it has less reason. It is almost always a sign of some intellectual inadequacy on one side or the other: at a certain level of intelligence the clash of generations simply ceases to exist." What produced the cult of youth in politics, Mosley added, was ambition and the instinctual desire of the young to escape from a failing society. "The older men and also the bogus young of the present period become discredited because they are trying to work policies doomed to failure." Mosley, *My Life*, pp. 134–135. Both factors no doubt explain Mosley's exploitation of this theme at the beginning of his career. One of his first political acts was to give a speech to the League of Youth and Social Progress in which he denounced "these old dead men with their old dead minds embalmed in the tombs of the past." Ibid., p. 128. For Mosley's later use of generational rhetoric, see my chapter 3 and Sir Oswald Mosley, *Mosley: The Facts* (London, 1957).

Credits

ILLUSTRATIONS

Maurice Barrès in the 1890s. Bibliothèque Nationale.

Henri Massis. Bibliothèque Nationale.

Jacques Rivière about 1920. Bibliothèque Nationale.

Ernest Psichari about 1912. Bibliothèque Nationale.

Alain-Fournier about 1910. Bibliothèque Nationale.

Portrait of Henri Franck in 1905 by Jacques Briss. From the frontispiece to *La Danse devant l'arche* (Paris, 1912). Bibliothèque Nationale.

Henry de Montherlant in the 1920s. Roger-Viollet.

Pierre Drieu la Rochelle in the 1930s. Roger-Viollet.

Marcel Arland in 1929. Bibliothèque Nationale.

Jean Luchaire on the bench of the accused in 1946. New York Times News Service.

Jean Prévost about 1930. Bibliothèque Nationale.

Youth Movement group around 1900. Archiv für Kunst und Geschichte, Berlin.

Youth Movement group on a hiking expedition in 1909. Archiv für Kunst und Geschichte, Berlin.

Youth Movement group singing in their "nest" in 1911. Archiv für Kunst und Geschichte, Berlin.

Walter Flex during the Great War. Courtesy, Mr. Wilhelm Heinz, Director of the Walter-Flex-Gedächtnisstätte.

Ernst Wurche at the front in 1915. Courtesy, Mr. Wilhelm Heinz, Director of the Walter-Flex-Gedächtnisstätte.

Fritz von Unruh in 1920. Bildarchiv Preussischer Kulturbesitz.

Ernst Jünger during the Great War. From the frontispiece to *Im Stahlgewittern* (Berlin, 1927).

German veterans marching in 1930. Bildarchiv Preussischer Kulturbesitz.

Karl Mannheim. From the jacket of *The Sociology of Karl Mannheim* by Gunter W. Remmling (London, 1975). Courtesy, Routledge & Kegan Paul Ltd.

Rupert Brooke in 1913. The Mansell Collection Ltd.

Scherill Schell photograph of Rupert Brooke in 1913. Courtesy, Rupert Brooke Trustees, King's College, Cambridge.

Rupert Brooke's grave on the island of Skyros. Courtesy, Rupert Brooke Trustees, King's College, Cambridge.

Love and Death by G. F. Watts. Tate Gallery, London.

We Are Making a New World by Paul Nash. Imperial War Museum, London.

Siegfried Sassoon in the early 1920s by William Rothenstein. The Mansell Collection Ltd.

Wilfred Owen with fellow officers in 1916. Imperial War Museum, London.

Erich Maria Remarque in the early 1930s. Radio Times Hulton Picture Library.

Henry Williamson at a meeting of the British Union of Fascists in the late 1930s. Radio Times Hulton Picture Library.

Vera Brittain at a meeting of the P.E.N. Club in the 1930s. Radio Times Hulton Picture Library.

T. E. Lawrence with his brothers when Lawrence was an undergraduate at Oxford. Courtesy, Professor A. W. Lawrence.

Sir Oswald Mosley addressing a meeting of the British Union of Fascists in the late 1930s. Courtesy, Sir Oswald Mosley.

Miguel de Unamuno in 1917. Alfonso.

Ramiro de Maetzu in the 1920s. Alfonso.

Pío Baroja about 1900. Courtesy, Mr. José Alfonso Sánchez.

Azorín about 1920. Courtesy, Mr. José Alfonso Sánchez.

Ortega reading the news of the outbreak of the Great War in August 1914. Courtesy, Mrs. Soledad Ortega.

Ortega in 1925. Courtesy, Mrs. Soledad Ortega.

Ortega after his speech calling for the "rectification" of the Republic in December 1931. Courtesy, Mr. José Alfonso Sánchez.

Giovanni Papini. From Giuseppe Prezzolini, *La Voce* (Milan, 1974). Courtesy, Professor Giuseppe Prezzolini and Rusconi Editore.

Giuseppe Prezzolini. From Giuseppe Prezzolini, *La Voce*. Courtesy, Professor Giuseppe Prezzolini and Rusconi Editore.

The first number of the Florentine journal *Leonardo*. From Giuseppe Prezzolini, *La Voce*. Courtesy, Professor Giuseppe Prezzolini and Rusconi Editore.

Benito Mussolini leading the march on Rome in October 1922. Roger-Viollet.

The union of older and younger generations in the Fascist militia. Roger-Viollet.

Adolfo Omodeo during the Great War. Courtesy, Professor Pietro Omodeo.

Antonio Gramsci shortly before his arrest in 1926. Courtesy, Istituto Gramsci.

The first page of Gramsci's *Prison Notebooks*. Courtesy, Istituto Gramsci.

QUOTATIONS

Grateful acknowledgment is made for the use of material from the following:

Vera Brittain, *Testament of Youth*, 1933; by permission of Victor Gollancz Ltd.

Rupert Brooke, *The Letters of Rupert Brooke*, ed. Geoffrey Keynes, 1968; by permission of Harcourt Brace Jovanovich, Inc., and Faber and Faber Ltd.

T. S. Eliot, "Gerontion," from *Collected Poems 1909–1962*, copyright 1936 by Harcourt Brace Jovanovich, Inc.; copyright © 1963, 1964 by T. S. Eliot; reprinted by permission of Harcourt Brace Jovanovich, Inc., and Faber and Faber Ltd.

Antonio Gramsci, *Quaderni del carcere*, 1975; by permission of Giulio Einaudi Editore.

T. E. Lawrence, *The Letters of T. E. Lawrence*, ed. David Garnett, Jonathan Cape Ltd., 1938; by permission of the Letters of T. E. Lawrence Trust.

Index